Highway

Praise for *Red Sun: Travels in Naxalite Country*

'A book that every MP, MLA and minister should read before entering office. Needless to say, sociologists and bureaucrats should treat is as compulsory study material.' – *The Hindu*

'(An) excellent book ... *Red Sun* is an important book, not only because it warns of the grave situation in Chhattisgarh and elsewhere, but because Chakravarti manages to humanize the conflict. Rather than the tactics of guerrilla warfare or the euphemisms of the defence specialist, ordinary people, largely caught up in events over which they have no control, are at the heart of this book.' – *India Today*

'Chakravarti's descriptions are interspersed with reflective comments, but no political theory. That is his strength, for the book raises grievous questions. Why has our political system created masses of desperate people? ... *Red Sun* should be read widely, especially by those mesmerized by newfound wealth.' – *Outlook*

'A fascinating work of reportage ... *Red Sun* proposes no easy answers, but the author succeeds in his aim of "tearing the veil" off a crisis from which we have averted our eyes for too long.' – *Mint*

'Ear-to-the-ground accounts that showcase a refreshingly keen eye for detail ... [Chakravarti] serves up an impressionistic travelogue, peppered with riveting dialogue and engaging cameos of people ... suspecting rebels, confused bureaucrats, smug politicians ... he meets on the journey.' – *Hindustan Times*

'Chakravarti is a gifted writer ... *Red Sun* is an important work, because it chronicles a forbidden India whose reality we deny.' – *The Telegraph*

'Chakravarti adopts a questioning attitude ... The result is a remarkably objective book on a domestic threat that is often underplayed by the Indian government.' — *Far Eastern Economic Review*

'The sombre story of India at war with itself.' — *Deccan Herald*

'A disturbing vision of a country splintered by the unevenness of development ... [*Red Sun*] manages to breach the walls of silence and denial that fortify middle-class preoccupations, and makes you think.' — *DNA*

'*Red Sun* is a meticulous account of Chakravarti's travels in the prime Naxal-affected areas of the country ... he successfully puts into perspective a complex issue that, for many of us, is as disconnected from real life as space travel.' — *Business World*

'Chakravarti ... brings back a story which is as poignant as it is dreadful. Unlike many other armchair "opinion makers" ... he tries to understand the phenomenon from a perspective that can only be described as humane.' — *Tribune*

'This book is an eye-opener, and Chakravarti, through his superb command over the language and the subject adds a human touch to a pressing issue. A must read.' — *Sunday Mid Day*

'*Red Sun* is an excellent primer for those who know little of an India where Naxalites live side-by-side with the poor ... [and] a prized possession for people who want to work on the subject in future.' — *Down to Earth*

Highway 39

Journeys through a Fractured Land

SUDEEP CHAKRAVARTI

FOURTH ESTATE • *New Delhi*

First published in India in 2012 by Fourth Estate
An imprint of HarperCollins *Publishers* India
a joint venture with
The India Today Group

Copyright © Sudeep Chakravarti 2012

ISBN: 978-93-5029-334-8

2 4 6 8 10 9 7 5 3 1

Sudeep Chakravarti asserts the moral right to be identified as
the author of this work.

The views and opinions expressed in this book are the author's own
and the facts are as reported by him, and the publishers are not in any way
liable for the same.

All rights reserved. No part of this publication may be reproduced,
stored in a retrieval system, or transmitted, in any form or by any means, electronic,
mechanical, photocopying, recording or otherwise,
without the prior permission of the publishers.

HarperCollins *Publishers*
A-53, Sector 57, Noida, Uttar Pradesh 201301, India
77-85 Fulham Palace Road, London W6 8JB, United Kingdom
Hazelton Lanes, 55 Avenue Road, Suite 2900, Toronto, Ontario M5R 3L2
and 1995 Markham Road, Scarborough, Ontario M1B 5M8, Canada
25 Ryde Road, Pymble, Sydney, NSW 2073, Australia
31 View Road, Glenfield, Auckland 10, New Zealand
10 East 53rd Street, New York NY 10022, USA

Typeset in 12/14 Venetian301 BT at
SÜRYA

Printed and bound at
Thomson Press (India) Ltd.

To an India where people don't have to be hurt in a hundred ways, or die, to exercise freedom of speech and expression, and to live with dignity and identity.

And so, to peace.

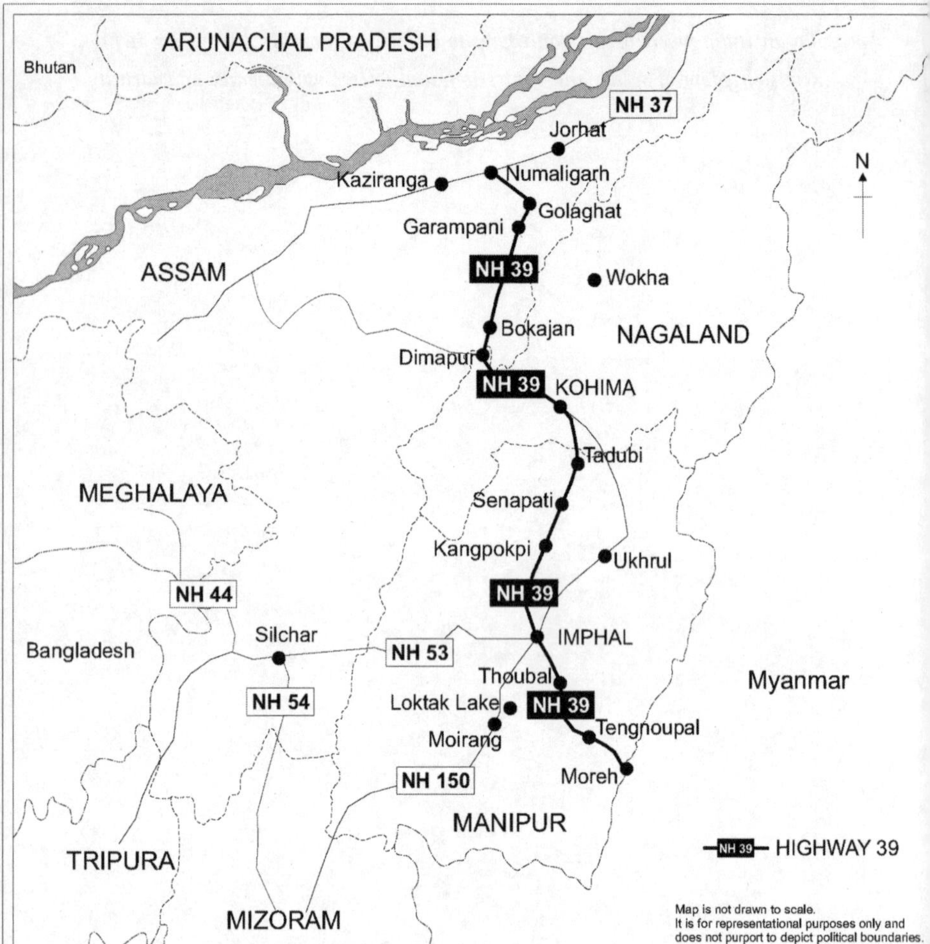
ARUNACHAL PRADESH
Bhutan
NH 37
Jorhat
N
Kaziranga
Numaligarh
Golaghat
Garampani
NH 39
ASSAM
Wokha
Bokajan
NAGALAND
Dimapur
NH 39
KOHIMA
Tadubi
MEGHALAYA
Senapati
Kangpokpi
Ukhrul
NH 44
NH 39
Silchar
IMPHAL
Bangladesh
NH 53
Thoubal
Myanmar
NH 54
Loktak Lake
NH 39
Tengnoupal
Moirang
NH 150
Moreh
MANIPUR
NH 39 HIGHWAY 39
TRIPURA
MIZORAM
Map is not drawn to scale.
It is for representational purposes only and does not purport to depict political boundaries.

Contents

Introduction	ix
1. And so, to a place where brother kills brother	1
2. Spiritsong: Journeying to the grave of Angami Zapu Phizo	13
3. 'Madam, do you want an honest answer? I don't consider myself an Indian'	26
4. A visit to the Promised Land: it's 3:20 p.m. in Nagalim	40
5. Tea with a general: 'So you think you can wear us down? I say, bullshit!'	49
6. A brief interlude about fat cats and futures	67
7. A story of butterfly wings, frogs' waists, and the zigzag line to justice	72
8. 'People listen to those with guns. It's not nice, but that's how it is'	92
9. A.O.I., Alphabet Soups, and other delights of a ceasefire without ceasefire	105
10. The day 'Caman-do' took away a little girl, & other stories	120
11. Find a scapegoat, frame him, kill him. Then, kill some more	131
12. The lament of Brahma	144
13. Surprises in Dimapur: old friends, new lights, and freedom at dinner	159

14.	And then the shell landed	168
15.	Into the cloud mountain: where rulers and rebels hold court	176
16.	The system of factions, and the game of winner-takes-all	195
17.	Stories of fire, fear, and loathing—and a party in surreal Imphal	209
18.	'The heavens are filled with smoke from smouldering pyres of your dead sons'	221
19.	Of fasting and steadfast ladies	245
20.	About a one-Act play of omission and commission (parentheses included)	252
21.	Interlude: 'Dial *456*452# to know about India's freedom struggle'	264
22.	Republic of India: Version Imphal 2.0.1.0	271
23.	'Who told you this is a tourist place?'	280
24.	In praise of Vision 2020: 'I sing softly-softly, nah, brother?'	288
25.	Walkabout in Moreh: the Wild East, and other stories	299
26.	'National integration through cultural interaction'	307
27.	Imphal-Delhi-Imphal: tea with a bureaucrat	317
28.	Interlude: walkabout with Meitei soul	331
29.	'General weakness. Pain in private part after electric shock'	336
30.	What Uncle Muivah thinks, Uncle Muivah does	342
31.	Mr Muivah's difficult homecoming, and other ongoing stories	361
	Postscript	369
	References	372
	Index	376
	Acknowledgements	387

Introduction

It is tempting to say this book took hold of me on account of Asangla Angelica Sangtam, but that would only be part of the story. An urge to write about what India calls its 'Northeast'—a tag for a region that today comprises eight states, and several hundred ethnic groups, tribes and sub-tribes spread over roughly a tenth of India's landmass—happened for other reasons too.

India is a country that excels in blindsiding itself with what could be called attitudes of geography and demography. Governance plummets if the place is both far enough from New Delhi and lacks the heft of population to contribute sufficient numbers to the equation of government formation in New Delhi. The more notable ones of these governance blind spots in these past decades—even accounting for the mostly positive recent churn of 'reformist' India—lie in this region that abuts a busy junction of boundaries and countries: China, Bangladesh, Myanmar, Nepal and Bhutan. A vanishing trick, as it were, is perpetuated on what today amounts to nearly forty-six million people.

Anyway, to Asangla. This petite student would speak freely to my friend Jean-Christophe Gardaz, or J-C as we called him, imbuing this Swiss computer specialist with initials of some irony; he being a devout atheist, Asangla a devout Baptist. But she would not speak freely to my partner and I; devout Indians that we were. It was disturbing for me and jolted the sense of Indian-ness that my generation, born a couple of decades after India became independent in 1947, was conditioned from our childhood to take for granted. It was as if this girl mocked our urbanity, aspiration and assumption to be global citizens of a rambunctious democracy, severely imperfect and corrupted though this democracy was. She was a walking talking conscience of India's haphazardly buried recent history.

Asangla is Naga—her mother is of the Ao tribe, her father was of the neighbouring Sangtam. We are talking about 1995. The Government of India was still two years away from inking a bizarre ceasefire agreement with the largest of the Naga rebel factions, the Nationalist Socialist Council of Nagalim (Isak-Muivah). Operations were on against this group and a rival breakaway of the NSCN, the Khaplang faction, in the Indian state of Nagaland and several districts in the neighbouring states of Manipur and Arunachal Pradesh. (Naga tribes have lived in these parts for several hundred years—perhaps several thousand, but oral histories of indigenous peoples don't travel well with the schema of politics.)

It took a couple of years for Asangla to thaw, for her to be able to take me at face value, and accept that all 'Mainland' Indians—those of us not from the 'Northeast'—weren't the enemies of her people. And that, at least some us cared about the war in which soldiers from my country had for three decades killed, maimed, raped, tortured and scarred—both physically and mentally—tens of thousands in her homeland and that of other tribes in the region; most of the victims civilian, not armed rebels. (Here, I am not counting the to-my-mind pointless deaths of several thousand police, paramilitary and military personnel in the nearly five decades of Naga wars and other rebellions in the Northeast caused by political arrogance and ineptitude, let alone the several rebellions of the Mainland.)

Asangla's distrust was rooted in the horrors that Jawaharlal Nehru's India visited upon her people when some Naga leaders led by Angami Zapu Phizo proclaimed a 1951 plebiscite as proof that

Nagas wanted to be independent from India. Nagas would stand their ground, they said. They had been trying to make a case for a separate identity and separate lands since 1929, when a group of Naga elders petitioned the Simon Commission in London to let the Naga Hills be. They weren't part of the Crown's Indian dominion, they formally claimed. They were not of British India or an India to follow. They were of several Naga tribes. And, as Nagas, they were happy to be on their own land, left to their own devices.

Nobody listened to them at the time, the soon-to-be rebel icon Phizo said. And now they offered the plebiscite as further proof of intent.

An angered Prime Minister Nehru sent in paramilitary and the army to dominate the situation, unwilling to let slide political gains that India's newly free leadership had spent recent years accumulating, largely in frenzied diplomacy to cobble together the idea of India.

I first read about these things in detail in *Strangers of the Mist: Tales of War and Peace from India's Northeast*, a refreshingly opinionated and informative book by Sanjoy Hazarika, a friend from our time as journalists for American newspapers. (The book was published in 1994. Nearly twenty years later, the cover of my copy of the book has faded, but the title is still apt. The people and ideas of 'northeastern' India that Sanjoy wrote about continue to be strangers to much of India and the world.)

I also read in *Strangers* an excerpt from the 'Chaliha Report' that formed part of the Bishnuram Medhi Papers. Sanjoy had accessed these at New Delhi's Nehru Memorial Museum and Library. In mid-September 1953, Bimala Prasad Chaliha, president of Assam Pradesh Congress Committee, wrote a report to his colleagues about what should be done in the Naga Hills.

'THAT THERE SHOULD BE NO BLOODSHED IS RECOGNIZED,' the Chaliha report urged in capital letters. It continued:

'1. That the present impasse in Nagaland should be resolved.
2. That the differences should be settled amicably and peacefully by negotiations.
3. It being understood that the negotiations will take place if the Congress party accepts to discuss the Naga Independence Issue...'

Nehru and his ruling Congress party went the other way. Indeed, as I read, Nehru wrote a note to Medhi, Assam's chief minister at the time, in mid-May 1956, when the war in the Naga Hills was in full flow. The note was written after a meeting with top Cabinet ministers, officials from the external affairs and defence ministries, and the chief of army staff. Among other things, it prepared the ground for further action by invoking things beyond the core Naga question—'...much more to it than the mere military approach', Nehru put it. 'These Naga troubles and revolts have a larger significance for us in the international sphere and they give a handle to our opponents everywhere. More particularly, of course, Pakistan takes advantage of them.'

China's play in the subcontinental game had yet to begin in earnest—Mao's empire was several years from offering training and logistics support to Naga rebels. But the proximity of what was then East Pakistan and the spectre of India's arch enemy offering sanctuary and supplies to any school of rebel thought were enough for Nehru to take a firm stand with the Nagas. This set the template for future action in the region both by his regime and several that followed, including the template of massively exceeding the 'vanilla' brief of combat by wilfully including civilians as what is in the lexicon of conflict chillingly termed 'collateral damage'.

'There can be no doubt that an armed revolt has to be met by force and suppressed,' I read further in Nehru's note to Chief Minister Medhi. 'There are no two opinions about that and we shall set about it as efficiently and effectively as possible. But our whole past and present outlook is based on force by itself being no remedy ... Much more must we remember this when dealing with our own countrymen who have to be won over and not merely suppressed ... It may be that the present is no time for the political approach, because it may be construed as a sign of weakness. But anyhow our minds should be clear that and even now onwards we should do nothing which will come in the way of that political approach and we should let it be known that we want to be friends with the Nagas unless they revolt against us.'

The trajectory of that intent from war to winning over has travelled a great distance since the 1950s. Nagaland is today a state of India, and has been since 1963, the result of a 'political approach' that bulldozed rebels and civilians without discrimination and engineered factions among rebels to accept India and its Constitution. Sixty years on from the beginning of the Naga wars, though, India is still trying to 'be friends' with the Nagas even if the idea of revolt among them is much diminished.

And, India is also trying to 'be friends' with people of Manipur of nearly every ethnic and political hue.

And...

And...

And...

The story of the 'Northeast' is still the story of our times, the unfinished story of India's integrity.

~

The region has been delivered courtesy of the Government of India one part misunderstanding, one part annoyance, and one part callousness.

Naga resistance quickly coalesced into organized insurgency, and at the time of writing this exists in the form of a ceasefire, not formal peace. And there is still hurt. Much of the festering anger stems from Nehru permitting the outright massacre of combatants and civilians and domination with a degree of brutality that ranks among the more disturbing in the modern world. And, following the British practice in nearby Malaya, and predating America's atrocities in Vietnam in following a scorched earth policy, Nehru's approach permitted the corralling of tens of thousands of villagers into little more than concentration camps. Rape, torture and death were attendant, routine corollaries. To prevent the outside world from getting wind of this, the government continued with the British system of the Inner Line Permit, which in this case prevented media and the general public from gaining access to the Naga Hills.

(India also has the dubious distinction of being a post World War II country to strafe and bomb its own people—as happened with the Mizoram rebellion in 1966—in addition to Xeroxing the brutal land campaign in Nagaland for Mizoram, but that's another story altogether.)

It seemed like a mockery of Nehru's own speech at the time of India's freedom: 'A moment comes, which comes but rarely in history, when we step out from the old to the new, when an age ends, and when the soul of a nation, long suppressed, finds utterance.' He also said, 'Freedom and power bring responsibility,' and that, 'the service of India means the service of the millions who suffer…'

Since this rousing speech we seem to have travelled the road to deceit; to wilful, often-repeated junctions of self-destruction.

With increasing interaction with my Indian friends, it gradually dawned on Asangla that some of us didn't think she was either 'Nepali', 'Chinese', or simply, 'What country are you from?'—queries those from the 'Northeast', India's far east, routinely encounter. There existed sufficiently pluralistic Indians who opted for the neutral, 'Where are you from?'

And so, J-C's apartment in the Nizamuddin East residential area of New Delhi, where Asangla sometimes visited, became a frontier of sorts in our relationship: a place of détente. It helped that my parallel and conversational deconstruction of India's past and India's political pantheon brought closer our world views. Names like Nehru, Vallabhbhai Patel, Govind Ballabh Pant, Indira Gandhi were those who had done much wrong to many of their fellow Indians alongside their doing right—dazzlingly right, as we were taught through school textbooks prepared by government agencies. Some of my elders among historians, journalists and writers—the first tribe I encountered through my chosen course of study at university, the others on account of my chosen profession—had also helped to reduce the polish of self-respect applied by government propaganda, a sort of aggressive whitewash that often accompanies nation-building.

Peace was sealed after I helped to get Asangla and J-C married, short-circuiting a crooked Delhi lawyer who had taken them for a ride for several months, citing their disparate nationalities to delay their wedding. Besides, that Asangla was Naga automatically implied a possible rebel background, and made 'security clearance' mandatory. All that sorted, I stood as a witness to their wedding in a court room in south Delhi.

In gratitude, Asangla gifted me a shawl of the Ao tribe, typical of her mother's village near Mokokchung—the largest town in the Ao region. Twice destroyed by the Indian Army, the town has witnessed numerous attacks by Indian forces, its inhabitants marked in ways that could keep judges at the International Court of Justice or any court to judge war crimes greatly occupied, should they ever be moved to acknowledge barbarity in these parts.

The shawl is of wool, woven richly in crimson and black. Asangla and J-C remain friends, though they are long gone into the expatriate wilderness of the world. And every time I draped the shawl, with the cocooning warmth of it came Asangla's telling of her story—the history of her people, of her mother and her father, of what they endured as youngsters. And why she and others like her sometimes were so angry and hurt. Why many hesitated to call themselves 'Indian' even as they could not deny India's proximity and the gradual, impelling—even compelling—mesh of the modern day in which Indian politics and the Indian economy offered their undeniable attractions.

Besides, I had promised Asangla that someday I would try to add to the telling of the story of her people, bring more of these stories to the 'Mainland' and beyond, so that people would understand more, misunderstand less. I realized much later that it was as much to understand her story, and stories of people like her, as to come to terms with yet another dark side of the country I love—and am also exasperated and horrified by in equal measure.

There have over the years been other nudges to travel this road, some forcefully outright, some subliminal.

I recall a friend at my college, whom I shall call K, because to name him would immediately identify him as someone in the upper echelons of Manipur's power structure. A Meitei from Manipur, he was resolutely cheerful despite losing his mother in an attack by a prominent rebel group from that state. That group felt that his father, a politician, had sold out to 'India' and, besides, he wouldn't dance to their tune. From that I learnt of nationalistic Meiteis who continued to be deeply angered by India's formal absorption of Manipur by treaty in 1949—and what they felt was continual denial of due respect by Indian leaders of Manipur's ancient heritage and identity. Of course, movements that took to arms in the late 1970s were also deeply suspicious of Naga intent, a reality brought about by cynical policymakers who carved out the states of Nagaland and Manipur in such a way as to include vast chunks of homelands of a few Naga tribes in Manipur. More of this in the book.

This brings me to my friend K's ironical world view. Alongside his evident good humour and otherwise liberal outlook, this bon vivant would keep his distance from a fellow 'Manipuri'—say, a Naga from the Tangkhul tribe that called the sprawling Ukhrul district of Manipur home—because he was different culturally, and hence, politically. The Meitei, largely converted to Vaishnavism in the eighteenth century on account of growing evangelical influences from Bengal aided by a Meitei king who mandated conversion, mostly live in the bowl of Imphal Valley. The Meitei stood apart from the Naga and several other tribes—of the Kuki, for example, among a list of more than thirty tribes and sub-tribes—which continue to live in the hill areas that surround Imphal Valley; the Valley forms just about 10 per cent of the landmass of the state.

The Tangkhul, I would learn much later, are called 'Elder Brother' by many Meitei intellectuals wistful of a once-unified past that describes them as coming down from the hills in the times before local written history to set up home in the less-topographically daunting Imphal Valley. But that sentimental ingress did not preclude the natural, ongoing suspicion between the 'hill' and 'plains' people, now also separated by religion—the Tangkhul and other tribes are overwhelmingly Baptist, the Meitei overwhelmingly Hindu-Vaishnav—language, and ethnic identity. Moreover, the same urge that drove Asangla's people to take to arms against India to carve out a Naga homeland spilled over to Manipur, with the Tangkhul spearheading a significant aspect of the latter-day rebellion against India—NSCN (Isak-Muivah) has a large Tangkhul component, and one of the leaders, Thuingaleng Muivah, is Tangkhul. For this faction of NSCN, 'Nagalim' includes the hill areas of Manipur—an idea that is anathema to the Meitei, who see in the Naga rebel construct a conspiracy to diminish Manipur in general and the Meitei identity in particular.

Much blood has been spilled over this. And so, while I didn't like it, I understood my Meitei friend's wariness with non-Meitei Manipuris even in the relatively calm climate of St Stephen's

College in Delhi, far removed from the temporal and political battle zones several thousand kilometres to the east. I knew then this 'Northeast' was a complicated place, made more complicated by the quite haphazard division of British-ruled India into India, Pakistan and Burma that further fractured homelands. But it seemed entirely too complicated to pay attention to. I realized only much later that I was displaying the time-worn 'forget it, too complicated' brush that 'Mainlanders' apply to any Indian territory east of Darjeeling; and Darjeeling already seems plenty east.

Perhaps I was at the time consumed by what was happening in the hubs of Delhi, Mumbai and other metropolitan areas, as I worked my way into journalism. My chosen profession opened my eyes to both the maelstrom and the magic of India: along with all the progress, there was enough indication right near Delhi of the myriad political and policy failures of India. The time of my relatively young adulthood was only a heartbeat away from the mayhem that would ensue in Punjab after Indira Gandhi ordered an attack on Sikhism's holiest shrine, the Golden Temple, in Amritsar. It was to cleanse the temple of pro-separatist rebels, but the damage to the shrine cost that prime minister her life. That was in 1984.

Just as that was winding down, mayhem ensued in Jammu & Kashmir in 1989, when Benazir Bhutto as prime minister of Pakistan permitted the intelligence apparatus of her country to export terrorism outward from the Kashmir valley. (I would hear her admit as much at a conference in New Delhi in 2003 I designed for the *Hindustan Times*, an organization I worked with at the time.)

But, unlike these two conflagrations which raged and in the case of Kashmir continues to have implications well beyond India's immediate geography, the goings-on of the so-called 'Northeast' were strangely muted to us elsewhere in India. Attention would only be drawn by the grossest of events—as with the wake-up call of Assamese angst in 1983 when, in a burst of anti-Bangladeshi immigrant anger, men, women and children were butchered at a place called Nellie.

I saw the standoffish perception continue well into the late 1990s, India then in the throes of a consumer boom and making early claims of having arrived on the world stage. I recall a colleague in Delhi, from my days as an editor with *India Today*, being posted from Delhi to Guwahati. The appointment was made by a vindictive senior editor at the magazine over a point of prestige. The rest of us could do little except offer our colleague advice of making a good go of it—there was so much to write about in northeastern India, many of us told this colleague who was nearly in tears over his perceived banishment. This is as much an opportunity for you as the magazine, we urged him. Learn more about this region and tell our readers. (Ironically, it worked so well for him that in a few short years appreciation for his work got him back to the 'Mainland' and 'mainstream' media!)

But largely, the Northeast remained 'Outland', a kind of region I described in my 2008 book on India's ongoing Maoist rebellion, *Red Sun: Travels in Naxalite Country* (Viking/Penguin; revised 2009 edition, Penguin). To me 'Outland' is out of sight of the majority of Indians in 'Inland' and, therefore, outside of any easily digestible construct. Like the poor of India in the heart of India, the identity-conscious in the country's eastern periphery too have been trodden to the limit. For decades, governance in the region has been driven largely by the principle adopted by rulers of India that, while the region has strategic significance in geopolitical terms, the people who occupy these spaces exist merely as pawns in that scheme, more ethnic artefact than thinking species with definite identities and aspirations. And, besides, as I alluded to earlier, these spaces accounted for a minuscule number of Lok Sabha seats—and so were perceived to be of little consequence to national politics and creation of government in New Delhi.

While in the case of several 'Mainland' states, regional aspiration was addressed first by creating states along linguistic lines (as recently as the early 2000s, Chhattisgarh, Uttarakhand and Jharkhand were carved out of Madhya Pradesh, Uttar Pradesh and Bihar driven by cries of stifled development), in the Northeast, the demand for identity and development frequently attracted violent government crackdown. When insurgencies developed, counter-force was a natural—and by rights, legitimate—reaction.

'In the northeast ... the Indian government responded to ethnic insurgencies mainly through force,' I read in an essay by Rajat Ganguly in *The State of India's Democracy*, a 2007 volume co-published by The Johns Hopkins University Press. (The piece drew on strategic affairs writer Kanti Bajpai's earlier work 'Diversity, Democracy and Devolution in India' in *Government Policies and Ethnic Relations in Asia and the Pacific*.) The essay not only stresses massive operations against the United Liberation Front of Asom in 1990 and 1991, but also mentions several other identity and development-led movements and insurgencies in the Northeast that around the time felt the force of India: '... Bodo, Naga, Tripuri, Gorkha ... and Manipuri'. At best, it continued, like the operations in Kashmir, the ones in 'Indian northeast have temporarily weakened the insurgents and allowed the government to keep violence within an acceptable level'.

I have heard and read many commentators and scholars call this phenomenon many things, but perhaps the most memorable for me remains Sanjib Baruah's description of the Government of India's approach to these aspects of India—especially in the Northeast—as 'durable disorder'. (The New York-based scholar expands the idea in his 2005 work *Durable Disorder: Understanding the Politics of Northeast India*.)

Very simply: there were stories to be told. Stories that had to continually confront India's grand conceit of being the 'largest' democracy by also pointing out that it needed to be a 'good' democracy, an 'effective' democracy; a place where people didn't need to take to arms, or be butchered for asking for simple rights to identity, livelihood and respect mandated by the Constitution of India.

~

I did not manage to carve enough mind space, as it were, to pursue independent research and writing till I took a sabbatical in 2004.

My chosen profession as a journalist had been largely kind to me; and as first a correspondent and then an editor in various incarnations with both global and Indian publications I had travelled much of the country and some of the world. A near-ringside view of India's economic reforms since 1991 was for me a great revelation, as India visibly unleashed its positive energy. As a card-carrying member of urban, 'privileged' India, I was on a roll. Though 'Outland' India was never far from my thoughts, I confess even that distance was occasioned both by the pressures of a job and the seductive allure of being a media person in Delhi.

I was finally able to break away. I planned to write some novels and short stories but also pursue narrative non-fiction—telling stories that can do with all the telling. *Red Sun* came of this space: what I gauged as an urgent need to break through the mall-stupor of Middle India and tell it how poverty, corruption, displacement and denial were creating vast pools of negative energy across India. The Maoist rebellion was just one of the more visible and distressing versions of it.

I continue to research and write about the Maoist rebellion, and have extended my research and writing to the convergence of business and human rights—a conflict zone of the present and certainly of the future. And with the publishing of *Red Sun*, I had the required space, the bandwidth to pursue the stories I had for long wanted to, stories of neglect and conflict from the 'Northeast'.

During a road trip in Manipur and Nagaland along Highway 39

in 2008, the approach and the title of the book fell into place. This highway through its routing offered itself as a broad sutra for storytelling both about conflict and the coming out of conflict.

It's not much if you look at the distance, 436 kilometres, from a tiny outpost called Numaligarh along the southern bank of the Brahmaputra in Assam, near the well-known rhino sanctuary of Kaziranga, to the border with Myanmar, at Moreh, in the state of Manipur. It's a mere child in a country that boasts highways from Kolkata to the borders of Pakistan—the Grand Trunk Road—its template built centuries ago by Emperor Sher Shah Suri.

But Highway 39 appeared to me like few others: a living, festering snake of a lifeline that winds through a landscape of both romantic and brutal history, continuing bloodshed, immense rage, and desperate hope. Besides touching a deprived part of southeastern Assam, specifically a sliver of Karbi Anglong district, Highway 39 joins Dimapur, Kohima, Senapati, Imphal and Thoubal—past and present touch points of conflict with India. Highway 39 travels through geographies that manifested India's malaise of wilful blindness; if you will, a sort of highway to governance hell. Here, buying peace with government jobs and government dole, as India continues to discover, does not guarantee peace or people's unfettered loyalty to the Republic of India.

Manipur, which had not seen war since its squabbles with colonial Britain, is today home to several dozen insurgency groups across the tribal and religious spectrum—a direct result of New Delhi's political mismanagement of ethnic and tribal identities, and imposition of the pincer-like Armed Forces (Special Powers) Act that permits the Indian Army, its agencies and paramilitaries to perform duties that combine a soldier's and that of a modern-day Gestapo, with impunity and immunity. Life in the state is nearly at a standstill. The state's capital Imphal, as an Israeli visitor and former soldier recently told me, reminds him of the West Bank. The state and the people are deeply stressed.

'Welcome to Psycho City,' a wild-eyed, hopped-up youngster greeted me at an open-air rock concert in Imphal in the summer of 2008, the time I began to travel for this book. 'We would like to leave,' the improbably named Nightingale Singh, a student at the city's Raja Bodhchandra College told me. 'What are you doing here, man?'

The area near my hotel had been under curfew for three years, a result of several grenade attacks on soldiers as they patrolled a nearby market, Ima Keithel. Commonplace tales. The concert at which Nightingale and I met had to go without a billed marquee name, Bangalore-based Raghu Dixit Project, a band that counts folk and fusion songs in Hindi in its repertoire. A couple of major Meitei rebel groups had for years put out a fatwa against anything Hindi in Manipur. As the national language of 'colonial' India, it is unwelcome in the local rebel construct.

I told Nightingale I wanted to tell stories from here and elsewhere along the highway—and the vicinity of the highway. Before melting into a luridly decorated tattoo stall at the periphery of the concert, part of the popular Roots Festival that for some years annually travelled the Northeast, he told me I would find more stories than I would be able to tell in a lifetime. He smiled his lopsided smile. 'Remember, man. *Psycho City.*'

Eastern Assam, which Highway 39 slices through for a brief stretch, was until 2011 home to two major and three minor insurgencies, from the Karbi and Cacharese people, in various levels of surge and surrender: again, as elsewhere in this region, anger a result of ill-governance, administrative apathy, wilful ignorance of tribal and regional pride, of identities, histories and hopes. Development and income levels here count among the lowest in India, agriculture continues to be among the most primitive, education fractured, industries practically non-existent, business more subsistence and trade-related than what ought to form the core of a modern system.

In this melting pot of mandated mayhem and mess, people continue to die of conflict even as they yearn to come out of conflict. And there was dual irony, as I also learnt in the years prior to beginning the book. As much as the administration that rebel groups reviled across the 'Northeast', they too indulged in forms of extortion and corruption, putting the squeeze on common people they had sworn to protect. And the other: rebel groups which claimed to fight a particular cause could sometimes be fighting themselves—most visibly among the Naga rebel groups. In that same summer of 2008, two major factions indulged in a kind of fratricide not seen for two decades. These shambolic displays of cause and effect are also part of this story.

The 'Northeast' was for long not in as intense a geopolitical sweet-spot as Jammu & Kashmir; that would have brought global attention. Nor is it at the heart of India, like the Maoist rebellion—misunderstood as that battle too has been for its impelling force; a battle for the forgotten, ignored, reviled and conveniently written off. But an assertive China at its borders, and prospects of trade and business with Southeast Asia have in the past decade or so compelled official India to greater interaction in these parts. It is essentially a soothe-the-natives approach that geopolitics has made imperative: cool conflicts; provide play to aspirations, offer hope or we lose the empire sort of thing. And, even with a rampaging economy of conflict that lives almost entirely on Central government dole—and one that survives and thrives on the absence of firm peace: security deployment, security-mandated contracts, skimming off development funds meant to uplift broken zones and people—there is a momentum of progressive thinking and economic aspiration that is gradually spreading outward from cities like Guwahati, Shillong and, to a lesser extent, places like Dimapur, Kohima and, even, Imphal.

There is recognition that all Indians are not enemies. There is an appreciation that while the Indian state can be a productive tool of economic and development leverage, the 'Northeast' must trigger its own economic energies. As the government's Vision 2020 document for the region asserts: 'Critical to the progress towards prosperity in NER is its liberation from economic imprisonment.'

There is a growing recognition that, as an economy of conflict is seductive for those who live by it, peace must therefore be fought for; the vultures of war must be subdued, or more generations will be lost. There is hope too in certain quarters, in these blasted, hurting regions as much as in some pockets of policymaking Delhi, that the 'Northeast' could be a productive bridgehead of ties with Thailand, Laos, Cambodia, southwestern China and, more foresight and peace willing, with Myanmar and Bangladesh.

And there is growing official recognition that, if these regions are not reclaimed, they will be utterly lost to India: the same countries that profess partnership with India could drive a cleaver through it, with India's abject help.

And so, Highway 39 seemed to me like the region it travelled through. Broken, but not entirely dispirited; corrupted but fiercely hopeful; so not-India, and yet, tied to its future. (Sections of Highway 39 were re-numbered in 2011 as the National Highway Authority of India goes about streamlining its system—and today, some sections form part of the futuristic Trans Asian Highway that is to link India and Southeast Asia. And yet, for me, there was no better name for the book. To delete Highway 39 would be to delete a tormented history, a seething present, and an uncertain future.)

~

It became clear to me early on that to attempt an omnibus book on the 'Northeast' would for my purpose be impractical. If the world often has difficulty grasping the enormity of India, both on account of its geographic and ethnic variety, that logic extends to the mini-universe of its northeast. Moreover, my purpose from the beginning was to bring more stories out of the confines of the Northeast, and, equally, away from seminar rooms in which names, faces and histories are sometimes reduced to statistics and polite noise; I have attended enough seminars to know that this also is a truth.

And moreover, I would not be the first one to bring India's northeast 'out': excellent academic work, commentary, investigative work in both conventional and electronic media in general—and increasingly robust 'northeastern' media in particular—long and short fiction, poetry, and plays are quite abundant for people of the region and those interested in the region. Protest icons like Irom Sharmila of Manipur, for example, are widely known in the Indian 'Mainland', driven by reportage in print, on the Internet and television. But, generally, there isn't much news or views beyond what is occasioned by a 'news spike'—the killing of a 'VIP'; violent protests; fighting among rebels groups; the 'suspension of operations' against one rebel group or another, or the ongoing grosser human rights violations by police, paramilitaries and the army. And, there is still not enough writing and discourse about what drives the dynamic of protest and hurt in these parts.

As with much in the Indian subcontinent, there is still space to humanize a story. To tell it from the points of view of the players and participants—often, reluctant players and participants. As a storyteller, that is what I set out to do.

But, to tell these stories for the ease of both the telling and comprehension of readers I was compelled to stay away from the micro-ethnic melting pot that the 'Northeast' so often is. And so, I had to make some choices.

Highway 39 offers in its broad sutra a slice of Assam, Nagaland and Manipur. But even within this sutra, this thread, I was compelled to keep away from (only for this volume, not for any future endeavour!) representing every ethnic entity and aspiration on this route. The Karbi people of Assam, in my opinion, occasion exclusive works; and I hope to soon live and work among them to understand this more fully. And 'greater' Assam, of course, is its own special universe, a whole series of books on its own. It was not possible to represent people or stories from every Naga tribe for the sole purpose of being seen as politically correct. As this is not an ethnographic study, I have taken the approach of spontaneity. In Nagaland, for instance, if I met a victim of India's excesses who happened to be of the Ao tribe, so be it. Were a bureaucrat of the Lotha tribe, fine. Or Angami, Chakesang, and so on.

In Manipur, if a particular story I was pursuing took me to the lands of the Tangkhul Naga tribe, it was natural. The core narrative of Manipur and Imphal Valley is incomplete without the Meitei. But to look for stories among the Meitei Pangal—Muslim Meitei—simply for the sake of political correctness could amount to more words. I have similarly been constrained to refrain from a deep dive into the Kuki ethnicities in Manipur; in the slices of life I hoped to offer readers in an attempt to contribute to greater general understanding of issues and aspirations, an omnibus approach could muddy the scope. Besides, I didn't want to simply parachute in and out of people's lives, histories, miseries for the sake of it; these had to bind into a larger narrative.

This may not be the perfect approach, but to my mind there really isn't a perfect approach, only practical ones that attempt to bring untold stories—or humanized versions of told stories—to audiences that are not otherwise accessed. And, in both broad and specific terms, show everyday instances of life and death in this roiled and yet deeply aspiring region. How the people of these parts have paid a heavy price for simply wanting to be themselves. How the Republic of India has extracted that price. And how the Republic of India continues to pay a price along with the people it has tried so very hard—and often, brutally—to make its own.

My travels took me to these everyday situations, everyday truths. In the course of several visits over some years, I met rebel leaders, and security and government officials. I met everyday people living everyday lives, whether these lives were shattered by incomprehensible death or shuttered by equally incomprehensible policy. I attempted to follow the thread of some histories of conflict and, equally, the thread of some histories of conflict resolution.

Each layer, each step of the journey brought me closer to these truths and realities. As I learnt, there are many truths and realities in these parts. I sincerely hope *Highway 39* acquaints you with some of these.

Goa
January 2012

1

And so, to a place where brother kills brother

Dimapur railway station is a mass of sleeping, dozing humanity at two in the morning. Except for a couple of dozen people on Platform 1, the only one with a shelter and a low-ceilinged waiting hall, the remaining several hundred seem to be from what is known in these parts as Mainland India. Call it Neverland India if you will. Many hardliners do here, in these places east of Bengal; people for long at war not so much with India's idea of itself, but India's idea of why they should be Indian.

Labourers and fully armed troops wait to catch a train home from this plains town that is the commercial hub of Nagaland; or to another place of employment or deployment. A prospering India, and a troubled India, has ample opportunity for both.

I'm headed first to Kohima, the state's capital deep inside the Naga Hills, and I am stuck.

No hotel in Dimpaur will let me in this late into the night, not even the ones that have earlier welcomed me. Not de Oriental Dream, the quirkily named but hospitable establishment where I hold a now useless reservation. Certainly not the state-run Saramati, the creaky, musty, supremely polite place that firmly shutters its entrance at 9 p.m. And I'm unable to find a taxi driver who will brave Highway 39 to reach Kohima; indeed, any road to any part of the state except the immediate environs of Dimapur.

This is partly because there is prudence in avoiding hilly roads in pitch dark, negotiating hazards like seemingly infinite drop-offs and wrecked tarmac that mock both a quick car and quick driver, and deride as impotent even the aid of robust headlights. And part of it is born out of long years of knowing well the strange animal of conflict. After decades of war and a decade of tense peace wrought by a bizarre ceasefire between India and two main Naga rebel groups—groups that have an ironical history of mutual bloodletting—danger lurks around here.

The previous time I visited, a year earlier in May 2008, one such group had been battling a faction that had broken away just months earlier.

Over April and May that year, the streets of Dimapur and nearby villages had become a battleground. Young Naga men from a breakaway faction of the largest Naga rebel group, National Socialist Council of Nagalim (Isak-Muivah) (NSCN-IM), claiming to fight for Naga honour and freedom for Nagaland from India, had in combat uniform and armed with automatic weapons, abducted or chased down and killed their former colleagues from NSCN-IM—similarly dressed and armed young men who also claimed to be fighting for Naga honour and freedom from India. Twenty people had died in a matter of weeks, among them a student and a bystander. By July, the number of dead from such skirmishing would rise to a hundred.

'Much damage is committed in reducing our noble cause to a cheap struggle,' the influential Naga Students Federation, a conglomerate of twenty-two tribal students' bodies, admonished in a scathing statement that, while angrily criticizing Naga rebel factions, was careful to not permit India's stake among the Nagas any leeway. 'Perhaps,' the statement chided these 'national workers' whom India calls rebels, 'the nobility of our struggle is reduced to an embarrassing state.'

But that was only a small part of a sordid tale in the sordid history of the region.

I am stuck in the dead of night because my train from Guwahati, the Rajdhani Express, the only train on which I could get a reservation, was three hours late. This is generally regarded as being 'on time', going by the train's record of travel from New Delhi and onward to the trading and oil town Dibrugarh in the far east of Assam—and so, quite nearly the far east of India. It's not unknown for trains in these parts to arrive half a day, even a day after they are scheduled to, for a journey of about 2,500 kilometres from New Delhi. A relatively quick train like the Rajdhani is supposed to take thirty-nine hours; slower trains take fifty-three—on time.

My immediate journey from Guwahati to this commercial hub was just a tenth of that distance, traversed comfortably in a little over four hours, even with the continuous chatter of my co-passengers, two Central Reserve Police Force officers carrying on about real estate investments in their home in the faraway Gangetic plains city of Lucknow, close to the longitudinal centre of India. Another universe.

Dimapur has the only railway station in Nagaland. It's also the only one its southern neighbours from Manipur can productively use to reach the mainland. The alternate station for Manipur at Silchar, the tea town in Assam not far from India's south-eastern border with Bangladesh, means a minimum of a day's travel on an absolute horror of a road; and, anyway, to get from Silchar by train west to the mainland, requires laborious changeovers in Guwahati.

Resigned to temporary homelessness, I crunch into the back seat of a bug yellow Suzuki Alto sub-compact taxi in the parking lot of Dimapur station, having arranged with the driver to be off at 4.30 a.m., or first light, whichever is earlier. It is suffocating in the muggy late-August heat if I keep the windows rolled up. Roll one down even an inch and squadrons of emphatic mosquitoes pour in.

The young Nepali taxi driver has it worked out: he looks at me disdainfully, sprawls on the pushed-back driver's seat, covers himself from head to toe with a filthy cotton sheet, and begins to snore.

Wide awake, I dream of the nearby Naga Hills that touch me with a physical force each time I see them.

As a long-time Himalaya addict I've had a fair share of the slow, winding rides and hikes through the now denuded foothills in India and Nepal to reach relatively more wooded areas and then to the great heights of the snowline. In my adoptive home of Goa, cradled by the Western Ghats that parallel the Konkan and Malabar coasts, evergreen is a way of life—at least where zealous miners of iron and manganese ore let ancient forests and hills alone. These blue-green hills, dwarfs to the Himalaya but of a still handsome height, continue to provide a rush for the senses, water for rivers, and a soothing ecological cocoon to residents.

The Naga Hills have begun to do the same for me, and added dimensions of its own beyond physical characteristics. The prospect of spending a few days or weeks nestled in the mist, the clouds, cloaked by a determined history and a largely indeterminate future makes me both greatly excited and deeply concerned. Travel here means confronting the truths, lies and bloodshed that have shaped modern India. It means confronting the reality that people whom I was instructed to revere since my childhood, names we as Indians read as streets, stadia and institutes of learning, faces we saw in history books and on increasingly rare postage stamps, treated other citizens—people these revered names and faces glibly insisted were citizens—with brutality that rivalled any other in these modern times.

The feeling had consumed me again just days earlier as I chatted with Temsula Ao, the Naga writer who is also dean at North-Eastern Hill University at Shillong. Among other things, I was curious to know if some of her stories were rooted in personal experience, or were derived from hearsay—stories that travelled across Naga regions and generations, riding equally on despair and anger. It was a mix, she told me: some personal, some carried. Then she smiled and said gently, as cold rain fell outside her heated office and we sipped from cups of strong, sweet tea: 'Part of my anger is there.'

The stories, she insisted, personal and otherwise, simply had to be told, like the one about young Apenyo in 'The Last Song'. It's set in 'troubled times' as Ao writes in this story from *These Hills Called Home: Stories from a War Zone*, and is about a girl who loved to sing. It was a time when the Naga independence movement 'was gaining momentum by the day and even the remotest villages were getting involved, if not directly in terms of their members joining the underground army, then certainly by paying "taxes" to the underground "government".' Apenyo's village, no different from so many across the Naga regions, was preparing to celebrate a 'double Christmas', with the inauguration of a new church. As the pastor led the congregation in prayer, and Apenyo, the best singer in the village, rejoiced in anticipation of leading the choir that would begin as soon as invocatory prayers ended, they all heard the sound of gunfire in the distance.

'...*Very soon the approaching soldiers surrounded the crowd, and the pastor was commanded to come forward and identify himself along with the gaonburas. But before they could do anything Apenyo burst into her solo ... and not to be outdone by the bravery or foolishness of this young girl, and not wishing to leave her thus exposed, the entire choir burst into song. The soldiers were incensed; it was an act of open defiance and proper retaliation had to be made ... the crowd, now overcome by fear and anger, began to disperse in every direction...*

...Only Apenyo stood her ground. She sang on ... as if an unseen presence was guiding her ... as if to withstand the might of the guns ... In desperation, Libeni rushed forward to pull her daughter away but the leader of the army was quicker. He grabbed Apenyo by the hair and with a bemused look on his face dragged her away from the crowd towards the old church building...'

This haunting story draws me in like none other in Ao's book.

'There was chaos everywhere,' she writes. 'Villagers trying to flee were either shot at or kicked and clubbed by the soldiers who seemed to be everywhere ... Libeni was now frantic. Calling out her daughter's name loudly, she began to search for her in the direction where she was last seen being dragged away by the leader. When she came upon the scene at last, what she saw turned her stomach: the young captain was raping Apenyo while a few other soldiers were watching the act and seemed to be waiting for their turn. The mother, crazed by what she was witnessing, rushed forward with a growl as if to haul the man off her daughter's body but a soldier grabbed her and pinned her down on the ground ... The small band of soldiers took their turn, even though by the time the fourth one mounted, the woman was already dead.'

And then, it was time for apex butchery; the description imprinted firmly in my mind's eye. '...Returning to the scene of their recent orgy, the captain saw ... the two women, both dead. He shouted an order for his men to dump them on the porch of the old church. He then ordered them to take positions around the church and at his signal they emptied their guns into the building. The cries of the wounded and the dying inside the church proved that even the house of God could not provide them security and save them from the bullets of the crazed soldiers ... But the savagery was not over yet. Seeing that it would be a waste of time and bullets to kill off all the witnesses inside the church, the order was given to set it on fire...'

For me, travelling in these parts is a little like being buffeted by a wrenching history of conflict and a desperately yearning future; and for temporal dessert, some twisted reality as well.

~

There they are, the Naga Hills, to our left, nearly as soon as we cross the sluggish brown snake of the Dhansiri and turn to the south-east for a few kilometres. Soon we will take a sharp left, turn due east and let the heights take us in.

Dawn arrives over the hills like light caressing the world, touching the scattered clouds with flecks of orange and red. A layer below, around the still shadowy midsection, a sarong of mist drapes the green. The air is moist, cool, and smells of the earth and bamboo. It rakes my face pleasantly. The concrete nightmare of Dimapur is behind us: on either side are teakwood plantations; further on, the hint of evergreen. Tendrils of mist dance on the highway. It is quiet in the early morning. I can't help thinking: the tranquil beauty of it all can probably make an atheist wonder if there is a God, and if he, or she, ever took a course in applied art before attempting anything as advanced as Creation.

The taxi driver fortunately has eyes only for the road. He calmly chews on pata and tamul—paan leaf and betel nut—energy for the two-and-a-half-hour mostly uphill run to Kohima. He inserts a USB drive into the innards of an MP3 player by the dashboard, and shoots me an enquiring glance. Not now, I request him. Wait till the morning is less lovely. He smiles and shakes his head. He seems cheerful enough after his nap, bright-eyed at 5 a.m.

Even the time, Indian Standard, is part of the day's allure. To our very near-east, in Myanmar, it is 6 a.m. To our west, in the intervening mass of Bangladesh, as it were, further away than Myanmar as the crow flies, it is 4.30. But it is 5 a.m. again further *west*, back in India in Kolkata—and the same time two-and-a-half thousand kilometres even further to the west, by the border of Gujarat abutting Pakistan. The bizarre application of IST has time and again driven groups of well-known persons from the 'northeast', more recently the Assamese film-maker Jahnu Barua, to demand a different time zone, for the daylight saving it would bring and, with it, more efficient use of time and greater productivity. Perhaps the effect of managing different time zones in an already chaotic country has kept India's rulers and administrators from enforcing it, but it is difficult to not give in to the sneaking suspicion that time, too, is on call at the all-knowing altar of the Republic of India. It is entirely conceivable that, were India to stretch a further thousand kilometres on either side, from, say, Iran to Laos, for a show of government-mandated unity it would still be under the paternalistic embrace of IST.

There it is, to my left: Diphupar Gate at the '4th Mile', soon after the turn to Dimapur's tiny airport and Nagaland's only, nestled between the highway and the hills.

On a summer night the previous year, 10 May 2008, here at Diphupar Gate I had watched several thousand women from numerous Naga tribes, sickened to their hearts with bloodshed from Naga killing Naga, gather for a torchlight rally. Many carried candles, but most staves of green bamboo split at one end to hold small containers of oil feeding the flames of protest. Traffic was at standstill. This stretch of Highway 39 belonged to the ladies, there at the call of the Naga Mothers' Hoho, or apex association, of the Dimapur area.

I had walked into the charged throng; and the ladies, young and old, allowed me, an obvious stranger. Two middle-aged women stood on an open-top truck by a building that advertised the Nagaland Muay Thai Institute. The ladies were positioned behind a couple of microphones on stands, connected to a battered amplifier and further, to two large loudspeakers fixed on top of the driver's cab—the ensemble powered by a car battery.

I had walked in mid-speech. A stout lady with glasses was speaking in a mixture of Nagamese and English.

'Ekta request koribo,' she spoke in a strong voice over the crowd that stood in respectful silence. She raised her pitch. 'Stop this killing! Stop this fighting!'

She turned her anger on the Naga rebel factions, taunting them to kill her if they wished. 'Aru ki koribey? Amakey maribey?' That brought a wave of laughter, but it was quickly stilled.

Her voice seemed amplified in the ensuing silence. 'If you love your brother and sister, father and mother, son and daughter, *stop* this fighting, *stop* this killing.'

People around me had begun to wipe their eyes. I stood transfixed.

She spoke of how the next day would be celebrated everywhere as Mother's Day. 'Only Dimapur-ay nohoi, Nagaland-ay nohoi, whole *world*-ay hoi.'

'It is up to us mothers to talk peace. We will have to go door to door. How many more children will we give birth to,' her voice dropped to a choked whisper that the speakers carried to every ear, every heart in the gathering, 'to see them die?'

She started to cry, and we cried with her.

Then it was time for payer. The second lady on the truck led the crowd, in Nagamese, and then English.

'Dear Lord,' she intoned, and the ladies repeated after her. 'Take away our garment of fear. Give us your garment of peace and hope.'

I looked around. The ladies had their eyes closed in prayer. Some covered their eyes. A few shook with sobs.

'We pray to you. We give ourselves unto you. In Jesus' name, Amen.'

They marched on slowly towards St Anne's Church down the road, for a few minutes of silent prayer.

I watched it flow, this river of light.

~

The landscape is richer as we come closer to the hills. Hemmed in by the highway on one side and the hills on the other, the plains narrow to form a triangle past Chumukedima, or 'Chumu', as locals refer to the small, increasingly urbanized village in charming diminution. Fallow fields give way to a mix of badlands of tall grass broken with now-dry depressions and the occasional patch of vegetable on higher ground. The land undulates gently as it approaches the hills. A shallow gorge opens up to our left, cleaved by the Dhansiri—we shall soon follow the river for several kilometres as we begin our climb to Kohima near the sharp turn-off for Patkai Christian College. It's as if the highway, fifteen kilometres from Dimapur, squeezes shut the valley.

It's killing country.

Six days after the mothers marched, the smouldering anger of NSCN-IM exploded on the breakaway faction, the one that has abducted its cadres. The dominating group hadn't been able to swallow the split in the first place when, in late 2007 a hundred of its officers and cadres broke away under the leadership of Azheto Chophy and set up camp at Vihokhu village in the shadow of the hills under the flag of NSCN-Unification. Vihokhu isn't far from Dimapur; it is on the side of Highway 39 that ultimately converges near Patkai Christian College.

The breakaway had been a massive blow to the prestige of IM, not only as an organization, but because its own general headquarters, or Oking, lay just a few miles away at Camp Hebron—named after the Old Testament holy city of Joshua and Abraham, among other biblical luminaries—accessed from the opposite side of the highway. Besides, Unification cadres strutting about in Dimapur, a place IM has long held to be its backyard, was galling: several Unification cadres were camped there, and many more were spread around Chumu. This affected IM's notion of territory for control of both tactics and 'taxation'—imposed subscription on salaries and sales that feed rebel engines. They were equally upset with the kidnapping and eventual execution of an IM cadre by the Unification faction from the vicinity of the heavily patrolled IM training area of Mt Gilead—another Old Testament geography of significance to ancient Israelites and, as incongruous as it may seem, to the stolidly Baptist-influenced NSCN-IM.

It had hurt its sense of prestige some more because the Unification faction almost immediately after its breakaway made overtures to the Khaplang faction, or NSCN-K, which had parted ways with the then-undivided NSCN after a series of brutal pre-emptive strikes a decade earlier, in 1988. The union of breakaways was, for all practical purposes, made public on 7 May 2008, when NSCN-K released its reconstituted list of kilonsers—ministers—in which Unification members were awarded key positions.

Conflict quickly escalated. On 16 May 2008 around 5.30 a.m., IM cadres ambushed and chased down a group of their former colleagues. After a fierce gun battle lasting nearly seven hours, fifteen Unification cadres lay dead.

Just about a fortnight later on 3 June, IM attacked the Unification camp at Vihokhu. More than a dozen Unification cadres died. In another attack three weeks later, the camp was entirely overrun. Most managed to escape, but ten Unification cadres are believed to have died.

This yet again underscored a recurring theme—gratefully leveraged by Indian intelligence operatives and policymakers—of Naga sovereignty and identity: From fighting India to fighting one another.

We roll up to the checkpoint past a massive gate designed in the Naga fashion of crossed beams curling inward at the top. This is where my 'Inner Line Permit', issued a few days earlier in Shillong, the still-charming capital of nearby Meghalaya, needs to be shown for entry to the Naga Hills. Dimapur and its 'plains' environs remain free zones, but no place else. Every non-Naga citizen of India, with the exception of political bigwigs, Indian Army troops and paramilitary, needs this paper to travel to specified districts in Nagaland, for a specified time. Colonial British used it to restrict entry into the hills with a view to prevent rampant inroads of people from the plains—basically, people from elsewhere, and people unlike them or the Nagas. The Government of India used the ILP, as it is known in speakeasy acronym, to prevent news of its campaign of butchery against the Nagas in the 1950s, '60s and '70s from getting out.

This is 2009. Nobody stirs to stop the taxi, to check the piece of pro-forma paper I clutch in readiness as proof of being a law-abiding citizen—abiding by Section (1-4) of The Bengal Eastern Frontier Regulation 1873: ancient, misused, but nevertheless, a law.

I'm through. Not too bad, I think. This is largely thanks to the relative absence of conflict, at least of the kind sponsored wholesale by the Government of India—shoot, shell, bury alive, set alight, cut open, molest, rape, torture, and pen into concentration camps a people to ensure they remain Indians. As well: raze villages, destroy food stock, scare people into the jungle where, for lack of patriotism as New Delhi deemed it, they often starved or died of disease, sometimes both.

My driver, perhaps to soothe my disappointment at not being stopped for checking, but more likely to break the monotony of a near-continuous series of hairpin bends and sharp turns that pave the broken way to Kohima, turns up the volume to raucous Bollywood pop.

The morning dies.

2

Spiritsong: Journeying to the grave of Angami Zapu Phizo

I play a memory game of places as we careen through absolute jungle which moves away only when the hills change from a steep to a gentle slope, or when the road forces it, or the jumble of a waystation village carves from it a defiant and dusty existence.

I say it aloud: Dimapur-Chumukedima-Medziphema-Piphema-Sechü-Kohima.

'You missed Pherima,' the driver reminds me, and cackles. 'It's between Medziphema and Piphema.'

He is right. I briefly toy with the idea of quizzing him about the Assam Rifles outposts strung out along our route—Foxtrot Company of 20 Assam Rifles at Medziphema, Alpha Company at Piphema, and Charlie Company at Sechü. A cheap shot, I let that go. And, anyway, he might again put me in my place; tell me of a few I have missed.

Traffic picks up. We are soon into an endless line of trucks, buses, army and paramilitary convoys, and cars. At Piphema, about halfway to Kohima, as we stop for a quick breakfast of boiled eggs with red chilly powder, and tea, downhill traffic of a similar nature is dense as it passes us on the way to the plains. The princes and princesses of politics and bureaucracy will soon follow, to spend a day of administration and intrigue in Dimapur, or to be on time for the infrequent flights to the transportation and shopping hubs of Kolkata or Guwahati. When the skies are somewhat overcast, as they are now, Nagaland's chief minister, Neiphiu Rio, too would have to drive down—or up—in a motorcade of SUVs, sacrificing a helicopter ride. His colleague farther south along Highway 39 in adjacent Manipur, Okram Ibobi Singh, has it a little easier, jetting in and out of the fairer weather and larger airport at Imphal; but most of the rest that Ibobi Singh professes to administer have no recourse to but this highway for travel or commerce.

It's such an artery that when there is a snarl-up, chaos ensues. This could be because of that area of perpetual landslip just below Kohima, or the frequent blockades on account of political protest along the stretch from Kohima south to Imphal (for the formation of a new district, or protest against it; for delayed elections to various councils that, on paper, administer hill districts; extra-judicial killings—take your pick). The protesters could variously be angry Naga residents of Manipur's northern hill districts; or their counterparts from the Kuki tribes; or the 'plains' Meiteis who are often seen by the hill people as encroaching on their turf and lives; and, anyway, many in Manipur live in perpetual angst against the State and its often ham-handed administrative and policing paraphernalia. When a blockade happens, prices of essentials, food and fuel—mostly trucked from the refinery of Indian Oil at Numaligarh, at the northern end of the highway—shoot up along with tempers. Then, everybody curses this lifeline, and sometimes, deathline, of a road.

Usually, the Meiteis and Kukis of Manipur blame the Nagas of both Manipur and Nagaland. The Nagas in turn blame the Kukis or Meiteis. And, usually, they all blame India.

Kohima arrives almost as a surprise, a distant view of kindergarten buildings that, in the nature of such places from Shimla to

Darjeeling, look a lot prettier from far, or at dusk, at night, at dawn. That is when pinpoints of electric lights and mist hide the merciless daytime views of overgrown, creaking habitations—squalid, teeming, overpopulated mini-metros draped across hills that seem ready to plunge with the entire sprouted mess into shadowy valleys and be done with it.

The entry to Kohima, strung roughly north to south on a series of ridges and slopes shows exactly that: clusters of shanties and tiny shops on either side of the road as we arrive at a three-way junction. On my right the highway, now little more than churned-up asphalt decorated with impressive potholes, slopes further upward on to the southern aspect of Kohima and its majestic backdrop of Japfü peak, hidden this morning in a mantle of cloud. The highway then travels through the region known as that of the southern Angami tribe, to Mao Gate, the marker of another, eponymous Naga tribe and into Manipur. The jumble of shops directly in front of us at the tri-junction also houses the Dream Café, a tiny, friendly place of coffee and conversation with excellent views of the eastern valleys and hills.

But today I take a left to head towards the main market area and Kohima village. The commercial Razhü Gate area—which my driver, evidently taken in with the sycophantic Congress party template of naming just about any significant public place or building after members of the Nehru-Gandhi family, calls Rajiv Gate—is open for business. I stop only to collect some newspapers from a stationery store crowded with schoolchildren making last-minute purchases before class.

~

We move on past Kohima village. It had nearly died during the Naga wars with India, and earlier, during colonial India's war with Japan. The cemetery full of Allied troops and officers, a trimly maintained tourist attraction in Kohima that features in brochures and guidebooks, is now behind us.

The Naga dead from the wars with India are more discreetly held, buried in memories that pass on from one generation to the next and resurrected in memorials not spoken of in tourist literature. Implicit defiance against India remains fresh across Nagaland and all the Naga regions.

I first came by it some years earlier on the way from Kohima to Khonoma, Naga rebel legend Angami Zapu Phizo's home village. A few hillsides away from Kohima, it was a bastion of Naga resistance at the time of British domination in the Indian subcontinent as it was during the time of Indian's brutalizing of the Naga regions. Phizo, who died in 1990, had known both times.

'Nagas are not Indian: their territory is not a part of the Indian Union,' I read on a marker along the twisting track made almost impassably muddy by May showers. 'We shall uphold and defend the unique truth at all costs and always.'

The quote was ascribed to Khrisanisa Seyietsu, who held office from July 1956 to February 1959 as the first president of the rebel Federal Government of Nagaland. It wasn't an old marker either. The Reverend V.K. Nuh, general secretary of the Council of Nagaland Baptist Churches, formally unveiled the commemorative in February 2007.

At picture-postcard Khonoma, by the tiny grocery that caters to visitors and locals alike, a large block of basalt hosts the flag of free Nagaland and a memorial decorated with wreaths of flower and pinecone. Placed in 1997, it remembers forty-six people from Khonoma who died fighting India between 1956 and 1992. The text, as ever, is stark: 'These men and women of Khonoma gave their lives for the vision of a free Naga nation. We remember and salute them and still hold fast to their vision.'

The Government of Nagaland knows of these declarations of sadness and pride, and won't mess with them. It knows of the furore that this would cause. The Government of India and its agencies won't mess with these either. It would reopen barely healed wounds. It might destroy peace—a restless, even ludicrous peace, but peace nevertheless.

They maintain a similar distance from Phizo's grave.

There will always be flowers on it, I know, fresh and dried. There may even be some bouquets for both a leader and a legend who earned immense admiration and respect; and a broken man ultimately defied by many of his own people, ridiculed by many for being away, aloof abroad. He remained in sanctuary in the United Kingdom even as lives continued to be destroyed in the name of the movement he helped to begin and coalesce; even as an India-machinated state was born in 1963 out of facile agreement; even as new rebel factions, most emphatically the NSCN, evolved out of the construct of the Naga National Council (NNC)—Phizo's child. These latter-day rebel leaders barely disguised their contempt for 'Uncle' Phizo, a leader who led from the comfort of a home in Bromley, Kent.

Phizo, his legacy unreconciled, lies by the sprawling, helter-skelter concrete warren of Nagaland's Secretariat. He was brought here from England in 1990, permitted the reconciliatory journey in death to the homeland he fled in 1956 with the help of India's freshly minted arch-enemy Pakistan, and a well-known Baptist missionary, Michael Scott. I sometimes wondered why a son of Khonoma was not at home in Khonoma, but was instead interred with ironical ceremony in a suburb of Kohima, by the entrance to the gates of the Secretariat, a symbol of government—indeed, by extension, the Government of India—that he stood against for so long.

'Isn't Phizo a son of Khonoma? Shouldn't he be there, at home?' I once asked a senior bureaucrat in the Government of Nagaland. I could picture in my mind's eye the memorial that would perch on the highest point of the lip of ridge that dominates the village, surrounded by the comforting maze of green hills, lush terraces of paddy, the horrors of war now made over to the sounds of peacetime: a carpenter at work, a farmer calling out to another, the free laughter of a child carried on the breeze. The image of kelhoukevira: in Angami, the-land-where-life-is-good.

'Phizo is a son of Nagaland,' the elegant Naga lady had replied in an accent moulded by several years at good private schools, and Miranda House, an elite college of Delhi University. 'He belongs to us all. He belongs *here*.' She had nodded her impeccably coiffured head to indicate Phizo's grave, located in the direction behind her padded leather chair.

In Nagaland the feeling is never far that, even as India thinks that Nagaland belongs to India, the Nagas have believed, all through fire, retribution, rebuilding of their homelands and a patchy reconciliation with India, that Nagaland has always belonged to the Nagas. India will at worst remain an entity of compulsive power; at best, an entity of convenience.

Phizo's grave is a living testimony to this.

The first time I saw the grave on a summer day some years past, the sombre grey-black blocks of unpolished granite, assembled in the shape of an arrow aimed resolutely north, I knew that emotion. There lay wreaths of lilies and orchids, their white-yellow-violet-fuchsia offering both innocent, unmarked respect of the public and deliberate statements from rebels. One wreath had pinned on it the visitor's tag, marked in black felt-tip: 'C-in-C Naga Army'. Beside it were offerings of rebel commanders of the 'Ao Region', 'Chakesang Region', 'Angami Region' and 'General Officer Commanding the Northern Command, Naga Army'. I didn't hazard a guess as to which rebel faction these may have been from—all factions claim to be the real Naga Army, and all carve out 'regions' according to specific tribal zones of the Nagas.

The open presentation was important, though, irrespective of factions. So too was the importance of the message the wreaths celebrated. The memorial stone perched on the arrow didn't mince words about Phizo's place in history. Under the mark of a cross etched in stone were also etched these words:

A.Z. PHIZO
FATHER OF THE NATION
HERE RESTS THE MAN
WHO GAVE HIS ALL
FOR HIS PEOPLE
16: 5: 1904 – 30: 4: 1990

At the base of the memorial, 'commissioned by Funeral Organisation Committee on behalf of the Nagas', was a more resolute statement from Phizo, first in Angami, then in English. I always picked first the words in Angami; for me its alienness was somewhat reduced by the use of the Roman script, and so I would read words that I didn't understand, and yet somehow I understood their power.

Urra Uvie
Urra kha mia tsülie
Lho
Ungumvümia sü
Upecütsie zo

Our land is our
Heritage.
To none shall it be surrendered:
As whetstone our opponents sharpen
Us.

~

I am drawn inexorably to Phizo's grave. Inexplicably, I feel I cannot enter Kohima and not visit what in modern Naga lore is not merely a grave; it's a touchstone to history.

We drive past Kohima village to begin a short, sharp descent before the stretch of blacktop towards the Secretariat and 'new' Kohima, my personal journey to be touched by the spirit of the hills. As I travel again to Phizo's grave, I think about what I read the previous day while travelling to Nagaland. It was a conversation recorded in a book, *My Journey in the Nagaland Freedom Movement*, by Biseto Medom Keyho, and published in 2008—a year ago. The conversation is between Phizo-in-exile in the United Kingdom, and visiting Indian prime minister, Morarji Desai.

They met in London in June 1977, Desai riding high after the Janata Party's resounding defeat of Indira Gandhi's Congress in the general elections. Desai had initially disagreed to meet Phizo unless the Naga rebel leader formally accepted the Indian Constitution as his guiding doctrine. The meeting came about nevertheless, on Desai's understanding that Nagaland would not be on the agenda. But to expect Phizo to not mention Nagaland was either foolishness or arrogance. Keyho's book excerpts the fascinating, often belligerent conversation that underscored yet again India's official position of not remotely considering any manner of freedom for the Nagas. Nehru's dictum of India's unity at any cost had now passed seamlessly to the man who came to rule the empire of India after his daughter, Indira.

This is reportedly how the conversation went:

Phizo: I have come to meet the prime minister of India because my people have been suffering for a very long time. And you have become the prime minister of India for only about three months. I am not blaming you for our sufferings—that I want you to understand, but I thought we could find a way to bring about an end on the matter.

Desai: The Nagas are not suffering. And if you talk about Nagaland, I shall not talk with you. I told your niece Rano that I am prepared to meet you as a person but not about Nagaland.

Phizo: In 1947 when the British were about to leave their Empire a Naga delegation went to Delhi to meet Mahatma Gandhi because our situation may not have been understood by the Indians. And we explained to Mahatma Gandhi that the Nagas are not Indians and Nagaland is not Indian territory. We submitted the points of discussion to Mahatma Gandhi earlier as his secretary asked us to do so. I think his secretary was Mr Pyarelal. We asked Gandhi if India will attack Nagaland when it became free. Mahatma Gandhi said, 'If you say that Nagas are not Indians and Nagaland is not Indian territory then the matter must stop there. We also do not want the British and they are going. India will not attack you. She has no right to do so and I will sacrifice my life for you before any Naga (is) shot.'

Desai: From where the meeting took place?

Phizo: In Delhi at Bhangi Colony. Mahatma Gandhi was assassinated soon after. If he had lived a few months longer the Naga problem would not have arisen but if we do what Mahatma Gandhi would have said were he alive there will be no difficulty.

Desai: Why have you brought up Mahatma Gandhi's name? I know him better than you. I will not follow him. I will do everything what I consider to be right. Now, what more do you want to say?

Phizo: I have come to meet the prime minister of India because the Nagas have been suffering for a long time and we must find a way out to end the trouble.

Desai: I told you the Nagas are not suffering. I know everything. And there is nothing to discuss. Nagaland became a state in India in 1960 [it became a state in 1963], before that it was in Assam.

Phizo: How could Nagaland become a state in India?

Desai: It was the Nagas who came and asked for a state and it was given to them.

Phizo: But that is an argument and I (didn't) come here to argue with you. The Government of India may claim something on their part and the Nagas uphold something on their part, and there may be a wide gap between us. But the problem is more serious than an argument and I wish that we could find a way and go into the matter more deeply.

Desai: No. I will not talk about Nagaland. And if you want to talk about Nagaland, this is the end of the meeting.

Phizo: I am 73, and you are older than me. How long are we going to be here? Even if you and I do not agree today that is not the end. So, we must find a way to solve our problem, and the sooner the better. Are you not as good as the British who have given freedom to India?

Desai: Why you talk about the British now? Who are they? It is said the Aryans came to India and all that, but what is the use talking about the past? We are already here—and what else? You are a foreigner. You are staying in a foreign country. You receive reports and talk about it. I have all the reports, and there is no problem. I know everything. I am the prime minister of India and nobody needs to tell me that there is a problem.

Phizo: We the people of Asia fought against the white imperialists. And how could we Asians now fight and kill each other?

Desai: Why bring up Asia? It is India.

Phizo: Will the prime minister of India exterminate the Nagas?

Desai: Yes, I will exterminate all the Naga rebels. There will be no mercy.

Phizo: Is not that horrible?

Desai: We are protecting our citizens. Only a few Nagas are giving trouble, harassing the people in the villages—that we cannot allow. We must protect our citizens. And I will exterminate all. There will be no mercy.

Phizo: Whether we are few or many I thought we could go into the matter deeper.

Desai: I told you I shall not discuss Nagaland and if you want to talk about Nagaland, this is the end of the meeting. What more do you want to say?

Phizo: Well, my meeting you today, as it is, is more in the nature of making an acquaintance with you as our case is a long-standing one which we cannot decide in a day. I have some Naga colleagues with me including my daughter and son. I want them to come and meet you and hear from you what you have said to me. Can I go and bring them in?

Desai: Yes.

Phizo: I have told the prime minister of India that the Nagas are suffering terribly for so many years.

Desai: The Nagas are suffering because they are persisting on [sic] independence. You and all who are outside are welcome back to become Indian. But if you want to talk only Naga independence I won't talk to you.

Khodao Yanthan [Naga leader accompanying Phizo]: When you were elected prime minister, because all through your life you fought, the Nagas thought you will be the man for the final settlement of the Naga problem.

Desai: What is there to settle? ... I will have absolutely no leniency on rebels. If you want to persist on [sic] independence I will have nothing to talk ... I will certainly exterminate the Naga rebels. I have no compunction in that.

Phizo: Mr Prime Minister, will there be further opportunity for discussions?

Desai: What discussion? There will be no discussion.

~

The Naga National Council is today a faded remnant, with statements occasionally emanating from the UK. It banned the book by Biseto Medom Keyho as it contains several exposes of the pettiness that engulfed NNC and several branches of the Naga 'national movement'. But NNC still has cadres. Even if they are small in number—much smaller than either NSCN-IM or the Khaplang-led faction of NSCN—they still have weapons enough to be taken as a pressure group, as spoilers and stakeholders in the future of Nagaland. Their leader, Adinno, Phizo's daughter, is the puppeteer heir, ruling from the UK. She is often painted as an object of derision by other rebel factions, including those that split during her stewardship. Her pronouncements in rebuttal are equally derisive, equally shrill. It's a personality-driven, egotistical, roiled mess.

I recall a late-night conversation in Kohima with a former NNC heavyweight railing at me as he once claimed to have railed at Phizo.

'What are you doing in London?' the elderly gentleman, now an anti-corruption activist-academic flung his arms about in recreating his animated conversation with the 'father' of his nation. 'Come back here and fight.'

'You have to be with the people. Come *here.*' The gentleman had pointed towards his worktable, laden with administrative and legal papers, reference books, classics and adventure novels. 'What can you do by being away? *Nothing.*'

'They are all corrupt.' He had shaken his head, fury suddenly dissipated, segueing to his other favourite topic, besides Phizo.

'The leaders here are among the most corrupt we have. The most corrupt in India.'

There it is now, Angami Zapu Phizo's grave, washed by the scent of young pine, serenaded by the sirens and busy red beacons of government cars that stream in and out of the Secretariat, on either side Kohima grown like a frantic, ambitious amoeba, marking once-forested hills with rude slashes of construction.

I go to make my compact with history.

3

'Madam, do you want an honest answer? I don't consider myself an Indian'

'I am a first-generation entrepreneur from here.' Neichute Doulo spreads his arms to include the geography. 'So I am sometimes invited to speak at various forums.'

We are at the terrace that fronts his single-storey house, perched on a lip of hill overlooking Highway 39 as it winds its way south past the southern Angami regions towards Mao Gate. In this quiet preserve in the southern suburbs of Kohima, Neichute can on clear days look across the rolling hills to the south-east and to his own tribe's homeland, of the Chakesang Naga. Indian soldiers and paramilitary left emphatic imprints there during the war to ensure Nehru's wish that the Chakesangs, like other Nagas, remain with India. Of course, this wish fulfilment had led, at least from what I read in some books of history and journals, to the standard government modus operandi for subduing political aspiration at the time: beat-rape-maim-kill-burn.

We stand looking that way, silent for a while. A sharp breeze envelops us in its late-morning embrace. It muffles the sound of his children playing, the sounds of the kitchen, and the rare sound of birdsong.

'Once, at St Xavier's College in Bombay, a lady in the audience asked me whether I feel I am an Indian. So I told her, "Madam, do you want an honest answer or just an answer?" She said, "Definitely I want an honest answer."

'When I told her that I don't consider myself to be Indian, she got very annoyed,' smiles the founder of Entrepreneurs Associates, a microfinance organization focused on farmers and the unemployed. 'This was in 2002, I think. I was asked the same question in 2003 in Pune. There were senior army officers present, including the former general officer commanding of the Eastern Command—he had then been retired for a year. His wife had very good memories of Nagaland; he too. I told them the same thing. But I said that I am not in any way an Indian, in the same way I don't feel like I am an American or Chinese.' Neichute explains that he also told them he had not directly experienced any 'bad things' from the Indian Army; and that he had not seen most of 'our struggle' because he was born in 1972. 'It so happens that being Naga is my natural assertion.'

Fair enough, I respond. Being Bengali is my natural assertion. And because the history and political structure since the time of India's independence haven't yet offended the sense of identity of the Bengali people who live in India, and that of my own, being Indian has also become my natural assertion.

Neichute interrupts softly, looking at me: 'Yes, but we were not allowed to read our own history.'

'Why?' I know the answer, but the query is reflexive.

'Because we don't have it in our textbooks. In our school it was offensive to mention Naga history. I studied in a Jesuit school and all the priests and teachers were from mainland India. They were also nationalistic, perhaps from their point of view rightly so, and nothing of our history was actually discussed. But when we were in college—here in Nagaland—some of our lecturers, who were Nagas themselves, would sometimes discuss this away from class.'

He leads me back to the wood-panelled living room. His police officer friend who was present when I arrived, Chinese Chakesang—'Shee-nay-say but you spell it as Chy-neese, nah?'—is having tea. He has to return to work soon, he explains with a smile of apology as we take our places on a sofa set around a low, polished wooden table.

Neichute's interest in Naga history grew when he was in Class 12 at school and during the early years of undergraduate study. Nudged by peers and teachers, he began to read a number of books on Naga history; one that struck him was a book by Nirmal Nibedon, a journalist who wrote what is now considered a classic, a gripping account of the Naga wars called *Nagaland: The Night of the Guerrillas*. His interest sparked, Neichute dug around in the archives of *The Assam Chronicle* for articles from the time of the war. He also went back to Thetsumi, his home village in Phek district of Nagaland, which shares boundaries with the Naga-concentrated Senapati and Ukhrul districts of Manipur, and asked the 'old people' about what actually happened.

'Many of our old people were not willing to talk. Then I found out that many people in my village were tortured—it is part of the history.'

'Why do you think the old people did not want to talk about the past?' I ask. 'Was it a forgetting they were experiencing, forgetting something so horrifying that…'

'The old people felt that educated Nagas of the younger generation were not giving due recognition to our struggle, that we only talk about employment in the government sector, have a good life, live in the cities; our historians are so complacent with the jobs they have in their universities and their colleges. So, many elders felt it was out of context to share their story. But they were so happy when I was inquisitive, and gradually began to tell me things. I could sense the inner joy when they could share their anguish, their hope, with me. And I thought in a way it could also be a healing … a healing…'

Taken with emotion, Neichute stops to search for words, and uses the silence to pass around a plateful of pear and orange.

'Healing process?' I offer, after an appropriate gap.

He nods emphatically, joined by Chinese. 'Yes, a healing process for them.'

Mute, I share with Neichute a section in a book I'm carrying, *Nagaland and India: The Blood and the Tears*, by Kaka D. Iralu. In it is reproduced a letter dated 3 August 1957 to the United Nations Organisation signed by Khrisanisa Seyietsu, Kedaghe (President), 'Government of Nagaland'. It makes for harrowing reading.

> *Within the years, from January 1955 to July 1957 ... 79,794 houses have been burnt down and also 26,550,000 maunds of paddy rice have been burnt down and destroyed by the Indian armed forces ... 960,000,000 rupees worth of things have been lost through this fire destruction in six hundred twelve villages out of eight hundred fifty two Naga villages, approximately...*

The letter then details various other atrocities committed upon Nagas—and it is difficult to suppress extreme discomfort whenever I read it, as I do now.

'1) *The ladies are very often intended [taken or villagers asked to supply] from all Naga villages. The elders are shot to death when refused to supply them with intended ladies...*

4) *The Naga women and girls are made naked and raped publicly every day.*

5) *Young girls with young men are arrested together, and their shameful covers [clothing that cover the genitals] are taken off and forced them to make intercourse publicly in the Church buildings.*

6) *The Naga virgins, aged between ten and fifteen years are raped to death by the Punjab Regiment...*

8) *The glory of the mighty forces of India is to commit sodomy by making unusual sex with the Naga boys through the rectum...*

13) *The daily practice of the mighty forces of India is to pierce the Naga victims with red-hot iron, even to their shames...*

14) *Shave off the Naga victim's hair and the chilly powders are applied all over their bodies. Forced them to eat one-fourth seer of chilly powders at the point of bayonets...*

15) *The innocent villagers are arrested everyday, and are ordered to dig out their own pits of six feet deep ... they are put with heads upside down in their respective pits ... For instance, the terrible drama was made to the twenty two unfortunate victims at Mukhami village border by 9th Gurkha Regiment, on January 7, 1957...*

19) *...one Naga Home Guard Videlhoulie, Kohima Village, was shot at Kohima village wet cultivation on July 12, 1957. When the victim was beheaded, his own sister named Duonilhouü was forced to carry the head up to the Kohima police thana...*

21) *The Naga victims' legs, hands, fingers and even their testicles are broken and grinded everyday, everywhere in Nagaland...*

25) *The indigenous Nagas have three meals a day. They have been living now from hand to mouth. Their wealth has totally been lost ... The nations of the world should not turn a deaf ear to these entreaties of ours today...*

~

'I began to feel very strongly.' Enough to pass up an opportunity to join the Indian Air Force, Neichute adds. It would have otherwise been a natural step up from being an active member of the National Cadet Corps' Air Wing.

'I am not so much interested in human rights issues or political issues but I do believe after reading our histories that the fight Nagas have is legitimate,' he continues. 'In the 1950s and 1960s, Naga villages did not have a modern system of governance; Nehru may have felt that we may not be able to survive on our own at that time. He could be right. He could also be wrong, because at that time...' Neichute repeatedly taps a forefinger into the arm of the sofa.

It could have gone either way? I suggest.

'*Yes*. It had not been experimented. Burma was such a young nation but it was coming up. People say it is a wrong kind of nation, but it is surviving. Of course, in Africa we have seen tribal fights and social conflicts and yet, Africa has also survived, some countries have thrived, and they were in a worse position than we were—because our social capital was very good. Our older people may have been illiterate but they were wise; the local governance we had at that time was in some ways better than what we have today.'

Neichute is in flow, and drawn by his telling, I lean forward on the sofa spontaneously. I see Chinese adopt a similar posture.

'Anyway,' Neichute resumes an earlier line of thought, 'I began to feel very strongly that I am not an Indian, but that does not mean I am an enemy of India. I am also not an ultra-nationalist,' he clarifies, to maintain distance from those who take to arms. 'I feel it is very important to reach out to Indian people. I have met many Indian people who are willing to listen, and who also respect our struggle. That is when I realized: this is why India is great. I found so many Indian people wanted to know the truth without making a value judgment.'

Chinese has left for his office with an offer of help were I to ever get into trouble. 'Any problem, anytime, please call me.'

I feel no fear here in my travels, I had replied. I feel no resentment. I feel at home.

'That is good.' He smiled. 'But things can happen.'

Noting down his mobile number, I joked in return, 'I know where to find you.' I meant the most prominent landmark in Kohima besides Japfü peak, and the neon red cross, made famous as an image by the photographer Pablo Bartholomew. The enormous white-painted police headquarters is the most visibly lavish construction in Kohima.

'I can't miss it,' I said to cackles from both Chinese and Neichute.

Now, done with a simple tasty lunch of rice, chicken stew, boiled squash, and fiery paste of fermented fish, Neichute and I resume the thread of our discussion over dessert.

'Local pineapple,' he explains proudly, as I wax ecstatic about the quality of fruit. 'There's so much we can do, nah? People have different jobs in life, and I feel I should help people come up economically.'

To hear him tell it, Neichute's leap of faith with entrepreneurship came after a brush, literally, with a professor of economics from southern India who would taunt folks in class—in Nagaland: 'You Nagas have no mind for economics, because it involves mathematics, statistics.'

'I felt very angry with that. So I told the professor in class, "Sir, I don't like you." He challenged us. Otherwise, I was interested in history.' Neichute says he ultimately gave up a job teaching economics at Kohima's Baptist College to co-establish a microfinance outfit in 2000.

'While I was teaching, I began to feel very strongly that Nagas need to do business, they need to work. I enjoyed teaching very much but this need to change our culture, say "no" to government money, began to influence me a lot. So I resigned, and with some of my friends who felt the same way we formed what we call Entrepreneurs Associates.'

They decided they could help in several ways but the first and most important was the way of microfinance because banks, Neichute says, are wary of doing business with Nagas in general. Personal loans are provided only to government employees. Car and housing loans are becoming more prevalent, but largely limited to Dimapur and Kohima. Banks rarely invest in Naga-run businesses.

'They say people don't have collateral,' Neichute laughs, 'which is true. As our land is tribal, it cannot be sold or mortgaged, or transferred from a tribal to a non-tribal.' Providing microfinance, which precludes the need for collateral, seemed like the answer.

The seed money, Neichute tells me, comes from a partnership

with ICICI Bank Ltd and Axis Bank, and a lesser one with State Bank of India. Entrepreneurs Associates takes term loans from them and combines that with savings from its members to channel funds to prospective entrepreneurs. The organization has also convinced some local companies to refinance loans. The minimum loan amount is Rs 5,000 for an individual who either has an idea and needs capital, or wishes to consolidate and expand an existing business; the maximum ranges from Rs 100,000 to Rs 500,000 depending on the bank providing the loan. The term of the loan runs from three to six years, again depending on the bank.

Neichute reels off examples of beneficiaries in Dimapur and Kohima: a grocery shop, a garment shop, an iron fabrication unit, a restaurant, and some small hotels. In a range of a four- to seven-hour drive from Kohima, Entrepreneurs Associates supports initiatives to breed mithun, a type of buffalo endemic to Nagaland; several piggeries; orchards raising oranges, pineapple and soon, kiwi fruit. (From a conversation with Hekani Jakhalu, a friend of Neichute's, I know this sort of enabling is a growing trend. Hekani, a trained lawyer, returned from Delhi in 2005 to promote 'life skills' for people to run small businesses through YouthNet, a Kohima-based organization of which she is the director. She is also engaged in trying to figure out through a survey how many Naga youngsters live outside the state, in India, and what occupations they are engaged in—with the ultimate purpose to help with counsel for 're-skilling', and also to gauge if their skills could be re-purposed for use in Nagaland's economy.)

But the going is not all smooth. Telling it, Neichute comes close to losing his temper. He snaps out a series of statements, and the force of these lead his two young daughters, who peek into the room, to quickly withdraw.

'We NGOs are limited; our resources are always limited. A lot of the time funders don't listen to us—they may also have their own agendas. The government has resources but they don't listen. Our organization doesn't have FCRA [clearance to receive overseas funds in accordance with India's stringent Foreign Contribution Regulation Act]. When we thought of applying for it, intelligence people came to our office three or four times. So I got very annoyed and didn't apply ... I used to speak very openly about my feelings as a Naga, my phone used to be tapped...'

'So they thought it was just a racket to get money?'

'Yes, and also, help the Undergrounds.'

Have you during work for your projects come in touch with the Underground? I ask.

'We have not faced trouble.'

Not necessarily trouble, I clarify. To much laughter from Neichute, I give examples about how even Maoist rebels in India sometimes differentiate between 'good bourgeoisie' and 'bad bourgeoisie'. Some initiatives backed by UNICEF in areas of Maoist influence, for instance, are okay by Maoists. But they want to be seen as approving such projects: a sort of we-have-decided-it's-okay-for-the-people—a kind of propaganda victory.

'I have interacted with them,' Neichute says quietly, 'but I am not so popular with the Undergrounds.'

Why?

'I don't like to meet with them.' He softens the blow. 'Most don't pressure us for donations and things. They see that we have given help to so many youths. They also see us as people who have struggled. So even without talking there's a good relation with us. Some Undergrounds have asked money from us. But we say that we are not here to make money to give you. We made that very clear.' He sighs. 'So far there has been no trouble.'

So they tolerate you, I suggest. There are always issues in an area in conflict, or an area which has recently come out of conflict. Nagaland in that sense is a halfway house, a work in progress, but there is no real resolution. And here, I say, let me flip the proposition. Have you faced pressure or trouble from government, local as well as agencies such as paramilitary or army—or do they too tolerate you?

'No, that has not really happened. SIB [State Intelligence Bureau] came a few times. It was like harassment. So four five of us got together and went to meet the local boss, I think his name was Joseph. We told him, "Look sir, your boys keep coming to our office to ask how much money we have received from foreign agencies. We have come here to tell you that, number one, we don't have FCRA. Number two, we have not applied for FCRA. Number three, we have not received a single paisa from government agencies. So if you need to know about our activities, let us know: you can come any day and we can have some tea together." After that they stopped coming.'

~

'I feel very strongly that we need to build the economic pillar of Naga society,' Neichute says. 'It is not healthy either for New Delhi or for Nagas to have a relationship that we have at the moment: a relationship of dependence. It is not only dependence, but co-dependence.' He smiles. 'Some politicians and bureaucrats in Delhi also depend on the dependence of Kohima, of Nagaland, on the present system.'

I had seen the previous year's official figures before heading out to Nagaland. For the financial year ended 31 March 2008, the state government received Rs 2,996.02 crore (nearly Rs 30 billion) as revenue. Just eight per cent of this came by way of tax and non-tax revenue raised by the state government. A tiny portion of the remainder came from Nagaland's share of Central taxes that the Government of India divides among various states; the bulk, more than Rs 2,300 crore (Rs 23 billion), came to Nagaland as grants-in-aid from the Government of India.

'It's a lot of money to fool around with,' I tell Neichute.

'Oh, a lot,' Neichute snaps. 'If money comes to Nagaland, money also goes to some people in Delhi—so everyone benefits. But this is not healthy. Number one: when statehood was offered to us, policymakers told the Nagas that we were tribals and, because the great leaders in India loved tribals, we were told everything will be provided for free. So, we don't have to pay tax. Whereas when the British first came and controlled us in the nineteenth century, they said we have to pay two rupees per year per household as tax. When the Government of India came and annexed and ruled over Nagaland they said, "We will not give you any tax burden; we will give you a special development fund. We will build you roads; we will build schools which we have destroyed in the war." All this seemed rosy at the time.'

For the few Nagas who said 'no to India's hegemony'—Neichute mouths words familiar in conversations in Nagaland—it became difficult to fight against that flow. Many went with the 'flow', explains Neichute. 'Mostly young Nagas who had studied in India, and became the bureaucrats, the politicians, the nouveau riche.'

'We are still not paying tax.' He raises his voice. 'Our state is a 100 per cent non-revenue state. All our economic planning has to be according to what is being envisaged in New Delhi. This is not at all right. So much money is wasted ... People in government are interested in how much share they should get...' Neichute splutters to a stop.

Well, look at the police headquarters, I remind Neichute in an attempt to undercut his anger.

'You can't miss it.' He barks a laugh.

It is difficult to also miss several other pointers of waste—and outright illegality. Before arriving here, I was browsing through the Comptroller and Auditor General of India's report for 2007-08 on Nagaland's finances and use of funds. The report details several dozen cases of routine financial inefficiency, impropriety and fraud.

I read about how Rs 214 million sanctioned under the Technology Mission for Integrated Development of Horticulture in North Eastern States was 'misappropriated/ unaccounted for'. The report suspected 'misappropriation' of nearly Rs 22 million released by the Director of Agriculture to the District Agricultural Officer, Tuensang, for 'implementation of schemes'. Even though nearly Rs 120 million worth of 'new infrastructure' for District Headquarters at Dimapur was 'lying idle since September 2006', Government of Nagaland went right ahead with constructing infrastructure at a new site. Besides, the government incurred an 'avoidable interest payment' of almost Rs 71 million.

The report mentions loss of revenue running into tens of millions of rupees because a supplementary agreement favoured the 'sole selling agent' of the State Lottery. It records how none of the five working public sector undertakings—state-run units—finalized their accounts for the financial year ended March 2008 in time, and that their accounts 'were in arrears for periods ranging from nine to 26 years as on 30 September 2008'. The report dispassionately records the relatively trivial detail of the overpayment of almost Rs 38 million, because two different contractors were paid for the same work, to fix a four-kilometre stretch of road.

But even the sedately worded CAG report couldn't hide its temper with this one. As I read: 'Scrutiny of records of the EE [electrical engineer] Electrical Transmission Division, Dimapur revealed that the Department foreclosed the project in May 2005 after incurring Rs 32 crore [Rs 320 million] towards construction of buildings and procurement of machinery and equipment ... The building so constructed and machinery & equipment procured were lying unutilised at site for the last two years as can be seen from the photographs given below: ... This has resulted in an infructuous expenditure of Rs 32 crore apart from the objectives of the project remaining unachieved.'

'A lot of government funds are being spent on construction and not actual development,' Neichute fumes. 'You look at our roads, they are horrible. Roads are needed much more than such a tall government office. Many of our school buildings are almost falling down. Our colleges are government colleges, where human development is not being prioritized. The Government of Nagaland employs 127,000. To run a small state like Nagaland, now with better communications and Internet facilities, I don't think we even need 20,000 people—if people are willing to work.'

I call it the Mizoram Bribe, I tell Neichute, a strategy adopted in the state far to Nagaland's south in a bid to conclusively end conflict after treating civilian populations first to utter administrative callousness and famine and then, when many protested and took to arms in 1966, to utter barbarity.

Neichute doesn't smile. He shakes his head. A lot of money is also wasted in Nagaland because Nagaland isn't permitted to do the planning, he says, which has to be in conformity with what Delhi wants—and Nagaland can't do the planning because Nagaland doesn't have the resources. 'So it's a waste for taxpayers in India,' Neichute says. 'Their money is being wasted in Nagaland. And because we don't pay tax here there is no transparency ... there's no accountability—it's not our money. But, you see, were we to pay taxes, we would question why such a grand police office is being constructed when in our hospitals people do not even have a place to stay.'

It's a very brave thing to say in Nagaland, I offer. Indeed, it would be brave to say such a thing nearly anywhere in the 'Northeast'.

Neichute brushes away my concern. 'I keep mentioning this in my talks. It is important for Nagas to pay tax. We say that people are corrupt but how do we judge that they are corrupt because they don't pay income tax, no property tax. Where is the system to assess whether someone is corrupt or not? And since we don't pay tax and all money is free from Delhi, even if a secretary or politician has got five-six government cars—they buy the latest cars in the market—it is okay.

'I also ask people to say "no" to this money by any means. And the only way to say "no" to this money is to say "no" to government money—and all this money is government money. People look for government jobs because they want the money, not because they want to work; they want pension. It's a trend.' Neichute wags a forefinger in warning. 'And it's a crime, actually, by Christian ethics: getting money without working is a crime. And we are all Christians here. So I feel this culture needs to be changed. We *must* rise and say we want to do business, and generate growth and income and job opportunities for others. At the moment we are only looking at New Delhi to provide us jobs.' He slaps the coffee table in front of him. 'This is *wrong*.'

4

A visit to the Promised Land: it's 3:20 p.m. in Nagalim

The way to Hebron is through Beverly Hills.

Were you to travel south from Dimapur towards Kohima, the turn comes at the 5th Mile, a mile after Diphupar Gate. The way to Camp Hebron, NSCN-IM's main 'ceasefire' base, general headquarter for its civilian administration and military, or Oking, is through a district of plush farmhouses redolent of similar places in and around New Delhi. To local wags—and in Nagaland, most residents I come by appear to have a sense of humour born of living in a whirl of conflict, corruption and politics—the area is known as Beverly Hills. It's a code for where the fat cats, both established and arriviste, take up residence. Often, their second. Sometimes, third, even fourth.

Around the tenth century AD, as I learnt from an Archaeological Survey of India brochure, this area along the Dhansiri River that marks the eastern boundary of present-day Dimapur was settled by the Kachari tribe. According to the Archaeological Survey, the name Dimapur is derived from 'di', 'ma' and 'pur', together adding up to mean 'the great town on the bank of the river'. It still is for some, I see as I pass several grand estates of Beverly Hills, enclosed by walls and imposing gates. I pass Rio Villa, named after Nagaland's chief minister. His family owns major real estate holdings in a handsome radius around Dimapur, including two major 'resorts'; I have visited both. One even has a public-funded waterway, part of an irrigation project, running through it, and a motor launch to take visitors sightseeing. If nothing else, it exemplifies creative use of money.

The landscape is less typically Nagaland and more typically Assam, as it were, with fields of paddy and small forested patches, houses of mud and thatch. These plains, with occasional bands of badlands carved by long-dissipated rivers and rivulets, were scythed out of the state of Assam and awarded to Nagaland when it was given the status of a state of India in 1963. And the long-dormant Dimasa people of the area had yet another set of overlords after the British and the Assamese.

The journey is along winding roads, moving steadily deeper to the southwest, abutting both the homeland of the Zeliangrong tribe in Nagaland and Karbi Anglong district of Assam. After fifteen minutes, the complete absence of police becomes evident; and even paramilitary and army personnel and vehicles. No patrols, no convoys. By tacit understanding, this is NSCN-IM territory, and 'sanitized' by its forces, as more than one insider has told me. Every now and then an off-roader goes past me in either direction, many of these being Maruti Gypsys and Mahindra SUVs popular in these parts, mainly the Bolero and Scorpio models. Most vehicles are without number plates. Security, secrecy, chutzpah—whatever.

The clusters of hamlets thin and, eventually, there are none. After an hour, I come upon Camp Hebron. There is a security post by a large Naga-style gate with a barrier across it. A Naga Army cadre, in camouflage combat gear and carrying an AK-47 rifle, welcomes me with a smile, and checks my ID. My host, Captain Akhan, the adjutant of the camp, is reached on a mobile phone to verify our appointment. It is early afternoon.

The camp is set on a series of knolls, and we follow this topography as we drive without Naga Army escort. We pass a series of neat huts along narrow but well-tarred roads, with neat signs pointing the way to the administration office, offices of various kilonser, or ministers, and similar signs that mark a well-laid-out camp. A sign guides me to the GHQ—general headquarters—of NSCN-IM. It's an acronym I find easier to use than the organization's formal name, NSCN/GPRN. It helps me avoid confusing them with their rivals, the Khaplang and Unification factions, which have for the moment coalesced into NSCN (Unification), and use as their acronym, GPRN/NSCN. The different word orders legitimize claims by both factions of the Naga armies run by these organizations; the apex Nationalist Socialist Councils of Nagalim run by both; and the Government of the People's Republic of Nagalim (the root of the acronym, GPRN), also claimed by both.

On such confounding subtleties are battles fought for Nagalim.

From even this gentle height it is easy to see that the site is well chosen. Ravines and defiles mark the extremities of the camp, which is mostly on a rise, unlike the relative flatlands at the ceremonial gate. On three sides are dense forests, but the areas nearest to the camp are cleaned of foliage, forming a figurative moat that offers both visibility and denies concealment to intruders. Lookouts can scan the surrounding countryside for several miles. Over and above this line-of-sight, this Naga Army prides itself on its networking.

'How good is your intel for movements of the army and security forces, and major tip-offs?' I had asked a top NSCN-IM officer.

He had replied, deadpan: 'About half an hour ahead of the (Indian) army.'

Indian Army and police officials freely admit to the networking and intelligence-gathering prowess of their on-ceasefire foes, who use far lower-tech methods than the 'jungle drums' available to

India's security forces, intelligence services and police—for instance, their ability to listen in on conversations. The Naga armies have their own, ear-to-the-ground methods. The reason is quite simple, really: the Naga armies have held out this long, during war with India and the relative absence of it, because they have the home advantage.

Two young, sharp-eyed and stern-faced IM cadres, one of them a girl, stop me at another checkpoint. There are no smiles here for me, just a businesslike inspection of intent, and meticulous, slow scanning of ID. Nearby, more cadres, young women and men, bristling with automatic weaponry, sit watchfully.

As ever, reality sinks in only after seeing it. This is a state of ceasefire, not surrender. And it is vastly different in tone and content than, say, the terms of agreement that kept Nepal's Maoist rebels in designated 'Peace Camps' after a deal was signed between them and the caretaker government of the day in 2006. In Shaktikhor Camp near the Chitwan area in southern Nepal, for instance, only those guarding the perimeter or senior officers' areas carried weapons openly. When I visited that camp in July 2009, the remainder of the weaponry (only what was not in placed in secret caches, as I was told repeatedly by insiders) was stored in temperature-controlled containers. These were supervised by personnel of the United Nations Mission in Nepal, created especially for monitoring the camps and the peace agreement, and agreed to by all parties—Maoist rebels, and an alliance of seven political parties ranged against the king of Nepal.

There is no international observer for the peace process in Nagaland or the Naga regions. At any rate, thus far India hasn't permitted any overseas organization to peer into what it considers its internal affairs. It cannot, however, prevent Baptist church organizations from the US, the UK-based Quakers, and Dutch non-government organization KREDDHA, an acronym which translates as International Peace Council for States, Peoples and

Minorities. The inroads these organizations, especially the religious, have made into Naga society, politics and psyche run deep, and, from the buzz I have picked up from the Indian side and from books of history, are willing to play both 'plotboiler' and peacemaker.

Some pieces of paper signed in 1997 marked the absence of war between the Government of India and NSCN-IM only within the state of Nagaland, but did not bring with it the trappings of peace. Ceasefire or not, NSCN-IM continues to function as a regular force, running drills, organizing patrols, recruiting more to its ranks to a level that would be of concern to India. Besides, while NSCN-IM is admittedly under ceasefire with the Government of India, technically it remains an enemy.

GHQ is about a kilometre in from the gates of Hebron. It is an organized sprawl of office huts, barracks, mess area and parade ground. The training area for recruits and regulars is further to the south, beyond a couple of low hills, but I've been told I won't make it there yet. In fact, for a 'non-Naga', especially one such as myself with no kind of dealing—political or administrative—with NSCN-IM, to make it even this far is an exception.

I get down from the car in an open area near the adjutant's office. Captain Akhan is there in welcome, with an orderly on either side. He is a compact wiry man in olive-green combat tunic with the Star of Bethlehem sewed on to a collar, and a dull-metal pistol holstered at his waist. His handshake, typical of an army man's, is firm, brief. He dismisses the orderlies who react to his command by snapping together their heels and throwing smart salutes. The captain then ruffles the heads of two lean German Shepherds that have meanwhile loped up to him, wolf-like, from behind a barracks. They don't bark as they fix me with unblinking eyes, but they haven't yet been taught to not wag their tails in front of visitors.

'What are they called?' I ask, impressed at this display—as I guess I am supposed to be.

'King and Queen. They listen only to me,' Captain Akhan says, in fluent English. 'Sit,' he snaps at the two, and they immediately follow the order. 'They don't eat till I say so. They will attack if I say so.'

'Nice.'

'Please come in,' he invites me into his office smilingly.

It's painted green, and Spartan. Captain Akhan sits behind an unassuming plywood-topped table of steel, painted green, on which he casually places the 9mm pistol. I take a chair from the three ranged in front. To my right is a closed cupboard. Behind him, to my left, is a framed message in homely needlework: 'Joy is Love, When it is Shared.' On another part of the wall is a poster of the UN's Universal Declaration of Human Rights. That shares space with a photograph of V.S. Atem, a legend in the Naga armies; he was longvibu, or chief of army, from June 1969 to July 1999 in various incarnations of rebel groups. He held the rank of lieutenant-general, and is credited with whipping the undivided Naga Army as well as its incarnation as NSCN-IM into one of the best-trained rebel forces in Asia.

To my left there are five clocks. In 'Nagalim', where we are, a clock shows it to be 1520 hours. In Washington DC it is 0744; Tokyo: 1848; London: 1042. These are the three capitals of residence, transit, and leverage. And in Bangkok, for long a place of refuge and transit for generations of Naga rebel leaders, it is 1647 hours. Some of the times are a bit off, but the need for such diverse timekeeping is by itself an indication of the organization's world view.

The pride of place on the wall behind the captain, unsurprisingly, belongs to the flag of Nagalim, a light-blue background with three ribbons of red, yellow and green curving from about mid-section to the left and arcing to the right. The white six-pointed star, the same as on Captain Akhan's tunic, is at the top left corner of the flag. At least the design appears to be common to all factions of Naga rebels.

Captain Akhan turns out to be forty, but this is an army, he explains, that ranks its officers on the length as well as merit of service. Having joined at thirty, he isn't doing too badly as captain, and adjutant of Camp Hebron. He stays in camp, occasionally visiting his family resident in Dimapur. We trade banter about the perennial issue of balancing work and home; but he gets a distant look once in a while, a man who clearly misses being with his family and his two daughters whom he tells me so much about.

His mobile phone wakes. The ring tone would seem a little out of place in any army camp except that of the Baptist-driven Nagas. 'The love of God is the greatest love of all...' I hear, before he brusquely taps a key to take the call and carries on for several minutes. Mostly, he listens attentively, and sometimes interjects or queries in Nagamese.

My eyes are drawn to a stack of brown paper envelopes on his desk, the mark of office stationery—in particular government stationery. They are neatly addressed both in type and immaculate handwriting. They are too far for me to see names and addresses clearly. There's also a stack of writing paper nearby, and files, the same as any government office. I'm reminded again about what several insiders and security experts have told me, that NSCN-IM has honed to perfection a legacy of the old days: records. Paperwork of the organization is legendary. It knows who is tasked with what, and which organization or person is to 'donate' how much to its coffers. There are stories of cadres being in the jungle for several years, and then returning to a major administrative camp or, say, a camp like Hebron, and finding his service record updated.

There's more, and not all of it to do with paperwork. In most parts of Nagaland, and in many of the Naga-majority areas of Manipur and Arunachal Pradesh, NSCN-IM has the clout to decide who wins and loses in a particular constituency in an election—in a village or municipality, to the state assembly, or to Parliament. It has a stake in bureaucratic appointments. Its support for a chief minister can, in these fragile political times, maintain or break a coalition.

An emergency has arisen, the captain tells me after ending his conversation. I won't be able to stay in camp as long as we had planned, but first, there's lunch. I don't complain; I have a soft spot for Naga food.

On our way to the mess hut, I see more than a dozen young cadres on a time-off, horsing around as youngsters will. Some of them seem as young as fifteen or sixteen. They briefly stop when they see Captain Akhan. He shouts out something in the Tangkhul dialect that makes them smile, but they wait for us to be out of sight before bursting into laughter.

We are the only ones in the mess hut. Here they eat twice a day, early morning after drill, and late afternoon, before sunset; the sun sets 'early' in these parts.

Lunch—dinner for the camp—is superb. Sticky rice, fried pork tossed with ginger leaf, tear-inducing chilli and fish chutney, some light daal—Nagas of all cuts have over the years developed a soft spot for the very Indian daal—boiled cabbage and, for me, the pièce de résistance that would have pride of place at any table in southeast Asia: small freshwater crabs basted in sesame oil, and tossed with red chilli and basil. We eat in the Naga fashion, with our hands.

'You folks should open a restaurant at Hebron gate,' I say between mouthfuls.

'Why?' Captain Akhan stops, hand paused over his dented aluminium plate; mine is of melamine. Evidently, such crockery is either kept for visitors or the captain is putting on a show of a happy camper.

'It could be good PR.' I smile. 'People say they are afraid of the Naga army, and with some of the recent incidents in these parts, maybe some public interaction would do your organization some good.' I couch it as a joke, but the captain accepts the point with a smile.

Later, over a cup of green tea, we talk about his organization and what it could do. But the captain is cagey. I am to meet a superior officer later in the day, and he would rather the 'brass' answers my questions for the record.

5

Tea with a general: 'So you think you can wear us down? I say, bullshit!'

By the time I reach the general's two-storey house, it is pitch dark, and past 7.30 p.m. The electricity too is out, a frequent occurrence even in Beverly Hills for those who are unable or unwilling to maintain immense generator sets at their estates. Illumination is provided by Chinese LED lamps brought in from Myanmar, the country that is the succour of a supply chain for all northeast. Two weeks-old pups go playfully for my ankles as a helper lets me into the short driveway. There's a modest lawn to the right. A narrow path leads us to the main living area.

It's an unpretentiously decorated house, as far as I can see. There's a large space divided into two, I see by the harsh white glare of the LED table lamp. There's a smaller formal area to receive visitors, replete with simple wooden carvings of animal figurines, totems and a crossed set of Naga spears. An empty bit of floor occupies two-thirds of the room. Several dozen plastic chairs stacked against the far wall supply the answer; the space appears to double as a mini-hall for frequent meetings. There's an old AK series rifle on the wall. It has the feel of a memento, not a weapon in use. Across from where I am seated, a staircase reaches into the shadows of the first floor. After a few minutes, Major General Phungthing Shimrang, number three in his army, and convenor of its Ceasefire Monitoring Cell on behalf of NSCN-IM, descends from it. He carries a LED lantern.

'Sorry,' he says as he warmly shakes hands with me. 'The power goes off a lot here.'

He comes across as a no-nonsense person, and I've been told he hates people beating around the bush.

Besides, I know he is busier than usual: the local papers in the past week have been full of talk of reconciliation among various Naga rebel factions. Representatives of three political groups, NSCN-IM, GPRN/NSCN (the 'Unification' group that thus far is led by the 'Khaplang' faction), and representatives of the Federal Government of Nagaland had met for the first time in Dimapur just the previous day under the banner of a church-supported, doggedly optimistic 'civil society' group called Forum for Naga Reconciliation. A very big deal, considering the two biggest rebel groups had been slaughtering each other in and around Dimapur a year earlier. And FGN—the smallest and relatively shadowy lot, but with still a fair bit of bite from cadres and weapons—has for long carded itself as spoilers by using the name of Phizo and claiming that, as it alone retained the name of the long-ago, undivided 'parent' organization, it spoke for all Nagas with the authority of legacy.

A bigger deal yet had been the presence at the meeting of the youngest brothers, Jonghan and Wanghying, of reclusive GPRN/NSCN Chairman S.S. Khaplang. The brothers had made the trip from their base in the jungles of Myanmar, along with some colleagues of the Naga Yuya, the apex Naga body in Myanmar controlled by Khaplang. This 'track-two' initiative involved for some a walk across international borders with the help of a colossal surveillance wink courtesy of India's intelligence apparatus; and being present in Dimapur under the benign glare of the governments of Nagaland and India. It may seem unusual. But the game, I learn more with each visit to the region, is among the trickiest being played out in this part of the world. Trickier in some ways than the several preparatory meetings and, howsoever incongruous it may seem, football matches between teams of rebel factions played as an ice-breaking gambit in the resort town of Chiang Mai in northern Thailand. As I visit the general, Forum for Naga Reconciliation has been going flat out for peace for a year under the guidance of its charismatic convener, the Reverend Wati Aier.

At the state government-run Saramati Hotel, where I had stayed on a previous occasion but which was barred to me this time on account of the reconciliation meeting, representatives of the three factions had stood for photo opportunities in front of a banner that declared: 'Naga Reconciliation: A Journey of Common Hope.' Later, uniformed cadres of NSCN-IM and GPRN/NSCN had together sung songs—again for the benefit of the media and by extension, the public.

It seems like a good swing-in for a conversation with Gen. Phungthing.

'I saw in today's papers this big picture of all the groups together, NGOs, and one paper carried a photo of cadres in combat dress singing a song for Nagalim. For me as a non-Naga it meant a lot. But when *you* see a photo like that does your heart sing? Or do you look at the photograph and say "Okay, nice photograph".'

The general laughs out loud, and then replies obliquely. 'See, you are asking a person who has always gone to war: "When you see blood, how do you feel?" In the same way, to a doctor seeing blood every day the blood does not matter any more. Seeing a picture like that makes you think. How? Why? How long can you go on like this? Why should our people be so hard ... so indifferent? Or, why are our people not in a position to understand the root of the issues?'

He shows an upraised palm in supplication of his point about differences among groups as well as demands related to Naga autonomy. 'It is good if we can reconcile—reconciliation as a process must go on. One way or the other it will have to come one day or the other. But it is a process. It will never be in a position to overtake the issues. Even if our struggle comes to a positive conclusion, at that time also the matter of reconciliation will always be there. If we are together, no doubt it makes things easier. We can move together, struggle together, fight together, we can share together.' He shrugs, his casualness masking a tone of warning. 'But at the same time, if we are just playing together without any reason ... it's like fire and petrol—they can never work together. It can explode. These things must always be kept in mind.'

Well, I say, if you want to look at a reconciliation process, look at Nepal. The Maoists and their former enemies haven't really worked things out yet except getting rid of a corrupt and megalomaniacal king. It's been more than three years since the absence of war, but continuing squabbles, tensions and threats show there is also the pinch of peace.

In any movement that leads to conflict, Gen. Phungthing replies, the Naga, the Cambodian war, the Vietnam war—'wherever it may be'—when the movement is on, you don't have time to think much about the end. 'But when the dust has settled, you think: he is walking on that line; I'm walking on this line. You come together—you have no more the process of winning that war, you're thinking of how to move forward.'

He doesn't articulate the key queries, and that isn't surprising: these are make-or-break matters involving 'face'; and even to talk openly about it could convey aggressive tonality. But I don't carry a similar baggage of history, politics and diplomatic endeavour. And so, I wade in:

If at all there is reconciliation, how will it work? Will all organizations be equal even if their numerical strength and firepower are not? Will a new umbrella organization be created to accommodate representatives from all factions? Will past transgressions, including killing of cadres of one organization by another, be forgiven; or will there be some manner of compensation, such as an apology to the families and, in addition, some monetary benefit? Will groups continue to deal individually with the Government of India for ceasefire and settlement, or will the umbrella group handle this responsibility?

Will Nagaland be enough? Or is Nagalim a must, by taking back chunks of traditional Naga territory partitioned first by the departing British Empire and later, India? And will the leadership of each of the factions be able to accept as equals the leadership of the other factions?

Moreover, moving away from the rebel planetary systems, what will happen to the existing political leadership in Nagaland? Will politicians be willing to cede power to rebels in a democratic set-up? Or will guns and a deliberately corrupted and shaky democracy coexist, as it does now? And will the Government of India, should it perceive Naga unity as being entirely too threatening as it did in the 1940s, '50s and '60s, permit the reconciliation process? Or will its various agencies, even as the general and I speak, be working to sabotage the talks to their own ends—ostensibly, for the greater good of the idea of India, to uphold which, evidently, any amount of death and domination is the norm?

These aren't by far all the issues that will need sorting out, I submit to Gen. Phungthing, but these will need to be the bare minimum for any reconciliation process to make sense, to have any purpose.

'As you said,' the general says, 'it is harder to keep peace than it is to keep war, because everyone will have their own way of influencing it. [That's how] geopolitics comes in, foreign policy comes in.'

India has now undertaken peace initiatives with almost all her neighbours, he continues, she is a growing power. But India came about not by consensus alone, but also by force. After the British left there were princely states, the general says, and the home minister at the time, Sardar Vallabhbhai Patel, conveyed to several states reluctant to join India that they will be forced to.

'And he used force. Only the Nagas defied it. There was no treaty at all with either the British or India, not only with Nagas in India, but also in Burma. The Nagas in Burma have never accepted [the division by the British of Naga territory between Burma and India]. When they went to Panglong—I don't know whether you know about the Panglong Agreement in Burma…?' He stops, eyebrows raised. I nod to acquiesce.

General Aung San, the father of Nobel Peace Prize winner Aung San Suu Kyi, had in the 1940s initiated a series of conferences in Panglong in the Shan State of Burma with ethnic Burmese tribes—among them the Kachin, Shan and Chin—for the unification and eventual independence of Burma from British colonial rule. To this end, he had for a while even allied with Japan during the Second World War and headed the Burma National Army—in an echo of what Subhash Chandra Bose did for India's independence with his Indian National Army. But Aung San decided to support the British war effort when it became clear to him that the Japanese were not keen on ideas such as independence for areas it had conquered. The momentum for unification peaked with the Panglong Agreement in 1947. The Naga tribes on the Burmese side of the border, numerically lower than the tribes Aung San had wooed, disagreed with this assumption of unity and protested with their own plea for independence. Then, and later, such protests have fallen on resoundingly deaf ears, the same as in India. The Nagas, for all practical purposes, had become geopolitical playthings.

I can sense Gen. Phungthing's agitation. So I decide to lower the tone of our conversation a notch, and talk to him about the Naga construct within the present-day geopolitics of the region. How does he see Nagalim panning out? I ask. Does he foresee India and China playing political football with the idea of Nagalim?

'I would not say that,' Gen. Phungthing replies, and smoothly deflects the query to make his own point. 'Every nation will want to have its own rules. One is because of the politics of it, and the other is because of the economics of it. So definitely, everyone would want to see spheres of influence everywhere. A Naga is no exception—Nagalim is no exception to that. Naga people are at the moment at a very crucial stage; and if you look east from India to Southeast Asia, this area becomes the centre of it. [Former Prime Minister] Narasimha Rao used to talk about a "Look East Policy".'

I tell him of a joke I'd recently heard at a seminar, that if New Delhi had pursued its so-called Look East Policy with as much vigour as it has its Overlook Northeast Policy, things might have got better a lot sooner.

'They just overlook it,' the general guffaws, and calls for tea before returning to the conversation. 'They think that anything the Centre says will be acceptable. The policies they have made do not realistically have anything to do with the Northeast. From that point of view the "Look East Policy" may not have a very bright future.'

When it comes to Nagalim, he argues, the basic search is for freedom. 'When you say "freedom", people may express it in different forms. We are talking about our rights. You can call it self-determination. The question is: how can the Naga people be kept separated by an imaginary political boundary which has been created? Even in India, the Nagas are divided for administrative convenience—the division took place during the British rule, but it is still being practised. It was always a question of divide and rule. Now, when the Naga people want to come together, is there anything wrong? *No.*' He thumps an arm of his chair. 'That's a basic human right.'

He then puts a more progressive spin on things than traditional Naga rebel doctrine, developed before the battles with India began: that Nagas want freedom and they want to be left alone. 'This world of politics goes on,' the general admits. 'We cannot be isolated. We must also be a part of the world. But at the same time I cannot be put into subjugation, to accept whatever someone else says—which is never liked by the Nagas.' To some extent, he says, when the British came in the nineteenth century, the conversion to Christianity gave the Nagas the point of view of religion; they were made to take part in it and become Christian. 'You may say that when we became Christian, the warrior spirit, the fighting spirit, may to some extent have died down, because we began to understand more from a religious point of view that we should not fight.'

But faith and identity are two different things, I offer.

'Ya, that's what I am saying.'

So, what gets to you is that the criticism of your claim of nationhood comes with a paternalistic tone?

'That's right. One book [by an Indian writer] mentions that in Nagaland there is nothing else, only jungles; we have come to civilize them. Like the British said to the Indians: we have come to civilize the Indians. You see ...' He leans forward a fraction. 'Those who have understood the Nagas, the [idea of] the Naga nation, will not accept that—though they may be few. No ideas grow overnight. Even when Naga villages fought with each other, it was because of territory—they wanted to be free of domination by another: "nobody should come and dominate over me"; that's the spirit they had. Each village was a kind of republic in itself. With time the feeling grew.'

This last is standard Naga nationalistic discourse. I have heard it and read it many times, but it bears repetition precisely because people—policymakers and politicians in particular—from the 'Mainland' and even several immediate neighbours of the Naga people in Manipur and Arunachal Pradesh, dismiss it. As we sip tea, I try to swing the conversation to more touchy subjects.

For instance, I have for long wanted to ask someone from the Naga armies how it felt to treat the Indian Army and paramilitary as soldiers, as combatants; and have them in turn treat Naga rebels as terrorists and 'bandits'—a common Indian Army appellation for an enemy, a hangover of colonial nomenclature. How did it feel to do battle between soldier and soldier, and see India's forces extend their war to Naga civilian populations, burning villages and towns, raping, molesting, torturing, killing, even burying people alive. So I ask the question. It touches a nerve.

'There have been Sikh, Maratha and Gorkha soldiers over here. We haven't undertaken guerrilla operations in their villages in Punjab, Maharashtra, Darjeeling or Nepal and burnt their houses down and treated their people as part of our war.' He smiles, and then sighs deeply. 'I have always felt that the Naga warrior or the Naga army has not been treated with the same honour on the field of battle as the Naga army has acknowledged them as fighters, as warriors. I have found that to be a great mismatch in attitude.

'Those who have written books have called Nagas so many things: separatists, underground, rebels, secessionists, and nowadays, there is the use of the word "terrorist". Even the Naga movement has been termed a demand—"the Nagas are demanding this". Nagas have never...' He looks away for a moment, and recovers. 'So now, the relatively small groups of people who are fighting the Indian Army are "terrorists".'

He stays quiet for a while. 'We played with some ethics,' he resumes. 'We never retaliated against people when the India army tortured our people more than we expected. They did that because they thought it was the only way of teaching the Nagas. So many Indian generals have said to me in Nagaland and other places "that at that point of time we violated so many human rights, but we thought that was the only alternative to make the Nagas understand". *We* have never done that.'

Before I can fast-forward things to the present day, he goes on.

'Even now, we do not agree to killing of innocents, bombing places, indiscriminate killing—we don't accept that. We have always given our enemies honour. That has not been accorded to us by the Indian armies. They think that just by putting fear into the public's mind they can root out the Naga movement.'

Gen. Phungthing's phone rings, the ring tone a smart riff on an acoustic guitar. Interesting music, I say, and he laughs out loud before taking the call. He speaks in Tangkhul dialect, and listens more than he talks.

When he is done, I steer the conversation to the ceasefire, the bizarre animal he has monitored for a dozen years on behalf of NSCN-IM, in the manner his counterpart, Lt. Gen. (Retd.) Mandhata Singh, does on India's behalf as we speak. There's a ceasefire agreement on paper, but the ceasefire doesn't extend outside Nagaland, even though large indigenous Naga populations exist in the hill districts of Manipur contiguous to Nagaland and similarly, the districts of Tirap and Changlang in Arunachal Pradesh. Where does it go from here?

'It's a headache.' He laughs. 'We should find a way out to solve this politically, because the Indian government has said it is not feasible militarily. The world over that is the reality: even if I fight I know tomorrow I have to sit down and talk. They may defeat me or I may defeat them; or there may be a stalemate. A time will come when we will have to negotiate. So, when the ceasefire was declared [in 1997] we thought we would give the best we can; the first commitment our leadership had given was that we would leave no stone unturned to find a solution to the Naga political problem.

'The ceasefire,' he adds, 'became more a discussion on the non-issues.'

Much of this discussion, I learn from him, other Naga Army officers and functionaries, and Indian military and government sources, has involved nitpicking on which party had broken ceasefire rules, from firing upon or killing one another's troopers in Manipur to issues of Naga Army personnel found with weapons outside designated camps in Nagaland. It is no secret that NSCN-IM and GPRN/NSCN, with which the Government of India has maintained ceasefire since 2001, continue with training and patrolling. I have seen personnel from both groups carry handguns in 'civilian' areas, testimony to continuing tension with India's forces as well as between one faction and another. NSCN-IM's Alee Command, its overseas forces, is still a reality; it maintains a few camps in Bangladesh, the same as GPRN/NSCN maintain armed camps in the territory of Myanmar along with its 'ceasefire' camps in India. But Gen. Phungthing's point, I understand, is more that core political issues are not being addressed. Real and perceived violations of ceasefire arrangements have instead taken precedence.

The general talks about skirmishes in Naga areas of Manipur and Arunachal where the ceasefire technically does not apply—and yet care must be taken to not escalate conflict, keeping in mind the ceasefire operational in adjacent, contiguous Naga areas of Nagaland. He begins with an incident in Ukhrul district of Manipur in August 2009, when NSCN-IM cadres and Assam Rifles personnel came face to face. People died on both sides and both sides claimed provocation by the other. I've heard several versions of the incident, and I'm waiting to confirm the version closest to the truth from a security official who did a postmortem of it, but for now I keep my peace and listen to what Gen. Phungthing has to say.

'This is not the first time. I can give you a list of all my people killed by Assam Rifles. And yet we have not retaliated—at the moment—because of the commitment the leadership has given.' But at one time they used to retaliate, Gen. Phungthing says, even as recently as 2004, in Manipur. 'You say we have no ceasefire in Manipur. When we ambushed a convoy of CRPs'—Central Reserve Police Force troopers—'they said no, no, we should not do this. Okay, we accepted it. But what about *you*?'

He is working up to a temper now. 'They think [India's Home

Minister] Chidambaram is very strong, he can solve this issue. We say "good, if he can solve this issue then good". But he cannot force me. Just because Mr Chidambaram threatens me … oh Mr Chidambaram just because you are the home minister I should salute you and surrender arms!' He dismisses it with a flick of a hand. 'We are not concerned about that.'

Recently, he says, Government of India representatives talked about Sri Lanka to the Nagas. 'They said, "See the Sri Lankan armies have defeated them [Tamil Tigers]." You may to a certain extent have wiped out the LTTE, [but] the cause is not yet wiped out. The cause is not yet discussed.'

It's the same thing with the Nagas, Gen. Phungthing froths. 'The question is: did all the Nagas surrender in 1960?'—which led to a process culminating in the declaration of Nagaland as a state of India in 1963. 'Did the Shillong Accord [of 1975] solve the Naga issue? When some of the Sema groups [rebel units dominated by those of the Sema or Sümi tribe] came and surrendered, and some from them became Rajya Sabha members, was the Naga issue solved? *No*. When [former chief minister] Hokishe Sema took Naga matters from foreign affairs to home affairs, was the Naga issue solved? *No*.' The general is referring to the time when Nagaland affairs were, for several decades, administered by the Ministry of External Affairs, and supervised directly by Nehru—ironically for India, it's a factoid Naga rebels recant when claiming Nagaland was not a part of India.

'When a crisis came in 1988, with Khaplang—today you call it IM and Khaplang—[the split] was actually plotted by some of our Naga politicians and the military intelligence; this is well known. The Naga area is so small. What you are speaking today will be known tomorrow. So who are you trying to fool? [The intelligence] tried that, and it didn't work to solve the Naga issue. They are using them today'—he waves a hand and furiously continues in a disjointed manner—'the reconciliation process…' He shakes his head.

It is indeed no secret that India's intelligence services and the home ministry play the game every which way with each faction, and try to tap into separate points of leverage within each faction by using those with political ambition. The purpose is to weaken a faction by fomenting dissent or trying to split and gathering in what the Chinese regime colourfully calls 'splittists' to further use as pawns in this intensely localized derivative of a Great Game construct. I've personally seen such a 'play' happen as recently as 2009, but that's a story for another time.

'They tried to make [the Khaplang group] fight with us, thinking that as there is a ceasefire between the Government of India and NSCN-IM, we would not do anything to them; so they used a third force. Whereas in the [ground rules of the ceasefire] agreement it is said, "We will not support GAP"—groups of armed persons—"which is inimical to each other".'

'Are you suggesting that these ground rules were intended to be broken from day one?'

'Day one itself,' Gen. Phungthing says. 'But now they are telling me, "See, you should not have relationships with the Naxalites." Why they mention Naxalites is because in the early nineties [before NSCN's ceasefire with the Government of India] we have gone and trained the Naxalites, the People's War Group.'

I am stunned. This is the first direct admission that I have heard of; there still are suspicions that NSCN-IM have maintained their links with the rebel conglomerate now known as Communist Party of India (Maoist), formed in 2004 with the merger of Communist Party of India (Marxist-Leninist) People's War and its allies, with another large faction, Maoist Communist Centre.

The general is in flow. 'Now they say you have relationship with this Sikkimese group, the new Gorkha organization'—the Gorkha Janamukti Morcha? I intervene—'Ya, whatever it may be ... [They say] "You are giving them training." Then they said you should not have relationships with the Khasis, with the Garos [the two major ethnic groups in Meghalaya], with this and that. So today, for the sake of peace we have left everyone out, to find a solution to the Naga problem. But what did the Indian government do? Maybe the home ministry thinks the Nagas are fools. They think they will make the NSCN-IM weak and when NSCN-IM is weak they think we will sign an agreement. They are all wrong.'

So it's like a war of attrition, I suggest. I know the government point of view—at least a prevalent point of view among some officials I have interacted with at New Delhi's Ministry of Home Affairs—that it is indeed a war of attrition, even to the point of waiting for the natural demise of the two leaders of NSCN-IM, Isak Chishi Swu and Thuingaleng Muivah, and even their arch-foe, S.S. Khaplang; the idea being to clean up should the factions splinter thereafter in a frenzy of ego and turf wars by the next level of rebel leadership.

'We have made it very clear,' Gen Phungthing says. 'At our last meeting [with the Indian side] we said, "You think you can wear us down?" We can wait.'

'And what they will do thanks to all you gentlemen,' I try a joke to temper the atmosphere a bit by pointing to the tradition of peace talks between Naga factions and India being held outside the country, in Bangkok, Amsterdam and sometimes, Zurich, 'is develop a taste for Thai and Dutch food.' We both burst into laughter. 'You need to take credit for introducing the Indian bureaucracy and army to these cuisines. Maybe Swiss cuisine too—whatever that is.'

Forgive me, I add, when the laughter dies down. A little gallows humour is sometimes good. But really, I persist, as an Indian citizen, not a player or party, I see the Naga peace process with India as yet another political circus in addition to the many that exist. I see a country that I love wilfully destroying so many bits of itself in several ways...

'We are not against Indians,' Gen. Phungthing intervenes. 'Why should we be against innocent people? We are fighting because the government policy is not acceptable to us … I keep telling all the [Indian] generals, you will go off tomorrow. But whatever you have done, sown yesterday or today, the next one may have to bear it.'

So where does NSCN-IM go from here? What does this Naga Army, twelve years into the ceasefire, see itself as? A guerrilla army? A regular army with a guerrilla mindset?

'We are always kept on the toes, not because of us but the enemy itself and the situation. Yes, if we are to resume fighting, the approach, the strategy, tactics, may change. Because in these twelve years the Indian Army must have definitely studied how Naga guerrillas fought with them. So I cannot say we will use today what we used yesterday.'

And meanwhile, I remind him, the Indian Army has also upgraded its skills and weaponry. The general would know better than me the significance of regular Indian Army presence in Manipur—the crack Mountain Brigade and other elements. The army's counterinsurgency and jungle warfare school in Vairengte, Mizoram, is accomplished enough for the US Army to have sent troops for conditioning and training. Besides, the general and his colleagues have reminded me that Assam Rifles have more than thirty battalions in the Naga areas. There is soon going to be one division of regular army. At Rangapahar on the outskirts of Dimapur the army has a corp command; a lot of troops were 'rotated' to Kargil, but they are beginning to come in, 'may be three army battalions here in Rangapahar,' as I am told by a NSCN-IM functionary, who also added: 'Rangapahar is looking after Manipur and Arunachal Pradesh also, so they will send in two divisions into AP because of problems with China.' Their awareness means the Naga armies know well what they are up against.

But a large force alone will not win a war for the Indians, I have also been told, both by Nagas and Indian security officials. The

Nagas have watched the demolition of LTTE on account of its chief Velupillai Prabhakaran taking the might of the Sri Lankan armed forces full-on instead of sticking to guerrilla warfare—which for decades had kept Sri Lankan forces at bay. The Tigers even engineered serious reverses for the Indian Peace Keeping Force when it tried to take on the Tigers on their turf. There are still red faces on account of Indian intelligence agencies having helped train Tamil Tigers in guerrilla warfare on Indian soil in an attempt to tighten the screws on what was seen as Sri Lanka's errant, arrogant leadership—and then, humiliatingly, have the Tigers turn against India.

'We will never go into conventional war though we have an armed force,' I am repeatedly told by Naga rebel leaders. 'We know what the enemy can do. And we also know where it cannot be.' Even if the Indian Army has terrain maps out here in Naga areas, there could be a missed feature like a stream, a patch of forest, sudden change of weather—numerous factors that could upset a plan and play into the hands of guerrilla forces at home on their land.

'Even now I will proudly say, if they come to the jungle we will fight them,' Gen. Phungthing tells me. 'No matter how much the government—they may send in a column of army, but they can never come in formation, they have to go like this.' He gestures with split hands, snaking them to resemble narrow trails wide enough for one person, moves them up and down to resemble fluctuating terrain. 'By the time they come in, I'm seeing only one. One thousand may come in, but I am seeing only one. By the time he comes further in with other soldiers I am somewhere else. Even if hundred people come searching for me, it would be like searching for a needle in a haystack. So they thought that by torturing and harassing the public, they would find us. But they failed to do that. This is never written, never told, in the Indian discourse.'

Our tea lies cold, untouched. The general orders fresh black tea from a boy who arrives silently; he must have remained in the shadows all this while. The electricity is still out. Tiny moths are urgently circling the LED lamps around us.

After asking for tea, the general returns to being livid, but using a different stream. 'Indian intelligence bureaus are so concerned about how many Nagas have gone out, how many are staying in all the cities. They have the details, the statistics—they want to track them. Sometimes we sit down to talk to them and joke: "How many Nagas are there in Delhi? More than ten thousand. How many houses? Which areas?" They know.

'The Government of India may say Nagas are Indians, but they think every Naga is a potential…' He stops and turns away his face. His fists, resting on arm-rests of the sofa, are clenched. 'In the last twelve years … this G.K. Pillai, when he was joint secretary in charge of the Northeast [in the home ministry; Pillai is home secretary as the general and I chat], we have quarrelled over this also. They say the army is not touching innocents, civilians. And we say bullshit, *bullshit* to you.' His voice has risen. 'I am using their language for us—"you bloody things". They say we are trying to give you peace. What peace are they trying to give us?

'Tomorrow they might catch you,' he points to me, 'because you have talked with me. What's the point of doing that?'

'You talk like this in your ceasefire meetings?'

'Yes, yes. I don't give hints.' He means that he speaks plainly. 'Just because the Indian government calls us terrorists doesn't mean we are terrorists. Even if they call me a dog—as they used to call us when they caught us … I was in their custody so I know how they treat us. I was in jail for six years.'

'How were you treated?'

'They did not treat me like a human being.'

'Were you physically harmed?'

'We were bound, chained. We were made to sit on the floor. Even today if you look at these bones you will find these bent'—he points to his legs—'up and down. Rollers. This was in the early

1980s. I was brought here [to Dimapur], then taken to Shillong, then Assam—I have visited four or five places. Some of our friends helped us to get released. In Assam I had twenty-one cases against me; in all, thirty-one cases. Enemy of the state, dacoities, this-that. These things are personal so we don't want to speak about it...'

'I'm sorry.' It's not my place to apologize, but I don't know what else to say.

'In the early days they would put pins out here.' The general shows me the spaces under his fingernails. 'Then they would rip out the nails. They would hang you upside down. They would beat you everywhere.'

As we walk outside to my taxi, he tells me, 'Take the Naxalites, the government is saying that the biggest threat to India is Naxalites. The prime minister is always saying it. They are saying they will send in lots of armed forces. There will come a time when these armed forces will say, "No, I will not fight my own people."'

Now they are taking Nagas from Assam and other areas, Gen. Phungthing continues. 'I say, "Good, take as many as you want." It is good in one way. We know also why they are trying to build up this IRB [Indian Reserve Battalion], Assam Rifles and others with Naga people, thinking that they will fight against brothers. Tomorrow, a time will come. We will ask pertinent questions to the Naga people.'

'Basically,' I intervene, 'what you are saying is: Thank you for training our people for us?'

'Yes!' Gen. Phungthing laughs.

The pups come rushing out from the garage, mill about our legs. I try to shoo them away, keep them away from the wheels of my taxi. The same boy who brought tea arrives and scoops the pups into his arms.

'Movements and revolutions do not come overnight, and neither do they die down overnight,' the general tells me as I get into the car. 'The harsher the response the more they grow.'

6

A brief interlude about fat cats and futures

By the time I reach my small room at Hotel de Oriental Dream, it's past ten at night. I'm tired and hungry. But it's too late for room service. I look wistfully at the menu. It invites me to go 'Soup Diving', then go to the 'Desi Non-Veg Disco', but perhaps learn to 'Noodles Un-Knot' before I did. Were I still with appetite I could always indulge in 'Sneaky Veg Biryani & Pulao' or a 'Casual Fling' with the Lay's brand of potato wafers.

I usually dismissed all of these to opt for Naga food, not officially on the menu at this Naga-owned hotel but well made should anyone care to ask. Sometimes, I opted for a set of Korean-style noodles made with instant noodles, a platter of wilting but bravely attempted sushi and a cup of ginseng tea. This is on the menu to please visiting evangelists from Korea, an increasing breed of religion-mongers in both Nagaland and Manipur adding to the occasional, vocal disquiet of the several existing Baptist and Methodist missions, and the Catholic Church.

A call from Mmhonlümo Kikon drags me out of the menu daze. 'I'm in town,' he announces, impossibly chirpy. 'Just drove down from Kohima.' I've known him to sometimes do that twice a day in an electric-blue Maruti Esteem with indomitable spirit—the car, that is; Mmhonlümo drives like a maniac, and the hairpin bends on Highway 39 between Dimapur and Kohima aren't kind.

'What are you doing? Don't tell me you're sleepy already. Come *on*, brother!'

He tells me some friends of his are at a lounge—I nearly choke in surprise—not too far from my hotel. He'll collect me in ten minutes, he says, and ends the call before I can protest.

In a play of it's-a-small-world, Mmhonlümo got in touch with me after reading my book on India's ongoing Maoist rebellion, *Red Sun: Travels in Naxalite Country*. Correspondence over email gave way to phone conversations, and when I mentioned to him my *Highway 39* project, he insisted I look him up in Kohima. I did, and after a steaming breakfast of very non-Naga alu-puri at The Heritage, the charming hotel on Officer's Hill that was once the deputy commissioner's bungalow, he invited me to visit his hometown of Wokha, the biggest town in the Lotha Naga region.

It helped too that the old college network kicked in. Mmhonlümo and I are both alumni of St Stephen's College, a long-time Delhi target of affection, envy and derision in equal measure. He and I attended several years apart. I'm middle-aged; he is a mid-thirties package of restless energy typical of the more radical of his generation here: caught between the inherited angst of Nagaland's terrible history and its uncertain future. A farmer, politician and activist, this is an impatient man in a troubled land.

We arrive at a nondescript office block opposite the fairly rundown Hotel Ne-Li and, using a side entrance to get inside, walk two floors up. Our destination is Purple Haze, the name lit up at the entrance in neon signage. Inside, the large room is packed. Patrons, mostly smartly dressed teenage or young men in their twenties and similarly aged, smart ladies, sit in separate groups at red-upholstered banquettes. The occasional spiral of cigarette smoke decorates the wash of dim, red-toned lights. At one table in the far corner from us—we're shown to a table near the entrance—a balding, trim gentleman sits with two stunningly attractive ladies, each arm on their shoulders. The Doors entertain as piped music from tiny state-of-the-art speakers.

I'm introduced to those already at table. There's Tsibu Haralu, Mmhonlümo's friend from his university days in Delhi, a large, jolly Zeliang Naga. He now runs a private security business based in Dimapur. There are two others, but I can't gather their names; the introductions are drowned out as Jim Morrison screams '*Come on baby light my fire*'. I'm made welcome with chicken tikka; drumsticks doused in spice and that India-wide abomination for such restaurant fare, orange food colouring; and a generous measure of Black Dog whiskey. Other patrons are drinking a sprinkling of whiskey, beer, cocktails—I can recognize glasses of mojito among a cluster of ladies—and red wine.

Nagaland is, of course, a state with alcohol prohibition, in Indianism a 'dry' place. And so, of course, every garbage recycler's dump in Dimapur and Kohima is piled high with empty bottles of beer and hard alcohol. State-run hotels in both cities display not-so-prominent signs dated 1989 on notice boards as to how importation of alcohol into Nagaland is prohibited—and blithely serve beer and alcohol in restaurants. An hotelier friend from Nagaland once told me how she and her friends have sometimes helped out by ferrying several bottles of imported spirits and wines from Kolkata to Dimapur, as a favour to ministers and people from the chief minister's coterie returning from a visit overseas.

Drink and conversation are flowing freely, easily. Tsibu, after discovering that I'm working on a book, talks sadly about betrayal among Nagas, 'both for the cause and against the cause'. He shakes his head: 'It's complicated.'

'Fat cats,' I agree, quite mellow; conflict and conflict resolution for the moment reduced to strands of colourful thought. 'Always, everywhere, the fat cats are responsible for the mess you see around.'

'Fat cats?'

'Wealthy and powerful vested interests, crooked politicians and bureaucrats—the usual scum.'

'Eh, brother, I'm a politician also,' Mmhonlümo protests, a forkful of tikka stalled in its journey, reminding us that he contested the assembly elections in 2008 in Wokha district, narrowly losing to a much older candidate backed by a major rebel outfit. 'Please don't call me names,' he says, a little offended.

'You're a fat cat,' Tsibu tells him happily.

'Okay, you're a *nice* fat cat,' I allow. 'A fat cat with a good heart.' I turn to Tsibu. It sounds more elegant in Spanish, I tell him. 'Gato gordo. Gato is cat. Gordo is fat.'

'Cat fat?' Tsibu is puzzled.

'Yup. That's the grammar of it.'

'You're a cat fat,' he tells Mmhonlümo. He then asks the DJ for a guitar, and requests the house music be turned off.

'I'm feeling happy, brother.' He turns to me. 'I'm very happy you are here, you're doing this book about our people.'

'About many people,' I qualify, feeling deeply relaxed, contented. 'Peace on earth, brother.'

Tsibu starts to sing *'Wind of change'*, a 'power' ballad by the rock band Scorpions, effortlessly plucking and strumming the acoustic guitar. His voice is strong, clear, without a trace of Black Dog.

The conversation has stopped. It's very late. A knot of four young ladies turns to look at us. The bald gentleman and his two lady friends come across to join us. We're all singing along loudly, passionately. I stop, embarrassed, realizing I'm the only one off-key. Mmhonlümo nudges me again into song.

'Where the children of tomorrow,' we sing, many unashamedly in tears, 'dream away in the wind of change.'

~

Minister of Home Imkong L. Imchen today insisted again that Nagaland is facing a problem of employment and not unemployment. If Nagas could specialize in things that non-Nagas are doing for us, there would be no problem of employment, he stated, addressing a student gathering at the 33rd annual conference cum freshers' meet commemorating Pou Jadonang's 78th death anniversary of the Zeliangrong Students Union.

Talking on the importance of unity of the Nagas, the home minister said people like Pou Jadonang and Z. Phizo had tried, during their time, to assimilate all Nagas as one. In this regard, he urged the people to tell the Underground brothers and sisters that Naga unity should come first, only then can a solution come about. He also asked the people to be clear about the proper definition of Independence as not only Independence from India but that of individual independence.

Stating that the Government of India's assertion that Naga talks should be within the framework of the Indian Constitution is a misnomer, he said this shows the GOI's lack of proper knowledge about the Naga situation as well as the Constitution of India. QUOTE Present talks are very much outside the Constitution of India UNQUOTE he stated, while adding that the talk can only be incorporated on the Constitution if the two parties agree.

—From the *Sunday Mirror*, 30 August 2009, departure area reading kiosk, Dimapur airport

7

A story of butterfly wings, frogs' waists, and the zigzag line to justice

I first met Luingamla, a chubby-faced teenager, one afternoon in June 2009 at the National Centre for the Performing Arts in Mumbai, where the cleft of the city's southern business district of Nariman Point meets the sea. She formed the introduction to the programme I had come to attend, 'Woven Tales from the North East'.

At the time of our meeting, Luingamla had been dead nearly twenty-five years.

In a small, darkened auditorium, Zasha Colah, curator of the city's Nicholson Gallery of Modern and Contemporary Art, described the story behind the image of a richly woven piece of fabric projected onto a screen, a fabric into which Luingamla had now been transformed. Luingamla was fourteen, Colah explained, when she was shot dead by Mandhir Singh, a captain of the Madras Regiment.

She was alone at home in her village in north-eastern Ukhrul district of Manipur, which the Manipur government spells as Naimu, but those of her tribe, the Tangkhul Naga, retain the traditional name: Ngainga. Her family was away at church, it being a Sunday. Luingamla among her six siblings did not possess adequate footwear to appear before God—the family was very poor—so she had remained at home.

In her calm way, Colah told the four dozen or so of us in the audience—a smattering of society ladies, designers, students, and the odd ones out like me—who had gathered for a series of talks and presentations on fabric and tradition of weaving in northeastern India, that Captain Singh and a lieutenant entered the girl's home. Finding her alone, they raped her. When she resisted, Captain Singh shot her dead.

The year was 1986. The hill regions of Manipur were gripped by counterinsurgency operations against Naga rebels by the Indian Army and paramilitary. The brutal behaviour that had characterized such operations in the 1950s and 1960s had lessened in volume, but not practice.

Zamthingla Ruivah, a teenaged neighbour, was nearby, but helpless. In time she became a master weaver, but the memory of Luingamla wouldn't leave her. 'Luingamla fought these men off,' Colah explained. 'Luingamla's spirit was strong. Zamthingla decided to capture her spirit through weave and geometry.'

There she was, Luingamla: on the screen in front of us, as a simple, slightly hazy studio photograph; and as Luingamla *kashan*, a sarong and a strip of shawl. The kashan had broad borders of black along the lengths hemming in two combs of white along the widths. Within this frame ran four strips of intricate weave containing sets of tiny inverted pyramids resembling butterfly wings in white and green, interspersed with similar shapes in crimson; diamond-back zigzag lines in white; and intricate diamond shapes bordering these strips delicately dotted, like a chain of beads.

The comb-like pattern, *rikshi-phor* or *phorei-phor*, signified 'the chastity of a woman', an explanatory poster that Zamthingla had got designed and printed in Imphal would later inform me. *Shongwui shili*, the 'design where a line of zig-zag indicates as to how to find the way for Justice from one place to another'. The tiny pyramids were *konghar-angachang* and *khaifa akashan*: 'the wings of butterfly and waist of frogs design signify places of judgment (courts) firmly for fair justice.' *Malum-mik* were the streams of tiny diamond shapes guarding the butterfly wings, waists of frog and the zigzag line to justice: these 'symbolize the eyes of the termite ... it signifies the never ending support of the Tangkhul Women Society and other such organisation [who] move unitedly, relentlessly help in finding the truth till the end of the struggle for justice'.

Before all this, of course, was the explanation for so much red in the kashan. 'Luingamla's kashan is 90% red in colour,' the poster explained, 'signifying Luingamla's innocent blood which was shed for the cause of women's dignity and honour. It also signifies the valour and unflinching courage of women.'

'On special days, such as 24 January, the death anniversary of the girl,' Colah continued with her careful delivery, 'the kashan is now worn as protest and solidarity. As soon as [protest] came in words it challenged the army and its sense of persecution. The army could not read the kashan, so it was allowed to carry on.'

She then introduced Zamthingla to the audience. The frail, demure lady inclined her head and accepted the applause. A few minutes later her understated dignity was further reinforced by Sentila T. Yanger, a well-known fabric and weaving expert from Nagaland, during her talk. 'The strength of the woman has gone into that fabric,' she explained in reference to fabric woven by Naga ladies in particular, and ladies of the northeast in general. 'These are woven mantles of self, stature and merit' woven by women for men and women alike.

As the event ended, in the crush of the foyer I had asked Zamthingla—her sister helped with translation—for permission to visit her at home in Imphal, to talk at greater length away from the tenor of the 'society' event. (The co-host from the Morarka

Cultural Centre had at one point introduced dancers from the Sümi tribe of Nagaland, moving to a weavers' song, as 'dancers from Manipur'. 'Nagaland,' one among the audience had corrected, with some temper. 'Tee-hee,' the lady had trilled. 'Nagaland, is it?')

I know the story of Luingamla goes deeper than has been told here—the significance of it; the organization of it. I want to know more, I had told Zamthingla. She seemed sceptical—we had only just met; and Mumbai is a long way from Imphal. But she had agreed.

It is three months later, and I am at her door. My musician friend Rewben Mashangvah, who knows Zamthingla well, has brought me on his ancient, sputtering, battered Bajaj scooter that simply refuses to die. I'm nearly as fond of the scooter as I am of Rewben.

Zamthingla lives near the Meitei Church in Lamphel pat, in the northwest quadrant of Imphal, close to Langol Hills, a low range that marks the northern and western boundaries of this state capital. It's a small, neat house of exposed brick and aluminium roofing. The aluminium sheet that is the gate opens to a well-tended, tiny garden. Rewben, who will also act as translator this September morning, and I are seated on a sofa. Zamthingla sits on a stool. Her young son is at home—'Schools are closed because of strike, nah, brother,' Rewben explains. The boy plays kindergarten rhythms on a small keyboard.

I told you I will see you in Imphal, I gently tease Zamthingla. She is gracious enough to admit she didn't think I would show up. The story of Luingamla draws me forcefully, I tell her; and the story of what you have done for her.

'I had to do this for her,' she answers simply, slightly hunched on the stool, in that act even more diminutive. 'I had to do this for all of us.'

We travel back in time for a while, when Luingamla was fourteen, and Zamthingla eighteen. The daughter of Suilei and Lungshimla, recalls the master weaver, was gentle and loveable. What she tells me differs a little from what Zasha Colah said in Mumbai—that Luingamla was raped. There was an attempt at rape which the little girl resisted with all her might; Zamthingla herself heard the commotion, and the ensuing gunshots.

Zamthingla is overcome for a while. To carry on, she just hands me the poster she had made, the one with details of Luingamla's kashan. I read that Mandhir Singh '...taking advantage of the lone situation, forcibly attempted to molest and rape her maiden chastity and she firmly resisted with all her might and valour, the carnalist army captain was extremely outraged, pulled out his pistol and shot her death cold blooded. Thus the young budding virgin girl died shedding her innocent blood for the preservation of woman's dignity and chastity.'

The only scrap of information I have been able to cull is a few paragraphs from a page of an official gazette that records the death of Luingamla. It lists the 'Court Martial Proceedings against 2 (Two) army officers for the murder of Miss Luingamla ... of Ngaimu Village, Ukhrul Dist., Manipur'. This snippet also lists Mandhir Singh's rank a little differently to what Zamthingla and Colah have mentioned.

'On 24/1/86 at about 1.00 p.m. Miss Luingamla d/o Mr Suilei ... was killed by Army Officer,' the gazette observes with bureaucratic abruptness.

'For the murder of the said Luingamla, Lt. Mandhir Singh of 25 Madras and 2nd Lt. Sanjeev Dubey of 764 ASC Bn. attached to 3 B.U.H. II Ward tried by the General Court Martial at Leimakhong Army Brigadier Hq. The G.C.M. was constituted by 7 members of Indian Army Officer presided over by Col. Natarajan and one Lt. Col. as senior member and 5 other majors.

'The Court Martial commenced on 5th May, 1988 but was ... dissolved on technical ground and again constituted on 1st June 1988. The prosecution examined 17 witnesses including the villagers of Ngaimu.

'The defence produced 5 witnesses including the Major General P.L. Kukrety (Mike Section).

'The Court examined 2 witnesses as court witnesses.

'The trial was concluded on 11.8.88. The General Court Martial convicted the accused Lt. Mandhir Singh for life imprisonment and cashiering for the murder of the said Luingamla subject to the confirmation by the confirming authority under the Army Act. The co-accused 2nd Lt. Sanjeev Dubey was acquitted by the Court Martial.'

That's where the page of the gazette ends for me. It gets a bit muddy here. Singh was ultimately let off, I have heard. Nothing at all was done for Luingamla's family—and that is quite typical of the ham-handed manner in which India's forces have tried to deal with situations in these parts. For instance, from the locals I heard of an event from the early 1990s when the army badly beat up three men and two women in the area. By way of apology they were offered tea and a box of lipsticks each for the women.

Versions vary. But it doesn't change the fact that Luingamla was killed. And that it broke Zamthingla's heart and made her resolutely angry. So angry that she began to weave to fight India's army.

Luingamla's memory wouldn't leave her, Zamthingla says, no matter the passage of time—she speaks in a rush that Rewben finds difficult to keep up with. 'Luingamla's story had to be told.'

One day, she simply set about putting the thoughts about her young friend into her weaving. She wove by hand around six sets of fabric, including the kashan and the top cloth, and gradually a strong design emerged. Zamthingla took the design to the Tangkhul Shanao Long, the apex women's organization of the tribe, and explained to them her purpose and the story behind the design. The organization approved the design and initiated a plan to spread the design and its message.

'I then wove between twenty-five and thirty pieces to send to weavers across the Tangkhul areas, north, south, east, west.'

And the ceremonial, political fabric called the Luingamla kashan came to be.

'I now want to do a song about Luingamla with Rewben.' Zamthingla smiles. She gives me an A4 size sheet neatly crammed with romanized characters of the Tangkhul dialect on both sides, which Rewben explains is now more poetry than song.

'I have to work much, much more,' he tells Zamthingla. 'A song set to music is different from poetry.' He turns to me: 'Nah?'

'You're the boss,' I tell him, teasing, and he bursts into trademark cackle.

Before we leave, I tell Zamthingla what I plan to do next: I want to visit Luingamla's village. I want to see Luingamla's grave, and anyone from her family. I want to see how she is remembered in the village. Luingamla has become an obsession, I tell her; I have to see this journey to its end.

'Good,' she says, nodding. 'Good.'

~

In three days I'm off to Ukhrul. It's easy enough if there aren't shutdowns, landslides or violence: tickets are available at Kangla Travels just down the road from the Tam-pha, my very modest hotel in the North AOC area of Imphal. A near-continuous stream of convoys, patrols and the early-morning call to falling in of troops in several nearby barracks—a combination of Assam Rifles, a hub of Army Intelligence, CRPF, and the 2nd Battalion of Manipur Rifles—make it an intimidating place.

Buses leave within minutes of the other between 5.45 and 6 a.m. and then again at mid-morning from this busy tri-junction, for the three- to four-hour run of 87 km, mostly uphill, to Ukhrul. The buses return after their crews have rested for a couple of hours. There's no such thing as an evening or 'night' bus to these parts.

North AOC is also the main jump-off point for long-haul buses to Kohima, Dimapur, Shillong and Guwahati. The sun is up, the day switched on, and the place chaotic and loud, as all such places tend to be. Streams of autorickshaws arrive stuffed to the gills, as it were, with one of the most popular buys in the region: blankets of Chinese make from the trading town of Moreh at the border with Myanmar. This cargo, along with loads of aluminium clothes racks, plastic LED lamps, track pants, T-shirts, even bags made from rolls of plastic product casing, is briskly loaded onto buses, stacked perilously on the roof till the centre of gravity of these vehicles shift appreciably upwards. In a few minutes, the buses resemble trucks with windows for people to breathe from, or to spit out betel juice and vomit with which each bus will soon be decorated, along with dust and caked mud.

Police and paramilitary along the way will extract without fail a 'tax' from trader-passengers of such buses—certainly at Mao Gate, which marks the border of Manipur and Nagaland along Highway 39, and at every significant district and state border checkpoint that lies on the way to the final destination. Rebel groups that operate in the geographies of such transport will also extract their 'tax'. Groups of armed thugs that hide behind the acronymic fig leaf of UG—Underground—too will have a take. And so, the final sale prices of products vary from place to place, depending both on the length of journey (the economy of fuel and effort) and the intensity of it—which characterizes the economy of conflict.

My bus, of the Luoningthong company's service, is half-full. More passengers will board from the Chingmeirong circle a little to our north, from where we turn right off Highway 39 to head northeast to Ukhrul. A few more passengers join us at the Khumman Lampak stop, near a large eponymous stadium. This is an area with a large population of Manipuri-Nagas—my hyphenation an impolitic, if correct, indication of the ethnic cauldron and confusion in the state of Manipur. As we pass, the bus now loaded to maximum—I am crushed to the window on a bench that seats three—I see a sign on the signboard of an NGO office: 'Peace Through Development.'

It seems like a good idea.

My cynical mood lifts as we leave the mess of Imphal behind and cut through fields of impossibly green paddy as an amoeba-arm of Imphal Valley brings us to the eastern foothills; these also mark the end of Meitei concentration. I put away my sunglasses and with my bare eyes drink in the peerless colours of early-day. We begin our climb at Yaingangpokpi. But first, the bus stops to allow— well, there really is no choice—a convoy of Assam Rifles that emerges from a lane to cut into the traffic.

The bus attendant switches on a DVD player in the main cabin of the bus. Above it, a dusty TV screen blares a movie in Meeteilon that is more soap opera than cinematic enterprise. But it's entertainment for my Rs 70 ride. As in nearly all the local movies I will see—on buses, in homes, and on television during countless nights in tiny hotel rooms—government and conflict immediately mark their presence. In the first fifteen minutes of this one, there is a death, abduction, a fight, and a separation. Within the same timeframe, I hear the magic words: 'chief minister', 'home minister', 'minister', 'home secretary' and 'UG'. (Generally, this approach appears to work for romances as well.)

After an hour or so, we stop at the foothills village of Litan for a short break. Ladies rush to the bus offering boiled corn in its jacket, which they carry in a bunch, and great whorls of a dry dough-based snack.

Soon we are at Ramva, a tiny village on a ridgeline that combines a small but thriving market and a major Assam Rifles checkpoint. There's a barrier across the road—it is billed as NH 150, but if this ribbon-thin strip of tar is a highway then I must (an old college 'PJ' surfaced) be Cleopatra. I blame this giddy burst on the immense amounts of fresh air after the Dickensian atmosphere of

Imphal; and the exuberance of the movie. As one of several subplots unravel, the hero's friend turns into villain and back to hero's friend after beating back a dozen thugs with a Jet Li-like repertoire and grimaces to save the hero's sister, in the process getting severally knifed, surviving, and proposing marriage to said sister. 'Home minister,' I hear the hero's father intone as the family gathers around the hospital bed of this remarkable character, just as we draw up to the barrier.

The barrier is manned by D Company of 17 Assam Rifles. The bus empties. We all file in a line past an AR trooper without a weapon (he is backed up by a nearby guardroom that displays several barrels of automatic rifles) as he frisks every male passenger. Women are spared, but they need to walk across to where the bus will be parked, about fifty metres ahead, after checking. An elderly man and a youngster wander off from the queue to head towards a kiosk selling a typical jumble of bus-stop goodies, to be yelled at by the trooper.

'Idhar aa saley,' he demands. 'Main yahan kisliye khara hoon?' Come back you shits. Why do you think I am standing here?

The duo, blank-faced, return to the line after prompting by fellow passengers.

The ugliness soon dissipates. There is fortunately nothing more remaining of the movie except credits; and the landscape is as stunningly pretty as any in the eastern Himalayan foothills from Nepal on. From our height we can see the hills like waves moving to the east—lush, green, with some patches of jhoom fields of pineapple and vegetables—into the depths of Myanmar. Villages, always around a hill-top or along a ridge, flash their presence with the sun reflecting off roofs, remote in their traditionally strategic placement to make attacks difficult for marauders.

Ukhrul arrives almost as a surprise at the end of three hours, from rolling hillsides to a scattering of houses; a schoolyard with neatly uniformed boys and girls out at recess, bright red pullovers adding cheer to shirt-white and trousers and skirts of grey; a jumble of worn shops. All at once, a busy town strung along a ridge.

Rewben had told me his friend, Seth Shatsang, would be waiting for me by Hotel Oasis in lower Ukhrul. He would know the way to Ngainga and elsewhere. Sure enough, there he is, with a big smile and an exuberant 'Welcome to Ukhrul…'

Seth has a room for me at Oasis, owned by the family of a local Baptist preacher. 'The only room with an attached toilet,' Seth explains. That makes it the best hotel room in Ukhrul.

Seth is ready to leave immediately for Ngainga, preferring to keep a walkabout around Ukhrul until later, but he first suggests a quick meal. There is nothing by way of a place to eat at Ngainga, and we can't take for granted the hospitality of the village. I don't complain. A quick breakfast of rice, boiled cabbage, light chicken stew and fiery chutney of fermented fish with shreds of Raja chilli—the sort that might knock the sombrero off a caricature Mexican—turns out to be a fine store of energy; and it will keep at bay the damp. Ukhrul is at 6,000 feet and the clouds and chill are never far in September.

We are on a motorcycle Seth has borrowed for the day. It's dented, it rattles, and it spews smoke. Its mood matches exactly the state of the road as we turn left at the northern end of Ukhrul, having passed an enormous playground, the office of the local tribe's apex organization, Tangkhul Naga Long, and the bus stand. Beyond the large encampment of 17 AR the road becomes a winding track of uneven stone and mud, fresh from showers this past week. Seth points to a range in front of us—we're heading that way, fifteen kilometres west of Ukhrul—but before that there's a series of sharp descents and ascents and, always, the near-collapsed state of the track.

We come upon a stretch of mud every few metres. We soon develop a routine. I hop off, walk along the relatively drier section near the edge of the road that overlooks sheer drops, keeping an eye for relatively less sludgy sections to guide Seth. He then guns the protesting two-wheeler to slip and slide through shallower stretches of treacle-like mud.

As we cross over to a range of hills that cradles Ngainga, the track has become entirely muddy. We stop for a few minutes to recover, and soak in the sudden quiet that descends when the roar of the motorcycle cuts out. Ukhrul appears as houses peppered for several kilometres along a ridge, but thankfully not yet as dense as that of Kohima, or anywhere near the template of a civic disaster that Dimapur and Imphal have become. Luingamla's spirit draws us, and it is good to smell the air and the flash of wild herbs that wash over us.

We turn left at a fork instead of right, mistakenly going on for several minutes before being turned back by a friendly couple walking to Ukhrul. They tell Seth there's a sign at the fork that clearly mentions the way to Ngainga. When we arrive back at the fork, we understand why we missed it. A waist-high ridge of dried mud caused by the churn of truck tyres has obscured the sign, neat letters painted in black on a plank of wood that helpfully points: 'Way To Ngainga.' We need to wait several more minutes for a decades-old army surplus Shaktiman truck, hoodless, its engine screaming protest, that appears around a bend. Such ancient, battered trucks are the region's preferred beasts of burden. The mud reaches halfway to the wheels. Carrying a load of timber, the truck slides towards the drop-off, and is mercifully stuck. I walk past it, balancing on the edge of track and nothingness. Seth guns the bike towards the shoulder of the track, relatively less of a quagmire, and comes level with me.

As we painfully work our way towards Ngainga, armed with the knowledge, which offers little satisfaction, that most village approach roads in these parts are similarly nightmarish, I recall what a local bureaucrat had told me about how funds for road building—

indeed, any project—are typically used in the state. Ten per cent of the funds allocated for a road project 'goes' to the area's MLA, he alleged. 'UG' receives a skim of between 10 and 40 per cent. Ten per cent is marked to the 'concerned minister', meaning whosoever is in charge of the ministry; 10 per cent to the person who awards the contract; between 7.5 per cent and 10 per cent to the layer of 'concerned' bureaucracy; and, depending on the need and greed of whichever chief minister is up to it, 10 per cent to his appointed collectors.

The rest, between 10 and, on excellent days, a little over 40 per cent, goes to the intended project unless the ultimate scam is pulled: the project is shown as sanctioned, and either work-in-progress or completed only on paper, the funds disappearing along appropriated lines. Comptroller and Auditor General of India reports relating to Manipur and Nagaland are full of such indiscretions.

After several minutes we emerge on to a wide area carved from the hillside, to another fork. Seth points to the tiny houses of Ngainga up ahead in the distance. It has taken us three hours to come these fifteen kilometres. Both tracks lead to the village, Seth is certain, but we have to take the one on the left as on the right is parked an AR truck. In front of it is a further impediment of roughly chopped branches. Two troopers add more. A patrol must be about, and they have by this manoeuvre cut one route to the village, the last habitation on this section of the ridge. A few troopers sit on benches by the open tailgate of the truck, automatic weapons ready.

'Say you're here to buy shawls,' Seth nervously whispers.

That's what I do, reluctantly, when the two troopers by the barrier, one a Sikh and the other a Kuki as I discover from his name, come over to ask our business. They eye my mud-caked hiking boots and mud-splattered jeans.

'Achha?' the Sikh asks. 'Shawl?'

'Badiya shawl, paa-ji,' I reply, calling him brother in speakeasy Punjabi and using a mix of Hindi and English to praise the quality of shawls in Ngainga.

You don't seem like a trader, he tells me, looking me up and down. My fleece jacket is zipped open to reveal a navy T-shirt; my faithful orange backpack is with me; my sunglasses are pushed onto my forehead as we speak.

'Shawl designer,' I offer, a little weakly, mildly irritated with Seth for taking us down this path but I realize why he has done it; he may not want to be tagged by AR as a person showing writers or journalists around. I point to Seth and say he is a friend from Ukhrul. With that, and a cheery wave, we carry on.

We come upon the reason for the patrol further ahead. On a knoll on the left of the track villagers are out finishing a monolith. We pass under a newly constructed arch of planking and latticed bamboo to climb fifty metres or so to where the monolith is. Boys and girls mill around, and some adults, one of whom recognizes Seth. There's a flat area at the end of which is a small shed. More people are eating there, we see. Some come out to wash the traditionally designed plates—shallow bowls with a wide rim—from an open tank of water by the side. They are volunteers from the village, Seth's friend explains, participating in community work.

This work consists of erecting the monolith, which turns out to be a memorial on behalf of the Naga Army, the armed wing of NSCN-IM. On top of three tiers of concrete is a large slab of stone. Near the top of the obelisk is a circle in light blue. In the middle of it is a white six-pointed star, with two wreaths painted gold highlighting it. A foot or so below is a large rectangular space, chiselled smooth and coloured a dark blue. On it to the right is painted an inverted rifle. To the left is a message, somewhat in verse.

'We salute you fearless/ Officers, Rank and File,/ In you our pride and glory/ lies, you are the true sons/ and daughters of the soil, We fully acknowledge, you are/ here for our tomorrow,/ you are our proud history.'

And then: 'This monolith is dedicated to Naga National Workers who have laid down their lives and their all for the cause of the Nation.'

The memorial ends with an 'Unveiled by Brig. M. Joshua, GSO-1 N/A, On 27th Sept. 2009.' He is General Staff Officer of the 1st Naga Army.

It is to be unveiled the following day, the reason for the flurry of activity. To the left, partway down a slope, are four more memorials to people from the village, explains Seth's friend. These memorials are painted a simple green. Volunteers are putting final touches of beige and blue on the pedestals. One is for a Col. M. Ningwo, described here as the 1st General Staff Officer of the Naga Army. 'He was dynamic, and loved ideas, highly responsible, amicable but uncompromising on National Issues.' Maj. R.S. Shangam was '…a man of courage, tough and stubborn and practically a good fighter'. Capt. K. Mikrang's 'integrity was much respected'. Lt M. Shebna, 'One of the pioneers (Women's wing)' has inscribed on her memorial a message from Muivah. 'She served the cause of the Nation with unreserved commitment. Her undaunted courage under perilous circumstances was praiseworthy for all time to come. Nagalim shall be proud of woman like her.'

Muivah's words go beyond mere symbolism here. We can see the scattering of houses and shining roofs of his home-village, Somdal, from where we stand. It's on the next wave of hills from ours, farther to the west. Muivah has not visited Somdal for over forty years, the story goes. He pines for it, the story goes; he wants to see it again in his lifetime. That will depend on his organization, the Government of India, and the Government of Manipur.

A white Gypsy of the remaining AR patrol passes by us, towards Ngainga. The crowd coolly eyes them. Troopers in the off-roader are trying to be equally cool. The sound of Hindi movie music drifts up to us. I can't recognize the tune but it has an overload of violin and bongos and a piercing female voice. Then the track changes. 'It's from *Kal Aaj aur Kal*,' Seth identifies for me the movie the new track is from. I'm long past being surprised.

'Will they stop, you think?' I ask Seth's friend, who hasn't offered a name even after my asking. It is clearer now that he is a senior functionary of NSCN-IM.

'No,' he replies, lips drawn into a thin line, and tone turned chilly. 'They dare not stop here.'

It's another display, relatively minor but significant, of the twisted nature of India's ceasefire with NSCN-IM that operates within the geographical boundaries of Nagaland, but not anywhere else—certainly not in these parts, the Naga areas within the territory of Manipur. So the two groups will dance around each other, come within provoking distance of the other, try to pitch the other into triggering some sort of reaction, and mostly pull back short of outright 'action'.

We know what you're doing, is the point of the AR patrol. We have our eyes on you. We know such ceremonies are a ploy to both honour the memory of your dead, and also use emotion to nudge a few youngsters into your army.

Do what you have to, is the NSCN-IM response. We will do what we have to.

Seth's friend nods approvingly when he tells him that the story of Luingamla has brought me here. He points to a church, even at some distance the largest structure in the village. We should ask around for her grave once we reach the church, he suggests.

The towering toy-like façade of Ngainga Baptist Church—pillars, arches, four tiers of boxy rooms rising up to the spire all painted red, yellow, blue and white—comes to us after a steep climb. It is set about midway through the village in a large clearing which doubles as a soccer pitch and a venue for religious gatherings.

Small children, none seem older than six or seven, dressed in school uniforms of red, white and grey walk across the field, skirting a massive buffalo with grand curving horns that Seth explains would cost between Rs 45,000 and 50,000. The buffalo, nonchalantly going at the grass, and the children share easy camaraderie, but Seth and I give the animal wide berth to arrive at the back of the church. There's a trail leading down past a small school to the left.

Lessons are still on for older students, seated noisily across several tin, thatch and bamboo classrooms, at Scintilla School. It is 'sponsored' by the Ngainga Baptist Church, a sign proclaims. A local is on his way up a trail past the school, and Seth addresses him for directions to Luingamla's grave. The man offers to show us the way.

'Who is knocking at the door?' a female voice rings out in command at a lesson in English. The reply is silence: the children are distracted, all looking our way; the rooms are tiny, and the windows and doors are all open.

'*Who* is knocking at the door?' the voice asks again, then pokes an irritated, bespectacled face out of a window. I offer a nod and smile by way of apology as we pass by. Embarrassed, she returns the smile and ducks back inside. Peals of laughter ring out from the classroom.

After a five-minute walk up a rough stone and mud track we come to a levelled area at the very edge of the village, near a steep drop-off. There's some chatter with Seth as our guide stops in front of house—a shack. 'This is where Luingamla used to live,' Seth says.

I don't know what it looked like then but, I suspect, somewhat like now. It's a box with a sloping roof. The sides are of rain-stained planking laid laterally and nailed to larger pieces of vertical planks and some slim cylinders of tree; space made for a single window and door; aluminium sheets on the roof. The house sits on a raised platform of packed mud, the same surface as its floors. The people who live here don't look like they can afford Luingamla's kashan. It costs nearly seven thousand rupees, a tiny fortune.

Three young girls, the oldest about ten, come out of the doorway. All wear worn full-sleeved T-shirts and faded and torn track pants. They are barefooted. They shriek with laughter as I take photographs.

'Luingamla's nieces,' Seth explains. Meanwhile, their uncle arrives, brought by our guide from his house further up the slope, the one he built after getting married. There's no adult at Luingamla's former home. They are all out farming their terraced patches—some rice, maize, cabbage, some green leafy vegetable, chillies, maybe a little lemon, basic produce in this overwhelmingly agricultural economy of Ukhrul district—or, perhaps, tending to some livestock. Wungnaoshang, Luingamla's second brother and only sibling at hand, wears clothes as worn as those of the children: a checked shirt over torn blue track pants, and tattered canvas shoes. As we shake hands, Seth tells him my purpose. He wordlessly points behind us.

'Luingamla,' he says. We turn to look.

He points at a mound at the edge of the drop. It's about a foot-and-a-half high, three feet wide and about five feet long, of broken stone and mud. Sparse yellow wildflowers grow over it. Near the centre is a red plastic rose, kept in place with two small stones. There's no name, no marker beyond the jumble of stones and plastic rose. A black hen breaks through some shrubbery and skitters across the grave to take offence at a pup that has strolled across to us. I walk around the mound, stand by it. Now that I am here, I feel an unaccountable, perhaps even irrational, grief. It's a sad place, made sadder when compared to the relative pomp for the Naga Army's martyrs at the other end of the village.

Suddenly, for a few seconds, anger takes me. The Naga Army, I tell myself, is building grand memorials to their soldiers and their cause while *this* girl, who fought off a bullying officer—doesn't matter if he was of the Indian Army, *especially* as he was of the Indian Army, the shame of it—with bare hands and was killed for it, now lies in an unattended grave next to the hovel of the family. She is a hero in *anyone's* war, as much a victim of politics as a combination of random lust and bloodlust. *Why...?*

I realize Seth is gently shaking my arm. '*Look* at her,' I snap at him. 'And those chaps are building fancy memorials.'

Then, as suddenly, my anger evaporates. I am back at the heartbreaking hillside patch of poverty and memory.

We move a little away from the grave.

For three to four months after Luingamla's death, Wungnaoshang recalls, army personnel used to visit to see the house, the grave, and leave. Then the visits stopped. There was no apology from anyone, he says, 'the army or the government'. And, before I can ask, he says not a rupee was offered by way of compensation.

'Are you and your family still angry with the army and the government?' I ask.

'We were very angry and hurt, but over time our anger has lessened.' Wungnaoshang sits on his haunches, and we join him. With a twig he begins to scratch lines in the earth. 'The family has decided to forgive the killer. Let God be his judge,' he says softly, 'if man cannot be.'

The children gather around us. A toddler, also a girl, waddles towards us with the pup. She sits down on the ground, and the pup dutifully sits by her.

There's a moment of idyll in this setting, even among this grinding poverty and the memories that I repeatedly dredge up, so that I can take such tales outside—so that more may know of them, and some might try to understand a little of the history and politics before summary, often-ignorant and virulent, judgement is passed about the northeast by those of the Mainland.

When Luingamla was shot dead, at the other end of the country

I was a year into my career as a journalist, with *The Asian Wall Street Journal*. I learned to interview stockbrokers, bankers and bureaucrats in then-Bombay and New Delhi, quizzing them about the present and future of India, of the magic word 'potential' that seemed to colour nearly every nuance about India those days. It was three years before Jammu & Kashmir exploded into a heightened area of geopolitical manipulation by Pakistan and its allies; as mistrust, anger and hate began to build in a manner that is evident to this day. And, already, Luingamla's home and several places in this region had for more than four decades witnessed numbing churn.

In these parts, India, the country I love and despair of in equal measure, has for long been seen as absolute monarch and inveterate monster.

The AR Gypsy passes us as we prepare to leave at Seth's suggestion to avoid a downpour that seems to be only minutes away. Both of us would like to spend the night at Ngainga but at the same time, we are conscious of the imposition that might bring to modest homes.

There are four troopers in the Gypsy, and, this deep in the village, they have the sense to mute their preferred music. Their eyes are watchful, but the faces are of the desperately tired. The faces of the troopers by the truck too are mirror images of tiredness, I see as we again pass them. The eyes smile momentarily as I shake hands with the Sikh and Kuki soldiers and half a dozen others now returned from a foot patrol.

These are jaded troops in a jaded conflict zone, buffeted like their enemy counterparts and the civilian population between ceasefire and not, hair-trigger and not, as games of war and peace are played by other people. Those, the puppet-masters, know well the economics of war and the politics of peace.

Nothing else seems to matter.

8

'People listen to those with guns. It's not nice, but that's how it is'

I am on the Net, checking mail at Big Byte Infosys on the second floor of Embicy Hotel when the brigadier's call comes through on my mobile phone.

Anil Chauhan is the commanding officer of the Indian Army's 59 Mountain Brigade, crack troops currently headquartered in Senapati town. He is a man with a perspective and a mandated plan to watch over Senapati and Tamenglong districts of Manipur, which is pretty much the single biggest chunk of landmass in the state. This is deep inside a zone where he has to track NSCN-IM, several Valley-based Meitei rebel groups, Kuki factions, any activity of interest across the border in Myanmar and, by extension, be ready for any move, covert or overt, by China.

It's a bit tricky to take his call in the dingy but serviceable cyber café—I don't know if the friendly staff will turn surly were they to overhear my part of the conversation. So I move two flights down, to stand by a plaque that dedicates the floor 'For the Glory of God'.

'What are you doing hanging around Imphal?' the brigadier asks.

'If I tell you, you'll have to shoot me,' I joke. But I know he will wait till I hand over the package of Goan chouriço—fiery spiced sausage—I'm carrying for him; during an earlier telephone conversation he had let slip his fondness for it. Chouriço, various kinds of seafood pickle and marinade, and heavy, oversweet bebinca form my typical goodie-bag when visiting friends and acquaintances.

Why don't I come up to Senapati later in the day? Brigadier Chauhan suggests. He is having some people over in the evening, and it might be interesting for me to chat with them, get some opinions, check out the local colour. I can stay over at Brigade HQ, he offers. Sounds good, I tell him, I'll take an early-afternoon bus. It's only a couple of hours north; a half-hour more at the most, accounting for this wretched bit of Highway 39 that is often churned tar, stone and craters that resemble the sort explosive devices are primed to make. Driving and riding are both advanced art forms on this highway, and after several journeys I'm something of an adept.

I'm cheered by the prospect of travel. A chat with the brigadier will provide an insight into the complicated business of managing ceasefire in an area that technically doesn't have a ceasefire, and yet—it must! Senapati and Tamenglong, his 'patch', is also a complicated stew of ethnic mix, with one tense community sometimes just a rivulet-width away from another tense community. The stretch of Highway 39 between Imphal and Manipur's border with Nagaland at Mao Gate too is his territory of oversight. Whenever Naga groups want to make a point to folks in the Imphal valley, they can simply choke this vital supply lifeline. It has happened in the past. I have no doubt it will happen in the future: it's too plum an opportunity for grandstanding a cause—any cause.

I go back up to Big Byte Infosys to finish up, and then emerge onto the road. The Tangkhul Baptist Church is in front of me. By its side is the Kuki Baptist Church. They are joined in holy communion even as, in Manipur, Nagas and Kukis live in uneasy neighbourliness after years of bloody tribal pogroms in the latter part of the twentieth century that erased several villages and several hundred lives.

The walk back to my hotel, the Tam-pha, takes me past Hotel Imphal and just after, I see a sign for Manipur's tourism office. On a whim, ignoring a deepening drizzle as well as the impending journey to Senapati, I take the left turn to walk down a tamped earth track. I'm curious. In the course of several 'arrivals' at Imphal airport over the previous three years, I haven't once seen the Manipur Tourism kiosk in the arrival area open. It has stayed resolutely shut; designated staff perhaps afraid they would be held accountable for some fantastic notions described in brochures that, mysteriously enough, continue to be available and updated with newer photographs and better printing.

Your brochures told us, departing travellers may accost these hapless promoters of tourism, that NH 53 'links Imphal' with the 'railhead at Jiribam 225 km in the southwest'. But why didn't you tell us we would also require the service of a chiropractor; that the journey takes one day in good times, three days if it rains, and cannot be completed if it rains hard? Your brochure shows photographs of the Meitei, Meitei-Pangal, Naga and Kuki-Chin-Mizo people dressed in ethnic wear, standing side by side like happy mannequins, welcoming us with folded hands—you *will* admit it's a gesture a Naga or Kuki-Chin-Mizo wouldn't be caught dead doing unless the person was in the presence of sycophancy-hungry politicians from faraway Delhi; or Delhi's representative in Imphal, usually a former high-ranking 'spook-' or general-turned governor. Anyway, visitors might say, we haven't seen people dressed this way, all harmoniously together in public—and damn those Republic Day-chic dresses—we haven't seen these ethnic groups living and interacting harmoniously *anywhere* in this state.

Loktak—ah, Loktak—a traveller might sigh. 'The largest freshwater lake in the north-east region', a place of 'shimmering blue water', 'labyrinthine boat routes and colourful water plants'; and the bird's-eye view of islands of 'floating weed' on which people actually live. But you didn't tell us about the army camps; and the army people who try their best to not let us in, and will never let us stay.

I've had similar moments of epiphany looking at brochures of Chhattisgarh and Jharkhand, beautiful places beset by trappings of conflict, and the necessary lies such a situation would trigger to complete the suspension of disbelief.

As I walk in through the gates of Manipur Tourism, four police commandos, variously armed with AK 47s and ancient Sten guns, converge on me. Evidently it's a big day at office; a senior official is visiting, I can see his white Ambassador car parked at the entrance to the plain building. The guards won't let me get anywhere near it. They don't even bother asking me for ID. With impatient gestures one asks me to go away. With the neutral smile of a traveller I stand my ground.

The first time I walked into something as patently absurd as this was several decades back, when the tourism minister of India used to be a gentleman called H.K.L. Bhagat, long known to be a toady of Indira Gandhi, and accused of participating in anti-Sikh butchery that spread through Delhi after her assassination in 1984. I had attended a press conference called to tell foreign correspondents— I worked at the time with an American financial paper—that all was well in India. Bhagat had arrived wearing trademark dark glasses, accompanied by half-a-dozen elite anti-terrorism commandos in trademark black combat uniform and bristling with Heckler & Koch submachine guns, and smartly announced that India was safe for tourists. He had the good grace to not flinch when all of us had burst out laughing.

The last time was in December 2003, when the then chief minister of Jammu & Kashmir, Mufti Mohammad Sayeed, had explained to a group of visiting writers and travel industry professionals the phenomenon of army and paramilitary visible in their hundreds along the route from Srinagar airport to the resort town of Gulmarg, where we had arrived. Every small bridge on the way had sandbagged gun emplacements on either side. 'Don't mind them,' he said. 'Kashmir is peaceful.'

We knew an army operation was under way against insurgents at a nearby village, but we had been polite. Who were we to intervene in someone else's wilful delusion when all around was fresh snow, white and pure?

The guards are edgy as I refuse to budge, continue to smile, and raise an arm to point at the knot of people that now emerges onto the porch. Thankfully, a lady breaks away from the group to come towards us and asks me my business. I'm looking for travel information, I tell her. Brochures, perhaps a map.

'Oh!' She looks stunned. Then graciousness takes over and she invites me to accompany her inside. I nod at the group of people at the entrance. A smartly dressed gentleman looks quizzically at me—the lady explains to me as we pass that he is the tourism commissioner.

I'm brought to a nondescript room typical of government offices and made to sit in front of a lady. Her table is piled high with ancient files. Someone is deputed to bring brochures. These lie at another table; several hundred brochures, flat unfolded sheets, brand new from the printers. The lady I am seated across takes a sheet and with great precision folds it along the edges, transforming it into the folded accordion of a brochure. She hands it to me with a brilliant smile.

I can't help but smile back. These people seem to want to help. They would love to receive travellers to show off a land that is second to none in beauty, possibility of leisure and adventure, and the variety of its people and cultures. The kiosk at the airport is surely shut on account of honesty and embarrassment.

If only…
Two words. It usually comes to this.

I grab a quick lunch at Nikheel Café near North AOC bus stand. The plateful of large 'Diploma' Momo, larger than the usual steamed Tibetan-style dumplings used by students at a nearby school to celebrate success, comes with a bowl of glutinous soup. After wolfing it all down, and feeling it settle in my stomach like concrete pre-mix, I walk the short stretch to the Khoyathong area in search of a bus to Senapati. The ladies selling petrol in plastic filtered-water bottles outside the Indian Oil station are still about, I notice, patient under their mushrooms of both colourful and black umbrellas. The fuel station has stayed shut for several days: no supply. So the ladies dispense fuel, mysteriously procured from supplies that do arrive, I am told by the public and officials alike, for police and paramilitary, another link of subsistence in this economy of conflict.

On the rattletrap bus of Elvis Travels we head north past North AOC on Highway 39. On the outskirts of Imphal at Mantripukhri we come by the spanking new headquarters of IGAR (South)—Inspector General of Assam Rifles (South). The northern head lies in Kohima. It's a mid-sized bus crammed with passengers drawn from the Meitei, Maram Nagas, Kuki, and Nepali—rooted in these areas since the time of World War II and earlier, their ancestors a part of Gorkha brigades of the British colonial army and for many years the mainstay of Assam Rifles.

I drift into reverie as we pass the vast rectangle designated as Koirengei airfield to our right, a cluster of AR camps alongside open space that is gradually hemmed in by the Langol Hills to our left and Heinang Hills to the right. After Koirengei Bazar, across the road from two stone crushing plants, a police commando jeep stands guard over several trucks. I see the colour of money changing hands as we pass (but it could be the play of autumn light on my near-libellous sight). We are still in a narrow patch of plains, but that will disappear in a half-hour after we pass tiny Pheidinga Bazar, fourteen kilometres from Imphal, and then the market town of Sekmai.

Images from past journeys join me in reverie. A little more than a year earlier in May 2008, Rewben, a photographer friend Vidura Jang Bahadur, and I had stopped at Sekmai for a taste of the eponymous local brew, a clear distillate of fermented rice served with slices of sweet cucumber. Sekmai and the fiercely independent-minded village of Andro to the east of Imphal are resolute, alcohol-brewing holdouts in a state that had for more than a decade now mandated prohibition. Rewben enjoys his sekmai and had insisted we try it as well.

The firewater had rocked Vidura and I back on our heels in the tiny mud and thatch hut that served as brewery and bar, but it had somehow made the highway easier to take. We had taken along with us several plastic bags of the stuff and its sweeter cousin, atingba, to accompany the superb smoked fish wrapped in leaf that I had earlier purchased at Ima Keithel—The Market of Mothers—in Imphal.

We would soon reach the foothills checkpoint-town of Kangpokpi—KPI in soldier speak. Here, on a previous journey also in 2008, I had seen a bus driver being harangued and cursed by an Assam Rifles havaldar for taking a few seconds too long to stop after being flagged down for security check.

'Tujhe sunai nahin deta, behnchod?' the gentleman had asked of the Meitei driver. Can't you hear, sisterfucker?

The bus driver had sat rigidly.

'Bol saley, tu Hindustani hai ki nahin?' Nice, I had thought, fuming. It's a nice way to query a person about his nationality: Tell me, you shit, are you an Indian or not?

And, as I had prepared to get up from my seat, angry and embarrassed at this display and fully intending to yell at the trooper to behave, my neighbour Avia, an Israeli musician on a tour of the northeast as part of the Roots music festival, had put a restraining hand on my arm.

'Relax,' he told me, his young-old eyes urging restraint. 'These things happen. 'When I was in the army I had a gun and most others at the end of the barrel did not. People listen to those with guns. It's not nice, but that is how it is.'

I had launched into an explanation as to how this sort of threatening behaviour further alienates people.

'Yes, I know, my friend. But it's good to not make people with guns angry.'

Avia had told me some other things—he and his friends and fellow musicians from the electronic-reggae band Dub LFO: Dudu, Roy, Gai and Adi. Manipur was greener than back home in Israel, the West Bank and the Gaza strip. But it had the same feel, they said, of a place of disagreement and conflict.

The persistent drizzle breaks into heavy rain and then winds back down to drizzle as we near Kangpokpi. There's no army 'non-com' on this trip to intimidate our driver but the huge catfish he has in a plastic bag wedged between the dashboard and windscreen decides it has had enough of captivity.

The brown-black creature had been desultorily flapping a fin now and again during our journey past Sekmai, the Nepali village of Charhajare, Motbung, and Kalapahar—ready with banners for 'Shri Shri Durga Puja'—with the attendant stopping the bus with a sharp whistle; and to get it moving, a falsetto 'ui!' or 'oi'!

As we pass a wall near a curve up to Kangpokpi with a sign that politely suggests, 'Please join BJP', and another, more insistent one, 'Behold, for now is the day of salvation', the catfish heaves massively and slides off its perch. The bus stops with a screeching of brakes. The driver dives for the fish as it slithers across the floor, causing passengers seated in the cab area to yell, laugh and lift their feet in unison. It slithers into a recess, by the battery covered with a plank behind the driver's seat. We move on.

The rain-washed hills are green, lush, soothing. A snake of a river stays with us; downstream it would curve towards Imphal, now behind us, to soon become the Imphal River. We lurch around bends, moving closer to the river's source deep inside the Naga Hills—Manipur's Naga Hills. We cross a seemingly endless Border Security Force convoy near Tumoyu Khullen, heading south to Imphal; and, soon after, a convoy of more than a dozen trucks carrying LPG to Imphal, the city of perpetual shortages. Once we pass Taphou (a sign proclaims it as 'Taphou Kuki Village') and the surprisingly named Mt Everest College, the district headquarters town of Senapati is only a little way up the road.

The bus stops at the centre of a busy, mud-and-filth marketplace, buildings in the town deadened black with moss and the wreckage of time that rainwater has a merciless tendency to highlight. There's a machinegun nest manned by CRPF at the State Bank of India branch. As I walk left at the main market junction, uphill towards where I have been told the army camp is, two uniformed soldiers in a red Maruti van discreetly wave me down. It's my ride to camp.

I can't help thinking about the catfish.

~

59 Mountain Brigade is on a hill overlooking Senapati town. Troops have taken shelter in huts and lean-tos to keep from the pouring rain but as we make our winding way up to 'HQ' we are allowed to pass only after guards in raingear check the faces of the driver of the van and his colleague—a burly Sikh and a southerner—and diligently scan my ID. After five minutes we arrive at a worn two-storey structure sequestrated from an Assam Rifles battalion which in turn took it off the local Public Works Department. The PWD didn't miss it; the building had anyway been marked for demolition. Brigadier Chauhan and his senior colleagues have work

spaces on the ground floor, alongside the officer's mess. Upstairs is a library and reading room, and a couple of functional guest rooms. I am courteously showed to one.

As I look out of the window from the slim covered balcony, I see green-jacketed slopes across the river wreathed in low cloud, pine trees, and the downslope into town. The illusion of calm is quickly dispelled as a jeep and truck bristling with armed soldiers drive past in a growl of low gears.

I wander over to a bookcase along a wall outside the library—which is locked. It has a sprinkling of Agatha Christie, Ken Follet, Shobhaa Dé, Amitav Ghosh, Salman Rushdie and Jhumpa Lahiri, and Barack Obama's autobiographical *Audacity of Hope*. Nearby are books on Moshe Dayan of Israel and Gen. K.S. Thimayya, India's chief of army staff from 1957 to 1961. The war against Naga rebels was in full flow during those years; though not preparations to meet the heightened threat of war with China—this last, as I read elsewhere, despite Gen. Thimayya's caution to the government. There's Edgar O' Balance's work on the Yom Kippur war, *No Victor, No Vanquished*; books on warfare in the twenty-first century; Edward de Bono's works on lateral thinking; books on politics and culture of Manipur; encyclopaedias; and, quite fittingly for this part of India, the *Arthashastra* by Kautilya.

I head downstairs for a chat with Brigadier Chauhan, but I still have some time in hand. He has been out for an engagement and will return in a few minutes, I'm told by his 'G2'—head of intelligence—Major Gaurav. I use the time to stroll around the foyer. It's an exhibition of counterinsurgency and some velvet glove stuff in various villages and hamlets.

Photos of 'Operation Ijai' at Noney Market from May 2006 show photos of a lady and two boys behind a table stacked with gelignite sticks, detonators, loops of wire, and explosive material. 'Granular PUNCH', the label reads, and describes the manufacturer as an 'ISO 9001-2000 company'. There are photos of a 35 Assam

Rifles raid against a PULF (People's United Liberation Front, an Islamist group formed in 1993 by Meitei Pangal rebels) camp at Manou. The commanding officer of the same battalion is shown inaugurating a community farming project in Aziuram, and a community hydroelectric project in Namtiram.

Troops and the commandant of 22 Assam Rifles, Col V.S. Malik, pose in undated photos after its Ghatak—killer—platoon recovered 'WPN' and 'AMN' (weapons and ammunition) during 'Op Durga', though the photo caption doesn't mention from which group. In another image they pose with 511 kg of ganja seized during 'Op Red Poppy'. Personnel of the same battalion are shown at a ginger farming project at Awah Khul, and a community power project at Purul.

The mix of images is a sign of the times, a sign of the place.

The brigadier will see me now, an aide comes to tell me. I walk down the corridor to meet the compact, dapper officer originally from the Gorkhas—so far I have seen badges and emblems of the Sikh, Jat and Dogra regiments among this Mountain Brigade. It's a sparse room with space for a neat desk and a few chairs, a desktop computer, terrain and tactical maps on the wall, a small cabinet. Just as we seat ourselves a call comes through for him.

One of his officers is reporting a phone call received at a local landline number from a place across the 'eastern border'—Myanmar—as I gather from my host's staccato queries and responses.

'Find out now, why is that call being made?' Brigadier Chauhan speaks into the handset. 'I want to know the nature of the call. We can then decide to bring the chap in or track a wider net.'

He hangs up and turns to me with a smile. 'So, you finally made it. Tea?'

We get talking about keeping the peace and managing the tricky business of ceasefire with various groups—even the strange ceasefire agreement with NSCN-IM, quite an influence in his patch of the woods. It isn't the first time I've heard the brigadier's point of proven conventional wisdom that, should there be no force, no deterrence, entire areas will be ceded to whosoever wishes to claim these. That's why the Indian Army is present in force, he explains.

'The state police would not be capable of tackling IM,' he continues. 'In any case we all know that Manipur government is not a party to the ceasefire agreement. So legally they are free to operate against them—and so is IM. But IM doesn't operate against state police forces because they don't want to come into the limelight; but technically they can. [But] they should have the will, the equipment.'

'Isn't it tricky for people like you who operate in an environment of ceasefire but not in a zone of ceasefire?' I ask. 'It's a really thin line, isn't it?'

The responsibility for counterinsurgency operations, or 'CI', lies with the army along with Assam Rifles, he explains. 'What technique you will apply, what force—that is your business. And how you interpret a situation is your business.'

Maintaining law and order, Brigadier Chauhan says, is the job of the civil administration. 'But as you said, it's a thin line. Once you put on a uniform, whether you put on a khaki, OG [olive green], or Assam Rifles badge, you know what law and order is and you know what CI is. When you pick up a gun and go after a group to kill them it's CI Ops. When you're controlling a crowd or providing protection to a procession so that people don't throw stones at it, that's law and order.'

'Sure.' I absorb the lesson from a practitioner. 'But by "thin line" I meant parameters of the ceasefire. When IM or the Khaplang faction is present in Manipur state, technically the ceasefire doesn't apply. Correct?'

'Correct.'

Again, however, this can be left to interpretation, the brigadier explains. 'As far as IM is concerned they are very particular that they should not violate the ceasefire. They go to great lengths actually to see that at least here'—he means: in Manipur—'the situation is not disturbed.'

'But that's a good thing, isn't it?'

'That's a good thing. But they are doing it in a way that follows the letter of the agreement but not the spirit.'

It seems like a contradiction—and it is, the result of twisted terms of agreement of the ceasefire with IM. To be fair to the brigadier though, he isn't going about trying to annihilate Naga groups either. His job, as he tells me time and again, is to remind them that India's army is around in force, should that force be required.

9

A.O.I., Alphabet Soups, and other delights of a ceasefire without ceasefire

From what I can gather, Brigadier Chauhan has enough of a stew to deal with even without factoring in rebel outfits.

First are the ethnic clusters woven along Highway 39, all the way from Imphal north to Senapati. It may seem innocuous to an outsider, but a Manipur resident knows from childhood the significance—both positive and negative—of a multi-ethnic mix. On army maps, the mainly Meitei communities give way to mixed ones as the highway leaves the plains around Imphal to approach the hills. Kuki villages are marked with tiny pink flags, Nepali-majority villages with yellow, and Naga redoubts with green. Tracking the highway south-to-north: Kanglatunbi is Nepali, Thingsat is Naga, Motbung is of the Kuki, with four more Kuki clusters of Phaijang, Songlung, Kholep and Saitu.

Closer to Kangpokpi is Haijang, a Kuki village that has to its north the Naga village of Daili, and to the north of that, the Nepali village of Turibari.

To the left of Senapati is a big cluster with three colours nearly at arms length: Shongyangjang and Maokot are marked in Kuki pink; Dhoragari and Simili are marked yellow for Nepali, and the lone Naga holdout is Akutpa.

To the north and east of Senapati, the markers are all Naga green. Deeply forested Tamenglong district is almost entirely green with Naga concentrations.

A liberal sprinkling of rebels groups makes this stew more robust—and more roiled.

In terms of 'area of influence' or AOI, in the area that 59 Mountain Brigade work with their colleagues in Assam Rifles, NSCN-IM is marked as having influence over all Senapati and Tamenglong. GPRN/NSCN, or the Khaplang faction, arch-enemy and recent signatory to the reconciliation process among Naga groups, is shown as having influence along patches of NH 53, the road that links Imphal with the state's western boundaries. Much of this road lies in Tamenglong district, and this group marks the Vangai, Kaimai and Kaupru ridges as its areas of influence.

Among the Kuki groups, Kuki Revolutionary Army has as its AOI the southern reaches of Senapati district in the areas of Saikul, IT Road and Kangpokpi-Haijang. Their colleagues of the Kuki National Front (P) also operate in the Kangpokpi area and in Motbung to the south.

Then come three main valley-based insurgent groups or VBIG in army speak, which cling to hill refuges closer to Imphal Valley. The People's Liberation Army operates south of Sekmai and east of Tingkai. The United National Liberation Front, the oldest among the valley-based groups, works south of Sekmai, and along the Kaupru Ridge—an overlap with the Naga GPRN/NSCN. The Kanglei Yawol Kanna Lup, another Meitei group, works a place called Zouyantek and the Koupham Valley.

Alphabet soup.

If this were not enough, there are a whole slew of smaller ethnic outfits that work wherever they can take root, or visit for sanctuary. In no particular order they are, in an eye-glazing, mind-numbing stream: Zomi Revolutionary Army; United Socialist Revolutionary Army; Zomi Defence Volunteers; Zomi Revolutionary Force; Hmar

People's Convention (Democratic); the Islamic National Front; across from the North Cachar area of Assam bordering the brigadier's 'territory' is the Dima Halam Daogah; and also the Dima Halam Daoga (J) or Jewel faction, named after its leader.

And, into this astounding, confounding jigsaw is added the various groups' multiple equations with form, substance and reach.

For instance, take NSCN-IM. In Tamenglong and Senapati districts, in a little less than half of the total number of villages where IM operates, Naga people may need 'reassurance'—or it could be that they are threatened by Kukis or another ethnic group. So, IM, I've been told by insiders, maintain a presence in such a manner that they do not violate the ceasefire agreement. Cadres could be on leave, without weapons, in civilian dress—that is permitted under ceasefire agreement. Effectively, these villages will have one or two cadres in mufti.

They are the eyes and ears of IM. They have weapons too, I have heard from security experts. In their parlance, such a cadre is 'divorced from his weapon', and so, it conforms to a technical aspect of ceasefire. And, anyway, the army is not omnipresent. In these areas it operates what is called a COB, or company operating base of between sixty and hundred troopers to carry out regular patrols and 'domination'. But the army does not stay in villages. IM does.

The army is aware that, should the need arise, IM cadres can quickly get to their cached weapons; as quickly, two cadres in a village or hamlet can add up to ten or fourteen by triggering a network of a predetermined group of actors. This cellular approach is designed not only to operate against security forces but also against cadres of GPRN/NSCN, NNC, or any valley-based groups, or perhaps a Kuki group allied with GPRN/NSCN.

In relatively inaccessible districts of Manipur like Tamenglong, it could be anyone's game, I'm told, and army and paramilitary may not be the wiser. The vegetation is lush to the point of being impenetrable in some areas; and even tracks are fewer. Besides, government forces could be seventy-two to ninety-six hours—three to four days' walk—from a particular place or objective. Meanwhile, large groups or rebels can hide or disappear almost at will. And this is in the dry season. Monsoons further impede surveillance and operations.

Both IM and GPRN/NSCN send patrols out. But they aren't patrols in the conventional sense as there is a ceasefire on with both groups—even if such a ceasefire doesn't technically extend to Naga areas of Manipur and Arunachal Pradesh. They show up to display dominance in Naga-majority areas as well some areas where other communities need to be reminded that Nagas have 'reassurance'.

And, in these parts, alliances are as confounding as they are expedient. From my conversations with locally based army, paramilitary and intelligence officials the relationship between IM and valley-based groups appears to be purely of convenience. Army sources, for instance, point to an incident at the beginning of September, a couple of weeks before my visit to Senapati to see the brigadier. The army caught two Kangleipak Communist Party-MC cadres after a routine search of a van. The army claims to have found 'incriminating documents', including receipts for collections from other KCP-MC cadres. After interrogation it was discovered that the two had for the previous week been staying in Senapati at the house of a person whose brother is an officer in Hebron, IM's main camp near Dimapur. (Were such an incident, and the circumstantial evidence of IM 'outsourcing' revenue collection through another rebel group, brought to IM's attention, the group could easily explain away the suspected cadre as, say, being 'off the party line', gone rogue. He could also be shown to have been fired, or as being under suspension. Any reasoning, I hear from the Indian establishment, to finesse the accusation of IM spreading its wings or violating ceasefire protocols.)

I've heard numerous accusations of IM taking money to provide sanctuary, though anyone I speak to in the course of researching this book, both from the region and not, remain unwilling to go on the record with such assertions. Typically, these come with a request to remain anonymous; and also with a plea: we do this for the sake of ceasefire. But, anonymously, they would have no problem mentioning, say, that two 'valley-based' militants were caught in the hills, but there could be twenty still about under the benign protection of IM. Whenever pressure builds up on some groups in the Valley they find sanctuaries in the hills, I've been told. They could be harboured in rebel camps—ceasefire camps, but nevertheless a camp of rebels—but the army or AR may not know as they wouldn't technically be operating in and around such camps.

Kuki rebel groups have their own camps so they don't yet need that sort of 'protection'; instead, they would be in a position to offer such protection should there be a need for it. Using an approach similar to Naga groups, I have been told major Kuki groups offer sanctuary to allies of convenience in their ceasefire camps. (Several Kuki groups entered into a ceasefire an arrangement in 2005 with the Directorate General of Military Intelligence which was formalized in August 2008 as an agreement with Government of Manipur.)

The other conventional-wisdom conspiracy theory I have heard, and this is from rebel cadres and sympathizers, is that Kuki rebel groups—some as narrow as representing clans and sub-clans—were really constructs of India's intelligence agencies to use as leverage against IM. It served India's interests further that some Kuki groups allied with GPRN/NSCN—this provided added counter-balance to IM's influence in some areas. Equally, there's a conspiracy theory that IM splintered Kuki groups and brought some of these factions on their side, against GPRN/NSCN. It's a shifting, sliding, shape-changing equation that has overridden even the animosity between the Naga and Kuki peoples.

At any rate, the presence of valley-based groups in the hills for sanctuary, training or supply of equipment, is transitory and entirely need-based, as I am given to understand. It's a transaction. Groups may be at loggerheads ideologically but on the ground, monetary and tactical benefits can outweigh ideology. Something on the lines of: 'You want cadres trained? Fine, pay up. Need a dozen weapons for some operations over the next two months? No problem, pay and take. If you want to return them later in good condition once you've got your own supply through purchase or robbery we'll simply keep some amount of the deposit as rental.'

This may not happen at the organizational level, I am told, but at the local level. A local commander of one of the larger rebel groups could take such a call if so empowered by the parent organization, or simply decide to take the initiative and play satrap on the turf he controls. In a fractious environment, this local commander has a ready market. Some Manipur-based groups are as small as 'thirty people with ten weapons' between them, intelligence officials have told me.

(Elsewhere in India such a group would be treated as a gang, but on account of the boiling ethnic cauldron of Manipur such groups are now 'recognized'—acknowledged as entities by government agencies and forces. Besides, it pays to be circumspect. North-eastern India has a history of small groups growing into highly effective rebel outfits. This is true of the Naga areas and Mizoram, in Assam with ULFA and Bodo groups, and here in Manipur, the UNLF and PLA grew from tiny, determined bands.)

At any rate, should some groups need to generate revenue along with influence, there's evidently no harm in lateral thinking, selling sanctuary or weapons or both.

~

Sometimes, the strange nature of ceasefire can lead to skirmishing and tense fallout, as it did in the Ukhrul area on 12 August 2009.

That day a company of 23 Assam Rifles had a firefight with a group of NSCN-IM cadres between Shakok and Hundung Godah villages in the Phungyar subdivision of Ukhrul district.

According to a report of the Naga Peoples Movement for Human Rights, an organization quite open in its support for NSCN-IM, 'two NSCN cadres were killed, one of them in cold blood, and the other in circumstances that are highly questionable and suspicious'—this a standard allusion to torture. It also maintained that 'villages in and around the site were subjected to military operations, bombings, and arbitrary firings for the next few days'.

On the face of it, NPMHR's assertions are entirely believable given the history of brutality and butchery that has characterized Assam Rifles' efforts in curbing rebel movements in north-eastern India. Nineteenth-century sociologist and traveller Verrier Elwin coined for the force its motto: Friends of the Hill People. Banners and graffiti throughout the region have for years described Assam Rifles as either 'Enemies of the Hill People' or 'Killers of the Hill People'.

Similar sentiments would again be unfurled across Ukhrul that day and in the following days. On 13 August the bodies of Sgt Major Salmon Hungyo and Sgt A.S. Phanitphang lay outside the District Hospital, Ukhrul. Hungyo, dressed in combat tunic and pants, had a bullet wound in the stomach and a gaping head wound. Phanitphang, in a checked shirt and jeans, displayed two bullet holes in the torso and a bandaged, bleeding left arm. With the shirt removed, his body showed a frenzy of bullet holes and marks of being hacked. 'After being arrested and tortured at the site of the incident,' NPMHR claimed.

Word went around. Photos and videos spread by viral mobile telephony. By that evening, Ukhrul was awash in the light of torches carried by several hundred chanting, crying women. They led the men.

On the following day, 14 August, which NSCN-IM and other Naga rebel groups mark as the Nagas' independence day, all major socio-political organizations of the Tangkhul tribe, from the apex Tangkhul Naga Long to its women's and student bodies and the council of village chiefs, gathered to read out a memorandum they had written for Prime Minister Manmohan Singh, with copies to, among others, Home Minister P. Chidambaram, Home Secretary G.K. Pillai, and the joint secretary, northeast affairs, in the home ministry. The memorandum would later be submitted to the deputy commissioner of Ukhrul.

'We would like to understand if there is a ceasefire with the Government of India and NSCN-IM outside Nagaland or not,' speaker after speaker would legitimately urge, quoting from the memorandum, asking of this prime minister and his colleagues to erase India's past mistakes.

And then, the gathering further swirled the political waters with a dash of a human rights talk. 'This incident goes against all the norms and principles on which the Indian Republic is founded; and international norms and conventions.' And, how it is a threat to 'hard earned peace and stability', a manifestation 'of an unhealthy trend towards violence and confrontation', and exemplar of the 'callous attitude of Assam Rifles, the so-called Friends of the Hill People'.

The memorandum itemized the angst and urged action:

'A: Clarify once and for all whether there is a ceasefire outside Naga areas in Nagaland,' the memorandum demanded.

'B: Immediately stop the present military campaign.

'C: Immediately withdraw AR, Friends of the Hill People, from Ukhrul district.

'D: Guarantee the safety and well-being of the population of the area.'

All the while, the banners waved: Assam Rifles. Killer of the Hill People.

Stephen Ankang, president of Tangkhul Naga Long, moderated things a bit, but not by much. 'We respect the leadership of India, we respect the leadership of NSCN-IM,' he said when it was his turn to speak. He hoped that 'an acceptable solution will be found in the ongoing peace talks'. He was pleased so many people had turned out to show solidarity. 'Our unity is our strength.'

Then the rally of hundreds, banners held aloft, wound through upper Ukhrul and past the camp of 17 Assam Rifles—with its robust display of its emblem of crossed khukuri and sunburst in a fan above it—to the deputy commissioner's office.

Later, a memorial service was held for the two NSCN-IM cadres in a classroom adorned with posters explaining alphabets and water-harvesting techniques, as family fanned newspapers to keep flies off their dead. As the coffins were nailed shut, the gathering wept.

The drama and spontaneous public outrage fine-tuned by structured political response, did not escape Assam Rifles and their colleagues in the army and police. As I caught up with security officials over the next few days and weeks I heard versions of the operational aspect of the skirmish, including the talk that a major of the Naga Army was killed, but I have not been able to confirm it. Perhaps this 'information' was born of confusion; as NSCN-IM would have really gone to town had one of its officers been killed.

NSCN-IM cadres often move in a show of strength, security officials told me. Moreover, they said, the incident took place close to 14 August, a day of assertion for Naga armies. Around that time they would certainly be carrying out patrolling in force, perhaps to gather people for flag hoisting and other ceremonies. Such patrols are a clear violation of the ceasefire agreement, I was told—and in the same breath: 'although it doesn't technically extend to Manipur'. In a situation of this nature when government and rebel troops suddenly meet head-on, a firefight can ensue.

A mantra is drilled into the mind of soldiers in these parts:

security of self and that of colleagues is paramount. The nuance of ceasefire is secondary. As one armed patrol suddenly encounters another in this tense place the natural instinct is to open fire—for effect, and without warning—without gauging the nuances of whether the rebel patrol belongs to a group that is in some form of ceasefire agreement with the government. If an Assam Rifles or Indian Army patrol comes across a group of armed people, it may open fire, I'm told, if only because it has no way of knowing whether the other group will fire or not.

According to the ceasefire agreement (even the one that doesn't exist in Manipur!), NSCN-IM is supposed to alert Assam Rifles or the army if there's a patrol about, say, in area X, precisely to avoid chances of a clash. Indian forces may say: you can't be in area X as our troops are also operating there. At least that's how it's supposed to work; including in Manipur.

The assertion of the Indian side is that NSCN-IM cadres were not supposed to be there. The Assam Rifles patrol called upon a couple of more columns to surround Naga cadres. The firefight lasted for three hours—an indication, said those who I spoke to in the government, of how heavily armed the Naga patrol was. Technically—again the accursed term—Assam Rifles would be at fault only if they knew in advance of a NSCN-IM patrol and yet they ambushed them. But that didn't happen.

Again, a ceasefire is not peace, I was told by many security sorts. Clinically speaking, it's nothing more than an understanding 'between two belligerents'. Some army and Assam Rifles commandants may be more or less pleasant about it, but the definition remains inviolate. And, whatever may have been decided thousands of kilometres away where the chain of command peaks in Delhi, the person on the ground may have to make 'instant, go/no-go judgement calls'.

As for this accusation of torture by NPMHR: it is concocted. When an encounter is going on, troops have to try and move around, gain dominating positions. Who would have the time for torture? Of course torture *can* happen, I was told. If a person has information—and the Armed Forces (Special Powers) Act permits the Assam Rifles or the army to keep someone in custody for up to twenty-four hours before handing over to civilian authorities and the police—the person could be tortured to extract information. Technically it's a violation of human rights, but it could be done.

And so, it was not an engineered incident, the security establishment maintained, but a spontaneous one.

Spontaneity cuts both ways in this war of anger, suspicion and propaganda.

On 15 August, several bus- and carloads of people from Ukhrul were on their way to the villages near where the skirmish had taken place when they were stopped at a barrier at Shangshak manned by Assam Rifles. Along with the large bamboo pole across the road, there was also a stretched accordion of spikes.

The people were livid anyway. Word had gone around about the usual state overkill in such situations: clamp down on the area, restrict movement, manhandle locals to get information, intimidate them to minimize any trouble.

Neither side budged at the barrier near an Assam Rifles camp. Inches from the Assam Rifles camouflage netting that barely hid the machinegun nest, in pouring rain, the protestors from Ukhrul sang hymns.

In minutes it had become a public meeting.

'Let us go,' several dozen women chanted in response to prompting from a lady who raised slogans, amplifying them through a handheld mike and megaphone. Protesters held aloft torches: tiny canisters of kerosene tied to branches, and oil-soaked rags tied to bamboo staves.

'Remove the barbed wire and spike.'

'Do not persecute us.'

'Open the gate.'

Then a man screamed, a shout taken up by others: *'This is our land!'*

After several minutes of this, the commandant of the camp, a Sikh officer named S.S. Bhogal came out, talking into his mobile phone.

'Friends of the hill people,' a lady screeched. Then in Hindi: 'Sharam nahin lagta hai?' Aren't you ashamed?

The officer finally took the mike; his guards about him, automatic rifles at the ready, facing down the crowd.

'Baarish,' he pointed to the rain in a placatory manner. 'Hum bhi baarish mein khara hai.' Even I am standing in the rain, he said. I need an interpreter, he continued in Hindi, I cannot speak your language. Seeing the restless crowd he quickly gave up the idea of an interpreter and spoke to them in English.

'Firstly, I am not stopping anybody going to that area. I would like you to go but my request is, please reduce the numbers.'

Shouts of 'no, no' from the women.

'Secondly, DC-sa'ab has already gone there ... Okay, it is your choice if you want to go. I am giving an open commitment in front of everybody, nobody will be harmed. I have a doctor. If anybody is injured please bring them to us. If he needs to be taken to RIMS [Regional Institute of Medical Sciences] Imphal, we'll take him. Please restrict the number.'

More protests.

'None of our jawans are there.' The officer pleaded again, missing the inadvertent irony in his statement. 'We will not harm you, we will assist you, and we do not have any ulterior motives ... no hidden agenda to stop you here. Have a cup of tea and go.'

Screams of protest met this. 'No delaying tactics. We want to go now.'

The commandant gave in. The spikes were removed, the barrier reluctantly raised.

At Phalang village on the way to Godah, they sang hymns again, this time in the wash of battery-powered lights. They made it to the villages of the zone-of-skirmish. Point proved.

Upon their return to Ukhrul on 16 August they attended a special thanksgiving service for the 'safe return of peacekeepers'. That night, a torchlight rally of thousands was in attendance in the grounds opposite the office of the Tangkhul Naga Long.

'Naga people have been offended and insulted time and again,' a speaker's voice rang out, amplified. 'So should we stand up together and ask the Government of India: is there official ceasefire in our land or not?'

'The Government of India should immediately declare that there is ceasefire in Naga areas outside Nagaland.'

Pressure applied.

~

It is evening in Senapati. At 8 p.m., a young lieutenant from Brigadier Chauhan's staff shows up to escort me to the officers' mess for drinks and dinner. The brigadier's family is visiting from Delhi; the local superintendent of police and deputy commissioner are invited. Besides, there aren't many occasions to unwind, so his officers and troops will be pleased at this diversion even though the visiting General Officer Commanding of the Army's 3 Corps, for whom the celebration was intended, could not stay back till evening. In a sea of buttoned-down shirt-sleeves, pressed trousers and highly polished shoes, I stand out in my short kurta, travelling chinos and hiking boots. Normally I wouldn't be allowed into an officers' mess dressed this way, but my presence in this brigade headquarter is anyway an exception, so my attire is merely a matter of additional detail.

Plates of seekh kabab are passed around; and decorations of canned cheese and canned cherries for their short life together on a toothpick; and strips of carrots and cucumber with a yoghurt-based dip. Dinner—but not before measures of whiskey—is soup, three kinds of bread brought by the brigadier's wife from Delhi, baked beans, vegetables in white sauce, and custard. We eat well, watched over by a portrait of Paona Brajabasi, a Manipuri hero in battles against the invading British.

I chat with the younger officers, sharing some experiences from my trips along Highway 39: entertaining as a small measure of PR and large measure of conviviality. But the wit of the evening clearly is Nishit Ujjwal, Senapati's superintendent of police. He reminds the brigadier of his statement during a meeting from some months earlier, when he had asked the police officer to be careful: any surface you touch here, he had said, your hands will come away black as soot.

You're a philosopher, I tell the brigadier. The laughter is easy. The army doctor has brought his guitar from his room—it turned out to be the one next to mine. He and the young lieutenant practise the bars and the opening stanzas of a Bob Dylan classic.

'I say it's a dry state and I am following the law,' I offer, a bit light-headed now, sipping whiskey, thoroughly enjoying myself. 'Do you mind?' That brings more laughter and the SP's attention.

'When you go on patrol at night you have to look straight past,' he says. 'Or I would have to fill a few trucks with people lying on either side of the road, or weaving down the road.'

It's time for song. We walk to the porch and see a local band assembled there, formally dressed, wearing ties with the likeness of crossed daos with a spear placed vertically in between.

The brigadier is first up. He sings a Nepali folk song in a surprisingly robust voice, with little twisting movements of the hips and wrists—an officer of the Gorkhas at home with the culture of his parent regiment. After soaking up genuine applause, he walks up to the where the SP and I are standing.

'All the UGs are extortionists,' the SP tells me in a fierce low tone.

'I can understand they must have parallel sources of revenue because they are, you know, off-line, but they can't all be extortionists in the true sense of the term…'

'No they *are*,' he insists.

'No ideology,' the brigadier adds. 'No feeling for the nation state. There is no concept of the nation state as we might think it.'

Some Naga and Meitei groups may disagree with him; they were born of very strong and definite ideology and purpose. But it didn't seem to be the time or place to remind the gentlemen of it. Besides, the brigadier pre-empts my thought.

'The past is the past,' he murmurs to us. 'We have to live in the present. We have to plan for the future.'

The doctor is up next.

'How many roads must a man walk down, before you can call him a man?' he sings the Bob Dylan classic in a clear, melancholic voice, gently strumming his guitar.

At least we know the answer to this query. We join in for the refrain.

10

The day 'Caman-do' took away a little girl, & other stories

Basanta and Ranjeeta are upbeat. It's just after seven in the morning. The day is sunny and crisp, the damp of monsoons a memory. Even the battered Bolero off-roader of Human Rights Alert has stopped its wrenching sighs; the engine growls without missing a beat. To get out of Imphal is always a pleasure, the relief of breathing clean air, smelling it the way nature intended.

The valley, so narrow to the north towards Senapati, opens up in the south after Singjamei as Imphal's encompassing hills fall away. We pass the landmarks, small towns and smaller towns: Wangoi, Mayang Imphal, Sekmaijin Bazar. There's paddy everywhere, some green and young, some ripening with grain. We pass stray huts and picture-postcard lotus ponds, some tranquil cattle, and villagers engaging with their day. We pass the posts and patrols of Central Reserve Police Force—the 109th battalion—and Assam Rifles: there they are, resting along the paddies; at a roadblock ahead, keeping watch from the sandbagged rooftop of a commandeered telecommunications outpost, eyries of India in a place deliberately made alien.

It reminds us why we are on the road. Basanta and Ranjeeta work with Imphal-based Human Rights Alert. We're all off to see Vidyarani Chanu: they for their work; me, because it made me both angry and curious when I heard about her situation.

Vidyarani is eleven. She was recently arrested.

We press deeper into Bishnupur district, edging towards its borders with Thoubal district and beyond. At Sekmaijin Bazar we turn right to follow the gently twisting python of a sluggish brown river, the sun sometimes to our right, sometimes to our left. It is disorienting, but we do know we are now south of Loktak lake. We push in five, ten, fifteen kilometres, always following the river.

This place is poor. Few houses are of brick. The roofs are weathered aluminium sheeting, but the walls are little more than mud and thatch applied to skeletons of latticed bamboo—some walls are so worn you can see the frame. The signs for NREGS—the grandly named and corrupted National Rural Employment Guarantee Scheme—on walls of houses and shops gradually lessen.

Some walls have signs that urge differently: 'Get Out India. Long Live UNLF.'

Rushes of jobakusum—hibiscus in rich red, peach, white—that adorn the tiny yards or entrances of nearly every home offer bizarre counterpoint, careless beauty in the face of fear and death.

We are lost in this land of slippage. Basanta and Ranjeeta need to ask for directions after Phouakchong Bazar. We are past a small community of Meitei Pangal, and back on Vaishnavite territory. Some locals have killed a pig, and are cooking it by the river in a pit fired with straw and bamboo. It's a pre-wedding feast, Basanta explains. Children walk and skip towards the gathering, some holding large grapefruit, a few balancing on their heads fruit larger than their faces.

Everyone has heard of Vidyarani. We get directions, and these take us past the village of Khordak Ichin and, after more bone-rattling minutes on a road that has for long deteriorated to impossible track, to Nongmaikhong Mayai Leikai, Vidyarani's home village. A resident tells us her house is across the river. After half-an-hour or so of shouting to people across, explaining our purpose, a neighbour arrives with a flimsy boat, just planks nailed together. It can take two at a time, crouched low. Basanta goes across first; I follow.

But she is not at home, we find. The house is shut; the worn wooden door is locked. The walls painted a pistachio green show the mud layer through a peeling of time and weather, the tiny raised porch with a floor of mud has a rickety bench to the left. A tattered reed mat, what I know as *madur* from a childhood in Bengal, lies on the floor. A naked electric bulb, lit, hangs from a ceiling of wood slats and thatch. I step past a bush of red hibiscus to the porch to get a better look at a row of posters placed above head height on three sides of the porch. They are a quite typical mix of religious and Asian School of Sugary-cute. A small blond girl wipes her eyes; the message by her side proclaims: 'Without you my world is lost.' A buxom southern Indian shepherdess with goats in the background forms the next exhibit. A large poster of the goddess Saraswati follows. Then the door, with a 'YOU ARE WELCOME' invitation between two painted earthenware lamps, followed by an ageing poster, again of Saraswati, but this time with her sister Lakshmi and brother Ganesh. Thus embellished, the tiny house stands mute to horrors that have visited it.

Vidyarani's grandfather Salam Ningthemba Singh arrives after ten minutes or so to inform us the girl is at school. It's on the opposite bank, the one we had only just left. People were reluctant to tell us where she was, he apologizes by way of an explanation, until they had vetted our purpose. There's a larger boat half a kilometre from the house, he offers, and we can all return together. We do, crouched low as before, but without the imminent fear of toppling into water, as Salam expertly pulls us along a cable with rings on it. That is how we finally arrive at Immanuel Grace Academy.

Its exterior has the same rundown feel of the neighbourhood, simple dignity hobnobbing with poverty. Like the houses around, the school is straw, thatch, mud, and tin roofing. The mud walls have posters advertising telecom services from Airtel, the movie *Titanic*, the heavy metal band Scorpions, the Orchid Textile Centre in Yangon, Myanmar. The rusted gate is welcoming with a slightly relaxed variation of a saying from the Bible, the Book of John, 6:37: 'The one who comes to me, I will never drive away.' And so, Immanuel Grace Academy in all takes thirty boarders and three hundred students from nearby areas.

We are welcomed by Ningthoujam Ongbi Memcha, who describes herself as the wife of the founder of the school; he isn't around. Her description doesn't sound self-important, merely matter-of-fact. We are shown to a room at the northern end of the courtyard around which are classrooms. The blackboards must have at one time been black, the benches and tables new. A wing houses a decrepit two-storey hostel, with separate dormitory rooms for boys and girls. The room we enter boasts a worn sofa, where we sit. In front is a chipped table of plain wood, on the other side a bed with faded covers. To the right, there's a clutch of oversized, ancient microphones. We're all quiet as Vidyarani is escorted in by a young lady staffer at the school.

Vidyarani's head is lowered. The straight, lustrous black hair typical of her people covers her face. She sits on the bed. She wrings her hands. When she doesn't do that, the hands cover her face. As a comfort, her grandfather strokes her hair. But Vidyarani's hands never stop moving.

As Basanta prepares to question her, for a few seconds I'm overcome with emotion before I regain control. Watching Vidyarani is a wrenching experience. She is the same age as my daughter. She is of the same height. She attends the same class, 6. But my daughter has thus far not been abducted by police and detained illegally because the state is upset with her parents.

The document Basanta pulls from his backpack is a template from South Asia Forum for Human Rights, a Kathmandu-based organization not—unsurprisingly—on the list of favourites of the region's powers that are. 'Understanding Impunity,' goes the long-winded title. 'Failures and Possibilities of Rights to Truth, Justice and Reparation.' Highlighted by the peculiarly detached yet verbose manner in which such documents are described is the chilling and necessary purpose of it: 'A unified database design to capture human rights abuses committed by State and non-state actors and failures of guaranteed rights and the justice system contributing to impunity.'

The sections are straightforward. The first is to explain the principle of 'Informed Consent', all too often missing in India's due process across governance and business alike. The next records 'Respondent Information'. Another queries the details of 'Search and Seizure'. Things begin to warm up, as it were, from here.

Was search and seizure carried out with or without a warrant? Were witnesses present? Which agency in a bewildering array carried it out: the Army? Border Security Force? CRPF? SOG (Special Operations Group)? Assam Rifles? State police? Unified Command/Joint Operation? Or, 'Others (Please Specify)'? The following section pertains to 'Arrest and Detention'. And the next, 'Investigation', has a sequence that queries twenty-six separate kinds of torture, including choking; electric shocks; forced disrobing; forced ingestion of non-edible substances—not excluding faeces; forced to assault and/or sexually abuse members of the family, friends or associates; leg stretching; mock execution; pulling off nails or hair; sexual assault; the relatively moderate slapping, kicking, or punching; stubbing lit cigarette butts on the body; suspension by rope or cord, and the ever flexible category of 'Others (Please Specify)'.

And, of course, there is Section IX, which deals with the chilling holy grail of human rights nightmares: 'Enforced Disappearance and Fake Encounters'.

As Basanta explains what his organization does, what the document is meant for, Vidyarani hunches, draws in her knees, and assumes as foetal a position as possible for a seated person. I can't any longer see the message on her faded pink T-shirt—'Don't believe the type'—or the crucifix around her neck. The toes of her bare feet are tightly curled. The trembling of her crushed cotton capris suggests acute fear.

When were you born? Basanta asks her in Meeteilon.
''ninety-eight.' Her voice is barely above a whisper.
Class?
'Six.'
Basanta fills the rest with the help of her grandfather, turns some pages, a skip-to-next-question-if-these-don't-apply sort of thing. He is practised at it. He tries to coax replies from Vidyarani, but she freezes.

What community are you? He asks after a while.
'Meitei.'
For five minutes or so she replies to pro-forma questions, gently urged by Ranjeeta and the calm presence of her grandfather. But then she stops, spent, replying nothing at all to Basanta's stream of conversation and query in soft tones, an attempt to soothe her nerves as he traverses the geography of human rights fact-finding. Vidyarani looks now and again at him, then at me. She is terrified, and neither her grandfather's hand, which she clutches, nor the stroking of her hair by Memcha help.

Attempting another approach, Basanta decides to reintroduce himself, and tells her what he is doing and why he is here. He tells her that I am writing a book, and I am not a policeman; don't mind the close-cropped head of hair or Indian face. It helps. She resumes talking; her replies, though still halting, come more clearly. She still keeps her eyes lowered.

The 'caman-do' took her away, she says.
What do you study in Class 6? Manipuri?
'Mmm.'
History?

'Mmm.'

Geography?

'Mmm.'

Basanta turns to me after ten minutes or so of taking her through the section titled 'Arrest and Detention'. Her grandfather and Memcha having done most of the talking. Do you have any particular questions? he asks me.

Yes, I say, many. But first will you please tell her that I have a daughter who is as old as her. Grandfather Ningthemba and Memcha nod acknowledgement. When I go back home, I will tell my daughter about this day, about meeting Vidyarani.

And I want to ask her: when she was in custody, what was she doing, what was she thinking. Did she pray to God? Did she pray for her parents? What did she tell herself to keep her strength going?

'I wanted to see my parents,' Vidyarani whispers. Her composure, such as it is, begins to crack.

'Tell, nothing will happen,' Memcha gently urges.

'I was very scared.' Pause. 'I sometimes thought that the police will go to my house when I am not there. I thought if my parents got arrested they would be tortured. I was afraid for my two younger brothers. I was scared the police would arrest them.'

How old are her brothers? I ask, hating myself for taking Vidyarani back to the place she looks unlikely to escape from for years, perhaps never, a dark place where her mind now lives.

'One is in class 4,' she says, 'the other in class 1.'

Do you remember where you were kept? Did it look like a jail, with bars, or was it just a room?

'A room.'

Were you alone?

Basanta now explains: her two grandmothers were with her. They came to ask for her release, but when that didn't work, they asked to remain with Vidyarani.

I resume: Did the police tell her anything when they took her—when was it? Day or night?

In the morning, Basanta now takes over. Vidyarani has stopped speaking.

Did the police...

She was preparing to cook, Basanta says while consulting his notes, when she heard police commandos arriving. She was very scared. One of the commandos pointed his automatic rifle at her and at the grandmother. Since they could not find her parents, suspected of associating with People's Liberation Army, they took Vidyarani.

Vidyarani is crying silent tears. Grandfather Ningthemba gently wipes her eyes with a hand, then gives her a large light-blue handkerchief he has kept in the other hand all the while, as if knowing she would need it sometime during the interaction. The little girl clutches the piece of cloth.

She suddenly gets up and rushes out of the hut. The young lady who brought her in rushes after her. Memcha rattles off in Meeteilon, and Basanta translates, his matter-of-fact tone almost formal. 'She feels like vomiting.'

Memcha talks some more. 'She worries that if she speaks the truth something bad will happen to her parents. They are still in custody. So she is afraid to speak.'

'I understand,' I say; and it's partly a lie. I can understand why Vidyarani is afraid to speak, but I can never understand the degree of her trauma. We remain silent for a while. A young lady brings us small glasses of warm milk.

When did this happen? I ask. What was the date?

14 August 2009. A day before India's independence day. The school was on holiday from the twelfth, so Vidyarani had gone home to her parents. When the staff of the school heard Vidyarani had been arrested, they rushed to her home. Why had she been arrested? they asked. Memcha takes the story from here. She says

that when they saw Vidyarani, she was unconscious. They were told she had fainted. Memcha wanted her taken to hospital. The police declined—'denied that,' Basanta adds. They then insisted 'women police' arrive and, sensing the mood of the people, the raiding party decided to acquiesce. When the police finally tried to take Vidyarani, the people insisted they would first have to issue an 'arrest memo'. Memcha says she told them not to take the 'baby' because they could not find her 'mama' and 'papi'. The police then told her that Vidyarani's parents should surrender. Memcha and others still held on, asking the police if there was any law by which they could arrest a child.

How dare you talk like this? Memcha says she was asked. Who are you?

I'm the wife of the founder of the school where the girl studies, she replied. If you are taking her, she insisted, you should take at least one member of her family, the grandfather or grandmother. She said again that they would all try to arrange for the surrender of the parents, but they should leave the child alone. That didn't work.

How many police were there? I ask.

'It was a combined force of Assam Rifles and Manipur Police commandos. They came in Gypsies.'

Vidyarani was released on the evening of 18 August. She first went home. She reached Immanuel Grace Academy a day later. Before her release the police had already picked up her parents—which was why she was released. They came out of hiding to surrender, driven to panic with what might happen to their child.

What was she like when she arrived at school? I ask Memcha. Would she talk? Would she keep to herself? Avoid other children too?

When she reached home, Grandfather Ningthemba says, now wiping some tears of his own, she got down from the vehicle and fainted.

'I've seen a lot of change in her,' Memcha says. 'When we ask her to do something, even the simplest thing like cutting vegetables, she does not pay attention to that work.'

On 20 August they took her to RIMS in Imphal.

What was she like before her arrest? Was she a smiling, happy child? Was she playful?

'She was so active.' Memcha smiles in recollection. 'She loved to be with her friends. She had a good presence of mind.'

How do you see her now, after all this?

'She doesn't like to talk. She doesn't want to talk. She is afraid of other people.'

What are you trying to do to help her come back to normal?

'We keep telling her to not worry, that her mother and father will be released from custody some time.'

Does she ask often about her parents?

'She keeps asking if she can go to meet her parents.' The mother is in the central jail in Imphal, Basanta offers; just behind the main police station. The father is in Sajiwa jail to the northeast of the Valley, on the route to Ukhrul.

The two younger brothers, one four, the other nine, also have changed since their parents were taken away, Memcha tells us. They preferred in the beginning to stay at home; but now they stay at school as boarders. The school is now both family and sanctuary for the three children. The grandmothers visit as often as they can.

The boys arrive then. First into the room is little Sanamatum, the youngest.

How old are you? Basanta teases him.

'I don't know how old I am,' he smartly replies. Everyone bursts out laughing, and the boy laughs with us.

Which class? Basanta persists, ruffling his hair.

'B.'

Nursery-B? KG-B?

'B.'

Sanamatum rescues us from gloom; we laugh and cry as our hearts simultaneously warm and break. I turn to look for the other brother, Malamnganba.

'He is afraid of us,' Ranjeeta explains. The boy waits outside, reluctant at the calls to enter the room. It's okay, I say, don't force him.

He comes in anyway after a few moments. 'Class 4,' Malamnganba timidly announces by way of introduction. 'I am nine years old.'

Does Vidyarani talk to you both?

'Sometimes she cannot talk,' he says.

Do you try to get her to spend more time with you?

'Mmm,' he says, and stops. He lowers his head. 'I see a lot of change in my sister. She used to play with us. Study with us. Now she always speaks of our parents.'

Then he starts to cry.

Ranjeeta takes the boys out to the yard. As Basanta and I leave after a few minutes, we see them seated on some steps by the entrance. She hugs both the boys, all the while speaking softly to them.

I ruffle the younger brother's head, and for it I get a smile which lights up the day. I accord more dignity to the older boy and shake his hand. His grip is firm.

'Good luck,' I manage.

'Thank you.' He smiles. His eyes look directly, even defiantly, into mine. There's a sign by him, in the charming grammar of Immanuel Grace Academy. It's another saying from the Book of John, this time 10:11: 'The good shepherd give his life for the sheep.'

11

Find a scapegoat, frame him, kill him. Then, kill some more

The day isn't done yet.

South of Loktak lake as we are, we decide to skirt it travelling west, with a plan to complete a circular route for our return to Imphal. After the small market town of Kuimbi Bazar we reach Moirang. It's nearly 1 p.m. We stop for a tasty lunch of rice, lentils with spinach, fish from the lake, and fermented fish pickle at a no-name eatery near the town's main tri-junction. There's the narrow ribbon of road that has brought us from Vidyarani's village. To our right lies Imphal, forty-five kilometres north. To the left Highway 150, also called the Tiddim Road, stretches far southwest to the teardrop-shaped state of Mizoram.

We eat ravenously, released from the stress of the morning's interaction. But there's more to it. In my former life as a career journalist, my colleagues and I learnt early on to take 'time out' after absorbing someone else's tragedy—and all the horrors that regularly visit this region, this country, this subcontinent. In that I am kindred with Basanta and Ranjeeta, being in their own way recorders of stories and their tellers. We file away our own outrage and sadness for another time and place, and meanwhile soak up small joys when we can: for now a simple lunch to break the bone-jarring, mind-jarring journey.

Subhash Chandra Bose's forces visited here, too; Moirang was then a tiny hamlet. The Indian National Army, allied to the Japanese and the Germans, sworn enemies of the colonial British, has a memorial to it in this way station of a town in the centre of Imphal Valley, commemorating the place of that army's first raising of its flag on 'Indian' soil. That was in April 1944. Indira Gandhi as prime minister inaugurated a memorial and museum here twenty-five years later to mark that episode, a precursor to INA's participation in the Battle of Imphal alongside Japanese troops.

(When, in 2004, Manipur burnt more than usual, after Assam Rifles personnel abducted, raped and killed a suspected PLA member called Thangjam Manorama Devi, rebels too left their mark on the place, in partial revenge: they blew up a statue of a springing tiger near the gate. The complex, arguably the easternmost patriotic symbol of India within the geography of the Republic of India, is now guarded against those who feel the description of it being Indian soil is incorrect to begin with.)

In the era of INA, the area formed a strategic crossroads between the hills of Burma and Assam and, to the west, the plains of Bengal and the critical mass of Empire in the subcontinental heartland. The political geography is more fractured now. There is no war of industry and massive global scale, only localized wars of pride and prejudice, fought in the paddies, the hills, and the nearest torture chambers of captors. But the presence of the army and border security forces through the valley, in numbers beyond what is warranted for combating insurgency alone, underscores the continuing strategic importance of this area for India. Indeed, for any other player of importance in the region, and that primarily means China. In the geopolitically but not geographically distant second rung, there's Bangladesh and Myanmar.

The region's volatile politics doesn't escape us even at our wayside lunch. Behind our rickety bench is a wallpaper of the *Telegraph* from 18 February 2004, its northeast edition. 'NNC calls off Wokha truce meet,' the headline blares, informing us of an aborted attempt at peace between the Naga National Council and NSCN-IM. The 'strap' of the headline reveals the possible reason behind the cancellation: 'NSCN-IM accused of abducting leaders.'

We trail an army convoy on the way back, past the landmark towns of Ningthoukhong, Bishnupur, Oinam and Nambol Bazar, and watch a truckload of soldiers in battle gear glare at us. A few times, we swerve left and slow down to allow manically speeding patrols of army or Manipur Police commandos to pass: these are canvas-top Maruti Gypsy four-wheel-drive vehicles, somewhat differently configured from the one on which I brought my newborn daughter and her mother home from hospital: these ones have light machinegun 'nests' on the steel tube-latticed roof manned by a trooper wearing either biker goggles or sunglasses, flanked by colleagues in flak jackets gripping AK series rifles, heads covered in trademark, rakish black bandanas.

Just before Tulihal airport, in Malom, we reach the spot where ten people were shot dead by troops of 8 Assam Rifles on 2 November 2000 as they waited at a bus stop—a ramshackle shed. They were shot for reasons that remain shrouded beyond that of these AR folk being trigger-happy and vengeful to the point of being utterly warped by the state of conflict. The troopers were earlier attacked by 'Undergrounds'. This lot of AR chose civilians for reprisal. The youngest to die was a seventeen-year-old boy, S. Chandramani, the oldest a lady of sixty, L. Sana Devi. The event prompted an activist called Irom Sharmila to begin her fast to demand the abolition of the Armed Forces (Special Powers) Act from Manipur; the protest and demand continue to the day as we pass by Malom in September 2009. There's a simple arched gateway at the site of the killings. It leads into a small enclosure. The place has a name: The Ten Innocents Memorial Park.

I can't help thinking: Sharmila could have had her pick of time to begin her protest. That day, a day earlier, a year earlier, or a year later—anytime, really. There is no shortage of sudden death and reasons for protest in this valley.

~

At the major crossroads in Kwakeithel, in the southern suburbs of Imphal, I turn left to visit the family of Rabina Devi. She died as collateral damage, a death by structured insanity, the same as the ten mowed down in Malom. All Rabina had done was go to market in the heart of Imphal.

Just four days earlier I had stood where she had before her death while buying a clutch of bananas. As she had, I was surrounded by the inimitable colour and cacophony of Ima Keithel to my left. On the other side were the choked lanes of Paona Bazar. In between the shadow of a flyover loomed; the structure named after Bir Tikendrajit, a famous warrior of Manipur and hero of the Anglo-Manipur War of 1891, who was hanged for treason by the British. The route west from the flyover would have brought Rabina here from her home in the outskirts.

I had walked down to the spot from Hotel Tam-pha after an early breakfast of freshly made paratha and chana at the smoky, dim Taj Hotel just opposite, run by a friendly Meitei Pangal family. I threaded a short way to the west and then cut south, taking M.G. Road—as ever, there's a road named after Mahatma Gandhi when imagination fails and irony does not.

A stack of canoes and kayaks was placed by the slim strip of water that runs along the western wall of Kangla Fort; once a moat, now a place of sport. A poster announced it as a site for state-level water-sport competitions over some days towards the end of September and early October. Young girls paddled along, drawing smooth, powerful strokes along the water. I had watched for a few minutes this activity so resoundingly 'normal' that it seemed a like a radical space-time shift away from the daily civic hell of Imphal.

On the road, trim girls and boys dressed in Sports Authority of India tracksuits wove their way past police commandos; sports being the one instance in which India appears to have got it right here. Focus on sports, and some youngsters will jump at it to take their mind off trouble in their homeland; use sports to break out of the somnolence of despair that deep, continuing conflict can bring. And they have. Girls and boys from Manipur have for the past several years scored big in boxing, archery, soccer, hockey, and weightlifting, bringing some joy to their state, and providing several candidates for India's national teams. World champion boxer M.C. Mary Kom, a policewoman and mother of two, has for the past five years collected several international gold medals.

In Manipur she is as much an icon as Irom Sharmila.

Normality.

My walk shortly brought me to the area of Thangal Bazar.

The place resembles a civic disaster zone, as I had seen and felt on every visit to Imphal—certainly since the frequency of my visits had increased since 2007. Open sewers brought all imaginable filth to this premier trading area of Imphal. Mounds of garbage and multiple species of faeces ribboned the lanes and cheek-by-jowl rise of houses with shops below. Going deeper into the bazar, groceries, sweetmeat shops, stationery outlets and medicine stores gave way to the wholesale-trade heart of this ravaged city: stores for automobile parts, hardware, vast storehouses of rice, wheat, onion, garlic, potato—every face owning or manning these of a Marwari, a Sikh, and those with features from India's northern plains. I heard language and dialect from these ethnic zones: Punjabi, Marwari, Hindi, Bhojpuri. Folks from Bihar and Uttar Pradesh were setting up a pandal for the upcoming Durga Puja festivals near a junction. The fruit sellers all spoke Hindi or variations of it. 'Mainland' India in mainland Imphal.

I wound my way through Thangal Bazar to emerge in the northwest corner to reach Ima Keithel. I followed the filth, crossing a line of garbage and a bridge over an enormous open sewer, and turned left to find Bir Tikendrajit flyover dead ahead. There, facing the spillover of the main market, sat Imas in neat attire, some with arrow-straight marks of sandalwood paste rising from the bridge of the nose to the forehead. They set up shop on what I couldn't help calling the Flyover Road, selling banana, betel, fresh and dried fish, eel, snail, greens, water chestnut, from impeccably clean sheets of plastic, such little islands of order in the chaos. Their faces were calm, their eyes, in the manner of those who keep market, all-seeing. Near us was a broken, once-white statue of Hijam Irabot, another Meitei hero.

All around us—every few metres, it seemed—were Manipur Police commandos in their brown uniforms, stationed or strolling in twos and threes, in jeeps parked near crossroads, their automatic rifles at the ready, their caps spelling the word 'Commando' in an italicized scrawl in case anyone doubted their identity.

Like I had, Rabina may have noticed the sponsorship of the flyover in Bir Tikendrajit's name by Aircel, a prominent mobile telephony service in Manipur. She may have seen posters on the flyover advertising a '30-day Compressed Course MBBS in Shillong'—whatever the merit of such a crash tutorial in medical basics. Alongside, she may have also noticed posters that urged in bold capital letters: STOP OPPRESSION. STOP SILENT KILLING. STOP EXTRA JUDICIAL EXECUTION.

Perhaps as a resident she was inured to such schizophrenic missives, unlike me, a visitor for whom such a place seemed bizarre in the way dignity, desperation and death came together so carelessly, so seamlessly.

With such utter terror.

Here, as she stood on 23 July 2009, Rabina and her unborn child were shot dead.

On 23 September, I had at the same spot seen her family perform a simple, dignified ceremony to mark the passing of two months since her death. I had held back from introducing myself, not wishing to sully the moment with the intrusion of an interview. Those who performed the ceremony, dressed in traditional funereal pink and white cotton, and the handful who watched, had tears. Nobody knew why, and nobody had told them why a bullet marked Rabina out.

The only reasonable explanation—if ever it can be called reasonable— was that security personnel had fired shots to cover a staged encounter taking place a few metres away in a chemist's shop, to make it look like there was an exchange of fire while the police were under attack, and a shot hit Rabina. The police version says she was accidentally killed when police fired at a 'fleeing youth'.

I had also seen the family of that 'fleeing youth', Chungkham Sanjit, offer prayers for him near Maimu Pharmacy, one among a series of chemists' shops at the Kangla Fort end of the flyover, the same morning as Rabina's family offered prayers for her.

Nobody, not even his family, denies Sanjit had once been associated with the People's Liberation Army. Twice arrested and freed, he was, his family insists, detached from his former comrades and since 2006 had worked at a private hospital as an attendant. The police insisted: He tried to flee, he had a Mauser 9mm pistol which he threw away. So, they had no option but to shoot, and kill.

Much like some of my fellow citizens I had seen horrific photographs of the cold-blooded, point-blank killing of Sanjit by Manipur Police commandos, published just weeks earlier by *Tehelka* magazine. The article was headlined, 'Murder in Plain Sight.' The introduction chillingly led off with: 'In Manipur, death comes easy.'

And so it does. The series of a dozen photos in the magazine showed a composed Sanjit—hardly a 'fleeing youth'—being first surrounded by a posse of commandos at a small communication centre, and then being escorted to nearby Maimu Pharmacy. He was then dragged in—and dragged out, dead. A photo shows a dead Rabina placed on a truck. Photos show her sarong, a purple and pink striped phanek. Sanjit, wearing a black shirt, blue jeans, and a dazed expression in death, is placed by her. Photographers crowd the truck. Close-ups of Sanjit, and Rabina's bare feet and phanek.

No Mauser 9mm. No explanation.

I saw a few more photographs that did not make it to the *Tehelka* story, perhaps for reasons of space, perhaps for reasons of propriety.

One showed Rabina lying at the feet of a policewoman. Rabina's body was limp, curved in death. Her face was covered with a thin white cloth, bloodied. A pool of deep crimson nearly reached the polished leather boots of the policewoman, her face a study of consternation.

Other images showed a bloodied and dead Sanjit sprawled on his back at the far end of Maimu Pharmacy, on some old cartons and medical junk.

And on a building adjacent to the pharmacy, for years—and even on the day I watched Rabina and Sanjit's grieving families offer prayer—I saw a large billboard advertising the Congress party. On it a stern-faced chief minister with folded hands, Okram Ibobi Singh, marked space only a little less prominent than his boss, Sonia Gandhi, she with her trademark waving hand. It was a public display of a reach that political and media circles in Imphal—indeed, nearly everywhere in the region—insisted keeps Ibobi in power. This proximity to 'senior leadership', and what in politics is often called the TINA Factor: There Is No Alternative at present to Ibobi. Above Ibobi and Sonia soared the Congress pantheon, some members with impeccable and others with iffy records in relations with the public, democracy, and human rights. From left to right: Mohandas Gandhi, Abul Kalam Azad, Vallabhbhai Patel, Jawaharlal Nehru, Lal Bahadur Shastri, Indira Gandhi, and Rajiv Gandhi.

Exhibit A on a normal day.

~

The family Rabina married into lives in the west of Imphal, at Lamsang, almost due west from Bir Tikendrajit flyover, along Kangchup Road. The low house is situated opposite a school. The entrance is down a small lane off the main road, but I wait to allow a police jeep that comes lazily down the road to pass. The police do this quite a lot in this patch, I've been told. I turn to look at the signboard for the school, half-expecting the police Gypsy to stop. It doesn't. After a minute or so I cross over to the house, the back of which faces the road. I enter through a medium-sized iron gate into a space covered with tin sheets supported by bamboo poles—to accommodate a recent spurt of visitors that the main house can no longer absorb.

Large reed mats on the mud floor contain a scattering of toys, some plastic chairs, a table, a tatty sofa. A small boy in earrings, silver anklet and long hair prances around, watched over by an elderly lady and a young man. The young man turns out to be Thockchom Chinglensana, Rabina's husband. The lady, Thockchom Ungbi Memi, is his mother. The little boy is Rabina and Chinglensana's first born: Russel, two-and-half years old.

As Rabina's father-in-law, Thockchom Damu, arrives from the depths of the house, I get up from my perch on a plastic chair to greet him with folded hands, the same as I had his wife. Chinglensana and I managed a brisk handshake. And Russel, well, he got his hair tousled by me, much to his irritation, and laughter from grown-ups.

As Damu, a wiry man sparsely dressed in a vest and dhuti, settles in a chair, his wife settles down by his side. Chinglensana collects Russel in his arms and moves away from us, but not out of earshot. As patriarch, Damu has the role of key spokesperson.

First, I offer by way of introduction, I am very sorry about what happened. We heard about it even in my home on the other side of the country in faraway Goa. People would talk about what things had come to. 'Has the family received any apology or explanation on behalf of the government?' I ask next.

'There has been no clarification from the government,' Damu replies in a measured tone, in his naturally rasping voice. 'No clarification, so no apology.'

What would you all want to do now?

'I want to support the present protest by Apunba Lup,' he says. 'They are demanding the punishment of personnel involved in the incident, and the resignation of the chief minister.'

Apunba Lup, the coalition of citizens' groups has done more. It has forced the shutdown of all educational institutions in the valley—a controversial decision to force the hand of government into retreat and Chief Minister Ibobi into resignation—but it hasn't yet had any effect beyond public outcry to let children off the hook, not ruin their education. The government has with alacrity grasped this slim straw and is trying to gain a propaganda victory. Government-sponsored billboards in Imphal show images of schoolchildren. Advertisements on local television channels begin with cutaways of images of life in a 'bandh'. The word 'Life' flashes in large text, followed by black and white images of a boy and girl sitting forlorn on the steps of a school; walking down an empty corridor at a school. 'Make education a free zone,' the government advert urges, quite correctly for a change. 'Insure their future.' Classic, clever propaganda.

'Is anyone helping you?' I ask Damu.

'Nothing much,' he allows. 'Some civil society people came to show their support.'

'Have they offered to file a case against Manipur Police?'

'One lawyer and his team came and offered to file a petition on our behalf. That petition is already filed in the High Court.' A judge of the Imphal bench of Guwahati High Court had asked the police to file an FIR, or First Information Report, on the basis of the petition. But the director general of police filed a counter suit in front of the division bench challenging the order of the court, insisting that the initial order was set out by a single judge; it merited more judicial minds to consider filing an FIR, claimed the top policeman of Manipur.

'Do you believe you will get justice?' I ask Damu.

'Earlier we had full hope in the petition we had filed. Now...'

He lapses into silence. After a while a young girl brings us black tea in tiny plastic glasses. It's the moment for Damu to recover, and for his wife to wipe a tear. Chinglensana, dressed casually in a black vest and white Bermudas, has moved to the far end of the courtyard. He watches Russel tearing around the place, now shooting us all with a plastic toy weapon, a science fiction offering from the manufacturing-meisters of China; now showing off skills on a tiny tricycle, the red of it and his yellow vest and orange shorts a loud streak in an overcast day. Chinglensana's expressionless face now and again comes alive with a smile at the antics of his son.

'Please,' Damu tells me gently. 'Your tea will get cold.' His wife points to it with a small wave of her arm, and a smile.

It takes me a few seconds to respond to the household's decorum and sense of hospitality. I see it and experience it wherever I go in my travels: courtesy beyond measure.

'I am sorry,' I continue, with intent couched in polite words. 'You must forgive me if I ask a question that can hurt or offend you.'

Damu is gracious. 'We accept that you need to get some points to tell your story.'

'Thank you.' I plunge in. 'When the tragedy happened, what did you feel? Did you all feel the pointlessness of it? Did you feel anger? There obviously is grief, but who is your anger directed at? Who did you, or do you, feel most angry at?'

Damu considers this for a few moments. His reply comes without waver: 'I am sad that this chief minister is the head of this state.'

'Has the chief minister, anyone from his office, any minister, anyone from government, or the police, have they come here to ask after you?'

'No one has come. Some members of Opposition came to show their solidarity.'

What have these Opposition members done after coming to show their solidarity? I ask.

'I don't know. One MP came from Delhi also, from CPI(M), and some BJP MPs from Maharashtra, but I have no idea what they have done.'

'Do you feel that politicians, even from the Opposition, seem only to be talking, not doing anything?'

'They might be doing something in their own way, but we don't really understand what they are doing.' Damu holds out his hands, palm upwards, in a gesture of helplessness.

'What will you do now?'

'We are in a lot of confusion. We are focusing on the petition that is filed in the court.'

'The day the tragedy happened,' I pursue my query, and notice Chinglensana has gone still, 'was Rabina alone or was someone from the family with her?'

'She was with her son.'

I'm stunned. Nothing I had read or heard about the incident mentioned this fact, a two-and-half-year-old child seeing his mother alive one second, and then bloodied and unresponsive, the next.

'How did Russell reach home?' I manage in a strangled voice, stealing a look at the boy. Unsmiling, he has his toy weapon pointed at me.

'The incident happened around 10 a.m. We came to know of it on ISTV,'—a local channel. 'Maybe as the mother had already died, some kind-hearted passer-by kept the boy with him and then later gave him to the police. We only found out where he was at 4 p.m. His uncle went to the police station to claim the boy.' Damu's voice cracks.

Russell's grandmother smoothly intervenes, sparing her husband the embarrassment of grief in front of a stranger. 'He used to ask for his mother a lot. He still does sometimes. He keeps saying, "My mother is coming". Sometimes, he looks at his mother's clothes, and remembers her. He cries a lot then, and asks for her.'

'What do you tell him?'

'We say something to distract him. What else can we do?'

I ask for permission to take their photographs, and particularly that of Russell. When he is coaxed to sit on his tricycle by his grandmother, prop for the photo-op, he bursts into tears. His father picks him up and cradles him, croons to him, strokes his hair to calm him.

'He has changed,' the grandfather says, looking at his grandson. Then he lowers his eyes. 'We have all changed.'

12

The lament of Brahma

Irengbam Arun, the portly, feisty editor of a paper in Meeteilon, *Ireibak*, phones me one afternoon to check if I'm interested in seeing a play that evening. 'It will be an interesting experience, that I can guarantee you,' Arun chuckles.

Sure, I tell Arun, delighted to attend. From what little I know of him, the expression of mirth guaranteed handsome satire, several knives artfully stuck into the thick hide of The Establishment. The play, *Leibakki Wa*, an adaptation in Meeteilon of D. Vizai Bhaskar's searing Telugu play *Brahma Raatha*, is being staged at Jawaharlal Nehru Manipur Dance Academy, a short walk from my hotel; and, at any rate, I haven't planned any appointments for the evening, having decided on a time-out from interviews and continuous travel to soak up some quiet, read a book on aspects of Sanamahi, the ancient Meitei religion that draws so much from nature.

But the play draws me too. I had met the director, M.C. Thoiba, at Arun's office a few days earlier. He had with him proofs of the brochure to show Arun. I knew the Banian Repertory Company and the director would be sticking their necks out, leveraging the corruption of 'Brahma's Writ' to comment on the current play of Manipur's business of politics.

The show starts five minutes late, allowing the crowd of a hundred and fifty or so to settle in. The setting is stark: two single-level rectangular platforms to the left and to the right as we see the stage, and a three-tiered platform at the back.

The lights slowly fade in on three men in the empty space to the front of the stage. Dressed in dhuti and wearing the sacred thread, the divine astrologers wield large stylized pens made of bamboo staves, and go about, all avant-garde, scribbling on large reed mats. They are engaged in reviewing and writing the fate of people in heaven. Brahma the creator imperiously enters after a while, bejewelled and in colourful silks, looks around to check if all is well at the office, and exits with a harrumph.

Other key characters then begin to arrive one after another. The first is a contractor who has landed juicy government deals with the help of bribes. He carries a sackful of gold, jewels and cash. He offers to bribe the astrologers so that in his next life, he can return to earth again as a contractor, more powerful and successful than he had been. The senior of the team is outraged, but the youngest of the three appears interested. A schoolteacher arrives next. She was a teacher at a government-run school but spent all her time conducting private tuition—a more lucrative proposition. After much weeping and pleading, she is told in her next life she will be a teacher at a private school.

The 'contractor' returns in a double role as 'minister', played by an actor whose body language reminds me so much of Roberto Benigni in *Life is Beautiful*, and with little prompting talks of all he had done, the power he wielded, the bribes he received, the lives he affected. After a harangue that has the audience in splits, he asks the three astrologers to close their fists tight—he demonstrates: really tight. Then he asks them to open the fists.

He smiles. 'If you close your fists,' his tone is of a know-all teacher, 'you cannot take anything. If you keep them open you can take anything you want, as much of it as you want.'

I keep up with the plot because Arun, seated by me, whispers translations of key conversations and explains key moments. But the acting is so lucid and the context so clear that, Arun's translation, though very welcome, seems supplementary.

The minister speaks on to the awed astrologers about how wealth should be shared. Give some here, he says, give some there—in a reference to those overground as well as those 'underground'. There is an interruption of sorts, when his narrative suffers from the laments of a series of lesser mortals who arrive: a fisherman in search of a better life, a farmer's wife who yearns for her husband to return. Brahma, who has meanwhile returned on stage, listens with growing alarm. But he can do little; he has delegated the task of deciding fates to his writers of fate—and they are so inescapably corrupted by the minister.

Narada, the eternal jester and troublemaker to the gods of Hindu mythology, walks in about then, holding a skull, and urges Brahma and his pack of astrologer-writers to divine from the skull its fate when it had held life. Brahma touches the skull and screams and recoils in disgust. It comes from Loktak lake, one of the three astrologers interpret, and tellingly pauses. There is a hush in the audience. The area around the lake has for long been known for both real and faked encounters. The reference cuts as deep as any.

The play goes into flashback—a police officer arrives, touches the feet of the minister and begs to be promoted in spite of his bad record; then the person who the skull belongs to, a 'common man' dressed among other things in a Ho Chi Minh goatee and beret, arrives to demand development and fundamental rights. And I briefly slip into a reverie, recalling parts of a conversation with Arun at his office. It's difficult not to think back with the play nearly a mirror of our chat.

'When you ask a young child "what is your aim?" he will answer either that he wants to be a police commando or he wants to be an armed revolutionary. Because,' Arun had smiled, 'these armed people are the most powerful people. Imagine a child growing up in that situation. These two are the role models.'

We had gone on for a bit to talk about trauma among the youth, and even among those of his generation, because of what they had seen and experienced for so long. Arun, eager to avoid that subject as it would draw attention to the personal, had politely and briefly gone off on a tangent of affirmation and self-belief. We are a society located at the crossroads of South Asia and Southeast Asia, he told me. 'We have cultures from both our east and west; we have absorbed religions from these cultures, and from these a unique culture has grown. People are very proud of their heritage here. They are not accustomed to being subdued.'

'Nobody is,' I agreed.

'They have been a regional power here, minor or otherwise, for several hundred years; which is why the British used Manipur as a buffer between Burma and India.' He had leaned forward, moving away a writing pad and ballpoint pen. 'The energy is there. We have such energy. The problem is: how are you channelling that energy?'

I see you and your colleagues on TV, I had replied. I read what you write—at least what is published in English. You all sound so angry even with your restraint. You cannot very well hide your anger, your disgust. It comes through even as you speak softly, write softly; the words, on TV or doused with printer's ink, spit fire. Arun had nodded agreement.

Is there an end to this? I pursued. Where does it go from here— the violence? Does it end if Ibobi Singh ceases to be chief minister? Or is it so ingrained in the political culture that there can be no break from it?

'There is no political culture as such,' Arun had replied. 'Earlier we had politicians with ideology. After independence politicians have largely grown out of the bureaucrat-contractor nexus. Retired bureaucrats, contractors, businessmen, moneyed people ... in the US also you have moneyed people, but at least they sometimes offer vision. Here they are only out to make money. So, there isn't a political culture as such, just chamchagiri and all that.' He steepled his fingers. 'Ibobi Singh is here because he has the full support of Sonia Gandhi.'

But she is not stupid, I countered, surely she can see the damage someone like Ibobi can do—has done.

'She is not stupid,' Arun agreed, but for a different reason altogether. 'Ibobi gives some numbers. We have two MPs in Lok Sabha, one in Rajya Sabha. Ibobi gives them Congress MPs. Ibobi gives them Congress MLAs. He brings them back to power. Ibobi gives money for the elections of other states. And he keeps the middle people'—intermediaries—'in the Congress high command happy. And because of the support he has, Congress MLAs cannot raise their voice. If they rebel against Ibobi they are out in the wilderness without…' He paused to sip tea. 'And here, as it is happening everywhere, without money you cannot do any politics; you cannot be part of electoral politics.'

Arun had received a call then. The ring tone of his mobile phone was from the distinct piping soundtrack of a Sergei Leone 'spaghetti western' classic starring Clint Eastwood: *The Good, the Bad, and the Ugly.*

It felt good to share laughter.

The Ho Chi Minh lookalike who is soon to be a skull at Loktak lake—I can't think of the character as anything else—loses his cool after a long argument with the minister, and attacks him. The police officer, newly promoted, disentangles them. The minister screams invective, and orders Soon-to-be-Skull taken away and finished. Not jailed. Finished. The police officer drags away Soon-to-be-Skull.

The play ends with Brahma's lament, and his proclamation that he has reclaimed the right to write fates. But a suggestion made earlier in the play comes back to haunt him. Even with his four heads and four pairs of eyes, will he be able to see wrongdoing?

Arun and I remain seated far beyond the applause and the curtain call. We don't discuss it but it feels like breathing room before it is again time to look beyond the reality of make-believe, and the step back into the make-believe of reality.

~

The mood stays with me the following day, my day of departure from the current series of travel. The weather plays accompaniment: it resolutely blocks sunshine.

As my autorickshaw driver stops for checking at the security barrier at the entrance gate of Tulihal airport, a trooper of Central Industrial Security Force walks up. From his name I can tell he is from Tamil Nadu—a fellow Mainlander. My genial 'Namaste bhai-saab' and a show of ID and ticket are enough to bring a smile in reply. An 'Indian' by feature and name, I am evidently not a security risk in these parts and immediately waved through. For those like him, I am an insider.

We pass occupants of the vehicle directly in front, a white Maruti 800 sub-compact, who are still being checked by security personnel. The occupants are outsiders within this perimeter of secure India: an elderly Meitei couple, a young boy and a lady who looks to be his mother. The luggage of these Indians is on the road. One trooper checks their documents, another noses though the tiny trunk and under the seats. A third peers into the bonnet. There is a long queue of cars, SUVs and autorickshaws behind us. Afternoon is a busy time at Tulihal, with several flights to Guwahati, Kolkata, Delhi, even a 'hopper' on this day to Bengaluru, a major destination for many youngsters from Manipur in search of education and jobs.

After checking in for my Jetlite flight to Kolkata I walk towards the Nescafé counter, which also sells tea. It is one of two remaining refreshment kiosks in the airport, the second being inside the security hold; the small restaurant shut down several months earlier and nobody appears keen to revive it. Staff of several airlines are buying beverage for government officials and those similarly inflated with political tyre pressure, so to speak. The rest of us, of course, buy our own.

A paper cup of lemon-flavoured instant tea in hand, I drift towards the massive LG television set in the waiting area before the security enclosure. Over several visits I had seen on its screen a range of events from Formula 1 Grand Prix car racing to Prime Minister Manmohan Singh glibly assuring television networks that his government was doing everything to solve problems in politics and the economy, conflicts from Maoism to Manipur, and festering issues with Pakistan and China.

I settle down on one among a shaky row of blue-upholstered seats to wait for my flight to be called. The channel is switched to ISTV, and it is running a commercial break for a movie in Meeteilon, 'Now Showin' at Pratap Talkies in Imphal.

'No Peace, No Hope, No Justice,' the screen flashes in English. 'Only False Encounters.'

'No Mercy. Only Torture.'

'What is the Answer?'

'PANCHAA.' The screen shows a burly, angry, determined youngster. 'Panchaa is the answer,' the advertisement prompts in a final flourish.

I can't help thinking: Panchaa would have my vote in a flash.

～

On the plane I meet Astad Deboo, the dancer from Mumbai, who has made Manipur a frequent stop for several years. Several of his performances have included practitioners of thang-ta, the impossibly fluid Manipuri martial art. Once a curiosity, Deboo's encouragement for eleven years has seen Manipuri performers travel India and the world as part of troupes that showcase Manipur and India. They are brilliant; I've seen a performance. I tell Deboo of a time, in the autumn of 2007, when I saw a group of leaping pung-cholom drummers from Manipur hold captive a rapt audience at the South Street Seaport in New York, a loud shout away from Wall Street, and felt inordinately proud to be an Indian.

Deboo smiles, deeply pleased. He is these days working on a show with pung-cholom dancers, and invites me to a performance at the Old Fort in New Delhi on 6 October 2009, days away. Then, as the aircraft readies for departure to Guwahati and Kolkata—where I will stay on for a couple of days, and Deboo will connect with a flight to Mumbai—we talk about Manipur. Deboo turns sombre. Culture cannot feed everyone, he says.

'Those who can leave—leave,' he tells me. 'Many kids are going out, making a life for themselves elsewhere. And I can't blame them—there is nothing here. Every year the situation gets worse, much worse.'

The fact that several places in Imphal and elsewhere in Manipur get electricity for three hours a day—if they are lucky—is less of a worry than paying a bribe of more than three hundred thousand rupees, as one his performer's relatives was compelled to recently, to be taken on as a jawan at the local recruitment office.

Assam Rifles or Manipur Police? I ask.

Deboo waves it away, reclines his aisle seat, and slips into a nap.

I have the window seat. The deep blue of near space above us and the white sea of cloud below us, spun outside the cocoon of the jet, are soothing. Till I return again to the hinterland of Highway 39 to look inside histories, lives and perceptions, try and take stories from these lands to people in the 'Mainland' and beyond, so that they understand more, misunderstand less.

India versus the rest is somehow easier to tell. The lines, grooved as they may be in blood and ashes and resentment, are clear. But the stories of blurred lines are always more difficult to articulate: stories of a Vidyarani, a Rabina, a Sanjit. Stories of deliberate misunderstandings and callousness that people in power inflict upon their own; when protector morphs effortlessly to predator.

In the flurry of activity in the past days, the visit to Chungkham Sanjit's home had lain buried in my mind. As I play back the conversations in my digital recorder with a napping Deboo in the adjacent seat, look again in my notebook for impressions, the small house in Khurai Sajor Leikai swims into focus.

I had arrived at Sanjit's after traversing Imphal from west to east, running a gauntlet of narrow lanes to reach a patch of land covered with tin sheets and tarpaulin on latticed bamboo, walls along the dirt track reaching the spot plastered with posters of what I can only call the 'Sanjit sequence'. I saw all the images published in *Tehelka*, and two more that I knew of—Sanjit's body deep inside Maimu Pharmacy.

The 'Sanjit Joint Action Committee' was in session, as I soon discovered; that explained a few ladies quickly getting up to disappear into and behind the tiny house. The 'jeep' I arrived in, and my cropped hair, had evidently given the impression that I was from the police or an intelligence agency. Only the presence of some friends from Imphal, who immediately broke into Meeteilon to assuage any concern, had retrieved the situation. We all sat around a small table on rented chairs.

A young lawyer, who gave me his card but requested anonymity, explained the reason for their jitteriness, as a lady seated by him nodded vigorously.

She turned out to be Thongatabam Anita Devi, convener of the Sanjit Joint Action Committee, which comprised citizens from Sanjit's neighbourhood and the nearby localities of Khurai Chingangbam Leikai, Kongpal Leishram Leikai and Kongpal Ningthoubung Leikai. As the lawyer translated, Anita Devi spoke rapidly about her experience from the previous night—the night of 26-27 September 2009—when several jeeploads of Manipur Police commandos had come looking for her. She had managed to escape, using her intimate knowledge of the area's geography and the help of neighbours. She made her way to Sanjit's house. The police 'dare not' come here, the lawyer emphasized, saying it would have amounted to an insult to the grieving family. But that self-assurance did not seem to work for Anita Devi—she shook her head as the lawyer translated for her what he had told me.

'Anything can happen these days. That is why I went inside when you came,' she explained with a smile. 'A white jeep, like a police jeep'—then apologetically pointing to my head—'your hair...'

A flurry of motorbikes arrived with local youths; and soon, tea for all of us, brought by a Sanjit JAC member.

'So, you want to write about Sanjit,' the lawyer resumed, prodded by a sharp sidelong glance of a large lady who it appeared was still not taken with my intent, no matter that accompanying me were people with established credentials of not being either police or bureaucrat; and no matter that her colleague Anita Devi had appeared to accept my presence. Other Imas—mothers—gathered around us had tensed. The large lady unleashed a flurry of rapid-fire Meeteilon before I could reply.

Then I realized an error of commonsense protocol. I first offered my calling card, then a photo ID issued by the Foreign Correspondents' Club of South Asia—extremely handy for an independent writer. The Imas finally relaxed.

'Please tell Ima here'—I had requested the lawyer, gesturing at the large lady I instantly christened Grouchy Ima—'that just because my hair is short...'

There was an outbreak of laughter from assembled Imas, even Grouchy Ima, who rocked back on her chair with great hilarity.

With the ice finally broken, I had pressed on. Now that the incident has happened I was interested to see if justice would be delivered. Would people responsible for this incident be punished? Would the government assume responsibility for its actions? And what would common people do, and the Joint Action Committee, to create more awareness and demand justice?

The lawyer spoke for everyone, taking time out now and again to answer phone calls on his mobile phone and even that of other JAC members.

'We came to know that someone with a high-powered rifle killed Rabina—we have a copy of the post-mortem report that says so. We heard that Sanjit was killed forty-five minutes after this. We also heard three persons were interrogated before Sanjit was killed; they were asked if they had links with the underground.'

'See...' He unfurled a poster similar to those plastered on the lane outside, and we looked upon Sanjit, both alive and dead. 'We suspect he was killed because some police officers wanted a gallantry award.'

It isn't unknown in conflict zones. In Jammu & Kashmir army men, paramilitary and police have been held accountable for killing innocents by labelling them terrorists or terrorist sympathizers, all for plumping up their service records. Many security personnel have gone scot-free. Many missing victims remain untraced to this day, thought to be buried in forests or unmarked graves in Kashmir Valley.

'When his mother went to the police station to register a FIR they didn't do anything,' the lawyer continued as all eyes remained on us. 'Nothing happened either when she visited the deputy commissioner of police of Imphal West to ask the names of policemen who shot dead her son. They just pretended like they knew nothing about it.'

I looked around, and met tired eyes, the eyes of women appalled at the state of the world their children had come into and would soon inherit, and could die violently in the process of doing so. Sad eyes. Angry eyes. The lawyer's gentle voice carried on as if in the background, recapping the past several weeks. 'Agitation is going on for the last two months; and they finally announced a judicial enquiry after a month. And meanwhile, the DCP has told the court that the *Tehelka* photos are fakes. But we have said that is between *Tehelka* and the government, not between us and the government...'

Sanjit's mother came out of the house then. She hadn't come

towards us, but busied herself with a short broom, sweeping near the steps that led from the house to the yard where we were gathered. Our talk diminished out of respect for her.

An Ima, in my distraction I couldn't immediately tell which, spoke in fluent English. 'People keep coming and asking her the same questions. She is tired now. She is still very upset.'

Sanjit's mother was an island in her grief. People flowed around her. Her face expressionless, she silently moved the broom in graceful strokes, as if cleansing the space off intrusion. She glanced at us with a faraway look, and then away—I realized that she had looked beyond us to the posters of her son, the dead cause célèbre. With a slow, graceful turn she returned to what remained of her home.

We were silent. Some Imas wiped their eyes.

'We have done many things,' the lawyer softly resumed. 'We have gone for mass court arrest. We have talked with the chief minister and governor. But that was at gunpoint. Five of our JAC were arrested and six of Apunba Lup. So we decided to not talk with the chief minister. But there was pressure from police that unless we talk to the chief minister they will use NSA [National Security Act] against us. So we had to talk. We had five points.'

I had read of these. The first was that Chief Minister Ibobi Singh should step down from office. The qualifier was that he should surrender the home portfolio 'To someone who is very sincere,' I heard in the courtyard of Sanjit's home. 'We meant: the chief minister is not the right person to hold the post of home minister.'

That was a naïve demand, given the nature of India's—and Manipur's—tendency to sycophantic politics and dictatorial decision-making, but I kept quiet.

The second demand was for an enquiry by the Central Bureau of Investigation, as a judicial enquiry wasn't deemed as enough—unsurprising, as the state government routinely ignored the most damning indictment of its police and officials.

The third and fourth demands were related: the policemen involved in Sanjit and Rabina's deaths should be punished; and the area's DCP and superintendent of police should be suspended along with some policemen who had already been suspended.

And finally, the chief minister should call a special session of the State Assembly to clarify the position and make a statement.

'They said the CBI enquiry will take too long, so a judicial enquiry would be done,' the lawyer explained. 'And that will have no benefit as nobody acts on the result of judicial enquiries. The CM said he can't suspend police officers because they will go to court. As for me giving up the post of home minister, he said, "I need to talk to my colleagues, but most of them want me as the home minister."'

Square one.

Do you think any action will be taken? I had asked.

'We should go on agitating for one year, if it is required,' the lawyer had indirectly answered. 'People have come with an offer of ten lakh [one million] rupees for Sanjit's family. During police interrogation there was an attempt to induce a JAC member with money to withdraw from the committee. They have sent government employees to offer money and ask us to withdraw the agitation.'

Then he had leaned forward, some of the Imas too leaning forward in the reflex of conspiracy. 'This is confidential,' he spoke softly. 'We are going to attack the bungalows of some ministers and MLAs.'

'Attack?'

'Protest. Demonstration. We also want to write a letter to Sonia Gandhi, so that she can be reminded of the non-violence of Mahatma Gandhi, Jawaharlal Nehru, Indira Gandhi, Rajiv Gandhi.'

I couldn't help clarifying the situation. Nehru didn't exactly follow the path of non-violence—not after India's independence anyway. The Naga regions know well the brutal force of Nehru's precept of violence. Certainly his daughter Indira Gandhi did not.

Mizoram, Manipur, and Nagaland know it well. And her son Rajiv, even though he had attempted peace deals in Assam and Punjab, nevertheless had several blemished entries in the book of national conscience—where could one begin? Of these 'national' figures only Mahatma Gandhi truly had practised non-violence. And this Gandhi and the Nehru-Gandhis aren't related—though the Nehru-Gandhis haven't ever specifically advertised the fact.

There was laughter. There was more tea.

~

Astad Deboo is still asleep. Done writing notes for a time, I turn to look at the skies for a breather before I return to a book of poetry. It's by Robin S. Ngangom, the Manipuri poet who teaches literature at Shillong's North-Eastern Hill University. Slivers of cloud arrive as the aircraft begins its descent into Guwahati. As I briefly close my eyes the faces return insistently. The face of Vidyarani. The face of Rabina's husband and their son. The face of Sanjit's mother, mute in her grief. So many others; the dead and the living dead, caught between the state and those who take to arms against the state. So much anguish, so much anger.

> '...Childhood took place
> among fairies and weretigers...',

I read from 'A Libran Horoscope', a poem in Robin's book, *The Desire of Roots*.

> '...when hills were yours to tumble
> before they housed soldiers
> and dreaded chambers of torture.
> Childhood took place when boys built fugitive fires
> and talked of women
> until your friend adored a gun
> to become a widowmaker...'

I could show Deboo this, were he awake. Or another poem, 'The Strange Affair of Robin S. Ngangom', which I turn to as we prepare to land. I had already marked some portions of it with a highlighter some days earlier in Imphal.

> '...*Nothing is certain*
> *oil*
> *lentils*
> *potatoes*
> *food for babies*
> *transport*
> *the outside world.*
> *Even*
> *fire water and air*
> *are bought and sold...*
>
> *...Maybe the land is tired*
> *of being suckled on blood,*
> *maybe there is no peace*
> *between the farmer and his fields,*
> *maybe all men are tired of being men,*
> *maybe we have acknowledged death...*'

Take-off or touchdown, there is no escaping the thread of sordid history.

13

Surprises in Dimapur: old friends, new lights, and freedom at dinner

Rajib Barooah, a friend from my years at boarding school in faraway Rajasthan, insists that I visit his tea gardens in Jorhat before I head to Dimapur. I don't argue. I haven't met Rajib for a while, and spending a day on a tea estate can be a precious experience for visitors. Jorhat is also more or less up the road—following the course of the Brahmaputra along its southern bank, brilliantly blue and streaked with sandbars at this time of the year, late in October. Jorhat is also up the road from Numaligarh, where Highway 39 begins its journey south to Moreh. I need to be at this northern touch point, travel the highway from its beginning to its end.

Sitting by a pukhuri at Haroocharai Tea Estate, I realize this pit-stop is an indulgence the travel doctor may have ordered. Rajib's two children are away at boarding school elsewhere in Assam and college in Delhi; Mamli, his wife, is away visiting family in Kolkata. Rajib and I sit by this glorious pond in the early afternoon, serenaded by lazy geese and mynah and kingfisher, spooning grapefruit tossed lightly with mustard oil and shredded green chilly. Drinks of vodka and bitters are provided by attentive staff; they soon bring plates of fried rohu. Luncheon is yet to be. I guiltlessly take in this dose of burra-sahib, for me an occasional sin at someone else's invitation.

After a nap it is time for drinks and conversation with planters, businessmen and a sprinkling of army officers at Jorhat Club. I am deliriously relaxed living someone else's life; and they indulge me my hiking boots, work shirt and jeans at the gentleman's bar as we discreetly exchange news and information about the region.

Rajib tells me at some point in the evening that he has decided to accompany me to Dimapur. He hasn't been there for some years and, as the tea season has wound down, he has time to spare. 'Don't say no,' he cautions. 'The bus service on that route is notoriously unreliable.'

'Tomorrow,' I agree easily. 'I'm willing to be spoilt until then.'

Rajib and I set off around eleven in the morning, heading west from Jorhat towards Kaziranga—and Numaligarh. The green keeps pace with us, the curiously flat-top, telltale bushes of tea, endless acres of it, interspersed with farm and forest. The small town of Numaligarh appears to arrive almost in a blink. I realize I've been engrossed in catching up with news about old friends and, in between, replaying in my mind the chatter from the previous evening at the club. In this world of planters the key one seemed to be: United Liberation Front of Asom is in remission in these parts, thank heavens; and the newly appointed prime minister of Bangladesh, Sheikh Hasina Wajed, whose friendly attitude towards India will allow less sanctuary to ULFA and other bands of rebels and thugs masquerading as rebels. But there is a new worry for those with tea estates south and southwest of Jorhat. NSCN-IM, in its endeavour to spread influence and increase revenue, has started hitting on tea companies for donations—some planters have received 'demand notes'. The pressure, I'm told, gets more acute in the clusters along Highway 39, to the east of which only a slim strip of plains separates Assam and Nagaland. A planter had told me at Jorhat Club the previous evening: 'I don't envy those chaps. I wouldn't want to be there even if someone paid me.'

Numaligarh seems to be nothing more than truck stop and bus stop, its most famous landmark being an eponymous petroleum refinery a few kilometres south from the turn-off at Kamighat—and the highway-girdling span that proclaims the start of National Highway 39.

'Your happening highway.' Rajib grins as we pass the sign.

The distance of seventy-nine kilometres from Numaligarh to Dimapur passes quickly, and without incident. For long stretches the highway is smooth tarmac, and I'm shocked—I tell Rajib I can't recognize this as 'my' highway, so broken and pitted have I seen it in other stretches. The place names flash past, Rajib helping my habit of note-taking by translating from Assamese the places not represented in English. Together, we track the Dhansiri River, the sprawl of tea estates between Kamighat and Doigrung Bazar, the slim ribbon of the Rangajan River, the sign for the 10 Battalion headquarters of the Border Security Force at Golaghat junction. This is a relatively poor but for the moment relatively unstressed country, Rajib explains; conflict in these parts is settled for a time.

There is conflict, though, as far as the transportation system is concerned. There are hardly any buses on the road, and a couple of buses we see are nearly trashed with overuse; they are parked, broken down, as passengers mill about helplessly yet patiently, leaving it to luck to provide passage. I know well the feeling, and this day I am grateful for Rajib's offer of a ride.

After Golaghat, as we pass through a stretch of the densely forested Nambor Wildlife Sanctuary, the highway crashes into familiar stretches of near-total destruction. I sigh in relief; Rajib bursts out laughing. At Garampani we cross over from Golaghat district of Assam to the state's Karbi Anglong district, and again see flashes of tea gardens, the ones, I am told, NSCN-IM have included in its business plan.

Surprisingly—at any rate, surprising to me, fresh as I am from being incessantly checked in Manipur—we encounter only the second police checkpoint at Borpathar, the first being after passing the turn-off to Numaligarh Refinery. And then, the remainder of our short journey is quickly over: Bokajan with its Cement Corporation of India factory passes in a rush; Khatkhatti, the alcohol-shopping hub for 'dry' Dimapur comes next; and after nondescript Lahorijan, we are quickly past the border of Assam and into dusty, noisy, heaving Dimapur.

~

There's a surprise. An acquaintance from Kohima calls to say that Deirdre Boyd, the country director of United Nations Development Programme, is in Nagaland. Indeed, she is expected to be in Dimapur today, after spending several days in Kohima meeting government officials and NGO representatives, visiting projects. As a representative of a donor agency, in places like Nagaland, Deirdre would get the full treatment, equal to or more than what is usually reserved for an ambassador. I am told that Alemtemshi Jamir, the additional chief secretary and development commissioner of Nagaland, among the most powerful bureaucrats in the state, is personally showing her around.

Coincidentally, Deirdre calls minutes after Rajib and I check into my old favourite, de Oriental Dream. She is to judge a beauty contest at a local Naga cultural festival, she says with a somewhat embarrassed yet delighted giggle, and she is being quite heavily escorted by armed police as well as civilian government staff. That makes it difficult for her to breakaway to catch up with me. But Alemtemshi Jamir is hosting a dinner for her at Saramati Hotel, and she is certain he won't mind if a friend of hers shows up.

'Your friend, and a friend of his,' I remind her.

'No problem.' Deirdre is unfazed. 'I'm sure it will be all right.'

Rajib is thrilled at the prospect. He is rapidly re-evaluating his earlier opinion of Dimapur as a broken, no-hope town bound by conflict and corruption—much of it holds true—and is pleasantly shocked at the signs of life that Dimapur's streets and shops display. And, of course, the signs of efficient life at our quaintly named hotel. He can't get over it.

'*de* Oriental Dream,' he says every now and then, as he discovers that the room he has chosen for us has an air conditioner, a TV, room service, and en suite toilet that works.

I decide to shock him some more. As we have some time to kill before joining Deirdre's party at the Saramati, I take him to Purple Haze, the site of an earlier revelry. My disappointment at the lounge being shut down is lessened by the presence of a new watering hole that has opened in the two months since I last visited this building opposite Ne-ti hotel. The Zephyr Lounge welcomes us.

Rajib is taken with the mood lighting and elegant seating that wouldn't be out of place in metropolitan India. We are guided to our table by the polite manager. Eyeing the menu in a daze, Rajib orders beef teriyaki and shots of vodka. Getting carried away, unmindful that we have a dinner to gatecrash, he orders a takeaway of Penang lamb curry and fried rice. The teriyaki is delicious, the vodka uplifting. At a quarter to nine, I drag a reluctant Rajib to Saramati.

The party is in flow as we arrive at the hotel. It's in the sole restaurant closed off this evening to the public—Nagaland's key bureaucrat is holding court. The court is seated around several slim rectangular tables thrown together in a line at the far end of the large room; Deirdre is seated along one side towards the middle of the arrangement, Alemtemshi at its head. As Deirdre introduces me to him, and in turn I introduce Rajib, he graciously welcomes us both and offers drinks that a waiter rushes to serve.

Other guests, a dozen or so, come into focus. There's a pleasant surprise: two friends from Shillong are among them, Robert 'Bob' Lyngdoh, a former home and then youth affairs minister of Meghalaya and sometime rock musician, and Sam Shullai, a top drummer who shape-shifts with several well-known rock and blues bands. I first met Sam during his run with Soulmate, a robust blues act from Shillong. The story goes that Bob, a mouth-harp fanatic, once played out a classic, though not with mouth-harp, in front of several hundred exuberant youngsters. They expected a motivational speech for an end to conflict in the Northeast from this home minister. And so, the diminutive Bob dragged a didgeridoo to the stage, blew on it to expel the compellingly sonorous sound, quite like a chant of Tibetan monks the aboriginal instrument from Australia produces, and announced in all seriousness: 'Peace on earth, man.'

But Bob does have another side—I know from sombre conversations in his Shillong home, discussing his time as home minister during insurgency in Meghalaya; his function a meld of his personal liberal outlook and application of state power as a minister in uneasy stasis. The contradictions and the pressures of the job wrenched apart his life, his family. But Bob is here now in his jolly avatar, and with him quiet, smiling Sam. Like Deirdre, they have tiny crossed Naga spears pinned to their lapels—they are also arrived from judging the beauty contest.

Among the others there is a former member of the Bharatiya Janata Party (BJP) from Nagaland, Ato Yepthomi, and a deputy commandant of Nagaland's first all-woman battalion of police. Rajib and I complete the eclectic group. Except for the police officer, very conscious of being in the presence of a senior bureaucrat—she formally, delicately sipping orange juice—we are all quickly on our way to the place where conversation gets freer, and the space between point of view and argument begins to blur. Blame Alemtemshi—at some point he, prompted by Deirdre's 'Sudeep is researching a book', asks an innocent question: 'So, what is your book about?'

I want to get a sense of Nagaland's past and present, and a future, I tell him, and various ideas and forms of freedom that I would love to talk to you about. Our meeting is a remarkable and welcome coincidence; may I visit you in Kohima for a chat? As a joke I shamelessly add, 'One St Stephen's alumnus to another', knowing he is an indulgent member of the state's not insubstantial alumni network. Alemtemshi is smart: he offers vague assurances and evades the issue. But Ato the politician is hooked.

As we tuck into dinner—a variety of kebabs followed by northern Indian-style curries—Ato politely launches into incidents from the past, from the regions of the Yimchunger, and also that of the Pochury Naga. He speaks in low but firm tones of the Indian Army 'wiping out' all males of a village, a result of claiming 'Nagas wanted to be by themselves in their own nation'. I see Alemtemshi tensing—he sends a quick glance at Deirdre, but she too is smart, and looks politely on. I try to calm things by relating an incident that happened to me while researching a feature story in Jammu & Kashmir in 2002 for *India Today*, the magazine I worked with at the time. It was just before elections to that state's Assembly. I had run into a large pro-separatism election meeting at Handwara near the northwestern edge of Kashmir Valley. The crowd was chanting over and over again, 'Ish chahta azadi'. We want freedom. It was a slogan, a song, a dance, set to rhythmic clapping.

What do you want freedom from? I had smilingly asked them with the help of a translator when they took a break from sloganeering. You keep saying you want freedom, but can you define it, so I can tell my readers? Freedom from India? From Pakistan's rhetoric? From violence? The dynastic Abdullah political clan? Other political clans like the Sayeeds and Shahs? Do you wish freedom from corruption? From your spouses?

For a while there was silence, and I feared I had gone too far. But the Kashmiri sense of humour prevailed, and amidst laughter many from the crowd admitted that defining freedom was a very difficult thing.

Alemtemshi smoothly twigs on to this, and launches into a monologue as to how the 'very seventeenth-century idea of sovereignty does not apply here' and 'we have to define freedom and sovereignty in our own way'. He urges, 'Don't confuse freedom with sovereignty.' I had come by similar statements by Alemtemshi in a newspaper several months earlier when at a student gathering near Dimapur he had deftly sidetracked the definition of freedom as a lofty idea: 'Freedom also means freedom of thought, belief, action and freedom from want, suffering and joblessness.'

No nation is truly sovereign, I hear Alemtemshi telling Ato, and he then takes the conversation to another level as I watch, surprised at his candour. 'All these people,' he continues, 'they are all stuck in the past; they can't come out—Muivah, Isak, Khaplang, Kitovi [Zhimomi, top minister in the Khaplang faction]. All stuck in the past.'

Ato shakes his head, bypassing Alemtemshi's sharp yet telling rhetoric altogether to return to India's brutal mistreatment of those she ironically claimed as her own. 'We cannot forget,' Ato whispers, then raises his voice. 'We cannot *ever* forget.'

'How old are you?' Alemtemshi intervenes, more gently than I thought he would. 'You're from the 1970s? I'm from before.' He leans back in his chair, straightening his already impeccable 'Nehru' jacket. 'What have *you* seen? The life *after*. When I was four the army came to my village. I can tell you many things about what I saw, what happened to my people.' I realize what this is costing him—his tribal homeland, the Ao region, was terribly hit.

Alemtemshi then sighs and pushes away his glass. 'Let it be,' he says. 'We have to move on.' Ato begins to say something, but Alemtemshi raises a hand. 'If we have another peg,' he gently tells the younger man, 'we will begin to fight.'

He smiles. We all do. The lady police officer still has her face averted, studiously looking down at the tablecloth. Soon, we disperse, but not before Rajib plays face-saver. He is carrying several packets of tea from his estate, and he gifts a pack each to the guests at dinner. It's a kind gesture, but the curative properties of tea are not yet known to unravel the thread of conflict and the pain of emerging from it.

14

And then the shell landed

With great ceremony Y. Vandanshan Lotha pours me a measure of homemade blackberry wine into a small juice glass. Along with his wife Susieyana he makes the wine at their compact, simple single-storey home in central Kohima. This is around Minister Hill where the chief minister also stays; and not far from the official residence of the head of the ceasefire-monitoring cell from the Indian side, Lt Gen. (Retd) Mandhata Singh.

Van O Wine, they call it, and the label bordered in shiny metallic strip proudly proclaims it. If the fruit season is good, Vandan and smiling Susieyana keep themselves busy with winemaking, and sell it to friends and a few shops for between Rs 350 and 380 a bottle. This hobby is a little something to supplement Vandan's income as an employment officer with the Government of Nagaland. And it's also a little something to keep their mind off the fact that their youngest daughter Soyingbeni is dead, and Rebecca Senpilo, the 'middle daughter', as Susieyana puts it, damaged in the mind with the same blast of mortar that took the young one, who was then four and a half years old.

It didn't happen during the old Naga wars. It happened in 1995, two years before India's ceasefire with NSCN-IM. It happened in Kohima, which had for long ceased to be a battle zone. It happened just outside in the one-small-car-length driveway neatly set with small pots of orchid. Right by the place where Mhashan, Vandan and Susieyana's son, now sits framed with bright blue skies and October sunlight, gently strumming his guitar as two burly dogs keep him company, one occasionally yowling tunefully to the music.

It happened when Manmohan Singh was the finance minister, and his prime minister, P.V. Narasimha Rao, was boasting to the world that India had arrived.

'How is it?' Vandan asks after the wine.

'It's nice,' I say, sipping appreciatively. 'It is way better than anything they make in Goa.' That's honest enough. My adoptive home makes terrible, overly sweet wines that budget travellers buy in great quantities to take back home as souvenirs and gifts.

Susieyana laughs delightedly, and settles down to join us on the sofa set at the centre of the small, cosily warm living area.

'For your kind information,' Vandan tells me obliquely, formally, out of the blue, 'my father first joined the Indian Army in 1939.'

'Your health,' I reply lamely, caught off guard.

'When the first Assam Regiment was raised in 1939, he joined in the 1st Battalion. He studied up to Class 2. He was illiterate, but he could write his name. Then he was promoted to naik'—equivalent of a corporal in the Indian Army and the British Indian Army. 'Second World War came. He, the Late Yambamo Lotha, participated in the Burmese campaign. Then they came up to the Kohima Theatre.' The Japanese army had laid siege to the town, and controlled several key locations.

'My father died when I was very young,' he continues in his stilted manner.

'So I have not had intimate discussions with my father,' Vandan adds after a pause and a deep intake of breath. 'He then joined the Naga Army. So, such discussion was not possible.'

I put down the glass of wine. Arriving to chronicle a tragic death and the trigger-happiness of Indian officers and troopers way past the early decades of the Naga wars, I appear to have come by a wider tale with a strange twist.

I let Vandan spin out the story. He talks of 'that fateful day', 13 November 1944, when his father sneaked out of his camp in the 'Kohima Theatre' without informing his comrades, or his officer, a captain. He chanced upon a group of Japanese 'carelessly eating, drinking because there was for so long no counter-action from the British Indian Army, I mean, Allied forces,' as Vandan tells me.

'My father shouted "charge!" and thinking there was a big attack coming, they fled. After that he came down and told his captain, "Sa'ab, I have already sent them off." They didn't believe him but when they went to look, they found the area empty. Later, they came up from the side of Zubza and captured the area of the present-day Kohima cemetery.' During this time, Yambamo apparently killed seventy Japanese soldiers on his own, and was awarded the Military Medal. 'Bahadur Yambamo' by then had the Burma Star, and the Distinguished Service Medal.

'Phizo requested him to join Naga Army,' Vandan says next. 'My mother didn't want him to join as he was getting a pension of five rupees per month, and in those days five rupees was a lot. But he had to fight because Phizo had asked him. He told my mother he will come out after a few years, "because India will not give us the head"'—Vandan places the edge of a palm to his head—'sovereignty, "because India is too big and too powerful and we are too small. But they will give us up to the shoulder."' Vandan drops the palm to shoulder height, signifying India's strategy of thus far and no further.

'He was the first general of the Naga Army,' Vandan rounds it off, 'of the Federal Government of Nagaland.' Things click into place for me; Vandan's father is honoured even today by factions of the Naga Army. There's a Yambamo Lotha Brigade in NSCN-IM.

General Yambamo went to war with India and died of it. His former colleagues in the Indian Army went relatively easy on the family, Vandan maintains, even after his father joined the Naga Army. The gesture set against the 24/7 horror of the Naga wars seems honourable, if bizarrely so. Out of respect for a war hero, Vandan says, the Indian Army never burnt down the family house in Wokha, but ordered the villagers to dismantle it—thrice. Yambamo's wife and children were not tortured.

'I've been here in this house since 1981.' Vandan takes a sip of the wine. Susieyana tenses and looks out of the window; and I know what's coming. The tale of his father, as fascinating as it may be, was only a roundabout way to reach his hurt.

'There was a f-f-f-t sound,' Vandan says, pinning me with his stare. 'It was my fate to go through that, so it happened. The bomb fell in the midst of my family. Right here'—he points to the driveway. 'Fifth March 1995. There was some firing down there. There was some dat-dat-dat sound, then the sound of some explosions. Five past one in the afternoon.'

Please go ahead, he tells me, finish up the wine. I pour a small measure to buy him time and composure.

'The eldest girl'—Wonchibeni—'also got splinters. She is now studying law in Kolkata. The youngest one, who died, did not die from splinters but she was thrown back with such force that her head hit a stone. My son, then two, was also injured. My second daughter was crippled. She was six years old then.'

The doctors later told him that one-third of her brain matter came out in a wound caused by shrapnel from the two-inch mortar shell, Vandan says tonelessly, holding back his tears, but not Susieyana—she is freely crying into her handkerchief. The Mahindra vehicle from his office took several splinters and had its tyres deflated, so Vandan walked with her to the nearest hospital holding the injured part of her skull with his hand. Neighbours helped to carry the rest of his family: the youngest, fading fast; his eldest daughter; his mother who had her legs slashed, a vein ruptured, and who still carries several dozen bits of mortar shrapnel in her legs. And Susieyana, who until then was scared to see blood, but overcame her phobia to roughly bandage her mother-in-law's legs and do what she could for her children.

Young Soyingbeni was dead by the time they reached the hospital. Vandan later managed to take Rebecca Senpilo to NIMHANS, a top neurological-care facility in Bangalore, and later, to the Sitaram Bhartia Institute in New Delhi. She has improved, but remains motor impaired.

'I always believed I will not die unless I am destined,' Vandan announces defiantly.

'Has his sense of humour improved with age?' I ask Susieyana, to try and break the gloom.

'He has always been like this.' She laughs through her tears.

'Did you receive any gesture or apology from those who did this?' I ask them.

Vandan says the 16th Rashtriya Rifles 'continued to deny the mistake'. But a furious state government, headed then by S.C. Jamir, constituted a one-man enquiry commission led by Justice D.M. Sen, a retired judge of Guwahati High Court. 'He found there had been excess action, beyond operational needs,' Vandan says. 'One colonel in charge was given forced retirement, or dismissal. The [Nagaland] police chief then was Chaman Lal. The general commanding the 8th Mountain Division—General Patel I think—came [to meet me] with Chaman Lal. I have forgiven the soldiers, I told them.' Vandan chokes. 'But I have not forgotten. Christianity is one of the most strict religions. You have to forgive. But to forget…'

Susieyana clears the glasses, her face averted.

'Fifty-two splinters entered the vehicle, blocked mainly by the engine. Otherwise, I don't know what may have happened that day.' Vandan looks at me, his arms spread in a gesture of helplessness.

'My youngest died on the way to hospital. We were stopped at three places by the army.'

~

Justice Sen had been quite thorough. Brave even, given the time and place and the armed forces' and paramilitary's time-honoured initial response to anything: they did no wrong, acted appropriately, and it's all somebody else's fault.

As it turned out, Justice Sen ascertained a lot more.

The 16th Rashtriya Rifles, a force mainly used in Jammu & Kashmir to nearly as much bad blood as Assam Rifles face in the entire east, were on their way from Bishnupur in Manipur to Dimapur in a convoy of sixty-three vehicles strung out over five kilometres. The officers and men of Rashtriya Rifles claimed they were shot at and grenades were thrown at them. And so, they responded entirely in self-defence. Seven people were killed, all civilians; and twenty wounded, also all civilians. Vandan's family counted for an appreciable percentage of the casualties.

A report in *Economic and Political Weekly* from 1996, published a few months after the judge submitted his findings in March of that year, clinically lists Justice Sen's conclusions, based on several eyewitness reports and spot investigation by Kohima's superintendent of police. As the convoy passed through Kohima, it turns out that a tyre burst in one of the trucks spooked troopers in a particular section of the convoy into believing they had come under fire. They indiscriminately started firing bullets and mortar shells, and lobbing grenades. This continued for two hours. The Commission records 1,297 rounds fired by Rashtriya Rifles, and five mortar shells. Troopers also attacked property.

Nothing was recovered as incriminating evidence from the areas Rashtriya Rifles folk claimed they were attacked from.

It's a near-miracle that the five officers, fifteen junior

commissioned officers, and 400 regular troopers didn't all go berserk in a chain reaction, that some sense ultimately prevailed in command-and-control, or Kohima would have burnt again.

The judge looked into a couple of other incidents as well. There was one from January of 1995, when cadres of a Naga Army faction fired at the 15 Assam Rifles post in Akhulato in the Sümi tribal region north of Kohima. After more than an hour of exchanging fire, from a little before 4 in the morning, sixteen troopers went in search of the attackers. Not finding any, they forced people out of houses and burnt these down with kerosene as retribution for possibly harbouring the attackers. Then they fired at the wife of a farmer, killing her and blowing the hand off the three-month-old infant she was carrying.

Justice Sen held that Assam Rifles personnel were 'legitimate' in their initial response, but soon went completely out of hand, with 'unjustified' burning of houses and 'cold-blooded' killing.

The previous month, in December 1994, troopers of a patrol of 16 Maratha Light Infantry went berserk in Mokokchung, the main town of the Ao region. They were fired upon first by Naga rebels, and in an exchange of fire two each from either side were killed. Then the remainder of the patrol lost it. Using petrol they set fire to several shops and houses in the Police Point area of Mokokchung. Five Naga civilians were burnt alive. Four women were raped at gunpoint. Numerous people were beaten.

Justice Sen marked the patrol's initial response as 'fully justified and in no way excessive', but its subsequent overreaction as 'completely indefensible'.

As ever, the incidents marked the statistics of collateral damage, coddled by that other euphemism: fog of war. As ever, too, they marked the institutionalized dislike of a people.

Vandan brings me out to show where it happened. On the way I meet a shy Rebecca Senpilo, and Vandan's mother, who smiles toothlessly at me.

Vandan silently points out the perforations in the roof of the small verandah.

'She came and hugged me,' he speaks of young Soyingbeni. 'Then she went to hug her mother—over there.' He points to a place near a rusted iron pillar, a support for the roof. 'I felt something, something like sixth sense. I asked them all to go in. And then…' He looks at me, unable to go on.

And then the shell landed.

15

Into the cloud mountain: where rulers and rebels hold court

I wake to see heaven.

It isn't there in the room of Wokha's decrepit government-run tourist lodge, perched carelessly on a hill overlooking this town, the redoubt of the Lotha tribe. Heaven is just outside, bathed in the hesitant sharpness of new sunshine, caressed by a lingering chill from the deepest quiet of the night. It takes my breath away.

The peaks around us are misted over lightly, the warmth of the sun as yet inadequate to unravel the shroud completely. But the hills, as they cascade ever lower to the unseen plains to the west, where the horizon merges with the borderlands of Assam and Nagaland, rise from an ocean of white. They appear as hesitant islands here and there in the deep beauty and mystery of clouds that are as connected seas—each valley, every space between ridges an impenetrable white.

Belying the myth that no birds exist in Nagaland—residents have eaten all in their indiscriminate search for protein—I hear a songbird. But its tone is soft, perhaps awed by the day's heaven, perhaps muted by mist and cloud. There is no other sound. I close my eyes to absorb and save the image, the feeling, within me. A breeze touches my face as my favourite fleece travelling jacket cocoons me in its worn but comforting warmth. It's...

'Good morning, brother.' It's Mmhonlümo Kikon, jauntily emerging from his room. 'It's beautiful, isn't it?'

At another time I might have chided him for ruining the morning with understatement. But he is the reason I'm here, in fulfilment of a promise he made a couple of months earlier over revelry in Dimapur; so I smile instead. The caretaker of the lodge brings us fried eggs and tea. We settle on the steps in front of my room, like happy geckos letting the day wash over us. Bliss, such as it is.

'Yeah, a nice enough morning this late in the month of Nrungtsü,' I try to outcool him, showing off my very limited knowledge of the Lotha dialect, using the word for September gleaned from a calendar in Mmhonlümo's home in Kohima.

'So, brother, we'll go meet the DC—you remember?' he deadpans, outcooling me in turn. 'I have to meet him to sort out this issue with "IM".'

The leading faction of NSCN is a parallel administration here, much like many parts in the Naga regions and the deputy commissioner—DC—has to factor it in. As a local, and as a political aspirant among the Lotha tribe, Mmhonlümo has to try and play peacemaker, a soother of ruffled feathers. Whatever works. As ever, in his business it isn't enough to care; he needs to be seen to care.

We silently look upon the world, our modest but immensely satisfying breakfast done. Heaven is a fine thing as long as the illusion of it lasts, and it appears both of us want it to last a few desperate moments more.

I had pieced together the episode from recent reports in Naga-run newspapers and websites.

Residents of a village called Yikhum in Wokha district formed an action committee to protest alleged misappropriation of funds from the National Rural Employment Guarantee Scheme (now prefixed with an 'M' for Mahatma Gandhi, as if to sanctify the scheme's many proven ills in implementation). The fiddle had been committed by the chairman of the village panchayat and secretary of the Village Development Board. Villagers filed a Right to Information application with Nagaland's Department of Rural Development, seeking precise information about funds allocated and appropriated. The story goes that villagers were compelled to withdraw the RTI application under pressure from NSCN-IM. This happened in mid-September 2009—just weeks earlier as I visit Wokha in late October.

Yikhum villagers claimed that a former project director of the DRD and the local block development officer had visited NSCN-IM officials to put pressure on petitioners and protesters. So the 'action committee' with the backing of the villagers filed two petitions in the court of the deputy commissioner at Wokha, but these were turned down. Angered by this, action committee members burnt down the panchayat hall in the village in protest, on 16 September. This is significant as the panchayat hall is a symbol of government—the Government of India, as it happens.

The village chairman and Village Development Board secretary are said to have complained again to NSCN-IM functionaries, and this time NSCN-IM arrested one of the action committee members suspected to be the brain behind the incident. The NSCN-IM 'Town Command' in Wokha did this, in consultation with the central authority officer (CAO) in Wokha district—CAO is the equivalent of district commissioner or chief minister of a district in the IM setup. 'Town Commander' Major S.Y. Lotha was deputed to carry out the arrests on the order of the CAO.

Furious, on 18 September, villagers went up to the Town Command—I would soon see it, a nondescript building set on a rise in the middle of Wokha, across a small pond from which a road leads to Mount Tiyi College. Armed with daos, spears and whatever weapon they came by, villagers arrived in large numbers. Talk had it that villagers even managed to get hold of a grenade. They surrounded IM's Town Command. With the possibility of bloodshed looming—the Town Command would typically have ten to fifteen armed cadres; in case of major conflict, a brigade positioned about thirty-five kilometres away would be on call for reinforcement—the civil administration and civil society along with police defused the situation. But villagers insisted that their colleague be released by IM or they wouldn't budge. He was released.

That wasn't the end of it. The following day the person released asked one of his friends to issue a press statement saying that the civil administration and civil society had rescued him from the clutches of Major Lotha, the town commander. NSCN-IM was again upset, and arrested the two. When it became public in media, the organization clarified saying it was not an arrest, the two had merely been called in by the Town Command to have a 'discussion' to resolve issues. As I visit Wokha, one person remains in custody of the Town Command, and the situation is still tense, roiled by the implausible mix of corruption, a visible display of the influence of Naga rebel groups backed by arms, and the bizarre reality of some local government officials using a parallel administration to bail them out.

Why did NSCN-IM get involved? Technically, a complaint was made by the corrupt village chairman to the group—in its role as a parallel administration—after burning down of the panchayat hall which is paid for by the government. The complaint should ideally have been made to the deputy commissioner. But the complaint was, ironically, made instead to NSCN-IM. So, a simple matter of corruption and seeking refuge from justice and public anger became a complex prestige issue for the rebel group.

Such is the insanity of a conflict in limbo.

People's anger against both the government and rebels appears to finally have jostled the administration—the 'government' administration—to adopt face-saving measures. The deputy commissioner has taken up the petition of the action committee and conducted three hearings in the district court. But progress is slow. One or the other respondent is regularly absent. And the DC himself is 'busy', as I hear him say to a visitor: A Nagaland government-led culture and local-trade 'roadshow' in the district is scheduled for early November, and such preparation for Chief Minister Neiphiu Rio's move to gain popularity in each Naga region receives priority over everything else. So the DC is consumed, as are his most junior colleagues, the newly minted additional extra assistant commissioners—a unique species in these parts, indicating another aspect of Nagaland administration that is wholeheartedly approved by the Government of India: create government posts, give government jobs, buy peace. A purchase. A bribe.

Anyway, the news is that the panchayat chairman and Village Development Board secretary say they withdrew funds amounting to Rs 1 million, and gave it immediately to the project director. So, their plea is that they actually didn't take the money; they took it to pay off someone else. Now pressure is building up on the project director and block development officer to return the money to the village.

This happens only in Nagaland.

~

Will things change? I had asked Mhathung Kithan, Nagaland's blunt-talking home commissioner, a few days earlier, about the instance of dual administration that is also tied in with the state of talks between Naga rebels groups and the Government of India. Talk of 'packages' was about, aired primarily by Union Home Secretary G.K. Pillai during visits to the region in recent months. Such talk aimed at what such talk had aimed at these past twelve years: stay peacefully within the ambit of India's Constitution, or bust. Pressure talk. Stalemate talk.

'Things change,' Kithan had replied, lighting a cigarette and taking care to blow smoke away from me with a wave of hand, and continuing the same gesture to push some paper to the side of the table between us. 'One doesn't know whether any people who want independence will get it or not—and they may even agree to certain things short of sovereignty.' Seeing my raised eyebrows he smoothly clarified: 'Now these are all personal feelings.'

'Sure,' I had agreed, going with the Indian Administrative Service officer's gentle back-pedalling as his comments could be construed as being the official government stand. It was a small concession on my part—Kithan had opened up almost immediately, unmindful of a couple of visitors in his offices at the State Secretariat.

'Point here is what do *our* people want?' Kithan jabbed the cigarette in the air. 'There don't seem to be any clues, nothing indicating in any [degree of] clarity what our people want. If you ask me what *I* want, I know.' A wide smile. 'I am Naga. I know very well what I want. Any sensible Naga knows what he wants.'

I had let the point rest, riding a sense that the irrepressible bureaucrat would return to it during our conversation. Meanwhile, Kithan ploughed on, slamming rebel groups. 'All Nagas need to do is get rid of this movement. Nothing will come out of it. The whole movement has degenerated into individual or vested-interest groups trying to make hay or, rather, taking advantage of the situation, and feather their own nests'—he broke into Nagamese for emphasis: 'Eto hoye jaishe'. It happens.

'Except very few veterans of the so-called Underground—whether rightly or wrongly they have at least genuinely sacrificed everything—many have fallen by the wayside. Their objective is lost.' Most of the foot soldiers—young, driven, strongly indoctrinated—believe in the movement, Kithan conceded. But those who 'hang around the middle', they don't believe in the movement, 'only in enriching themselves and increasing their status'.

So where does it go from here?

'Parallel government has to go if Nagas have to go forward.' Kithan slapped the table. 'In whichever way. Say, this [rebel] leadership merges with the overground leadership in a new settlement. Lead the people as one body. But there has to be only one government.'

Any light at the end of that particular tunnel? I intervened.

He snorted, shaking his head. 'If the Government of India is willing to do it, human rights violations will be there.' He alluded to a theoretical strong-arm tactic of forcing the pace so that rebel groups have only two choices: return to fighting, or give up completely and formally join India's political mainstream. 'If they [the government] are ready to do that they can solve it.'

I had heard another top bureaucrat in Nagaland allude to a similar course of action. 'If the Government of India wants, it can settle this in two days'—the bureaucrat had admitted it was an exaggeration of sorts, but the general idea was correct. 'The leaders, except very few committed ones, will not go back to the jungle, because of their health, age, and the softness that has set in over the past ten to twelve years. And GOI—Government of India—knows where the leaders live, what they do, what they eat, when they sleep, who they meet, what they own, and have a fair idea of where they have their money. They can roll it up; shut it down. But that alone can't solve the problem.'

That conversation came back to me as I offered Kithan a weak 'But that won't really solve it, will it?', chilled at the prospect that it could have the opposite effect. While the Government of India's bulldozing of the rebels may put them in a defensive situation, the bloodshed and 'collateral damage' from such an operation could reignite Naga resentment and, in a worst-case scenario, a new Naga war, with nearby China gleefully watching a wedge being driven deeper into India's tense backyard.

'That's right, it won't really solve it,' Kithan agreed. 'But either *do* it, or *leave* it. Half measures will not work.'

Exasperation and anger spent, Kithan had lowered his tone. 'If this time the Government of India is really, really serious to solve it in the most understanding way, willing to compromise in the right sense of the term, it will also have to sacrifice, as will the Underground, who have to forego certain things. It has to be a package, where the ego of the Underground people will also have to be taken care of'—he slips into speakeasy Hindi—'basically, ego hai, na?'

But the Government of India is 'sticking to its position' and Naga groups are 'sticking to their guns', Kithan had shaken his head. 'That is not going to solve anything.' Then, unbidden, he strayed into territory I had been anticipating. Among other things, it again underscored the aching duality of wishful thinking and reality that many Nagas live with daily.

'I think many hardcore nationalists are also thinking the way many of us think: independence is not an answer now. Of course, I say if Nagaland were developed, if Naga people were able to stand on their own feet, if the government was good, we had fifty per cent of the officers with integrity, ten or twenty per cent of politicians with integrity, then even independence'—he slapped the table—'would be a reasonable demand.' This time he ignored my raised eyebrows. 'Whether the Government of India wants to give it or not is a separate issue, but as an individual I think that we have reasonable justification and we are not completely wrong in demanding independence.

'But today what can we *do* with independence?'—another slap of the table. 'It will be much better for us to remain with the Government of India, pull up our socks, clean our house and do real progress, real work for the people.'

The anger returned. 'I am sorry to say it but today Nagas are just like babies. India is carrying us on its back. We are eating whatever is being given. So what is sovereignty? You haven't even learnt to crawl, to use your thigh muscles or move your hands. So you are a nearly fifty-year-old baby.' He sighed, alluding to the birth of Nagaland as a state in 1963.

I had then shared with Kithan opinions I had heard in the course of several conversations and meetings. Among other things, that, on principle, people didn't wish the Underground ill because of their basic stand, to claim for Nagas both dignity and territory; and on account of India's grotesque manner in the past of dealing with that aspiration. But they were deeply disappointed with where the movement had arrived. And so, ironically, many people would not either forget atrocities that India's military and paramilitary committed, or forgive these; and yet, they somehow felt comforted with the presence of India's military and paramilitary as a counterbalancing force against the Underground. This, even in the current ceasefire mode.

Moreover, I hadn't sensed much clarity as to what 'freedom' would amount to. Needs seemed to be basic as in many other places in India, even in the Mainland, I had told Kithan: We want to be on par with other communities and people; we don't want to be dismissed as a sort of outcaste of the Republic of India. People want decent roads, jobs for their children, secure livelihoods. They want their pride protected. And they see the whole political process of ceasefire and negotiations as a circus. Younger people here as anywhere, I told Kithan, simply want to get ahead with their lives. They want to be successful.

'Let me ask you one question, as you're an Indian,' Kithan stopped me with a smile. 'Now this may sound funny because I am an Indian too, but for this discussion let's do a me-and-you.' He laughed. 'Just a figure of speech.'

I had joined in the laughter. 'Please go ahead. I'm comfortable with this reality.'

Kithan decided to immediately test my assertion. 'Should Nagas push for sovereignty or not?'

My response took surprisingly little effort and zero sense of shame—as I personally do not see seditious or criminal intent in righting historical wrongs. Independence for Nagaland may seem impractical right now, I replied in agreement with Kithan, especially as Nagaland didn't have systems in place, and perhaps the degree of professionalism and commitment that would be required to carry that dream forward. Perhaps, someday, if independence or greatly heightened autonomy is what the future holds out for Nagas, so be it. Besides, unless the Government of India adopts a brazen stance as China does with Tibet, it will find it difficult to brutalize Naga aspiration in the face of international public opinion this time around. But, in any case, Nagas first needed to come together to decide what was it, exactly, they wanted.

'For instance,' I passed the ball back to Kithan, 'do you see yourself as the home commissioner of independent Nagaland? Theoretically, all it would need is paperwork, but do you see yourself as belonging to an independent country?'

'It's like this.' Kithan had smiled his acceptance of the counter-query. 'We are just 1.5 million. But with commitment we can run the government, there is no problem. We would get enough funding. But [now] even with the Government of India's checks and balances we are not able to do anything—we are just swallowing everything. We are not ready. Look ...' He leaned across the table. 'Young people would like the problem to be solved, whichever way; they want things want to run smoothly. Here we are talking about elites. Among the elites leave out the bureaucrats—no, include the bureaucrats.' He shook his head, back to being exasperated. 'Why are people of the Underground respected?'

It was clearly rhetorical, so I waited for Kithan to continue. 'Because, number one,' he ticked off the reasons with a forefinger, 'they have guns. Second, all Nagas including myself, though I have my own logical reasons'—a look at two silent visitors in the room with us—'I still have my sentimental sympathy or my personal wish: if Nagaland were independent it would be good.'

He let me absorb that for a few seconds. 'How we use that independence or whether we would be able to survive is a different thing, but psychologically and sentimentally, I don't mind. So, we give them [the Underground] respect.' I nodded in understanding.

'Third, I feel for that kind of movement. I feel for independence, or sovereignty, or separate community of the Nagas—I favour that. But I have not been able to contribute to that. So if these people are fighting, okay, give them moral support. That's how two-three groups of people are thinking.'

Then he looped back to his earlier statement that Naga nationalist movements had degenerated.

'But no sensible Naga, even among bureaucrats, would as of today favour independence. In fact everybody would like to see the end of this factionalism, this whole Underground business. Difficult problem,' Kithan admitted, and pushed back from the table. 'I don't know if the Government of India is committed [to a solution]. But I do know that it is not stupid.'

'But are they being stupid about Nagaland?' I asked.

'Maybe I'm thinking too loud.' The bureaucrat sighed, waving a hand to urge me to take tea that had meanwhile arrived. 'Maybe they feel this is the right time to give a package and see what happens.' He sighed again. 'Even if we go today and commit in front of all the churches to straighten out, it will take ten years, maybe twenty years, because of the cancer that has got into our society.'

But you are the leaders, I said. Surely you can do something if you all try.

'Yes.' Kithan laughed his cynical laugh. 'We are the leaders.'

~

Mmhonlümo and I drop in at Mount Tiyi College after a visit to the deputy commissioner's office. My presence there was off-the-record, and anyway, the stultifying atmosphere of a government office under siege of paperwork and politics was enough to make me yearn again for fresh air.

I love the association of the college with Mount Tiyi. It is named after a hill in the Lotha region that, according to legend, is a repository of what several local publications politely term 'departed souls'. It seemed interesting to visit an institution that schools ongoing souls, as it were.

Chubatola Longkumer, the principal, warmly greets us in the open manner Nagas display to strangers who visit in peace, armed only with inoffensive curiosity. Her tiny office is in the rundown but neat old wing of the well-known local college. Across a playground a new, modern wing is taking shape, the concrete not yet yellowed with regulation paint. I look around as she offers tea, and laughs delightedly as Mmhonlümo and she practise the well-known Naga art of establishing six degrees of separation with the universe. As they trade names of mutual acquaintances, I look at framed prints of Indian icons on the wall: Mohandas Gandhi, Subhash Chandra Bose, Rajendra Prasad, Lal Bahadur Shastri. This place, about halfway to Mokokchung, the 'capital' of the Ao tribe—in the manner Wokha and nearby Longsa are to the Lotha tribe—was beset by Assam Rifles from the days of the British and more recently by India's official bestiality. But these icons, seen as being kind to Naga aspiration even though they solidly represent interests of the 'Mainland', sit naturally in this modest room.

It soon gets more convivial as K. Metha, a senior lecturer in history, joins us. Talk turns to the institution. Wrapping us in a grandmotherly smile, Chubatola allows the genial but intense history teacher to talk about the place, a pre-college to undergraduate institution that runs to twenty-two teachers and 350 students. Metha says a majority of the students are from nearby villages, from poor or relatively uneducated environments.

'The [state] education board often asks why, compared to

institutions in bigger towns, results here are relatively lower,' Metha says, and then spreads his hands in supplication. 'The point is that they have come up from a much lower base, and must therefore be given an opportunity.'

It's still the story of our times, as true here as it is in the 'Mainland'.

Mmhonlümo receives a call. A bus belonging to a local NGO, Centre for Youth and Social Action, that deals in raising awareness for prevention of malaria and HIV-AIDS, had been burnt a few days earlier, most likely a result of professional rivalry over funding and perceived success. Robin, the person who runs it, is distraught, Mmhonlümo tells us as he disconnects the call, and as a person who has opted to take his politics seriously—he says this to indulgent smiles from all of us—he must attend to the needs of his voters. It's time to leave Mount Tiyi College.

Robin is away on a sudden errand, we hear as we arrive at the rundown two-storeyed building that houses his tiny one-room office, past the hill from the college. A small bus sits outside on its rims, the tyres, like the bus—funded by Nagaland Aids Control Society—are burnt to a crisp. Neighbours tell us of Robin's problems with claiming insurance for the vehicle; about how the investigating officer from the local police station has come by to ask questions, but is as yet unable to provide answers from the clues a dumbfounded Robin provides.

Maybe he should ask the Town Command—the suggestion is at the tip of my tongue. But sarcasm won't solve this. I stay quiet.

We are rescued from the limbo of waiting for Robin by the administrator of the adjacent Springdale School which, as it turns out, was established by Mmhonlümo's family in 2002. His father, who started the school, has passed on; his mother lives in Dimapur with a younger brother, and another younger brother, an engineer, is posted by the government to Mon district. The school, Mmhonlümo explains, is run pretty much on autopilot by the principal and administrator. I'm taken on a tour in spite of my protests that I don't want to disrupt class.

'Learn and Lead', urges the motto of the school. The 'Thought of the Day', colourfully adapted from *Proverbs* 12:1 and meticulously written with chalk on a blackboard along a slim corridor of packed earth, is somewhat more blunt: 'Whoever loves instruction loves Knowledge, but he who hates Correction is stupid.'

Springdale School is a low, basic structure, a patchwork of brick, plank and thatch that works as a school as well as a hostel for about three dozen boys and girls who live in rooms behind the school. The principal is 'on leave' at present, the administrator who doesn't offer a name explains in broken English, but the school appears to be on smooth rails this Monday afternoon. Outside Class V, we overhear queries about the 'value breakup' of metre and centimetre. Tones of a lesson in flawless Hindi emerge from Class VII. Surprised, I'm taken and introduced to the teacher, Smriti Sharma, and her class of about twenty children.

'She is a Meitei from Agartala in Tripura, married to a Sharma—a Nepali—and teaches Hindi in Wokha,' Mmhonlümo grins as he tells me, matching the grins all around. 'Interesting, eh?'

I read on the blackboard a sentence typical of Hindi textbooks, as familiarly stilted and formal as from my long-ago days at school: 'Patna station par kavi ke swagat ke liye bahut badi bheed ikaththi ho gayi thi aur...' A large crowd had gathered to greet the poet at Patna station, and...

Another, a classroom marked VIII, was evidently discussing geography in response to questions in neat cursive marked on the blackboard.

'Why is "Indian Subcontinent" called so?'

'Which factors influence Indian weather?'

But the classroom is given over this afternoon to the school choir, practising for annual day functions the following week. A dozen girls dressed in sky-blue skirts, white tunics knotted with red ties, navy pullovers, spotless white socks and black shoes, break into giggles as we troop in and Mmhonlümo requests a song for the visitor—me. They hesitatingly break into song, and gradually gather momentum in rousing, perfect harmony.

'So many people who can't understand why we are so happy and free
We have crossed over Jordan to Canaan's fair land,
And this is like heaven to us...'

~

I think of it all on the ride back to Kohima, on Highway 61—a brief departure from my happening highway, Number 39. Conflicting and yet seamless images and impressions from Wokha that demand equal attention in my camera, my voice recorder, my memories. It is morning, and it is beautiful, quite unlike the pitch dark as I left Kohima for Wokha some days earlier. But there is a common thread: I am still in search of understanding, and with Mmhonlümo driving, we careen along hairpins that mark the highway.

As ever, reality is manifold. I recall Thungbeni, the feisty former president of the Lotha Women's Hoho, fire in her eyes and ice in her voice, telling stories of her longtime vocal and physical opposition to the heavy-handedness of both India's administration and of NSCN-IM.

What drives you, I had asked her. Rage? Anger? Desperation?

'All that you say,' Thungbeni replied, eyes flashing. 'And hatred. We must not forget hatred.'

Her voice had softened with another kind of pride as she spoke of her eldest daughter working in New Delhi, and two younger ones deposited at boarding school at a branch of Delhi Public School in Numaligarh, the small refinery town at the head of Highway 39. As I talked to her, I couldn't again help thinking that, if Indian policymakers had bothered to understand that Nagas too had hearts and minds, the wars wouldn't have been fought.

I recall Nyambemo Ngully, an elder of the tribe and a member of Forum for Naga Reconciliation, speaking in gentle tones about persistent rebellion, war, and the need for honourable reconciliation both among Nagas, and between Nagas and India.

There was Vyasan R., the freshly minted Indian Administrative Service officer in Wokha, wide-eyed with enthusiasm and at the same time burdened with schizophrenic reality, as he asked me with deadpan irony: 'So, have you visited the Town Command?'

I recall Mmhonlümo's aunt making available a room for me in her home in the dead of night—the gracious yet simple acceptance that her nephew's friend is like her nephew and, anyway, a guest cannot be turned away. On the morning of our departure, she stood in the courtyard of her home, bamboo racks laden with squash in the background, wishing me safe journey in Nagamese—'Bhal korey jaabi, deh?'—with the stern affection that a matron seems to employ effortlessly.

And I recall our stop at a memorial only a few minutes earlier, between the Lotha Naga village of Longsa and the Rengma Naga village of Kandiniu. Assam Rifles went to town here, but this time, nobody destroyed the marker that would have on another occasion immediately become the target of anti-India anger. The hurt of Nagas killed by Nagas went deep, and no faction, even one as powerful as NSCN-IM, would risk messing with that hurt. Below the image of crossed spears and mithun-head is a simple message:

'In memory of fellow innocent citizens who became the victims of bomb blast conspired by inhuman criminals on the ill-fated bus coming from Dimapur on 18th December 2000.

URENI MURRY
MARLYN TSANGLAO
BITHUNGO ODUYO
TSAMONGO ODUYO'

They died in retaliation for an incident earlier that year when Wokha villagers, angered by the heavy-handedness of NSCN-IM cadres, thrashed to death two of them (a reprise that could so easily have happened just days ago in an angry play of People versus the Town Command).

As Mmhonlümo and I spiral downward through the sea of mist, with weak, early light touching the tips of leaves and frequent rhododendron petals, there will be other reminders of this new-old Nagaland. From here to just before Botsa, Chief Minister Rio's constituency, the road will resemble a post-earthquake strip of tar; a close relative of Rio's is a contractor for the project, but the project, like so many others, will take its time, or will probably be completed only on paper. As we make our way to the new stadium that heralds the modern strip of suburban Kohima, we shall pass the homes of contractors, Nagaland's—as well as the Northeast's—premier citizens. I will learn to use a new and quite simple skill: try and tell which home belongs to a '2nd Class' contractor, which to a '1st Class' one; and no guesses for contractors of the 'Super Class'. But it is easy to get confused these days. Several large houses belong to bureaucrats.

Kithan, the tough-talking home commissioner, had stressed that part.

'Tell me, honest to God,' he had shot off in his typical no-nonsense manner. 'Today you see so many buildings in Dimapur and Kohima.'

'Oh yes,' I had agreed in anticipation.

'To whom do these belong?'

'I've been told, and shown, that many belong to ministers. I've been told that others belong to town planners, kilonsers'—here I referred to ministers in rebel administrations—'contractors...'

'Roughly, and it is my own estimation, of all these houses, eighty per cent belong to bureaucrats.' He slapped the table for emphasis. 'In Dimapur, the big buildings, shops or homes, belong to bureaucrats. Five per cent may belong to businesspeople. Fifteen per cent belongs to the ministers. That's the problem.

'Who owns most of the big tracts of land?' He had carried on. 'The bureaucrats. Farms are losing money but people are buying farms as an investment to park illegitimate money. And they don't care.'

He had nearly begun to froth. 'If I can earn one *crore* a *year* without lifting a *finger*, why should I slog my *ass* for a few lakhs?' He spat: '*Bullshit.*'

I had tried to make a joke of it. 'If all people speak like you, independence won't be too far off.'

Kithan had laughed, but it was strained. 'Every year they will be spending more than a crore of rupees to make a brothel out of our beautiful building'—he waved an arm about the room to mean Nagaland's Secretariat. 'It has become a source of income for some of our people. They won't bat an eyelid if you ask them to modify everything here. They will do it tomorrow because there is money in it.'

How does a person like you keep a job like this? I had asked, visibly astonished.

Kithan just laughed.

~

Mmhonlümo has promised food at a spot a few bends along the road, closer to Kohima than Wokha. There is a small eatery run by a fellow tribesman, he explains. In all likelihood we shall eat a simple breakfast of rice, pork, squash, dal, and pickle hot enough to make the devil canter in midwinter. It's something to look forward to, a soft landing between now and later, between the stunning scenery of the Naga hills and the sapping concrete of Kohima.

'What's up, brother?' Mmhonlümo queries my pensiveness.

'Nothing, brother,' I reply automatically, unmindful for a change of his driving, now one-handed, and conducted with supreme nonchalance. 'Sometimes this conflict business catches up. Please play that song one more time, neh?'

'Okay, brother.'

He thumbs his mobile phone again to life, playing a classic, cherished song that he copied off fiery Thungbeni's phone with a Bluetooth application the previous evening—she had it as a ring tone. And so, accompanied by haunting mist, long-forgotten Mahendra Kapoor achingly sings the hit from 1968, a time when I was a child and the Naga wars were already old. The song is from the movie *Kismat*. Fate. As we drive on, the words visit the absence of love and loyalty in a place of a million hearts:

> '*Laakhon hai yahaan dilwale, aur pyaar nahin milta*
> *Aakhon mein kisi kee wafaa ka ikraar nahin milta...*'

16

The system of factions, and the game of winner-takes-all

In Nagaland it doesn't do to meet one rebel group and not the other—at the very least, the main ones—so the call from J comes as a huge relief.

I've met him off and on at the residence of a mutual acquaintance in Dimapur. J is the public affairs officer of NSCN (Unification)—formed when a faction violently broke away from NSCN (I-M) and joined the rival Khaplang faction. Our conversation would typically be in the evenings, over sweetened tea, the pistol tucked into J's waistband glinting dully in the harsh light of a plastic Chinese lamp—the power seemed to be out most evenings in Dimapur. J's weapon was a ready reminder that the wounds of faction-fighting had not healed. Watched by two stony-faced, tense colleagues, the postgraduate in English literature from Delhi's Jamia Millia University politely checked me out for political beliefs injurious to the health of his organization. Satisfied that I carried nothing more than a notebook, recorder, camera and the urge to tell a story, he had promised several weeks earlier to carry my request for a meeting to his organization's leadership.

I am in Kohima at the end of October 2009 when the word

comes: Kughalu Mulatonu, the Emissary of the Collective Leadership and brother-in-law of Kitovi Zhimomi, the 'prime minister' of the united Khaplang faction, has agreed to meet me. The meeting will take place the next morning, the 30th, at Kehoi Camp near Dimapur.

'Are you happy, my friend?' J asks, solicitous as ever, over a scratchy mobile phone connection.

'Very happy, J. I don't know how to thank you.'

'You don't need to thank me. I'm only doing my duty.'

I'm excited enough to even look forward to the nerve-wracking drive down to Dimapur late at night, brave bad roads, bad drivers, and bad hairpin bends.

I turn left at Diphupar's 4th Mile turn-off, using Dimapur Central Jail as the first landmark to Kehoi camp. It is less fancifully named than the main IM camp, Hebron, but there are enough biblical markers to show me the way: heading south from Dimapur, I pass signs for Gilead Home, Manna Fast Food Centre, the Bethesda School and an obscured sign that shows only the first word: Papyrus—

Kehoi is a new home for this branch of the Unification faction. Its former camp at Vihokhu village, which we reach after passing the large bulk of the Referral Hospital, was completely destroyed the previous year by a wave of IM cadres bent on revenge for what they saw as an act of massive betrayal largely by Sümi members of IM. The landscape of these brief plains, a mix of great fields of harvested and soon-to-be-harvested paddy that stretch towards low hillocks, which in turn walk their way up to the forbidding bulk of the Naga Hills, camouflages so well the blood and animosity.

This is 'mian country', my guide tells me, explaining the numerous men we see wearing lace skull-caps, beards and lungis, seemingly an oddity in these parts. He refers to Muslim immigrants from Bangladesh who freely move about and live in this region. Here, they are largely retained by Sümi gentry to farm their lands. They go to Sümi schools, my guide explains, they learn English and the Sümi dialect. This, in the middle of contested Naga lands, is their home.

Thirty minutes on, past Vihokhu, I can see Kehoi in the distance, glinting roofs on a hillock at the base of the main range of hills, its location giving it a vantage for several miles. Spotting another landmark to Kehoi camp, I urge my driver off-road and onto a track of crushed stone and earth. A guard post quickly arrives, manned by India Reserve Battalion personnel. Troops here appear relatively relaxed; metal shields in the guard post with firing slits cut into them signify serious purpose, but the scene of combat boots drying in the sharp sun, and a trooper using a small fishing net to snare protein supplements from a nearby stream suggest an idyll brought on by a lull in fighting between the Naga factions.

We cross another stream over a wooden bridge. Rutted tracks lead us in switchback spirals up the hillock. It smacks of new-camp, still being shaped. A bulldozer busily flattens the track ahead of a sandbagged guard post. I can see makeshift huts of new thatch and woven bamboo, and new aluminium roofs. The Unification guard post looks new too, freshly arranged sandbags nestling a machinegun and a group of alert guards bristling with automatic weapons, mostly AK-series rifles. I'm expected, and allowed to pass after a brief check of ID and rapid exchange of dialect over walkie-talkies.

The camp looks quite empty. My guide explains that Unification cadres would be on patrol much like their former colleagues in IM, walkabout in the jungles and nearby villages to establish and maintain dominance. We arrive at a modest-sized clearing cut into the hillside. It serves as a parking lot—several Mahindra Scorpio SUVs are resident—and space for a number of huts. Cadres in full combat gear and AKs, their tunics with patches on the chest that simply proclaim 'Naga Army' but with the faction's distinctive red-and-green stripe, surround our car. A cadre escorts my guide and me along a dirt track, moving uphill till we come to another collection of huts. I'm asked to wait outside the largest one. Guards, fresh-faced youngsters, have taken positions around it. Our escort nods at the hut and then paces about with a handgun as I walk in.

~

Mulatonu is a small, dapper man, in a half-sleeved shirt and a tie held firm with silver tie-pin. A jacket is draped on the back of his chair, the only one behind a long table. Four chairs are placed before it. He rises and comes around the table to greet me with a tight smile. A regulation pistol is tucked into his waistband. Handshake over, Mulatonu settles back into his chair, behind him a Naga Army flag pinned to the bamboo weave that makes up the wall of the hut. A notepad, a pen and a notebook computer covered in brown cloth sit on the table. His watch—it looks like an Omega or Baume & Mercier, but I could be wrong—catches a little sun through the bamboo lattice work and winks at me. That is the only flash in his attire, all plain blue.

With his fingers steepled he fixes me with a stare, and I recall what I've heard about Mulatonu: he has a reputation of being matter-of-fact, very clever, highly astute, and, when necessary, quite lethal.

I don't mess about, preferring to quickly get down to business and keeping to a minimum my opening spiel about the privilege of meeting him and to be able to take the story of his organization to the 'Mainland' and elsewhere.

My use of the magic word brings a terse smile. 'We are also looking forward to meeting Mainland Indians, those who personally come to get a sense of the situation, so that people get to know the facts rather than confront themselves with emotional contradictions.'

I've heard the thought put in many ways, but not as colourfully as now. As I will soon discover, iron-fist-in-flowery-velvet-glove is the preferred modus for Mulatonu. How does his faction plan to take the movement ahead? I ask him. Things are extremely fluid, aren't they?

'It is true that people change, politics change and the economy changes,' he allows. 'However, every political leader of the Nagas—every Naga leader—has to know that with change things collide: perceptions, conceptions, strategies and ideologies.' Between the twentieth and twenty-first centuries there have been some 'strategic changes in the pursuit of Naga sovereignty', he continues, setting up the first hit. 'The flexibility in the change and the plight of the Nagas might have divided aspirations of the Nagas by some leaders—especially our counterpart, the IM faction.'

I understand, I automatically murmur, urging him on. He doesn't disappoint.

'We must be very clear that when strategies and ideologies collide, they don't coexist. If leaders talk too much about the strategies and leave aside the ideologies of the people and the cause—the nation—it leads to a downfall. I think the world is clear about the strategic misconceptions that have been undertaken by the IM group. But we will never do that—deviate from the ideological principles of the Nagas: that is sovereignty.' He smiles. 'We have the IM viewpoint that the strategic goal is economic independence. Mr G.K. Pillai, the home secretary of India, has created another synonym for it, economic packages. We call these strategic deviations…'

'From your ultimate goal?'

'We want the world to know there is a struggle, and that struggle is for sovereignty,' Mulatonu snaps. 'And we will never deviate from this principle, whether we achieve it today or not. It will be won even if it takes another thousand years.'

It's a slim window of opportunity; I move in. So, does he believe the exercise of reconciliation as undertaken by Forum for Naga

Reconciliation can ultimately be successful? Or is it merely a let's-try-to-understand-one-another sort of gambit?

Mulatonu answers in a roundabout way. He first trashes the 1960 accord which led to the birthing of the 'so-called puppet state government in Nagaland' three years later, and trots out the Naga nationalist line that all the Naga regions, both in present-day India and Myanmar, are not historically part of any dominion. Administration in British times, already quite scant, stopped at Zunheboto, a short distance to the northeast of Kohima. From there to the 'tens of thousands of square kilometres' extending right to the borderlands of Kachin regions deep inside Myanmar remained Naga. He then moves to pronounce judgement on efforts at Naga reconciliation, using the analogy of India and Pakistan.

'The British tried their utmost to unite the Hindu Congress and the Muslim League led by [Mohammad] Ali Jinnah. However, it could not happen and you had India, Pakistan, and later, Bangladesh. You see,' Mulatonu leans forward, agitated, 'reconciliation is a form of political concept; it is just a bypass, a pattern of bringing political parties together. However, if things do not go well, if there are clashes or crises between strategies and ideologies'—he stops to let the growl of an off-road vehicle fade—'this Forum for Naga Reconciliation will end there. We will have to see whether FNR is an emotional concept or a political, social and economic one. Unless and until this FNR is in a position to give leverage to political aspirations of the Nagas, it cannot survive.'

Tellingly, Mulatonu echoes the sentiments of the IM leader I met a couple of months earlier, Gen. Phungthing. (He had broken out into laughter when I quizzed him about his take on the photo-ops between different Naga factions that FNR meetings had brought about.) And, even as FNR attempts to move ahead, I ask of Mulatonu, there is also the Naga Common Platform. A senior politician, a driving force of the Naga Common Platform, had told me in Kohima just the past week that FNR is about 'spiritual reconciliation among Nagas'. Once that is done, I was given to understand, Naga Common Platform would step in and tell FNR the equivalent of 'Okay, well done, you've done your job. Now we will—because we can—deliver meaningful political solution.'

I also share the second point of view I heard during my other interactions with players: let FNR do its job, and if spiritual bonding evolves into a process for political settlement, so be it; let FNR be the platform to take it ahead. No harm in trying to see if it works.

Mulatonu cuts me short. 'Anybody trying to contradict the steps taken by FNR to be a motivation for political or economic affairs would be out of the loop, out of the book.' He ignores the loud pinging announcing a message on his mobile phone. 'There are some hints that some from the backdoor are trying to organize this Naga Common Platform.'

It is common knowledge that it is energized by the Nagaland government—senior members of Chief Minister Rio's party are the voices for Naga Common Platform. Mulatonu comes at that truth at a sharp angle, and pins that to a larger point. 'Now I would clearly convey my message to the so-called sponsors, the Government of India, and the puppet state government: *we* are the ones who have given blood and sweat for the sovereignty of Naga people. *We* are the ones who will settle the Indo-Naga political problem with the Government of India. Spectators have to remain outside the field and watch. We the players will play our own game and give the results.'

Eager for more insight here I shamelessly lay on some flattery. He's a bit of a born diplomat, I say, even though the way he talks would make him out to be anything but. Mulatonu laughs, but I can't gauge whether he is seemingly pleased or he has seen through my ruse. So I back-pedal a bit. 'But you speak with a great deal of frankness, and that is refreshing.' He is still smiling. It sets up my question.

Surely his organization must have a short- to medium-term approach besides the stated long-term approach of sovereignty. What is the Khaplang group's view on the way the entire endeavour, the game, could play out?

Sovereignty is not only the problem of the Nagas, he replies, quite unflappable. 'It is also the problem of the Government of India.' He explains it using a potent crutch of history: the sovereignty of India did not lie with Indians alone. It was the 'common problem' of both the British and Indians.

'It was the British parliament that stood up and said, "India should be given freedom." Why don't Indian parliamentarians, who have learnt so much from Great Britain, stand up in parliament and say "It is time to give freedom to Nagas?"' Mulatonu spreads his hands. 'When we have the capacity and the time to solve the problem, I think it will be very unwise to leave the problem that can be solved today as a problem for tomorrow.'

So what would be his strategy to make it so? I ask, at the cost of appearing naïve, to again drive at the issue of Naga reconciliation. Talks at this level take place between entities as much as between people. Among Naga factions even as the goal may be one, there are several approaches to that goal. Shouldn't these approaches move from several approach-avenues to a goal-highway, as it were, so that talks and negotiations become easier? If ever, in a gigantic leap-of-faith scenario, the UN were to come in as mediator between the Naga factions and India, wouldn't a uniform entity, or, at least, entities with broadly similar approaches and goals make more sense?

Mulatonu uses proverbs to dismiss the claims and actions of competing factions. 'Beggars have many bags,' he offers. 'Kings have only one royal seat.' I look politely blank. He tries again: 'And there is a common saying that a coward dies many deaths before he actually dies.' I smile to hide my incomprehension.

With an exasperated sigh he launches the attack. He refers to members of the Naga National Council committing themselves to the Constitution of India in 1975, with the Shillong Accord. This, I know, was designed to conclusively end the rebellion. The Government of India greatly pressured some Naga rebel leaders to join its club—but it ultimately led to the birthing of the parent NSCN rebel group, with leaders like Isak Swu, Thuingaleng Muivah and S.S. Khaplang perceiving the accord as a sell-out to Indian interests. And so, as a rebel, Mulatonu remains leery of the intent of those of the NNC 'group' who speak for a Naga future.

'If they are not satisfied living in the house they have created for themselves, they should break it,' Mulatonu snarls. 'They cannot exist in a Kohima transit camp of 1975 [a 'peace camp' where some surrendered rebels were rehabilitated] and say they are somebody—when they are nobody. Again, it would be very unwise for the Government of India to say these "peace-campers" or anybody [like them] are part of the [current] negotiating process.

'Secondly,' he ticks off the response on his fingers, 'the IM group has had talks with the Government of India for the past twelve years; more than seventy rounds of talks.' He taps the table. 'The loser does not get a trophy; he may not even reach the finishing line. *Seventy rounds* of talks in twelve years.' He shakes his head. 'What is the point of running without reaching the final point?'

I refrain from pointing out that he was recently part of that faction. And that, even the Khaplang faction, of which he is now a part, has been in ceasefire with the Government of India since 2001 without moving ahead in any significant manner towards the goal of sovereignty that Mulatonu so forcefully claims. But the time to flag that is later. Now is the time to gauge his reaction to the process of Naga reconciliation, and IM's repeated claim that it alone speaks in the true voice of Naga aspiration.

'So why should they claim the trophy?' Mulatonu continues. 'And when the Government of India has done so much—has fed them so much, fattened the IM with Indian masala—why should the Government of India say that IM exists?' He smirks to underscore the sarcasm. 'Every Tom, Dick and Harry cannot become national fighters.' This is explosive stuff in the atmosphere of Naga reconciliation.

I steer the conversation towards the what-if of Naga independence, and his faction's interpretation of Nagalim. (To my mind, this independence, though difficult, is not impossible. East Timor happened as recently as 2002, breaking its turbulent bond with Indonesia. The region around the Horn of Africa is going through country-birthing pangs as Mulatonu and I meet. Over time, maps could well change closer to home.)

'If, theoretically,' I begin, 'there is some day a free Nagaland—or Nagalim, or whatever you wish to call it—how will that work? Will it be the area that constitutes present-day Nagaland, or will it include contiguous Naga areas in present-day Arunachal Pradesh, Manipur and Assam?'

Mulatonu replies after a few seconds, and it surprises me with its sense of realism, the difference between 'party-line' rhetoric used to fill media, and the nuance of ground-level practicality.

'See, it would be foolish on the part of somebody to claim, "Everything is mine." I should be satisfied with "what *should* be mine". If you look at the map of Germany, you will see some Germans living in Austria, some Germans living in France.'

And some in Switzerland, I add.

'Switzerland,' he agrees. 'People have to differentiate between sovereignty and integration. What can be a part of sovereign Nagaland will remain intact as it is. What is not achievable [becomes] a non-issue. There are freedom fighters from Assam fighting for their homeland; there are freedom fighters in Manipur. They are giving their blood and sweat for the sovereignty of their homeland. Why should we try to pre-empt or pre-judge the sovereignty of the people fighting for their own [homeland], who are also in a struggle like us? But Nagas living in Arunachal—we call it Arunagachina, because it is a part of India; Nagas also claim a part of Arunachal as a part of Nagaland; China also claims it as China—are different.' Mulatonu grins, evidently pleased to have stuck this figurative stiletto into the abdomen of India's geopolitical claims, and then offers a palliative of sorts.

'I've given a clear instance of Manipur and Assam, where people are giving their blood and sweat like us, it would be political, and a non-issue on our part to claim that their land is our land, and their people are our people. We cannot do that.'

The implication of what he says sinks in. For instance, the Naga 'struggle' in Manipur is largely led by the Tangkhul-heavy IM. Agreeing to a Nagalim that keeps out of its ambit Naga territories in Manipur would immediately localize that problem as a Manipuri-Naga issue. It would also be a neat way of limiting the IM in a future Nagaland/Nagalim. It was a move held in check in this game of chess. The Government of India would be delighted with a play like this, as it supported its preferred divide-to-rule approach for conflict resolution.

Mulatonu reverts to rhetoric, and with a twist that Indian security mandarins are acutely aware of.

'But if in the name of peace and ceasefire, the Government of India tries to destroy the fabric of the Nagas, it would force the Nagas to take to a more violent struggle,' he says. 'And it would compel the Nagas to get involved with countries which are of more superior power than India. So India has to think specifically: does this problem have to be solved peacefully, or does it have to be solved violently? If it is to be done peacefully, there is no problem. But if it is to be done violently, with full-scale war, Nagas cannot bear the expenses. So Nagas will have to take the help of other countries—and the Government of India knows which countries.' That's easy enough. China. Pakistan. In weakened moments of India's neighbourhood bonding, some hard-line Islamist faction in

Bangladesh's defence forces and polity. Perhaps a disgruntled faction of the army in Myanmar.

Mulatonu is now in full flow. There are several hundred thousand graduates and postgraduates in Nagaland, he snaps. Why doesn't India realize the prospect such a human resource windfall can bring? Why doesn't India appreciate the natural resources of Nagaland? Why doesn't India realize Nagaland has enough tourism opportunities to benefit the economies of both Nagaland and India?

'Why doesn't India think of granting sovereignty to the Nagas and make Nagaland one of its most peaceful neighbours, rather than keeping it as a bedbug, by keeping it forcefully as a part of India?'

Speaking of sovereignty—I try another tack to gauge his faction's thinking—India may need assurances. Given geopolitical necessities in the region, India would probably look for assurances like it has from Bhutan, where the government is free to do what it wants, but for defence- and foreign affairs-related issues it seeks the advice of India. The combination of India's concern and paranoia over China may demand nothing less from a theoretical Nagalim.

Mulatonu is up to the game. 'If the Government of India says "we want [control of] foreign affairs, military/defence affairs"; suppose India were to deploy its armies in Nagaland more than what is there at present—if that infuriates China and happens to provide an invitational spark, will that benefit India and Nagaland?'

'No.'

'No. So, why not have peaceful relations among India and Nagaland rather than something that would destroy both India and Nagaland? If sovereignty is granted to Nagas that will only make the Nagas turn to India. But if this struggle carries on, it will force Nagas to go closer to China.'

'I appreciate this...' I begin, but Mulatonu cuts in.

'Nagas are very suspicious of the intentions of India. Secondly, I as a Naga leader feel the very weakness of India. Let's take the example of Sri Lanka. India failed with the LTTE and failed with IPKF. Take Nepal. India failed with its policy there.' He pauses as a cadre brings a tray full of orange-flavoured soda and tiny apples. At his invitation I take an apple: it's delicious.

'Take Pakistan.' Mulatonu delicately sips the soda. 'Every day Indian soldiers are dying fighting Pakistan. Its soldiers are committing suicide—theek hai?' He uses the Hindi phrase popular with Nagas, and twists the knife. 'This has come as a blessing for India, to solve the unemployment problem.' He waves a hand. 'Why doesn't India solve problems, instead of creating more problems? India has shown that it has failed to protect Jammu & Kashmir right from 1947. It had to accept the Line of Control with Pakistan. It has had to accept the Line of Actual Control with China. India could not stop China from taking Tibet—theek hai? If tomorrow China takes Bhutan, will India be in a position to defend the sovereignty of Bhutan?'

It will be difficult, I say. It is difficult to assert otherwise; nearly all security assessments of note in India and overseas don't give India's efforts a leaf's chance in a cyclone were that to happen.

'So tell me, which neighbour should depend on the Government of India to survive? If a war breaks out with China tomorrow, Nepal will never side with India, because Nepal knows India will not send enough support to protect the sovereignty of Nepal. So when India has failed to protect any or all of its so-called protectorate states'—Mulatonu stops for a sharp intake of breath, a habit he displays in mid-talk—'which neighbour should once again trust India?'

I remain quiet.

'India should protect its own sovereignty where it can,' Mulatonu says as a farewell message, 'and leave areas where it's not applicable.'

Our conversation over, Mulatonu guides me to the door of the hut and then retreats inside.

I take the opportunity to chat with the cadre who escorted me to the meeting—he turns out to be Mulatonu's PSO, or personal security officer—and his colleagues, some of whom lounge about in the courtyard, cleaning handguns.

They explain what is what. There are two 9mm handguns, and a .32 calibre one. One 9mm is a Smith & Wesson, the other a Spanish Star with Burmese army markings. The .32, also of Spanish manufacture, is an Astra.

Fifteen rounds in the magazine of the 9mms, I am told. The .32 holds thirteen. I heft each weapon in turn, as they all gather around, smiling, clearly amused at my curiosity.

For a few moments it's a schoolboy thrill for me. Then, suddenly chilled, I hand back the killing machines and take care to smile as I say my farewells.

~

In a place of conflict, as I have learnt the hard way over the years, it pays to smile. Especially now, as I know what their leaders know.

Reconciliation is a necessary eyewash, I had heard one Naga rebel leader say recently. In reality it is all about 'winner-takes-all', he had bluntly stated, when it comes to which faction will move ahead in the game to stake claim over every aspect of a present and future Nagaland.

I knew too from sources, and conversation with senior officials at the Ministry of Home Affairs, that India's security mandarins and 'spooks' knew well this subterranean, seething reality and, as always, were keen to leverage this towards an end where India emerged as the winner that takes all.

And so, Naga-versus-Naga would do just fine.

17

Stories of fire, fear, and loathing—and a party in surreal Imphal

It's a fairly long walk from activist and women's rights commentator Nandini Thockchom's office in Paona Bazar to Professor Arambam Lokendro's house. One of central Imphal's signature open sewers brings me north to the busy market crossroads of Wahengbam Leikai. Ima Keithel and Kangla Fort are to my right—the east. I turn left onto Sagolband Road, known for the cluster of booths that sell tickets for the interminable rides to Jiribam, Silchar and Aizawl; and the Aryan Theatre, Professor Lokendro's former redoubt, established way back in 1935.

I'm keen to meet the professor. At one time he along with Ratan Thiyam and Heisnam Kanhailal formed the troika of cutting-edge multi-form Manipuri theatre. The three hugely respected, elderly cultural czars have since gone their own ways. Thiyam is mostly in New Delhi, a formidable presence since my university days of attending stylized dance-drama performances in the capital's theatre hub around Mandi House. The maverick, reclusive Kanhailal works in Manipur. His radical production *Draupadi*, based on a short story by litterateur and tribal rights activist Mahasweta Devi, in which the character of Draupadi disrobes screaming protest at the dominating cruelty of men, is still a controversial talking point in these parts. And the professor, a former teacher of history at Manipur University, is by any account a vast, lucid repository of folklore, history, politics and commentary.

There is an added impulse as far as I am concerned. His elder brother Somorendro was the co-founder and later, chairman of United National Liberation Front.

After several hundred metres along the dusty road I finally find the turning into the slim lane of Meino Leirak. The house I'm looking for is a minute's walk away, behind a rusted gate painted green. There's a small crowd gathered in front of the low L-shaped house, on a space set apart from the packed earth of the compound with concrete flooring: it looks to be part open-air lounge, part rehearsal space. The elderly professor is seated at a large table overflowing with books, brochures and cups of tea. The others, mostly women—I recognize a few Meira Paibi leaders from the women's groups that have taken the lead in enforcing prohibition of liquor as well as political protest in Manipur—are ranged in a circle of plastic chairs around the professor. All wear serious expressions. It looks like a council of war, but as I discover, it's really to insist on peace.

The hopefully named Just Peace Foundation is meeting to discuss final points for the 'Festival of Hope, Justice and Peace' to commemorate Irom Sharmila completing nine years of her hunger strike. I already have an invitation to the events beginning 2 November 2009—two days away—at Jawaharlal Nehru Manipur Dance Academy. The invitation has a sketch of an angry face with blazing eyes, skirted with unkempt hair. 'Ushering in the 10th year of hunger strike against Armed Forces (Special Powers) Act, 1958', the invitation announces below Sharmila's portrait. Her name isn't mentioned anywhere. There is no need. In the manner of iconic individuals, Sharmila's face is well known here.

'Come, come.' Professor Lokendro is all smiles. We can't really talk today, he tells me. 'I forgot that we had called this meeting at the same time. So could we meet tomorrow morning, say 9 a.m.?'

No problem, I assure him. Meanwhile, maybe I'll learn something at the meeting he has going. He immediately involves me in his grandfatherly way, and from time to time looks to me as if for approval. I nod dutifully, realizing that he is taking the trouble to conduct his part of the conversation in English for my benefit. Those present address the professor as 'oja', for teacher.

Mahasweta Devi will be the chief guest, I see from the programme as the buzz of the meeting continues. She will also release a book on Sharmila, *Burning Bright: Irom Sharmila and the Struggle for Peace in Manipur*, written by my contemporary at college, Deepti Priya Mehrotra. Yumnam Mangol Devi, better known as Ima Mangol, a formidable and respected Meira Paibi leader will also be there.

Sharmila's brother Irom Singhajit walks in then, a stout, smiling man, dressed in a worn pair of trousers, frayed shirt, jacket and scuffed shoes. I know him from Deepti's book. He gave up his job in the state's agriculture department to look after his younger sister Sharmila, and fight her battles outside as she continues her protest in incarceration in a heavily guarded room in an Imphal hospital, fed these nine years through a plastic tube inserted into a nostril.

'We're in a critical condition,' Professor Lokendro tells me during a break in the meeting as others mill around sipping tea. 'The experiential reality we are facing now is quite a distinctive feature. It has its own dynamics and ramifications in many spaces. And, therefore, people sometimes find it extremely difficult to speak the truth.'

He lets me absorb this background—and his manner of speaking, which is to arrive cuttingly, if obliquely, to the point. 'The tension of our lives is such that violence, viciousness and corruption in the environment are undermining moral imperatives. You can imagine the conditions in which Sharmila ensures her struggle. The state,'—he waves a hand—'they just don't bother.'

Singhajit turns to us when he hears the name of his sister mentioned. He comes closer, but is content to let the professor speak of her; Sharmila lacks freedom, but not interpreters.

When she took to fasting, Sharmila 'took everyone by surprise,' Professor Lokendro explains. 'There were a lot of sceptics to her method. Many armed outfits were not interested in her, because the principle of non-violence is anathema to them—they think that the gun will solve all problems.'

He elaborates the purpose of Sharmila's protest. She was arrested on charges of attempting to commit suicide, under Section 309 of the Indian Penal Code. But she wasn't trying to commit suicide, he says; she merely wanted to protest, an urgent plea, really, to remove the Armed Forces (Special Powers) Act from Manipur. Till that happened, she wouldn't feed herself, or at best, not take food from her mouth—hence the nasal feeding through a tube. He made a film about her in 2003. 'Sharmila said in my film: "If I wanted to kill myself who would obstruct me? There's a (ceiling) fan, there's a lot of cloth; I could have hanged myself anytime. I am not saying that I want to commit suicide."' The professor bursts into laughter. 'She is aware of the nuances.'

Under provisions of Section 309, attempted suicide is punishable by 'simple imprisonment' for up to a year, or a fine, or both. So before a year of Sharmila's incarceration is up she is released and rearrested for attempting to commit suicide. It is now a nine-year-long ritual. 'It's a political use of non-violence,' he says, and with a smile drives home the irony. 'She has acted on one of the finest moral principles ever, designed by founders of the Indian nation-state.'

As Singhajit politely listens to what he already knows of his youngest sister, the professor maps a sort of trajectory of the protester in the making. He talks of how Sharmila wrote poetry in school, how she would travel everywhere on a cycle listening to people talking about human rights. Sometimes, she would display a stubborn streak of independence. She was once failed in school because she insisted on writing her exams using green ink. The professor talks of how she used to be found in Sanamahi shrines, lost in thought. Once she was discovered in a hill village near Imphal, and brought back, he says, by 'Meitei' security forces. 'A psychiatrist might ask: Is it some kind of delinquent derangement? Some trauma? I came to know much later than she was searching for some truth inside her—a sort of individualistic search for reality. She does not belong to the rung of young women who are attuned to the cultural trends of modernity; she doesn't use cosmetics, toothbrush or soap. She uses traditional toiletries, keeping alive pre-colonial associations.'

Later, as an intern with Human Rights Alert in Imphal, she was asked to go and meet a young tribal woman, a Kabui, who was raped by security forces in front of her father-in-law. It happened after a skirmish between insurgents and security forces near her village. When this girl related her experience to Sharmila, the professor says, it triggered an internal change in Sharmila. Then the Malom incident happened in early November 2000. And Sharmila the protest icon was born.

'So the state has created a living martyr,' I say to Professor Lokendro.

He nods vigorously, and bursts into his trademark cackle.

As the meeting breaks up, the professor asks Singhajit and me to walk with him to Aryan Theatre. They are doing a pre-final 'run-through' of a play to be staged to mark the tenth anniversary of Sharmila's protest, a trans-adaptation of Mahasweta Devi's *Hajar Churashir Ma*, a story set in the times of the Naxalite movement. The professor walks quickly, belying his years. Singhajit and I are slowed down because his battered Vespa scooter is giving trouble; we take turns to push it against the flow of traffic as the dust and pollution threaten to choke us. We arrive at the theatre after ten minutes or so of this.

The way in is between two shops, through a rickety wooden door that opens onto the centre of a hall the size of a modest house. The hall is rundown, mostly empty. Plastic and steel folding chairs are scattered across the packed-earth floor. The stage is to our right as we walk in. On stage, microphones are suspended from rafters. A large speaker faces the audience. The walls are blackened. Everything wears a dilapidated look. Professor Lokendro, who is greeted effusively by the director, S. Rajen, and his team, explains that the theatre burnt down in 1996, and hasn't really recovered. But it seems adequate, and the crew makes it resolutely pure in the starkness of poverty.

The three of us are shown to a front row of chairs. Before the lights dim, we are offered plates of kachori—'Made by the Marwaris,' the professor says with a smile—and rasogollas—another smile. 'Brought by the Bengalis,' we say in unison. Rajen asks the professor's permission to begin the rehearsal for *Lalhouba Amagee Mama*.

'Don't worry,' the professor tells him. 'Keep the rehearsal relaxed.'

Stage right—from the perspective of the audience—is the wall of a living room. There is a shelf with a few books, bric-a-brac, a phone. Simple cane furniture completes the minimalist ensemble. Stage left is a free space. At the back is a tiered platform.

The phone rings; a recorded crackle. A lady rushes in to take the call. She is lit with a spotlight as she mostly listens, occasionally responding in halting bursts of query until she is suddenly quietened. An elderly gentleman enters, followed by a younger man. The older man queries her in a garrulous tone until she, without turning, numbly delivers the news. The mood changes. Fade out.

The scene shifts to the back of the stage. Four men come in and lie down side by side on the stage, and are covered by stage crew with white sheets. The lady from the first scene is present, standing mutely by the side. A man in a police uniform standing on the top tier speaks loudly in a harsh, emphatic voice, ordering her to identify a body. She passes by two wailing women to a body at the end of the line. An orderly whips the cloth off the bodies. She touches the face of the corpse nearest to her and starts to weep. She slowly moves centre-stage and kneels, sobbing. Then she lets out a prolonged wail that ends in a scream. Lights fade.

Singhajit whispers to me that he needs to go home. I offer to leave with him—we shall in any case see the play a couple of days later. Miraculously, his scooter comes alive with a single kick of the starter. Singhajit and I laugh out loud with relief. On the way to Tam-pha hotel, I compliment him and his sister, the youngest of nine siblings, for the courage and dignity they have shown.

Singhajit dismisses it with a jerky wave, and quickly moves to right the scooter's wobble. He compliments instead their grandmother, Irom Tonsija Devi, the first in the family to take to protest—against colonial rule and then against India. I remember well a photograph of Tonsija Devi in Deepti's book, taken in 2007. It shows this frail but resolute centenarian seated by a tem, a weaving tool also used as a weapon in the old days.

'She was the brave one,' Singhajit insists. 'We are nothing.'

～

A few minutes after I reach my hotel, Nandini calls to say I'm invited to dinner at a friend's place, and that D, another friend, will collect me in a few minutes. The hotel is on his route.

'I'm cooking,' she says. 'It's Saturday night. We all need a break from Imphal. Come.'

I don't need another prompt; the room service menu at the Tam-pha and I have over several visits developed an acrimonious relationship.

D arrives punctually, and quite drunk. Without mishap we arrive in his Maruti 800 at a three-storey house in a lane opposite Burma

Bazar. The first-floor apartment belongs to Braja, who runs a school on the way to Tulihal airport, and an online art gallery showcasing modern Manipuri art. The spacious apartment has canvases on the walls. Colourful cushions are strewn around on casually placed sofas and divans. It's a den as much as public space.

Braja and his wife are friends of Nandini. There are two other couples, the men both doctors; someone there is a cousin to Nandini, but that is lost in the politely downplayed introductions. I don't pursue the point; I have been invited by Nandini but am still a stranger, and in Imphal identification is still worth some harassment, even an arrest, or a life.

But such concerns are soon brushed away with the flow of Scotch whiskey bottled in India, strong beer, and some wine from the Sahyadri Hills to the far west of India. For snacks there are bits of spicy chicken and a salad of chopped tomato, cucumber and onion. The conversation flows around me; and it's a pleasure to simply be ... away. I appreciate better what Nandini had told me during our chat a few hours earlier.

'I want to open a restaurant,' she had said suddenly, after she spoke of her activist husband Ramananda Wangkheirakpam having 'to go into hiding' to escape arrest some months earlier when their colleague and friend Jiten Yumnam was picked up at Imphal airport on charges of 'anti-national' activities—an open gambit by authorities to choke the protests and strikes by Apunba Lup; and Jiten was marked as a ringleader. Ramananda protests the misuse of land, unnecessary building of dams to choke rivers, the human rights violations. And Nandini is his partner in activism too. 'I'm tired of this,' Nandini had said. 'I want to research forgotten herbs, forgotten ways of cooking, recipes which our grannies remember but even our mothers are forgetting.' She had sighed deeply. 'Sometimes all this protest against the state is too much, too overwhelming—the politics of it all.'

The ladies begin to sing a popular song from *Yaadon ki Baraat*, a

Bollywood hit from the 1970s that celebrates a heart stolen by a paramour: '*Chura liya hai tumney jo dilko…*'

It feels all right: surreal Imphal.

Braja gets sentimental when I talk about my visit to Sekmai, and my fondness for its independent-minded people, the surrounding green, and eponymous firewater.

'So, do you like Manipur?'

'Yes, very much. But I don't like what's happening to it.'

He nods emphatically. 'Do you find Manipur beautiful?'

'It is utterly beautiful.'

He nods again. 'Do you think Manipur would be as sought after a tourist destination as Goa? Your place?'

It could, I reply without hesitation, preparing to add to it. Braja says it before I can: 'If everything was normal.'

'Yes, that would help.'

He smacks a fist into a palm. He sits there glowering at me, then shakes his head, as if to clear it. He reaches out to touch my arm in apology, and suggests that I sing. There's a chorus of affirmatives.

It's a bad move, I assure them. I've personally shut down two karaoke joints with my singing: one in Colombo, at what used to be the Oberoi hotel; the other at a club in the heart of Beijing. My rendition of a song by the Rolling Stones—'*I can't get no satisfaction*' both times—was so bad they temporarily cancelled karaoke and turned on house music to discourage me and others like me from taking to the mike. One of the doctors, tears of laughter rolling down his face, decides to sing instead. He's worse than I would ever have been.

The laughter stops short when Nandini announces that she is expected at the house of a senior bureaucrat for a little while—from the name I recognize he's a top official with Manipur administration. A good friend, L, is there, she explains, and she hasn't seen L for a while. Braja is outraged that we have to leave, and he is only partly mollified when Nandini tells him we'll return shortly. There's still her cooking to taste.

We drive to a large house along the southern perimeter of Kangla Fort, and cross a slim moat to reach it. The chief minister's house is across the road.

We enter a plush living room. The pride of place is given over to a large-screen plasma TV and home theatre system. There's a DVD of a Kylie Minogue concert on. Our host, a slim, gaunt man, surfs between the concert and entertainment channels on his direct-to-home service provider. He pauses to stand and greet us. L, who is the only other person around, points effusively to a bottle of Teachers and VAT 69 whiskey on the table. A Nepali manservant, unsurprisingly addressed as 'bahadur'—a despised term to the Nepali, as it is most often generically employed by Indians for domestic help or security guards of Nepali origin—soon brings glasses and platters of kebabs and sausage.

Our host is cautious, even more so when Nandini explains I'm working on a book partly set in his patch of the world. 'Are you a journalist?' he asks, suddenly tense.

'I used to be a career journalist.' My technically correct reply doesn't comfort him; but he can't now ask me to leave. I suggest that we talk about political and administrative issues another time, maybe at his office, and just enjoy the evening. That settles him somewhat. He seems more at home when a colleague, a senior official who works at the office of Chief Minster Ibobi Singh, arrives in a flourish of strong cologne and dapper Delhi-style weekend party clothing.

He is clearly at home here. He switches Kylie for some dance music I can't identify, and starts to dance by himself, and soon, in fluent Meeteilon, urges L to join him.

L turns to me. 'Come on, Bengali babu. Join us.' I decline with a smile.

'They've both had a terrible day,' L tells me when the dancing is done. I can imagine. Representatives of Apunba Lup and several other peoples and rights organizations met senior government officials earlier in the day to pressure them into taking concrete disciplinary action over the killings of Sanjit and Rabina, and to ask Ibobi Singh to resign. With schools and colleges still shut and Imphal Valley continuing its tense stand-off with the government, it was no-go at the meeting. And meanwhile, some Meira Paibi activists had thrown slippers in protest at the gates of the chief minister's house.

'So, it's time to party.' L explains the logic of the weekend: therapy by alcohol, music and company, a time-tested urban recourse made all the more on-edge for it being in Imphal.

Snacks and drinks done, all of us troop off to Braja's place, after L assures the bureaucrats their entry and exit will be discreet. There is nothing discreet about Braja's reaction, however. I can see he is livid to see us bring the bureaucrats home. His jolly party immediately takes on a stilted, formal tone, as friends and family become cautious about what they say to whom. The two bureaucrats react in a similar way. The senior one clearly isn't certain whether he should relax or not. The younger one decides to brazen it out; he wears his power as easily as his rich cologne. Nandini and I escape to the dining room for dinner. The stench of the dead party follows us.

The bureaucrats and L are leaving, and they take Nandini and me with them. It's close to midnight. In the compact car of L's hapless boyfriend we drive at breakneck speed along the now empty road to the airport to keep up with the black Tata Safari of the bureaucrats, with its tinted glasses. There's no accompanying security for them. This late, hopping from an improbable gathering to an improbable destination, they would in all likelihood have confused even a vigilant rebel. We're headed to a farmhouse L's mother is building near the airport. There's more to drink but it's now all desultory; L and her bureaucrat friends clearly want to move on elsewhere; and I feel like deadweight.

And so, suddenly, the evening is over. L's boyfriend offers to reach Nandini home and me to my hotel. Meanwhile, L and the bureaucrats have driven off at great speed back towards town. The taillights of the SUV slew briefly at Kwakeithel crossing and disappear round a gentle bend.

I glance at the expression on the face of L's boyfriend. It's firmly set, washed by the light from the dashboard. Dignity is a tough call in this universe.

18

'The heavens are filled with smoke from smouldering pyres of your dead sons'

'So, what were we talking about?' Professor Lokendro asks rhetorically. It is nine in the morning, and I'm back at his residence to complete our discussion, take it ahead from the previous day and beyond the scope of Irom Sharmila. We are seated, as before, in the courtyard. He waits for a noisy autorickshaw to pass in the lane by the house before he offers the answer: 'The emergence of heroes.'

But the professor, gaunt, bespectacled, intense, talks instead of the emergence of horrors, the moulding of mindsets from the 1960s as a reaction to what many Meitei intellectuals and youngsters perceived as trampling of a collective identity by Indian authorities. He tells me of an incident—'not many really know about it'—from 1969.

'I was a young person those days, interested in cultural activism and theatre,' he begins. After a meeting of his old theatre group, he says, and after a community lunch, his colleagues and he went towards the maidan that was there in those days, near Khwairamband market. The space is now a stadium. A platform was constructed for the visiting prime minister, Indira Gandhi, to give a speech. 'Statehood had not yet been granted to Manipur,' Professor

Lokendro says, referring to what would finally become a reality in 1972, when Manipur became a state of the Indian Union. 'In the 1960s a lot of socialist-inspired movements had taken root. They didn't like the political status—this sort of apprenticeship to Indian nationalism. The movement for statehood was very strong.'

Underground revolutionary movements had already been birthed five years earlier, and alongside, as a corollary, there were various people's movements for identity, for cultural nationalism, expressing their views as to how they were being treated as a minority; marginalized within India in general, and Imphal Valley in particular. 'The self and other, the centre and its periphery—these were being seen in the dynamics of Manipur in the future history that was developing.'

During Indira Gandhi's address there was stone throwing. 'Madame was hurt here'—he touches his nose—'by a stone. And the speech that came out from her after that ... the speech of Madame Indira Gandhi in the Manipur maidan in 1969, the kind of racist tone that she used.' The professor pauses to draw himself up, to theatrically turn a profile in uncanny imitation of Indira. '"Do you know who I am?"' he thunders. Then he relaxes the pose and smiles. '*Very* interesting.'

Some people were rushing forward just to listen to her, he continues, others were 'very angry' with her. The CRPF was responsible for security. They opened fire. Six people were killed.

'It happened while she was present,' Professor Lokendro shakes his head. 'This incident has been forgotten.'

He takes a call on his mobile phone. Unsurprisingly, it is to do with events related to the anniversary of Sharmila's protest. He listens and then offers instruction in measured Meeteilon. He smiles, and shifts attention back to me. It's time for another lesson in history, of how the relationship of India's administrative centre with the country's peripheries has changed. 'Why Manipuris,' he says, 'are regarded as rebels.'

AFSPA was introduced in the Valley in September 1980, the professor resumes, but the hill people of Manipur had already a taste of what it could do as they 'experienced the vehemence and hegemony of Indian security forces'. In 1951, a Naga of the Poumai tribe was the first 'Manipuri Naga to join Phizo's movement'. Over the years, many more followed, represented by all tribes from these southern Naga Hills. There were even meetings between Phizo and several political leaders of Manipur, he says, indicating Meitei leaders like Hijam Irabot, who he says was the first to introduce journalism in the Valley. But there was no joining of forces; Irabot, he says, was already a member of the Communist Party, and the communists had quite a different agenda—a social agenda. After Irabot's death in 1951—Irabot had by then been underground for some time—the social agenda was gradually transformed into a kind of national struggle.

'When Zapu Phizo was organizing the plebiscite in 1951...' the professor abruptly shifts planes to digress. 'It was such an interesting relationship they had in the early days. This kind of people-to-people relationship has been blocked.' It is an important point in these times of tension between those who are seen as being from the hills, and those from the valley.

'You know, not long ago Naga civil society people came to Imphal, and among them was a veteran of the Naga Army. During discussions with us—these were unofficial discussions with our civil society—he said a very interesting thing: all the time we have been thinking in a linear way. It is always Kohima-Delhi, Imphal-Delhi, Agartala-Delhi, Guwahati-Delhi. Not Imphal-Kohima, not Kohima-Guwahati, and so on.' This is largely true. Even sub-species of political economics like the Shillong-based North Eastern Council are still controlled by the Central government. The Central government's strict diktat of rule with each state—or union territory in the past—further compartmentalized the region. Now, ironically, the throwaway tag of 'Northeast' as labelled by India's political and bureaucratic leadership is gradually leading to a regional realization, if nascent, that there is a better sense of unity against being patronized by an always heavy-handed, often-callous, ruler. Call the ruler 'New Delhi'.

'It is really about the conduit of patronage: politics, revenue, military, security, development,' Professor Lokendro marks these off with his fingers. 'It's a mandated design. It's about how a big power tries to condition a people as to what kind of a value they want to impose on those people. Like a potter conceives a pot, they already had a preconceived design as to what they want a people to be.'

This is a general point about the region, but I want to draw him back to Manipur. How would you overcome this environment? I ask.

'That's it!' He leans forward, animatedly dragging the chair with him. 'That is the consciousness we are lacking. We don't have any spirited discourse in the public sphere. What kind of life are you leading? What is your social and political life? What are your economic and other lives? How is it all being conditioned? What are the changes? What are the influences, and what is the nature of patronage? And, what is the politics of culture behind this? Writers, poets, painters, musicians—they have to express these things—isn't it?—earlier than the common people.

'What should be the direction of change?' he continues, wagging a forefinger at what he considers to be the collectively somnolent, present-day cultural vanguard of Manipur. It's a controversial statement, but the professor is known for such opinions. 'Are you talking about quality of life? About liberty? About human capabilities? That has to be developed.' He spreads his hands in resignation and rasps: '*Where are you?*'

To be fair to the professor, I have heard this sentiment from others in Imphal, but not limited to cultural leadership in society and politics, and not underscoring the lack of discourse but its lack of focus and, therefore, its negative effect. Pradip Phanjoubam, the articulate editor of *Imphal Free Press*—which has seen staff killed by the Underground for refusing to kowtow to their diktat, and routinely been pressured by the administration and security establishment—talked to me of what he thought of as a vacuum in Manipuri thought and leadership. Specifically, to address the question: where does Manipur go from here?

'I think people here are really obsessed about the future and everybody is trying to define it in their own ways,' he told me in his office on New Checkon Road one evening during my previous visit a month and a half earlier in September 2009. 'And that also shows a leadership vacuum. People who are able should capture the imagination of the people with their definition of the future.'

But nobody seems to be giving up on the future, I had argued. You might say there are way too many forces at play—and in the Manipur of today that would be an understatement—but I sense great positive energy even in such pervasive gloom and cynicism as casts a web over Imphal Valley and really, all Manipur. There is a sense of people trying to desperately to reach out to a future.

'Yes.' He nodded. 'Nobody is giving up. They want a future.'

'So, what's your take on it?'

'Again, it's difficult.' He smiled, self-deprecating humour in his eyes evident even through thick spectacle lenses. 'I live in the same confusion—it's the same milieu as everyone else. And if I do come out with something nobody is going to believe it: I might say something, [chief minister] Ibobi would say something else, some other guy, and so on ... there's no consensus on what should be the future.'

What of the present protests against the government by those of the Apunba Lup? I had pressed. Any chance of leadership developing there?

'This time they haven't been able to influence many people,' Pradip said, a commentary on the fragmented, if utterly brave, nature of the protests. 'And I think people are at this point disillusioned with both the parallel leadership as well as politicians—legitimate, within brackets.' He smiled widely. 'If the government has been committing atrocities, insurgents have been doing the same thing. You don't really know who should be leading you. And so, every group is trying to take you to the Promised Land.'

He indicated a general lack of trust, of believability. 'You should have a definition of the future and also have the moral legitimacy to be able to convince people, for people to be able to believe you. That kind of leadership has been lacking here for a long time.'

But isn't that natural in an environment of such churn? I had asked. There are so many interest groups, both in the Underground and 'overground'. After a while there would be a natural cleaning of the chaff. Moreover, when faced with what is, for practical purposes, a dead-end, groups would logically begin to coalesce for survival when they realize they cannot be as strong or effective on their own. Better an uneasy alliance than annihilation. At least—I told Pradip—I had been given to understand by observers among media, activism circles and the security establishment that among some Meitei underground groups it was already beginning to happen. The Kanglei Yawol Kanna Lup, which had earlier broken from UNLF, had evidently, in principle, agreed to be united in purpose—even if a full integration seemed unlikely at this point.

Equally, there was already a concerted effort among a faction of Nagas in Manipur to effect an alliance with Kuki and Hmar groups as a working coalition of tribal 'hill people' against the administrative stranglehold of Imphal. And, if the splintered leadership of various 'aboveground' protests and even political factions in the Valley began to coalesce, Manipur should, theoretically, evolve iconic figures in the near future. Figures who would highlight both their ideas and their profiles.

Pradip acknowledged my argument but in turn offered a caution. 'There are so many different canvases at play here,' he explained, 'local, regional, national. For instance, now there is a divide between Nagas and Meiteis. Tomorrow if they suddenly make friends there are going to be certain other balances outside of that equation that will cause problems—and these will put hurdles before such a friendship. Even if it is not an overt friendship there will be a short-circuit somewhere and it will not happen as it was willed to be.'

Moving away from these churning gears to the desperate stasis of Imphal Valley, seemed to me to lack a momentum of change, even with great occasional outrage. The great public anger after the Malom massacre in 2000; the great outrage and churn of 2004 brought on by the Manorama incident; and since the summer of 2009, great outrage and organized rallies and protests by Apunba Lup after the deaths of Sanjit and Rabina have all been key, tragic touchstones in recent Manipuri history—cataclysmic even, from the perspective of local society and politics. But none with the force of sustained people's movements that could ultimately change the power structure of Manipur, force a change in political leadership of the state, and the way the leadership of India took the people of this state for granted.

And Pradip had been telling me even the Apunba Lup protests would not last long. It seemed logical: the leadership drawn from various activist and civil society groups was too fractured, and the state machinery too powerful—at will arresting some leaders and sending others into hiding—clinically denying a protest movement the critical gathering of steam. And, while the protesters were legitimately demanding a semblance of democracy, there were already protests against its imposition of the shutdown of schools and colleges to further pressure Ibobi's government. People for whom the protests were meant were grumbling against those who led these protests.

But it must recur, I had offered to Pradip in argument. All this anger of the people cannot simply vanish.

Pradip smiled, as if pleased to have led me to the spot. 'Each incident leaves residues of bitterness,' he explained. 'Individually they may not be able to command a mass movement but residues gather and sometimes it all explodes. I would see the Manorama incident that way. Women were being raped [by security forces], but proof against perpetrators was difficult to come by. But this [the rape and killing of Manorama] was open, it suddenly sparked something. Again, with the Sanjit incident—fake encounters have been happening for so many years, it's a known thing, but this triggered something. People knew there was something wrong with the police version but there was no way they could react. Then the *Tehelka* pictures came. [The lie] was totally exposed, and there was an explosion.

'That's why,' he said, 'the calm here is always tense.'

Then what else is there? I had asked him. There's no intellectual dearth in Manipur. There's no lack of political awareness. And people have no fear of even automatic weapons if they are angry enough—as the reaction, and protests to several incidents have shown. There is courage displayed daily, courage that comes simply from living in a place like this, a situation like this. With all this impetus, why isn't there a productive opposition to this government—or government policies in general?

'I have to go back to my earlier argument about the leadership vacuum,' Pradip replied.

'So the government is going to simply use AFSPA, NSA and all other acts to handle issues? Dampen all voices? Won't that backfire?'

'It would definitely backfire,' Pradip said animatedly. 'There's a total lack of imagination [by government] of how to handle issues. They have also been dismantling and discrediting their own institutions that can tackle these problems. Take judicial inquiries. Nobody wants a judicial inquiry now because you have treated it like dirt for so long. People are unwilling to come to depose for the Sanjit judicial inquiry, so you will have justice delivered by default. September 21 was the last date for submissions. The Commission extended the deadline to October 8. Then the hearing will begin. Again, in the hearing nobody will come out. So it is going to be only the police point of view that will be reflected.'

It's a chain reaction, Pradip explained. 'It's not easy to break a chain reaction, but either you do it or you leave it to god. It's a tall challenge but you still have to do it, break that chain.'

He had eloquently made that point in an essay in a book I had recently purchased, *Beyond Counter-insurgency: Breaking the Impasse in Northeast India*, edited by Sanjib Baruah, professor of political studies at Bard College in New York. At one point in his essay, 'Northeast Problems as a Subject and Object', Pradip wrote of insurgency being among other things related to administrative weakness and incompetence, and official corruption that 'continually tramples upon all sense of fair play and justice'.

'The initial reaction of societies exposed to such conditions is twofold,' he had written. 'One of awe and submission amongst the larger masses, and a general cynicism among the intelligentsia and elite, both dictated by the sense that if you cannot beat the system, join it. But the social mechanism is not a dead phenomenon, in thought or action. It is organically conditioned to transform itself to respond to any stimulus fittingly.

'Under a condition of constant and consistent abuse, it mutates and its reaction can become extraordinary, in extremity and cruelty. To a good extent, insurgency is also about such a transformation. Within a matter of a few years, moderate societies have become bloodthirsty. Insurgency in this way is a price that society pays for its neglect and insensitivities of the past.'

Basically, Pradip suggested, provide certain triggers, and a particular cycle of behaviour will emerge. Manipur is in a negative cycle. It desperately needs injection to bring about a positive cycle.

Do you see things changing at all? I asked Pradip.

'No.'

There seemed to be little to cheer as I absorbed Pradip's comments. A quick sunset in damp weather had added to the sense of gloom. Renovations at the *Imphal Free Press* office were noisy, and the trundling traffic outside, along the churned-up wreck of New Checkon Road near the Old Palace grounds added to the noise of sawing, hammering and drilling. I had opted for some gallows humour to lighten the situation.

'Why aren't you in jail?' I asked Pradip. 'You and your colleagues?'

That brought laughter. 'I don't know.'

'Look at that,' I said, pointing at a poster on the wall of his office. 'You have this poster here. It's the same one I saw on the walls of the government press at Kalibari, literally down the road from Ibobi's residence, the secretariat and police headquarters.'

It proclaimed a string of demands in bold capital letters, a mix of a litany of ills that plagued Manipur, and a plea for normality under a democracy for decades in remission: 'Stop State Terrorism. Honour Right to Life. Save Democracy. Stop Oppression. Stop Silent Killing. Stop Extra Judicial Execution. Uphold the Dignity of Women. Let us Carry the Meira Paibi Movement Forward. Repeal Armed Forces (Special Powers) Act.' It was part of the post-Sanjit, post-Rabina coda driven by leaders of the Apunba Lup—among them several well-known leaders of society and media.

'And you've been vocal with your point of view,' I added. 'Why hasn't the state come after you?'

Pradip had leaned back in the padded chair. 'Probably because there are so many people who are more radical than I am; and many have taken the law into their own hands, which I haven't done. I criticize [the state], but I haven't done that. And, I am trying to express a point of view, not trying to coerce anybody to believe in me.'

I state the obvious: 'It can't be an easy life.' Not easy for Pradip and nearly everybody else I've met in these parts.

'It's very, very difficult. Not just for me but anyone who tries to be independent, think independently. [There are pressures] not just from the establishment but also the counter-establishment.'

What keeps Okram Ibobi Singh going in Manipur? I had then asked Pradip, wondering yet again about this chief minister whose two terms in office had seen the biggest social and security eruptions in the past decade. He reminded me of Chhattisgarh's chief minister Raman Singh who, at the head of the BJP-led government, has presided, even gloated, over the killing and brutal forced corralling of tribal populations in the state's Dantewada region in the name of controlling the Maoist rebellion. 'Is it only Ibobi's closeness to Congress party satraps in New Delhi?'

'It would be one of the bigger factors, but you can't see an alternative at the moment. After Ibobi, who?' Pradip shrugged. 'That kind of thing.'

He said he had spoken to numerous people, including folks in the army, about Ibobi's stickiness beyond his closeness to the Congress leadership and underbosses. 'From their casual talk you can make out: they think there is nothing wrong with this man. There may be some sections of the army not so happy with him ... there was a story that came out about his links with the Underground—I think that was a plant by the army—it said [Ibobi] paid money to KYKL and PLA. But by and large I have a feeling that the army is quite happy with him; he doesn't do anything that is not in their interest.

'The army is a big political bloc here,' he told me as had others. It represents not just the defence ministry but also the home ministry's will. 'If the home ministry wants something to happen, the army is the instrument to make that happen.' Assam Rifles, a 'parallel influence', is very much within the army bloc.

'Maybe he's corrupt,' Pradip said of Ibobi Singh, 'but he doesn't interfere in their work.'

'So Ibobi continues?'

'Hmm.' The short answer to political survival in this conflict zone: if a chief minister tries to be independent, the Centre is not going to like it.

Pradip provided the example of Rishang Keishing, a Tangkhul Naga who was the chief minister of Manipur from 1985 to February 1988. In July 1987, NSCN-IM attacked an Assam Rifles post at Oinam in Senapati district, killing nine soldiers and capturing a large quantity of semi-automatic and automatic rifles and ammunition. Security forces went berserk in retaliation—called Operation Bluebird—molesting and raping several women, and torturing and killing men. Fourteen died, none of them NSCN-IM cadre.

Keishing 'actually used his office to get journalists from Delhi to come to Imphal at the invitation of the chief minister,' Pradip recounted, to expose Assam Rifles' retaliatory role using the fig leaf of AFSPA. That in turn deeply upset the state intelligence apparatus and, in particular, the governor at the time, Gen. K.V. Krishna Rao, a retired chief of army staff. Keishing, Pradip said, anyway had an adversary relationship with the general, perceived as being close to Keishing's own party, the Congress. Soon after the Oinam incident and his reaction, Keishing 'was taken off without any explanation', and summarily replaced by a loyalist, R.K. Jaichandra. By the time of Keishing's next run as chief minister, he was more chastened. As Pradip and I chatted, Keishing, a longtime Congress man, was ensconced in his second term as MP in the Rajya Sabha.

'State governments are weak, and they are made to feel powerless,' said Pradip. 'That has always been the case.'

It happens even with the seemingly all-powerful Ibobi Singh. When the army called a truce with the Kuki National Organization, an agglomeration of several militant organizations of which the Kuki National Army was the armed wing, the army announced what in its lexicon is called SoO, or Suspension of Operations, in the Moreh area, at a press conference in 2007. 'The army didn't even inform the state government before doing so!' Pradip laughed. 'The chief minister was bewildered. This won't happen outside the northeast.'

Take Nagaland, he added for emphasis. The Centre is conducting talks with both factions of NSCN. 'The state government is not involved. If an incident takes place in Nagaland, the state government is powerless to do anything.'

So it's all about the security establishment? I asked a question to which I already knew the answer.

'Ya,' Pradip stated with finality. 'And in that power structure the state figures quite low. The army or the governor is much bigger here than the constitutionally elected person.'

~

I share some of Pradip's conversation with the professor, hoping to draw him deeper into aspects of his own life and touch upon elements that drew his brother Somorendro and him into expressions of their own forms of Manipuri nationalism.

'There is politics and security in the smallest of details in Manipur,' he agrees. Glancing witheringly at a couple of mobile telephony towers on a building in front of his house, he provides an example from personal experience—but again, typically, coming to the point in his oblique manner. Some time ago he had been taking the help of a revenue official to demarcate land that belonged to his brother and his family. The officer told him the lane in front, Meino Leirak, was in fact 'under the purview' of the government, and that a twenty-five-foot-wide strip to the west of the existing lane and twenty-five feet to the east would be acquired by the government; of course, he would be compensated for it.

'I said, how can the government take so much land for such a small thoroughfare? He smiled and said he had been told the government had planned for future insurgency, insurrection, when big anti-riot vehicles and other paraphernalia could pass through. So,' the professor breaks into prolonged laughter and claps his hands in childlike glee, 'I came to know what is meant by security and development.'

He then tells me of the time he understood the way contemporary Indian polity functioned. That was in 2004 in the wake of the Manorama incident, when he led what he calls a democratic leaders' delegation representing a group of thirty-two conglomerate bodies to meet Prime Minister Manmohan Singh. Nine among the delegation met the prime minister to hand over a fifteen-point memorandum, the main pitch being the removal of AFSPA.

'He spoke to me so nicely about how simple basic freedoms, liberties of our own people *have been undermined*,' the professor lowers his pitch but not the intensity, 'by this Draconian law. He was so deeply hurt by the deaths; and Manorama's rape-sacrifice and ... he was very sad. I pleaded to the prime minister about the repeal of AFSPA. I can recall one thing I said to him: "Mr Prime Minister, sir, you are also from a minority community, and so are we. You can understand our suffering. You are the person who stated before the entire nation that you wanted to have democracy with a human face. May I add to your statement? I would like you to say: We will not only have democracy with a human face, but democracy with a human heart."

'He was softened. He kept quiet. We came out after forty minutes. Later, there was a statement about the review of AFSPA. A h-u-m-a-n-e law'—he spells it out—'that deals with the rights and dignity and lives of the people, would have to be put in its place. That's what he promised: a new law.'

It didn't quite work out that way. And the delegation got a sense of it even as it visited the prime minister. Professor Lokendro recalls with a smile the nature of political and diplomatic negotiations in the capital. These are very methodically structured, he tells me, in a psychologically designed environment that can go against those—'adversaries'—not aware of the intricacies of negotiations. If you are being denied something, it is done so you reduce the dimension of that demand—so the entire exercise is already graded: up to what the government or the other side will concede. And so on. 'So those of us from the northeast not wise in the intricacies of state—for instance, I pity our Naga brothers; for twelve years they are...' The professor shakes his head and laughs.

'We are being played around with. It is easy to play with us. Perhaps our minds are not as well equipped to deal with the working of Machiavelli, of Kautilya. So, [prime minister's] promise of a review came only as a response to the emotional breakdown of one of the Meira Paibi members of the delegation in front of the prime minister.'

It was only after that did they see a chit of paper being passed from the national security advisor at the time, M.K. Narayanan, to the prime minister, through the hand of the person who was translating from Meeteilon to English. Only after seeing this chit did the prime minister agree to the review. 'If we didn't insist as we did,' the professor maintains, 'they would have made us happy with something else and sent us off.'

They already had the review of AFSPA in mind—not the repeal, he says, but when to announce it was the issue. 'The moment was chosen by the national security advisor. The breakdown of the Meira Paibi provided that moment.'

A week after their visit, the prime minister visited Jammu & Kashmir. He used the same phrases he used with his delegation, Professor Lokendro says. 'You are people. Individual rights are denied to you ... the same thing.' He shakes is head. 'Some kind of phrase, some rhetoric, is important for people to consume.

'I came to know that the PM does not have a mind of his own,' he continues. Through the façade of calm I can sense his fury. 'I came to know that the power lies with Madame'—a reference to United

Progressive Alliance chairperson Sonia Gandhi. He stretches out the rest, syllables of absolute anger. 'But he is a beautiful front. He is nominated to the Rajya Sabha from Assam. He is a cosmetic of the nation-state. He is a shikhandi.'

That last is a strong one, an allusion to the character in the Mahabharata who, through subterfuge, aided Arjuna in killing the patriarch Bhishma. There are far ruder allusions to shikhandi: an eunuch; essentially, a person who cannot take a stand. So all that really happened, I recap to make light of this insult, was that the prime minister promised a review and he handed over Kangla Fort to the government of Manipur.

'No, the PM came down in November 2004, he handed over Kangla to the people—the removal of Assam Rifles from Kangla was one of the earlier demands of the civil society. But during the movement, the three-month agitation of 2004, repeal of the [Armed Forces] Act became a one-point agenda.' It was reviewed by the Jeevan Reddy Commission; a strong suggestion was made to do away with it altogether. But the government backed off, and suppressed the report. If it hadn't been for *The Hindu*, which placed the report on its Internet edition, the public wouldn't have known.

'The Indian state does not accept armed conflict in the northeast as armed conflict.' The professor unfurls a finger at me. 'They consider it to be a law and order problem. Even the Jeevan Reddy Committee struggles to describe it'—he paraphrases—'"A serious disturbance of internal order which necessitates the presence of the military." If it is acknowledged as a conflict, there are ways of intervention: there are international humanitarian laws; there is the international community...'

Naturally, therefore, the Government of India will acknowledge no such thing. The world must keep its hand off this mess.

I take the professor away from this, the AFSPA factor that overwhelms all discourse in Manipur. I'm curious about personal aspects of protest. After a minute or so, as we sip tea and the professor's anger cools, I ask him how he deals with what he has seen, and his brother Somorendro's life, his death. This would cut deep, and I apologize in advance should it offend him.

'No, no,' he assures me with a wave. 'Many people in Manipur have seen their family and friends lost in conflict. There has been a lot of violence, a lot of killings.'

He takes me back to the times of his forefathers. I know this history will be touched by the professor's politics and unabashed opinion, but that is what makes it interesting, less sanitized.

We encourage migration, he tells me, as ever coming at a delightful tangent. Our sisters and daughters give men who migrate to Manipur their language, children, and traditional culture. These migrants were accepted as sons-in-law. The 'jamai' culture, he says, was very strong here, and the tradition continues.

The Brahmins arrived in the fifteenth century. They were accorded very low status in the early times, the professor says, but because of their knowledge of rituals, of their larger world religion, they began to infiltrate society and culture. There was great contest between the indigenous Sanamahi religion and the arriviste Hindu religion about what he terms truths and realities—ideological struggles, really. Gradually, he explains, because of the growth of various ethnic communities, power of the state perforce became more extensive; 'and they needed a much more heightened ritual to theatricalize the authority of the body of the king as representative of the cosmos'.

'And the Brahmins were happy to oblige,' I chip in.

'The Brahmins were *so* happy to advise. They came without any practice on agriculture. No manual labour. They simply lived through scriptures and morality. They had to be associated with rituals through which they could live. They were kept as spiritual advisors, as priestly classes. Conversion of people into that religion was very important for them to survive. By the eighteenth century, when we were converted (to Hinduism), the state had to use force.

The monarch mandated it as the state religion—that was in 1720. And he had to punish the conscientious objectors of that religion. Then, in the 1730s, Tantrik priests came from Sylhet [in present-day Bangladesh] and said, "Oh your great land is the land of Shiva, the land of the Mahabharata, let us name your place Manipur".'

After the culture of conversions set, so did a discourse, says the professor, that Manipur was part of the Mahabharata, an essential component of new mythology. Arjuna had a child here, Babbhrubahana, by marriage to a local princess, Chitrangada. This narrative of Arjuna marrying a girl from here was accepted by those early converts, and it later became part of the Indian discourse. In his forefather's time, says the professor, they still believed in this history. To illustrate how deeply this attitude had become entrenched, he mentions what he calls the first civil society movement in 1934, the Nikhil Hindu Manipuri Mahasabha. They encouraged prizes for writing such history. In reaction, to disprove what to their minds was imposed mythology, Meitei radicals and Sanamahi practitioners—often the same—went to Orissa to photograph and document a village called Manipur, which records a legend, a tradition of Arjuna's visit.

'The religious resistance that has developed as resistance to the colonial authority of the state as well as Indian authorities,' the professor asserts, 'this fundamentalist development was essential.'

Part of it came about with a revival of the Sanamahi movement since the 1930s. Today, the professor estimates, a sixth of Meiteis practise Sanamahi. A form of communism merged with nationalism would soon follow.

Meanwhile, Professor Lokendro's family had begun to script their own interesting sidelight. His grandfather Meino Singh had married a daughter of a prince of Manipur, Surchandra, in the late nineteenth century. The professor's father, Dorendrajit, and another son who died, are of this union. Over time, the landed family—the princess had also brought with her titles to lands to add to ancestral holdings—under the British, who by then controlled Manipur and influenced its education, the economic system and attitudes, gradually transformed from gentry into middle classes. The grandfather was the first sub-inspector of police in the colonial regime; Meino Leirak, the lane that fronts the house we sit in, is named after him. 'A cultural transformation was taking place,' the professor explains. 'During this period, my forefathers spoke about the poverty they experienced in education. In spite of land, they were not able to adjust to the new economic system, the money economy. They were reduced. That was the period in which colonial ideologies were advocated. Even [Hijam] Irabot, who was a leftist, spoke of us being the inheritors of the great Arjuna.'

The family moved on. Lokendro and Somorendro's father initiated what the professor charmingly calls the family's 'ink-stained heritage'. Their father was a prominent poet and dramatist in the 1930s. He founded the Aryan Theatre. When he died in 1944, he left behind minor children, two sons and a daughter. A personal struggle began and, as the children grew to adulthood, merged with the sense of political awareness and Meitei nationalism. 'There was concern about the recuperation of their lost traditional heritage and the consciousness that developed in the 1960s, after Manipur was integrated into the Indian union,' Professor Lokendro makes his point. The discourse that emerged for the birth and growth of such national movements assumed a clear line: 'The independence that Manipur experienced for two thousand years.'

This passed on into the 1980s, he says, when 'local cultural nationalism' was unfolding, when the movement for identity and issues of marginalization of the people 'were being taken up by the underground—what are called non-state actors'. It became an immense point of controversy, 'not necessarily scientific', he allows, 'it was temperamental, sentimental'. The more the Indian establishment turned cussed about these aspirations, what he terms the 'Manipur project in India's culture, how we became part of

India's consciousness', the more it fed the emotional nationalism. It's as good an explanation as I've heard. And, finally, it brings the professor to the place of mirrors.

'My brother was secretly...' He takes a deep breath and looks away. 'He was the leader. I was not aware. I was completely a theatre person.'

In a rush, as if to quickly cover ground, to be done with unpleasant memories, he talks of being concerned with a kind of cultural activism, the dynamic of which was so overwhelming that he forgot his own family, 'the human treatment of my wife—she was simply suffering. We had four daughters. She was left alone to deal with the struggles of family life.'

'I was concerned with production—I did thirty-five plays. My brother also wrote plays, on identity, on women's emancipation. His plays were written in a conventional way, but we went into the experimenting mode. Jean Genet, all the existential literature—we were fed with it. Then Badal-dada [Bengali avant-garde theatre guru Badal Sircar] was such an influence in our lives; we had a workshop here with him in 1972.'

The professor speeds up his memory recall; compared to his generally sedate telling, he is now at near-frenzy. 'He told us about the clogging nature of the proscenium, he denied the proscenium'— the professor speaks of Sircar's disdain for the stylized arch that separates a typical modern stage from the audience, preferring instead free-flowing, interactive theatre spaces. '"We have to go to the people," he said. He chose *Spartacus* as our production; I played a part. Kanhailal, my friend and peer, interacted with him. He discovered the artistic exploration of the body of the Manipuri actor; and humanistic concerns of oppressed people—that was where he began his creative expressions. I was interested in political expression: I did Bertolt Brecht, for example, various things against the discourse of the state.'

He says he had an intuitive sense of the rebellion which was forming at that period, but he was not part of it. When he produced his play *Man Without Saddles*, he made the hero of the play hide in Bangladesh. 'Indian Army arrested insurgents and there was severe interrogation ... the representation of the resistance movement and the gradual decay of the oppressive authority, the existential conflict between the two was being portrayed by theatre. I wrote that play in 1971. It was produced in 1972. The whole movement became so strong later—in 1978, PLA started the first armed violence. I came to know,' he chuckles, 'that all the heroes were now hiding in Bangladesh.' But that happened a lot later; the professor nudges his memory back to the formative years for Somorendro and him.

Somorendro was in the political struggle, he explains, while he took to cultural struggle. 'He never talked to me about his revolutionary activities. He was lost to the family in 1969.'

A year earlier, Somorendro had helped to form the Pan-Manipuri Youth League, to press for the unification of Manipuris in Assam's Cachar region, Myanmar, and what was then East Pakistan—small Meitei populations exist in Bangladesh to this day. Professor Lokendro describes his brother as representing 'greater political integration not denying the use of armed struggle'. In plain language: if an armed movement is required, so be it.

But 1969 was a watershed year, in a sense. The government—specifically the Government of India—realized the increasing sweep of underground movements in Manipur. The Naga wars to the north were far from over even with the declaration of statehood for Nagaland in 1963. Meanwhile, India's war against Mizo rebels to the south, which began after the insurrection led by Mizo National Front in 1966—soon openly aided by Pakistan, which leveraged Mizo anger on account of government apathy and full-blown famine—was in flow. The barbaric template of victory at any and every cost to the civilian population that had thus far been applied to the Naga hills had been phased into play in the territory of Mizoram. The Imphal Valley was plumb in the middle of these zones. The government, which had for years largely limited itself to threatening and beating up radical students, went for the jugular of Manipuri nationalist protest—the incident of insulting Indira Gandhi at the maidan would prove to be a tipping point. Somorendro went underground.

Professor Lokendro and others gradually realized the depth of Somorendro's activities away from theatre. (As it turned out, he along with some acolytes of Hijam Irabot had already formed the UNLF in 1964.)

Meanwhile, the professor directed all his brother's plays. It stayed that way until 1975, when Somorendro came out as part of a general amnesty announced over 1974-75. He went right back to theatre and other forms of art, building a collective oeuvre that, by the end of his life in 2000, numbered over thirty full-length and short plays, and several scripts for radio and cinema. He had married Memchoubi, the fiery poet, soon after resurfacing, in 1976. They had four sons.

The underground movement soon splintered, the professor explains, moving away from Somorendro's 'political philosophy, the concept of an independence'. PLA was one such breakaway from the UNLF, which continued apace even as Somorendro formally retired from it. By then, he was a much awarded playwright, winning several accolades in Manipur and New Delhi. The plays kept hammering at themes that were still close to Somorendro, though. His 1992 work *Nong Tarakle* portrayed how common folk are squeezed by counterinsurgency operations. *Sak-Khangkhidaraba Lanmee*, in 1988, set up 'The Unrecognized Soldier' from earlier wars against the Burmese in the early nineteenth century, and touched upon the theme of factional fighting among revolutionaries.

That ultimately proved to be an epitaph. As Somorendro attended a seminar on women's courtyard plays in a suburb of Imphal in June 2000, he was shot at twice by a Meitei youngster who escaped on a scooter with the help of an accomplice. Somorendro died instantly.

I hear some of this from the professor; some I had already read about. I hear his voice now, again insistent. He speaks of his former friends and colleagues Thiyam and Kanhailal, criticizing what he describes in detail as their sell-out to the cultural establishment both in Manipur and New Delhi. It sounds like the voice of a bitter and angry person, but also of one who resolutely holds on to political views that have evolved over several decades. 'The work they are doing now has become anathema to me,' he says. 'I believe in resistance to the state—resisting the discourse of the state. For them, they are supporters of the state's social and economic paraphernalia of discourse; they are integrated into the stream of Indian cultural patronage. I do not take help from them, the ministry [of culture].' He snaps: 'I am not a salaried man.' He looks at the worn structures around the courtyard. 'I am as poor as I am.'

It is time to leave.

'What I am trying to say is that the presence of the Indian state in the northeast is absolutely contradictory to the development of indigenous energies,' Professor Lokendro wraps up, emphasizing each point with a slash of hand. 'And violence has become the way of self-determination. I try to look at things rationally, but in my heart of hearts, I am also a person fighting for resistance. I deny the nature of the hegemony of the state. I deny the development principles of the Indian state.'

Then he looks up at me, speaking once more of his brother. 'We are responsible for keeping his memories.'

Somorendro helps too, in his own way. He wrote a poem in 1989, translated into English in the year of his death. Before my visit to meet the professor I had read it alongside an obituary of his brother.

On your fields today
lie scattered the blood-drops
of your sons
to merge into your earthly substance
that it shall fecundate
the oncoming season:
Green Phige-clad mother
Oh beloved Manipur.

Your heavens above are filled with smoke
rising ceaselessly from smouldering pyres
of your dead sons.
The free wind had blown
and spread them afar
on the expanse of your sky.
It shall pour forth as rain
on to the remote corners
of hills and plains.

The long slumbered ancient seeds
shall be awakened afresh.
New sprouts shall spring forth
on your vast fields and fallowland.

One day at dawn
amidst the crimson rays of the sun
you shall change your faded cloths.
One day at dawn
amidst the crimson rays of the sun
your fond ritual garment green
shall be sprinkled with golden hue.

19

Of fasting and steadfast ladies

It's literally a picture of protest as the growing crowd—women, men, and even some children—await the arrival of Mahasweta Devi and Ima Mangol. The short driveway of the Jawaharlal Nehru Memorial Dance Academy is lined with a series of stark black and white images. Expectedly, there's an iconic one of Irom Sharmila: feeding tube in her nose, a rush of unkempt open hair, a hand brushing a cheek in an intensely feminine moment—but the overall mood is one of resoluteness. Other images speak of imposition and heartbreak. Listless children of a slain innocent. A wife mourning at the memorial of a husband. A mother at a son's. Police and paramilitary checking a youngster on a street, and a rickshaw-puller. A haunting image of women in mourning white watching from a distance as men perform last rites for the dead of a massacre by security forces.

There is no date, time or place to the photographs. There isn't any need. Here, everyone knows the when, where and how. It is in the DNA of every waking day.

Nandini's husband Ramananda, who has accompanied me for the evening's event, and I take in the photographs. We greet Professor Lokendro. His colleagues and several student volunteers are all gathered at the entrance. They move a little distance away to not get in the way. Ima Mangol has arrived. The tiny octogenarian receives a remarkable welcome, one befitting the cliché of a warrior, not the cliché of a grandmother: sustained, rhythmic applause as she approaches and passes by people lined along the driveway. Some greet her with folded palms, some rush to touch the ground before her feet. She accepts each mark of respect with dignified nods of her head, sometimes a smile; and, guided by Singhajit, Sharmila's brother, walks slowly and absolutely erect into the auditorium. The applause follows her in.

Such adulation and respect would seem unusual anywhere but here. Women like Ima Mangol—generations of Meira Paibi—have for more than a hundred years taken protest and outrage to the rulers of Manipur. These manifestations of *nupi lan*—women's war—have been both relatively small, and big. In 1904, several thousand women surrounded Lt. Col. H. St. P. Maxwell, the British Resident, over an order by him to renew the hated forced labour. Earlier imposed by Manipur's maharajas, the system of *lalup* forced males between the ages of seventeen and sixty to offer set days of free labour to be used at the pleasure of the administration. In a book I recently purchased, *Nupi Lan* by Karam Manimohan Singh, there is a telling of how Maxwell referred to these protesting women. 'It is very difficult to know how to treat a mob of wild cats like this, but I shall take care to disperse them next time before they become numerous.'

As it happened, Maxwell was compelled to call off *lalup*. In Manipur, this episode is referred to as the First Nupi Lan.

The Second Nupi Lan came several decades later, in 1939-40, over the issue of rice being exported from the valley by a compact of the British and Manipur's king, and executed by Marwari traders of the time. It created massive shortages of this staple, the move coming as it did after floods in 1939 that devastated crops. There were several recorded instances of starvation. Women took to protest. Khwairamband Bazar—Ima Keithel—was shut: an amazing occurrence for this institution that has, by some reckoning, been around since the sixteenth century. There are records from the time of this Nupi Lan, of police severely beating protesters—wading in with batons, boots; pretty much the usual.

Forward, a left-leaning journal of the time, describes the situation in its issue of 17 February 1940. The language is giddy but informative: 'Manipur State is in a ferment. Women are in the vanguard of a struggle against the autocratic State Government. Undaunted by lathi blows and bayonet charges, the brave women of Manipur are marching forward with a firm resolve to vindicate their honour and obtain justice. Saturated with the spirit of non-violence, they will not take defeat but will carry on till the battle is over. They are looking up to you for sympathy and help.'

A key player in today's 'northeast' was also at hand then to deal instant justice. A group of women who had gathered to petition the king was set upon by a contingent of Assam Rifles. Twenty women reportedly received bayonet wounds.

For me, what has happened since, in all the various moves to bring peace in Manipur through the decades of the 1970s, '80s and '90s, is an ongoing series of Nupi Lan. What happened in 2004 is Nupi Lan. If ten naked, middle-aged women marching to Kangla Fort screaming at the resident Assam Rifles and 'Indian Army' contingents to rape them as they did their 'daughter', accusing them of raping—and killing—Thangjam Manorama Devi—is not an act of war born in the deepest recesses of their minds where live humiliation, sadness and anger, I cannot imagine what is.

Mahasweta Devi's arrival triggers a flurry of activity. She is accorded equal respect as Ima Mangol. Josy Joseph, a Kolkata-based filmmaker who has for long documented Mahasweta Devi's work, holds her hand as she walks in escorted by Singhajit, and what seems like the human rights who's-who of Imphal, a mix that also includes several newspaper editors, and both established and upcoming Meira Paibi leaders. After a short ceremony to light a candle at a large portrait of Sharmila, the feisty tribal rights activist and author enters the auditorium. I take that opportunity to reacquaint myself with Deepti, my senior by a couple of years at college, and author of the book on Sharmila that Mahasweta Devi will in some minutes from now formally release. We had lost touch since our university days in the 1980s, but I remember her as a person with strong feminist views and utter disregard as to what anyone else thought of them—quite like her approach to the book on Sharmila.

Deepti initially looks blank. I explain—this process elicits a chuckle from Ramananda—that I had much longer hair those days, a moustache, and wore long kurtas and hippie-style beads; and offer my nickname, and names of mutual friends. Recognition dawns: 'You've changed,' she allows. I nod in submission.

It's time to enter the auditorium past a lurid anti-AFSPA poster. It shows a likeness of Sharmila crucified, in a desolate plain of sand, cacti and skulls. A likeness of Prime Minister Manmohan Singh—dressed in combat pants and combat boots, white kurta, sleeveless jacket, and trademark sky-blue turban—hammers a nail into Sharmila's feet. At Singh's feet lies the likeness of Justice Jeevan Reddy. The poster is headlined: 'Judicial fraternity of the planet unite against AFSPA, the lawless law!'

The auditorium that seats several hundred is nearly full. Ramananda and I find a seat at the back—Deepti has meanwhile headed off to the front seats, being part of the event that will begin anytime now, a little past four in the afternoon.

After the initial greetings to the ladies—Mahasweta Devi respectfully referred to as 'Ma Mahasweta'—and the audience, the MC swiftly gets the programme going with a song, a tribute to Sharmila. Within a minute I am completely overcome, along with people seated around me. The difference between them and me is that I can't understand Meeteilon. It hardly matters.

It's operatic, hypnotic. The impossible scales through which Naorem Ganga Tombi journeys is at once a lament for loss, and a celebration of spirit. The three violins, two pena—beautiful indigenous violin of Manipur that Tangkhul Naga also use, and call tingtelia—a bamboo flute, and keyboard appear awed by her voice; the players allow her to guide them through this sweep of pure emotion. When, after a few minutes, she nears the end, in a supremely controlled, mesmerizing cry of 'Sharmila-a-a-a-' that would shame to mortification an electronic echo-machine, I realize that I can't see very well. I'm crying freely. And the reason isn't Sharmila's chosen path and attendant pathos that this cause célèbre generates. I realize the singer has drawn from me emotion absorbed over several months of travel through lands wracked by misunderstanding, ego, rage, death, and continual disrespect; of meetings and conversations; of histories; of laments, and such desperate, resounding hope. People around me—grown men and women, children—are unashamedly in tears, transported by their own reasons.

~

The rest of the afternoon and early evening is a blur, nearly an anticlimax after this tour de force. Mahasweta Devi and Ima Mangol together release Deepti's book, *Burning Bright*. Deepti describes what Sharmila means to her, about how she got to know her over a period of four months in New Delhi over 2006 and 2007, when Sharmila slipped away for a protest at Jantar Mantar before she was arrested and kept in a series of Delhi hospitals under police custody. 'She has courage and determination that is beyond my grasp,' she says—and I disagree: Deepti did well with the book—and speaks of how she was gradually drawn in by Sharmila's compelling 'action', and 'so much willpower and spiritual energy' to decide to write a book about her.

The felicitations to Mahasweta Devi and Ima Mangol come next, in order of appearance as marked by Professor Lokendro and his colleagues—I recall this from the preparatory meeting from two days earlier at the professor's residence. Emphatically, the first representative is from the Sanamahi religion, then Zeliangrong, Buddhism, Islam, Hinduism, Christianity—both Catholic and Baptist. Mahasweta Devi then speaks at length, repeatedly describing the twenty-first century as 'Sharmila's century'. Her speech often borders on hyperbole, but I realize its relevance as a booster in a gathering of this nature.

What touches me, though, is Ima Mangol's speech, short and sharp, that Ramananda translates for me. She had sat rock-steady through more than an hour of the events preceding her turn. She speaks, as Mahasweta Devi before her, seated on stage on a chair fronted by a low table and microphones. Ima Mangol talks in measured, unwavering tones of the need for 'integrity in protest and resistance'.

She speaks of a legend that talks of the day 'northern gates' will be shut, and 'eastern gates will be opened'.

The inference is clear. There may come a time when India will be shut out. The destiny of Manipuri people lie in the east, with the east.

I leave partway through *Lalhouba Amagee Mama*, having already seen significant sections of the rehearsal. Ramananda reaches me to the head of the crowded lane near my hotel in Thangal Bazar—I had shifted earlier in the day from the Tam-pha to the slightly less claustrophobic Anand Continental, where Mahasweta Devi, Deepti, Josy and others among the visitors are staying. ISTV, the robust local channel, is showing the play live, I see as I switch on the television to catch up with the day's developments. I let it play on: news suddenly doesn't seem quite as important.

It's all a bit strange, though. There I had been in the heart of Imphal at an event that was doing all it could to expose the state and Central government and their agencies through speech, book, song, play and media. Over the next few days, smaller events would be held with the help of students at Manipur University, and human rights organizations: more talk, screening of movies on AFSPA, panel discussions on the state of rot and persecution in Manipur.

I wonder why the state doesn't ban it all, or brutalize it all, as it has so many acts of protest. Is it because the local police are stretched chasing after Apunba Lup, so it cannot spare more personnel to clear this relatively less aggressive protest? Or have some minds, police and bureaucratic, figured out that with the presence of people from outside Manipur at these events, a violent incident would further sully the profile of a heavy-handed administration?

Could some among the police or administration actually be in subversive sympathy—however far-fetched the notion—with the idea behind such protest? Or was it because they simply didn't give a damn because they knew in arrogant certainty that a few hours of non-violent talk, and song and dance would not change the status of AFSPA in Manipur, or the wretched reality of Manipur itself?

I receive a phone call. It's a full-moon tonight. In celebration, there is to be a recital of classical songs at L's farmhouse on the way to Malom, a place where the killings in 2000 triggered Sharmila's protest. Usual suspects from Imphal's power-society will be there. I'm invited.

I don't feel like going. Drained after several weeks of travel, all I want to do is sleep. Then I want to escape for a while the heartbreaking schizophrenia of Manipur. I want to see the face of my child. Touch the façade of normality that I have attempted to weave in a small corner of Goa, my home and sanctuary of several years. Be away from other people's wars, other people's fears, other people's futures.

But by now I know this too: I am at home here, and at so many other places, so many other points of humanity and history along Highway 39 and its roiled yet hopeful hinterland.

I can't wait to return.

20

About a one-Act play of omission and commission (parentheses included)

This easternmost region of India is littered with acronyms both grand and diminutive, threatening and peaceful. Undoubtedly, the one that draws maximum discussion and ire is AFSPA.

By itself, the expansion, parentheses included, is almost innocuous: Armed Forces (Special Powers) Act, 1958.

In practice, it is the single-most effective tool the armed forces and paramilitary have to do pretty much what they want.

It needed the death of Thangjam Manorama on 11 July 2004 and the subsequent storm of protest in Manipur for the Government of India to set up a committee to review the Act that is currently applied to all of the state barring the municipal limits of Imphal, Nagaland, much of Assam, parts of Arunachal Pradesh, and a strip of Meghalaya. A clone exists in Jammu & Kashmir. In November of that year, the Government of India set up a committee to review AFSPA, to be chaired by B.P. Jeevan Reddy, a former judge of the Supreme Court. Known in speakeasy as the 'Justice Reddy Committee' or 'Jeevan Reddy Committee', it had four other members—S.B. Nakade, an academician and jurist; P. Shrivastav, a retired bureaucrat and a former special secretary at the home ministry; Lt Gen. V.R. Raghavan, who earlier held the post of director general of military operations, and among the more well-known observers and commentators about the 'Northeast', Sanjoy Hazarika.

The genesis of it all lies in post-Partition mayhem and chaos. A slew of ordinances with the central emphasis of 'Special Powers of Armed Forces' were issued in 1947 to cover Bengal, Punjab, Assam and the United Provinces of the time. These were coalesced under one umbrella the following year. A few years later came the war against Naga rebels. In 1958, as I read in an annexure to the committee's report written by Hazarika, the home minister at the time, Govind Ballabh Pant, 'declared that "certain misguided sections" of the Nagas were involved in "arson, murder, loot, dacoity, etc."' He added, '"So, it has become necessary to adopt effective measures for the protection of the people in those areas. In order to enable the armed forces to handle the situation effectively whenever such problem arises hereafter, it has been considered necessary to introduce this bill."'

Pant, who is, along with his prime minister, Nehru, part of the pantheon of freedom-fighters-turned-rulers of free India that I was taught to revere as part of a state-mandated school curriculum, steered the bill that initially became the Armed Forces (Assam and Manipur) Special Powers Act, 1958.

Hazarika quotes opposition from some MPs to the bill, soon to become an Act. 'One of them, L. Achaw Singh of Manipur, described the proposal as "unnecessary ... an anti-democratic measure ... a lawless law".'

The MP from Manipur was prescient. The fig-leaf that AFSPA provided the army and paramilitary led to arguably the most shameful application of force and disregard for human rights and 'collateral damage' in independent India's history, arguably the strongest application being in Nagaland, then Mizoram—and since, in Manipur. Over the years, amendments led to the replacing of 'Assam and Manipur' with the parenthetical innuendo of 'Special Powers'. An expansion saw it applied to all northeastern states and territories with the exception of Sikkim, which had not been annexed by India at the time of the last amendment in 1972.

AFSPA is sprawling, but its sweep comes from just a few paragraphs of clinically worded bureaucratese:

'Any commissioned officer, warrant officer, non-commissioned officer or any other person of equivalent rank in the armed forces may, in a disturbed area,

'(a) if he is of opinion that it is necessary so to do for the maintenance of public order, after giving such due warning as he may consider necessary, fire upon or otherwise use force, even to the causing of death, against any person who is acting in contravention of any law and order for the time being in force in the disturbed area prohibiting the assembly of five or more persons or the carrying of weapons or of things capable of being used as weapons or of fire-arms, ammunition or explosive substances;

'(b) if he is of opinion that it is necessary to do so, destroy any arms dump, prepared or fortified position or shelter from which armed attacks are made or are likely to be made, or any structure used as a training camp for armed volunteers or utilized as a hide-out by armed gangs or absconders wanted for any offence;

'(c) arrest, without warrant, any person who has committed a cognizable offence or against whom a reasonable suspicion exists that he has committed or is about to commit a cognizable offence and may use such force as may be necessary to effect the arrest;

'(d) enter and search without warrant any premises to make any such arrest as aforesaid or to recover any person believed to be wrongfully restrained or confined or any property reasonably suspected to be stolen property or any arms, ammunition or explosive substances believed to be unlawfully kept in such premises, and may for that purpose use such force as may be necessary.'

There is a procedure for the aftermath of arrest. 'Any person arrested and taken into custody under this Act shall be made over to the officer in charge of the nearest police station with the least possible delay, together with a report of the circumstances occasioning the arrest.' The least-possible-delay aspect has come by Constitutional imperative and precedence to mean twenty-four hours. As a clause in Article 22 of the Constitution provides—the committee's report reminds us—that 'every person who is arrested and detained in custody shall be produced before the nearest Magistrate within a period of 24 hours excluding the time taken for journey from the place of arrest to the nearest court of the Magistrate.'

If this seems reasonable, the point that follows immediately after is not, and it is the one that is nearly always used to justify torture, molestation, rape and even the killing of innocents—though such events have been written off as nuances of conflict. This paragraph has protected rage, revenge and near-genocide in the Naga areas and Mizoram through the 1950s, 1960s, and later, relatively more isolated but no less numerous cases in both the hills and plains areas of Manipur and Assam. 'No prosecution, suit or other legal proceeding shall be instituted, except with the previous sanction of the Central Government, against any person in respect of anything done or purported to be done in exercise of the powers conferred by this Act.'

~

The committee arrived at its conclusion with some thought and deliberation—not ad hoc sentimentality. While its recommendation and aftermath came as no surprise to many, the exercise in official duplicity is a fascinating, and disturbing, lesson.

The beginning was positive enough, as described in the terms of reference of the committee. 'Keeping in view the legitimate concerns of the people of the North Eastern Region, the need to foster

Human Rights, keeping in perspective the imperatives of security and maintenance of public order to review the provisions of the Armed Forces (Special Powers) Act, 1958, as amended in 1972 and to advise Government of India whether –

'(a) To amend the provisions of the Act to bring them in consonance with the obligations of the Govt. towards protection of Human Rights; or

'(b) To replace the Act by a more humane Act.'

Going by its report, the committee over five months held thirteen meetings and conducted seventeen public hearings across the Northeast and New Delhi. They met nearly two hundred people ranging from the general public, relatives of victims of excess by security forces, lawyers, activists, students and tribal leaders; to senior bureaucrats and senior officials from the Indian Army, Assam Rifles, CRPF, and the Border Security Force, and received written representations from some state governments.

The security establishment unanimously—and unsurprisingly—recommended continuation of AFSPA. Significantly, so did the Ministry of Home Affairs in a presentation to the committee, even though it had technically set up the committee in the first place—pretty much giving the game away. And, so did the governments of Assam and Arunachal Pradesh—where the Act is applied in the southeastern districts of Changlang and Tirap. Meghalaya wrote in saying that the twenty-kilometre strip bordering Assam that was declared a 'disturbed area' and where AFSPA was in force could retain status quo.

Mizoram, where the key rebel group had signed a peace accord in June 1986, requested that in the event AFSPA is not to be repealed it should no longer be applied to this state as there had been no untoward incident warranting it. As an aside, the letter to the committee from the home secretary of Mizoram, C. Ropianga, poignantly mentioned: 'For the people of Mizoram, the Armed Forces (Assam and Manipur) Special Powers Act, 1958, leaves a scar on their minds, and all sections of people regardless of political parties to which they belong are against this particular Act.'

The state governments of Manipur, Tripura and Nagaland did not send an official response; though the committee records representations by officials of the rank of additional chief secretary and additional director general of police significantly telling the committee during hearings in Nagaland that the 'Act should be replaced with a more humane legislation since it had generated suspicion between the Nagas and others'.

The remainder—citizens and civil groups of various kinds without background of service or association with armed forces—recommended without exception that AFSPA's time was done and it should immediately be repealed. There was also a fairly large section of feedback—and this is a stinging commentary on all insurgencies and underground groups—that articulated the need for the armed forces and paramilitary to be present, to fulfil two functions. One: India's need to secure areas in this region almost completely bound by international borders. And two: to keep at bay what in jargon is called non-state armed groups who prey on the public for moral support, shelter, money and men—and sometimes, women and minors. But the armed presence of India, even these even-handed critics petitioned, should be without the aggressive prophylactic of AFSPA.

The committee absorbed all feedback, and based its conclusion on perception of the public, logic, and existing provisions in the Constitution of India as well as various laws of India.

It drew on the constitutionally mandated 'freedoms' in Article 19 of the Constitution, including freedom of speech and expression; freedom to assemble peacefully and without arms; freedom to form associations and unions, and freedom to move freely throughout the territory of India. It quoted Article 14 in Part III of the Constitution, which 'ensures to its citizens equality before law and equal protection of laws'. It invoked Article 21, which 'expressly declares that no person shall be deprived of his life or personal liberty except in accordance with the procedure established by law'.

Alongside, the committee pointed out that several existing provisions were adequate for the Central and state governments, security forces and the police to discharge their mandated, legally empowered functions. Article 355 of the Constitution already provides for the Centre's 'duty to protect every state against internal disturbance as well', and is hitched to Article 352 that details the obligation to protect the territory of India against 'external aggression or internal rebellion'.

The Code of Criminal Procedure, through Sections 130 and 131, 'make it repeatedly clear that where it is necessary to call in the army to disperse an unlawful assembly endangering public security, the armed forces so called in shall act according to the directions of the Magistrate though the manner in which the armed forces perform the task entrusted to them lies within their discretion'. The committee's report adds: 'Even where the armed forces are called in for meeting a more serious threat to public order or public security, or where the deployment of armed forces is required on a fairly long-term basis, this concern remains equally valid.'

Moreover, the committee pointed out, there is also the Unlawful Activities (Prevention) Act, 1967, as amended in 2004. The Act, the committee's report insisted, 'defines "terrorism" in terms which encompass and cover the activities of the nature carried on by several militant/insurgent organizations in the North-east states'. It goes beyond just the operational aspect on the field—which AFSPA restricts itself to—to include tracking and interdiction of terrorist networks, their funding, and so on. To bolster the use of armed forces and Central paramilitary, Section 49 of this Act already has 'expressly barred ... any suit, prosecution or other legal proceedings against "any serving or retired member of the armed forces or paramilitary forces in respect of any action taken or purported to be taken by him in good faith, in the course of any operation directed towards combating terrorism".'

And, as the Unlawful Activities (Prevention) Act is applicable across India, it would also not be seen as discriminatory, unlike AFSPA, which is selectively applied to a few states. AFSPA, as the committee bluntly describes in its report, 'has become a symbol of oppression, an object of hate and an instrument of discrimination and high-handedness'.

When the Justice Jeevan Reddy Committee formally signed on its recommendation to the home ministry on 6 June 2005, it suggested that AFSPA be repealed.

The ministry buried it.

Home ministers—both Shivraj Patil and his successor P. Chidambaram—and Prime Minister Singh have occasionally discussed AFSPA in public; such talk has remained in the nature of verbal balm to fob off complaints.

As I again read the committee's report on my way back from Manipur, I can't help recalling Professor Lokendro's jibe at India's establishment. Or his astonishment, mirroring that of many others, of the obdurate fondness of the security establishment towards AFSPA.

Tellingly, the governor of Meghalaya, Ranjit Shekhar Mooshahary, a former director of the elite National Security Guards, and director general of Border Security Force had just days ago on 1 November 2009 spoken of the need to remove AFSPA from the Northeast in general and Manipur in particular. In this he was joined by additional director of the Intelligence Bureau, R.N. Ravi. It made headlines nearly everywhere in the region; I had read about it first on the Internet at theshillongtimes.com from a poky cyber café at Imphal's Paona Bazar, literally a stone's throw from the spot where Rabina had been shot dead.

'The Act which has been in use for a long time is ineffective and there is need to revisit it,' the newspaper quoted Mooshahary as saying at the closing session of the Conference of Police Chiefs of the North-East, Sikkim and West Bengal in Shillong. AFSPA has been misused and would continue to be misused, he said. 'If the Act is removed, I think the situation would not worsen. In fact it will improve ... The Act has made the people vulnerable. The Centre could think of doing away with the Act or applying it in a modified way.'

(In January 2010, Mooshahary would go farther. Speaking at a conference of the North-East Region Commonwealth Parliamentary Association, also in Shillong, he tore into AFSPA. 'We cannot contain insurgency-related violence by alienating the citizens. We can do so more effectively by involving them ... This Act has alienated the civil society more and more with the passage of time ... and has lost its relevance in view of the emerging role of the civil society in violence-prone areas ... I do not subscribe to the view that we need to continue fighting insurgency and terrorism with the help of the Armed Forces [Special Powers] Act.')

Ravi, the serving intelligence officer, who stood to lose more than Mooshahary by going against the grain of conventional wisdom, told the media: 'We have every reason to do away with the Act and we believe that our police force can tackle the law and order situation.'

Earlier, in June 2009, the young Minister of State for Rural Development, Agatha Sangma, a member of the Nationalist Congress Party (NCP) at the time in coalition with the United Progressive Alliance government in New Delhi, met Prime Minister Singh, and handed him a letter urging him to either repeal AFSPA or withdraw it from Manipur. She had some impetus: while on a visit to Imphal that month she had visited Irom Sharmila at the Jawaharlal Nehru Hospital where she is kept under police custody. In September 2009, Sangma, an MP from Meghalaya, travelled rather far from the establishment to release, in Delhi, Deepti Priya Mehrotra's searing book on Sharmila and her circumstances.

Two years earlier in 2007, the influential Administrative Reforms Commission headed by veteran Congress party member Veerappa Moily had also suggested the repeal of AFSPA; in its place bolstering the Unlawful Activities (Prevention) Act with provisions to enable the armed forces to operate in the charged climate of northeastern India.

The net effect: status quo.

'The name is *so* important for them,' Professor Lokendro's livid sarcasm revisits as I read and research further. 'Armed Forces *Special* Powers Act.'

~

As it happens, for many it *is* important, and quite special. I've had serving army officers stationed in Manipur and elsewhere tell me without batting an eyelid they don't see what the fuss is about.

Sure we need AFSPA, I am repeatedly told. All we can do is hold a person for twenty-four hours and hand him over to the police. There can be no visible marks of interrogation, of torture—or the police won't take in 'the fellow'. We have to be careful about such things, I am told. It goes against conventions—the army officers mean the Geneva Convention as well as general conventions and internationally accepted practices of human rights—but we have to do what we have to do. 'We have the guy for twenty-four hours,' a senior officer told me. 'That's all we have.'

I have been told by several army officers that the police and intelligence folk have under the Indian Penal Code, Code of Criminal Procedure, National Security Act and the Official Secrets Act, more powers than the army does under AFSPA.

Few understood that the blanket permission to attack, kill, and destroy that the armed forces enjoy under AFSPA is a power far above anything else available in this land. In the years since 1958, under the cover of AFSPA, armed forces have turned their anger on civilians resulting in tens of thousands of civilian deaths—deaths of people who India, ironically, claims as its own. There have been uncountable number of beatings, torture and molestation; the razing and burning of several hundred villages across northeastern India. War crimes, really. The immunity AFSPA offers far exceeds the practical issues of handing over a suspect within a day to civil authorities. Several officers have also bluntly decried the police, saying in many areas the police and civil administration are hardly to be seen until the armed forces show up and reclaim territory from rebels and insurgents.

In his representation to the Justice Reddy Committee, a retired major general said that of 55,000 cases registered against the armed forces, there have been only three convictions. He meant it in defence of AFSPA, instead of what it can also be interpreted as: it is difficult for a complainant to take on the system. 'There can be stray incidents if a soldier goes amok,' he further offered.

I hear repeatedly: AFSPA is both paramount and appropriate. And, in the interests of national security, AFSPA should continue.

I have met a few army officers who are ashamed of the history of AFSPA. One such encounter took place at an unlikely venue: the Jaipur Literature Festival, which I attended in 2009 to give a talk about my book on the Maoist rebellion, *Red Sun: Travels in Naxalite Country*. I described in detail the mind-numbing atrocities the Chhattisgarh government had unleashed on tribals in Maoist-affected parts of the state, in the guise of a process called Salwa Judum—purification hunt in the Gondi dialect. I referred to the practice of state police and Central paramilitary threatening, killing, torturing, raping, maiming civilians, including children and the elderly; how villagers were being corralled into concentration camps; how villages and food stores were being destroyed and burned—the same as the armed forces had done in Nagaland and Mizoram. In fact, I suggested in gallows humour that the Americans had probably Xeroxed their anti-civilian brutality from India for their

Vietnam campaign. In Chhattisgarh you didn't need AFSPA, I said. Nobody prosecuted the police or paramilitary. There was no scope—democratic rights were routinely butchered.

The officer, a serving brigadier with experience of 'action' in the Northeast, and attached to one of the most prestigious regiments of the Indian Army, publicly acknowledged the pointlessness of AFSPA. He also said the Americans didn't learn anything from Indians—Indians and Americans had both learnt it from the British, who had perfected such tactics in South Africa during the Boer Wars, the jungles of Malaya and elsewhere.

That officer is today my friend, but that won't help repeal AFSPA, won't transform the approach that mandates military solutions when political solutions and commonsense administrative solutions would suffice.

And so, it continues. The Gods of Internal and External Security and The God of Unity at Any Cost have no time for Sanjoy Hazarika's heartfelt plea, recorded as an annexure to the Justice Reddy Committee's report:

> We hope that the report of the Committee will help in the process of reconciliation and democratization in the Northeast, create a space for dialogue and discussion, reducing conflicts and helping the region write a new chapter of peace, change and happiness in its troubled history. We also hope it strengthens the country's unity, integrity and security and creates an atmosphere for people to live in dignity, honour and peace.
>
> At the end of every dark night there is a dawn, however delayed. And for every day, there is a dawn, whether we see it or not.

21

Interlude: 'Dial *456*452# to know about India's freedom struggle'

Politics finally intervenes in my travels to nix Plan A.

I arrive in Guwahati, the region's gateway for trade and travel, on 24 January. I'm excited about a long, somewhat intense arc of journeying that will bring me to Imphal from the west. I plan to take the Inter City Express to Lumding Junction, spend half the night on the platform, and take the early-morning Barak Valley Express to Silchar: a day-long ride through North Cachar Hills of southeastern Assam to that tea and trading town. From there, I plan to ride a bus east to Imphal on Highway 53, forsaking for a while Highway 39 to get a sense of what is sometimes called the worst road in the northeast—and the competition is intense.

It will be nice to spend 26 January on the road, I think, see how this void of India deals with the country's Republic Day. In Delhi, of course, it is an occasion both for display of military mojo and officially mandated reaffirmation of India's faith in itself. There, as in capitals of Indian states, it takes place with the greatest of security preparation: as ever the sign of the times. In other places, further away from cities and towns, vestiges of administration are absent along with the thought contained in that much abused phrase, 'idea of India'. The battered road from Silchar to Imphal runs through such country.

I wonder about the upcoming journey on the late-afternoon hour-long bus ride into town from Guwahati airport. It's enough to keep my mind off the snare of traffic at Jalukbari Circle, which seems perennially decorated with the pilings of a flyover years in birthing. The bus route to Ulubari—I will get down before that near the local Reserve Bank of India office close to the station—takes us along the Machkhowa area by the stately Brahmaputra, though from this perspective and at this time of the year the river is more *chora*, sandbank, than water. Rusting steamers lie beached. The riverside eateries look tawdry in the fading light of day, missing the forgiving mask of neon that dark will bring. As the bus turns right towards Cotton College, close to my destination, a billboard advertisement to fund entrepreneurship by Assam's government asks: 'Are you an unemployed? Desirous to start your own venture?'

At least it's upbeat. This region can do with upbeat.

United Liberation Front of Asom has stepped in, I discover upon arriving at Guwahati station, a scene of chaos surpassing even the general state of chaos at large Indian railway stations. As I flew across the county from Mumbai, they blew up a stretch of railway tracks near Kokrajhar. So, all night trains across Assam have been cancelled for three days. Even the premier Rajdhani Express is being 'detained', I overhear railway staff talking. The deputy station master's office is a scene of bedlam: he's juggling irate passengers along with the information and logistics for several dozen cancelled and stranded trains.

Back on the concourse—equally a scene of bedlam—I check with travel touts as to night buses to Lumding that will enable me to make the connection to Silchar. No way. I ask about taxis: No way. I know flights to Silchar and Imphal have left hours earlier. And, anyway, in this region nearly nothing but air force planes take to the skies after dark.

Time for Plan B: direct travel to Imphal. I decide to take a 26 January reality check there.

Standing amidst the dislocation caused by explosive protest—literally—typical for this time of the year in these parts, I dial from my mobile phone the Gurgaon number of an Internet-based travel agency I use; it also accepts bookings over telephone. The efficient travel assistant helps me out: she can get me on an Indigo Airways flight to Imphal early the following morning.

'Will you pay by credit card?'

'Yes, but why are you shouting at me?'

'Sorry sir,' she continues to shout. 'You have to speak louder. There is a lot of noise where you are.'

'Yes,' I shout back, avoiding pedestrian traffic on the pavement as it rushes past me both to and from the station. 'I'm also trying to not fall into a sewer through a break in the pavement.'

She laughs and shouts, 'No problem, sir.' The interactive voice recognition system takes over. I tap in details of my card, and we're done. Within seconds, the reservation code and flight number are messaged to me. All I will need to do at Guwahati airport is show my ID and the text message to the reservation clerk and get an electronic ticket issued.

My country, the schizophrenic. Within minutes my travel plans can be both seamlessly demolished and resurrected amidst chaos. Technocrats call it India's ability to leapfrog ahead. But I so wish they would pay attention to the dead and deadening stuff the frog is leaping over—forgotten situations, places and people; areas of dislocation, of lamentable slippage.

All around me is a wash of hundreds of travellers; and commuting army, Assam Rifles and paramilitary personnel. Pedal rickshaws and autorickshaws live dangerously along the wheels of large army trucks. There's choking dust, gusts of diesel exhaust, blaring of horns, shouts by army men to pedestrians and all else to stand aside as they go about their business. The troopers look purposeful in black bandanas tied on the heads, automatic weapons at the ready. Convoys go rushing in and out of the large army transit camp building by the station with the improbable, cheery sign that invites: 'Home Away From Home'. From these parts India's forces are occupied fighting ULFA, keeping peace with Bodo rebels and those from Karbi Anglong and North Cachar districts, policing the border with Bhutan, tracking China from adjacent Arunachal Pradesh, and Bangladesh from Meghalaya and Assam—a laundry-list of security imperatives.

The Nandan Hotel in Paltan Bazar, Guwahati's travel and market hub, charges more money than I would usually like to pay for just a night's rest, but I've decided to give myself the evening off, indulge a bit. As I check in, a smartly dressed Assamese youngster who calls his sister 'sis'—equally casual-chic, and by his side—is trying to cajole the duty manager into allowing the bar staff to let him work his own cocktails.

'It's okay, bro,' she tells him.

'It's cool, sis, they'll agree.' There's a rapidfire exchange in a mixture of Assamese and English—I catch 'just etu fresh ginger mish-mash koribo lagibo; aru soda, to be added slowly over crushed ice. Hawbo?' They get their way.

Impressed, I order room service from Mexithachi, the signature restaurant of the hotel. But with a name like that, I concentrate on TV news instead of the food I'm about to eat. By dint of travel-habit I am already braced for the Thai-style green curry I have ordered to bring with it the flavour of salsa, and the oily orange plague of 'Manchurian' overtones that no person in Manchuria would ever have tasted.

DY 365 is flashing news about a drug haul in Bokajan, along Highway 39 in the Karbi Anglong district of Assam. The state's director general of police assures the people of Assam about having brought ULFA-related issues to bay. 'There have been some instances of violence, but the general situation is under control,' he mouths in the classic response of a lawkeeper in India.

On NeTV, Mrinal Hazarika, a leader of the pro-talks faction of ULFA, on the other side from his colleagues who have taken some lives with their explosion—along with ruining my Plan A—is going on about the sore point of who exactly is an Assamese. Those who have arrived in the state after 1971 clearly are not, he vehemently insists, keeping alive the explosive outsider/insider debate that has taken thousands of lives since the 1980s. Indeed, the debate helped to birth and prosper ULFA.

P.K. Dutta, the superintendent of police of Kokrajhar, where ULFA have blown up railway tracks, promises to 'relentlessly pursue' the perpetrators.

And veteran Naga politician S.C. Jamir is making a play for Nagaland upon arrival at Dimapur airport. Back from Mumbai after a stint as governor of Maharashtra, he explains to the camera: 'As a constitutional head, you are constrained or restrained. A politician cannot remain a governor for too long—I am actively with the Naga people for peace, progress and prosperity.'

The Congress politician is on his way to his home in Chumukedima—not the one in Forest Colony, Kohima, where one of his sons now live, as NSCN-IM have threatened to kill him if he ever crosses the Inner Line checkpoint to enter the Naga Hills.

'We have to approach the problem not through confrontation, but goodwill,' Jamir deadpans, this impeccably dressed and coiffed politician who for decades has stood stolidly against all manner of Naga armies and militant factions. 'After all, NSCN-IM, NSCN-K or Naga Army—they are part of the same society.'

Governor Jamir appears to be homesick at the right time. With all the talk about reconciliation, Nagaland appears politically stoked up and ready for the taking. How could he bear to be away?

~

The morning after is bitterly cold. In the grey early-morning light, people walk huddled into shawls and jackets. Along Mahatma

Gandhi Road, police stop milkmen on bicycles to check the large aluminium canisters they have slung on either side of the carrier. Explosives and weapons are sometimes transported in these. Sometimes, the canisters become bombs.

The autorickshaw I travel in to the airport is stopped thrice. We are quizzed as to our purpose.

The life and limb exercise. It's a nice warm-up to Imphal.

The cynicism leaves me on the half-empty aircraft. My flight is delayed by thirty minutes on account of fog in Imphal, but when we're aloft, I'm all but glued to the window, excited as a schoolboy at a sight I have seen more than once, but never tire of. The Airbus A320 banks right over the Brahmaputra to head southeast over Meghalaya. In minutes, we pass the airfield for Shillong at Umroi, the vast lake of Barapani further south. The distant sprawl of Shillong is draped over hills that have still managed to retain crowns of pine.

As the plane heads farther east, Meghalaya opens up. A deep, tree-laden canyon snakes its way south cleaving the harsh brown rocks of a great plateau. In the distance is a steep drop-off, and beyond lie the vast plains of Bangladesh. With the cascades of blue at this height, it's like watching the floor of an ocean: a continental shelf and the descent to abyssal plains.

Soon we are over Karbi Anglong and the Barak river system. The hills are sparsely populated. Specks of white and the shine of aluminium roofs flash from the green floor. The plane begins its descent fifteen minutes into the flight. In a blink, with the sleight of some cloud cover we are over the hills and south into the bowl of Imphal Valley. We curve wide over Loktak lake, heading west to circle back to Imphal, the shadow of the aircraft skipping across the expanse of water and blankets of phumdi, the floating reed-grass-mud islands.

Bump. Land. Whine of engines. Cut off. The utter stillness of the morning. Bright sunshine. A lungful of pure air drifting from the hills, fields and waterways.

The Manipur tourism office is still resolutely closed.

I ditch Tam-pha for the relatively more up-market Anand Continental in the teeming grottoes of Thangal Bazar. The window in my room opens immediately onto rusting grills guarding the privacy of a Meitei family. The smell of garbage and open sewers floats in with the morning breeze, but this location works if there is curfew on account of a shootout with any 'UG' group or grenade attack by one; or a general shutdown call by 'UG' groups. In this commercial zone, some grocer, some trader will always find a window of opportunity to work some business. If anywhere, there will be food here. Always, there will be some way out.

A few metres south of Anand, near a tri-junction of a sweetshop and the perennially overworked ATM of Central Bank of India, is the Cinema Paradiso. As I wait for some local contacts and friends to arrive, I settle for a cup of instant coffee and surprisingly good fried noodles at the cheery walk-up painted in canary yellow. Two young ladies at the counter handling box office and snacks are taking time out from college—there are no classes; educational institutions are still shut down.

For fifty rupees per person, the small theatre that seats fifty-four will screen a DVD of *The International* at 5 p.m. The next change is billed as *Avatar, 2012* and *District 9*. It will be fun to watch *District 9*, a movie about aliens on earth stuck in a heavily policed ghetto in South Africa that is more concentration camp. The irony of watching it in Imphal will be delicious.

My mobile phone company, BSNL, intrudes with a beep of text message. It's an offer for me to dial *456*452# to know about 'India's freedom struggle'.

'Imagine,' the text giddily urges me, 'how would be a life without Independence.'

There's a price to pay: 'Rs 25/m'. It's unclear as to whether the 'm' stands for every minute of patriotism, or every month.

Sounds like Plan C. I'm home.

22

Republic of India: Version Imphal 2.0.1.0

I wake at what passes for dawn on the morning of 26 January. It's bitterly cold. My tiny room is dark except for the flickering light from the small TV which I realize I was too tired to switch off before falling asleep. But I'm now glad I didn't; what's showing is surreal.

A programme rerun on Doordarshan-Northeast has Shillong-based musician Lou Majaw interviewing a retired lieutenant colonel about patriotism. At one point the officer yanks out a harmonica and starts to belt out some Bob Dylan. It's perhaps apt: Majaw considers Dylan to be god—in fanatical devotion he even holds a concert to mark Dylan's birth anniversary each May.

After settling his long white hair, a beaming Majaw asks the lieutenant colonel the reason for trouble in the northeast. That seems to be the purpose of the programme on this government-run channel. On cue, the retired officer instantly turns from musician to parrot. 'The insurgents and movements are just extortionists; they have no ideology. They just do it'—here he gestures to a pocket of his jacket—'to line their pockets.'

Would it be okay then—I mouth in parody of the chat show as the officer repeats the standard line I have heard from politicians, bureaucrats and security officials in all manner of media—if such groups did indeed have ideology? Would it then be legitimate to rebel against India, bolstered by ideology, as so many groups have done and so many continue to? But I'm not part of the chat show.

Majaw's guest launches into a harangue about the greatness of India. I can't help thinking: there must be something fundamentally wrong—or perhaps, fundamentally still raw—with the construct of India, if more than sixty years after independence from Great Britain we still need to try so hard, so institutionally, at patriotism.

Everything is shut, not on account of Republic Day but a shutdown call given by several rebel groups in Imphal Valley to 'boycott' Republic Day celebrations. But there must be, I'm certain, at least one place selling tea. Almost nothing except extreme natural calamity or total war has the power to prevent a tea stall from opening. And sure enough, I find one just round the corner from Cinema Paradiso, facing the wide open sewer that, like a canal, separates Thangal Bazar from Nagamapal Road.

It's actually a hole in the wall, from which a scruffy Bihari gentleman is selling sweet black tea with a sprinkling of rock salt. The small bridge across the sewer, a crossroads, and the area around the shop are teeming with Manipur Police commandos and regular police. I stand along with a few and drink welcome tea from tiny plastic cups, munch on freshly fried potato pakoras a helper is making, his back against the wall of the building the shop sprouts from. The teashop man tells me in Hindi he has the courage to open his shop when everything else is shut because there are so many police about.

A couple of police commandos are seated on a rickety bench. I join them, and look around. Across from the poky S.S.S. Hotel is a large billboard that offers the most publicly advertised recovery service I have come by. It's an advertisement for the SMARTI company, and shows a row of smartly suited men, and women in executive wear. 'The only debt recovery agent you can rely on. We stand firmly for a better Banker-Borrower-Relation.' Alongside a couple of telephone numbers are listed the firm's services: debt recovery, possession, auction, debt management programme, and a grievance cell.

'We ensure quick recovery and not resting in debtors account,' I'm assured. 'We analyse the situation, manage the decision and catalyse the growth.'

To live up to such a pitch in a city like Imphal, the firm would need to display great dexterity, great muscle and outstanding insurance for any chance at success. That will mean connections absolutely everywhere, including above the ground, and the underground. AG and UG: as ever, two sides of the same coin.

Refreshed with a second glass of tea, I walk southeast towards the main hub of Thangal Bazar where, at the tri-junction marked with a bust of Mohandas Gandhi, I can cut left to arrive at Mahatma Gandhi Road, down which the Republic Day parade is to pass.

Mohandas Gandhi's bust is garlanded with fading marigold and surrounded by piles of garbage. Groups of labourers and a few beggars, from their features all from 'Mainland' India, huddle around fires of worn tyres, plastic packets, plastic and jute sacking—breathing in the black smoke this warmth spews. A Border Security Force patrol stands guard near the State Bank of India branch and ATM—the snaking queues outside it missing today.

As I pass by the main State Bank office, I hear the synchronized sound of drums. It sounds like a march past and it appears to be coming from within the Kangla Fort. The parade must be preparing to move out. Then I hear from the depths of the bank building, a crisp military command in Hindi: 'Saavdhaan! Dayen murh!' Attention. Right turn.

Curious, I walk closer. Sheltered by the wall of the building which is also their camp, CRPF troopers in ceremonial dress are forming up in front of a flagpole. A guard in a pillbox, in full battle gear, tries to shoo me away with a loud 'chal hutt'—basically, piss off—and a wave of an automatic rifle. I ignore his admonition, tell him I'm a writer visiting from elsewhere, and slip him my ID. This soon brings another trooper, a smartly uniformed Sikh, Chal-Hutt's senior I see from the chevrons stitched onto his tunic. They are a company of the 143rd Battalion of CRPF.

'What do you want?' he asks me courteously enough in Hindi.

'I see you're about to start a flag-hoisting ceremony. I want to watch. I've never seen an Indian flag hoisted in Imphal.'

'Bas?'

'Bas.' That's all.

'Toh phir aiye,' he politely invites me. I rush in, as it appears my showing up has briefly delayed the ceremony.

I stand on one side of the cramped courtyard, as the troopers stand rigidly at attention in ranks three deep. Their commandant, a young lady, faces them, the flagpole in between. In Hindi, she tells them of how India became independent from 'British-log'; but that wasn't enough, she says. Now India also became a republic in 1950 'to protect our democracy that guaranteed equality for all'. She then talks about the 'shaheed'—martyrs—to the cause of India. And the shaheed of CRPF too martyred to the cause of India. She tells them about the idea of 'balidaan', sacrifice.

Sadly, more of you will die—I silently add—killed by those who disagree violently with what either India orders them to do or what India has reduced them to. And more of you will be asked to kill those who will die for their freedom from India, and for freedom from India's mandated poverty, institutionalized corruption, and arrogance of its leaders.

Such utter waste of lives, when mere governance would do.

The commandant nods. A senior trooper shouts an order to call the company to attention. She and the trooper then firmly tug the lanyard, and a neatly folded bundle of tricolour cloth already in place at the top of the flagpole unfurls, releasing a small shower of marigold petals. The small flag weakly flutters in the damp breeze.

When the gathering breaks into a rousing '*Jana Gana Mana* ...', singing the national anthem flavoured with all the accents of India, I can't help a lump forming in my throat. I accompany them, awed by the force of their singing.

When it is over, the lady leads them in a shout: 'Bharat mata ki jai.' They say it thrice: Victory to Mother India.

Then they march off to a nearby building, also of State Bank of India, to repeat the process. I follow, but meanwhile, the Sikh gentleman has found time to offer me a plate containing two gulab jamuns—their Republic Day treat. I wolf down the sweets in gratitude. We rush to catch up with the rest.

We gather on the rooftop by flagpole on the side facing the street. The ceremony is repeated. The flag unfurls its bits of marigold and the saffron-white-green colours of India. We again sing the anthem.

I look around. Three floors up all around us are the roofs or higher floors of other buildings, without exception peeling, blackened, and some broken. Only the mobile telephony towers on rooftops look new, shining; and few arcs of satellite dishes of direct-to-home television.

From a building to our left, two Manipuri children peer at us.

Then an arm clad in a red sweater-sleeve and bangles pulls them back from the window, and slams it shut.

~

The 'Underground' will evidently have to try harder to enforce a shutdown. The hell-or-high-water will of India's establishment is at present greater than the will of all underground groups put together.

Mahatma Gandhi Road is two, three and four deep with people, waiting for the Republic Day Parade to roll up. There are all manner of subcontinental races and faces here, but those with an oriental cast make up most of the number. It could be chasing the flag that brings them out. It could be curiosity. Or it could be the alleviation of the sheer grind of living in Imphal, where public aural and visual excitement provided by the government is typically the passing of official convoys with screaming sirens. Sometimes, the sounds are of public protest. Sometimes—though less these days—the sound of gunfire or a grenade going off.

I make my way through the throng towards the traffic circle in front of Kangla Fort. The circle presents an uncluttered vantage manned by a dozen or so police commandos and both male and female police. Incredibly, nobody prevents me, though the road is heavily guarded and at places where the crowd is thickest, plainclothesmen are about with long bamboo staves for crowd control—and they aren't being gentle, I can see. The opposite sidewalk, along the western wall of Kangla Fort, is entirely barricaded. There are no canoe and kayak enthusiasts in the moat-practice area today. The clutch of battered Tata Sumo variants and Mahindra 'jeeps' that make up the taxi stand for travel to the border town of Moreh is absent to make way for the parade.

The president of India must have arrived at her grandstand on Rajpath in New Delhi, and greeted the official guest of honour for this day, visiting South Korean president Lee Myung-bak. Doordarshan commentators would have got into the swing of things with their screamingly dull description of the grand march past of Indian machismo and prescribed unity. My pre-teen daughter would have risen earlier than usual on this school holiday to watch it on TV, to bolster the sense of her country she professes to love; though I know well that the daily explicit madness of India, what she sees on her travels across the country with her parents, and on TV, YouTube and in newspapers, utterly bewilders her, sometimes brings her dangerously close to heartbreak.

A few police Gypsys and Ambassadors scream up and down the route of the parade for a final security check. After several minutes, at a quarter past eight, the head of the parade that has poured out of Kangla Fort becomes visible at the north end of the road.

Soon, it is at the first of the markers, the three free-standing pillars of bamboo frame covered with visuals of flag, with various messages to develop fisheries. The structure displays visuals of Loktak lake, which most of an entire generation of Manipur residents have not seen up close, prevented by the presence of Assam Rifles camps all around the lake. The pillars are topped by replica cutouts of the Ashokan Lion capital from Sarnath. The dharma chakra, the so-called wheel of law that also forms the centrepiece of the Indian flag, holds up the lion, together merged in a colour we called tandoori-orange in long-ago days at university.

By half past eight, the lead vehicle that marks the chariot of the parade commander is much closer, fronted by a dozen soldiers who walk in full battle gear, with oval helmets, bulletproof jackets and a small forest of automatic weapons. They reach the next set of pillars.

One of the pillars urge: 'Be self-employed through dairy farming.' Another urges timely vaccination of livestock and pets 'for better health and optimum production'. The third, also carrying a message from Manipur's veterinary and animal husbandry department, has a socialist tone: 'Backyard poultry rearing by masses and meet demand for egg & meat.' It comes with a lurid visual of a man milking the likeness of a Jersey cow, with golden coins streaming from the udders of this magical creature.

Ten minutes later, the parade rolls up to Kangla circle. The watchful soldiers are followed by the parade commander, an impeccably turned-out officer of Manipur police. A superb marching band of Assam Rifles sets the pace. Troopers from Assam Rifles in full dress uniform, followed by CRPF, Manipur Police battalions separately of men and women, smoothly, crisply march past the awkward curve of the circle. They all draw cheers when they offer their salute, not to a 'VVIP'—an acronym mandated by the rulebooks of administrative protocol—but refreshingly, to bystanders. For a brief time spectacle supersedes politics.

The parade stops dead at five minutes to nine. Near a junction to the south, where Highway 39 turns towards Moreh, stands the lead vehicle, backing up the entire parade. There's much crackling of walkie-talkies from police personnel near me. A lady constable turns to me after a while—we had been chit-chatting once she figured that with my camera and notebook I wasn't a security threat that she may need to immediately deal with—and says 'gari kharab ho gaya' in adequate Hindi. The lead vehicle is kaput.

We wait under the benign gaze of a tiny, weather-worn marble likeness of a stern-faced Jawaharlal Nehru on the left side of the main gate of Kangla Fort. And, on the other side, the exhibit of an equally worn but real shell of a Folland Gnat F.1 fighter retired from the Indian Air Force. An increasingly sharp sun has broken through the light cloud cover. The crisp parade has entirely lost its charm, and by the time it shakes loose a half hour after stalling, crowds have begun to disperse.

I take this opportunity to walk across to the forbidden side of the road and make my way down the remainder of the now listless parade. Youngsters of the National Cadet Corps wait around. Some squat in the typical eastern fashion of rest. Groups of students from the D.M. College of Science wait patiently, as do their colleagues from Johnstone Higher Secondary School.

The leader of the drama troupe from the Nupee Lal and Khongjom War Memorial Society holds up a placard to shield her face from the sun. The back of the placard hopefully proclaims in unintended double entendre: 'We are one peace.' Groups of irritated dancers from several colourfully dressed Meitei cultural troupes follow. Young thang-ta and tae kwon do martial arts students in a small group have their heads bowed to the sun and wasted time.

The only sign of life seems to be in the Naga, Kuki and Hmar cultural troupes that bring up the rear. It's a serial mix of dancing, singing spectacle from the restless hills of Manipur in the seething valley. The thinning crowd cheers them as the parade finally picks up what seems like its last bit of steam for its short run to a nearby stadium, for the state's VIPs and VVIPs to offer benediction of nationhood.

At the tail of the parade, a few billboards offer encouragement. By piles of garbage along the broken walls of a cultural centre, the left-to-right grinning faces of Congress chieftain Sonia Gandhi, her son Rahul, and Prime Minister Singh announce in rhyme: 'Commitment of Congress/Development and Progress.' Nearby is a poster from the Manipuri movie *Bomb Blast.*

In another advertising dimension, a stunningly pretty local lady holding a black electric guitar showcases both the 2009-10 edition of the Manipur Idol talent contest and a social message: 'I would do anything for love but I wouldn't do that.' The message urges all to avoid unprotected sex and so, HIV/AIDS. It then adds: 'Be kewl.'

For the third dimension, the last Republic Day arch aspirationally announces that Manipur is the 'Gateway to South East Asia'.

And finally, to lay claim to the presence of a fourth dimension, a larger-than-life Mohandas Gandhi on a truck urges what to a casual visitor to Imphal would seem like a message of the greatest immediacy: 'Sanitation is more important than independence.'

23

'Who told you this is a tourist place?'

Across from my room at my hotel in Imphal is a young couple from Delhi, Khushboo and Akash Jain. She works as programme head with Jamghat, a NGO for street children. He is in the lighting business; he jokes that the trade calls it providing 'customized, turnkey illumination solutions'—in a similar vein to what makers of fancy pens call the devices 'writing instruments'.

They are visiting friends in Imphal on account of a wedding in their family. Both strict vegetarians, they speak glowingly of their hosts' sense of hospitality in going out of their way to provide all-vegetarian fare—even cooking food in utensils kept separately from the rest—in these joyously non-vegetarian parts.

We had got on well enough when we first met on the evening before Republic Day.

'How many checkpoints did you count?' I had teased Khushboo, the more talkative of the two, about their trip a day earlier to Moreh.

'I lost count after five,' she replied with a smile.

Then she had let a little anger pour. She says their taxi was repeatedly stopped, and they were rudely asked their business by both Manipuri police and Assam Rifles personnel all the way to Moreh and back.

'It was humiliating. It reminded me of Jammu & Kashmir.' She said it also reminded her a little of Assam, and of Nepal during the Maoist rebellion that ran from 1996 for a decade.

'You know how it is.' I had shrugged. 'If you're here, you have to get used to it.'

'I *refuse* to get used to it,' she snapped, as her husband looked a little alarmed. 'This is India.'

This is Manipur, I had gently corrected her. And this is an India of our making.

That had riled her, and her sense of Indianness, her pride at being an educated, successful professional in her own country. She rattled off about a friend of hers from her student days at Jawaharlal Nehru University who used to 'badmouth India all the time, like India and Indians are to blame for everything here', she jabbed at the faded carpet of her hotel room for emphasis. 'He has an MPhil [degree] but instead of doing something with it all he does is moan. Eighty per cent of the people from here look for government jobs and live on government funds, and then they rubbish India. It makes me *really* angry.'

Akash looked at me, a little embarrassed, wondering if his spouse's temper was getting to me. I welcomed it, actually; it provided an opportunity to talk things through. All she said is true, I told her, but that does not excuse India treating people badly and behaving with the same lack of morality the colonial British had displayed with their seemingly gratuitous divide-and-rule policy, and at the same time pour in money to feed an economy of conflict. Essentially, buy peace with the lure of government jobs and funds, encourage and overlook corruption, while continuing to treat locals with complete contempt, for overall strategic goals.

'There is corruption everywhere.' She had calmed down a bit. She talked then of a time she was asked to 'put down' eight million rupees for a government job through the Haryana Public Service

Commission. '"Leave your paper blank," I was told, "just pay the money." I decided to not do it. I couldn't do it.'

Then she offered me matthi and small kachori, high-calorie vegetarian snacks that Akash explained they carry everywhere, 'especially on my trips to China or a non-veg place like this'.

I decided I liked the couple. She was frank and unafraid; he quiet and unassuming. When I told them that I would visit Loktak lake a day after Republic Day, they readily agreed to come along. They had been turned back halfway by Assam Rifles troopers when they had tried earlier, they explained.

'How can they *do* that?' Khushboo had begun to fume again. 'This is India. We are Indians.'

They can, I assured her. Here, the Armed Forces (Special Powers) Act permits them to do practically anything they want: arrest, question, beat, torture, kill. Turning back tourists is a relatively gentle pursuit.

~

We set off early for Loktak lake. It's a wonderful day for a drive: the sun is out and sharp but chill winds moderate it. The sky is the clearest blue. I decide to put politics and conflict away—if the day will let me, of course—and plan on enjoying the outing as a tourist for the sheer pleasure of travel. We are headed southwest to Moirang Bazar, from where we shall turn left to loop around the back of Loktak to Sendra. We pass fields brown with straw— leftover from harvested paddy—broken by brilliant yellow splashes of mustard flower. These mitigate partly the view of denuded hills now brown in this largely dry season; the camouflage of green grass from the wet season hides for few months each year the general absence of trees.

The drive itself is smooth. After the clampdown for Republic Day it's as if both UGs and the security establishment have taken the day off, satisfied with various points each side has made. A dirt track leads from the jumble of Moirang into Ithing. It's a causeway, really, that splits the lake into two distinct waterbodies as it follows a ridge line of low hills for some kilometres. We arrive at the area marked in tourist brochures as the Sendra Tourist Complex, guest houses included—to find a large Assam Rifles camp.

The 33 Assam Rifles occupy two hills overlooking Loktak, including the 'tourist hill'. A musician friend from Shillong, Keith Wallang, is still angry from an abortive visit to Loktak a year earlier, when he says a major of the Assam Rifles rudely turned back his friends—all Meitei—and him with a 'Who told you this is a tourist place'?

The troopers at the sandbagged guardhouse by the barrier are quite polite to us. Perhaps it's because we don't have dreadlocks like Keith, a longtime fan of reggae legend Bob Marley. Perhaps, it's because we clearly don't look like we're from northeastern India. After showing our IDs, Khushboo, Akash and I are made to write our names, addresses, and mobile phone numbers in a worn register, and then sign it. We have to leave our car behind. Ordinary visitors have to walk up the hill to the viewing areas.

I understand better now why the tourism office at Tulihal airport is never open, and the shock generated by my visit to the tourism office in Imphal several months earlier. Somehow, 'Come to Loktak and visit the camp of Assam Rifles—the Friends of the Hill People' doesn't make the cut as a tourism pitch.

As we climb to the top of the hill, we see to our left troopers at an open-air classroom, seated four-by-four on red plastic chairs as an instructor talks to them. Behind the instructor is a white board on a pedestal; by its side is a lectern. The hill to the right is a mass of wood-and-aluminium and brick-and-aluminium barracks, the hilltop festooned with communications antennae.

Our first clear view of the lake from a height is past a guardhouse on stilts, a crude slap-up job of logs and roof sheeting. Lower down by the side of the lake is a jetty. Four speedboats with outboard motors are moored there. The boats are stenciled 'ARMY'. Alongside are two less-sophisticated boats that show wood ribbing, and no motors. On the jetty several kits of lifejackets, packs and AK-47s are placed in a neat line: evidently, a patrol is preparing for a regular sortie—or operation, I cannot know which.

We come by a few low buildings and tents: troop quarters. I'm distracted with all the security paraphernalia on display, so when we come upon some very honoured saplings it's with some surprise.

All along the steps leading up to a gazebo that is a viewing gallery are knee-to-waist-high plants that our collective botanic knowledge fails to identify. But those who planted these on 5 June 2009 are clearly identified on tiny boards in front of each sapling. There's one evidently planted by Okram Ibobi Singh, 'Hon'ble' chief minister; and another by I.N. Haokip, the state's tourism minister, also 'Hon'ble'. Other 'Hon'ble' planters include three more ministers; the member of legislative assembly from Moirang, M. Prithviraj; and his colleague from Thanga, T. Mangibabu Singh. The only non-honourable planters appear to be the state's principal chief conservator of forests, and the principal secretary (forest and environment).

Why would this lot—among them the chief minister and tourism minister—congregate at this army camp to plant saplings at great public expense? It's the great Indian photo-opportunity riddle, templated over several decades by several thousand politicians and public servants across the country. But at least there is some comfort: these fortunate saplings, protected as they are by an army camp, will at least have a chance of being saved from the invasion of goats, sheep and cattle.

Onward to the gazebo.

The mind-numbing beauty of Loktak surpasses the presence of the army, and the silliness with the saplings.

The view of phumdi past another guard post is truly awesome.

Alongside the playground of conflict this is also the playground of Sangai, the velvet-antlered dancing deer of the valley. It isn't seen often, but my mind's eye carries me to their home of phumdi. There are larger patches—irregular, circular and rectangular—on which are light bamboo and thatch houses of the lake's human residents, who live improbably on these floating islands of reed naturally compacted over years with mud.

There's a fisherman, in a bamboo hat redolent of Southeast Asia, punting along in his slim boat, casually balanced on the bow. I've travelled on one of these on Manipur's rivers, and I know from experience the trickiness of maintaining the centre of gravity in these simple boats. And there are three young girls, whose laughter drifts up to us as they bring back to their shoreline homes fresh lake water in aluminium pots, careful to first row a distance to be away from the muck of reed and waste of the shore. The haze at the horizon tricks us into believing the vast lake is larger than it is. It's a wonderful deception that extends to the range of hills to our east and west, and the occasional hillocks ahead to our north that mark the valley up to Imphal.

We step down from the gazebo and head to a pathway that takes us to a knoll several hundred metres away, passing several neatly painted, empty cottages for tourists that show grime and broken windowpanes. A couple of them look to be in better shape, and one is even being repaired: rest and recreation for visiting officials or their friends.

Out here in the late-January sun, with the quiet of the world around us, it's pure magic. Khushboo and Akash look at the kingfishers I spot for them; and the elongated bowls of ants' nests made with discarded leaves perched high on silvery tree branches made bare by winter. The young couple is delighted with our outing, and I am happy for us to have found these minutes of magic in Manipur.

Then the three yellow-painted excavators further along the

shoreline resume their diesel growling. The operators begin to remove clumps of reed and mud close to the shore onto dump trucks. We turn back, our moment invaded.

The gazebo is awash with Manipur Police commandos. I count a dozen before giving up. They are escorting a team from the Planning Commission in New Delhi, so a friendly functionary from the forest department accompanying them tells me. The burra-sahibs are being shown the sights of Loktak. Ignoring glares from the commandos I get closer to the cluster of officials. Khushboo and Akash hold back; instead, she begins to casually photograph the lot along with a sweep of the lake and its surroundings.

An official from the state's planning department is telling the visitors, in suits and blazers like many of their Manipuri hosts, how phumdi is being cleared to make it easier for armed forces to patrol the area. Part of the arrangement, of course, is to try and persuade the 'lake people' to move from their phumdi homes to brick and mortar structures on dry land. A relocation scheme is already in place.

And so, 'some of these lake people have two-two homes,' the official declares, and proudly adds, 'Their standard of living has gone up.'

The Planning Commission nabobs nod solemnly.

'Not all are ready to move to their land homes yet,' the official admits, and repeats, with greater emphasis, 'but their standard of living has gone *up*. They have *two-two* homes.'

The Planning Commission nabobs again nod solemnly.

They turn to leave. The entire party moves off in a flurry of action, shoes and boots rattling down the steps along the fortunate saplings.

Khushboo and Akash come by to join me; they had overheard some of the chatter.

Then I notice graffiti on a bench. It's mostly faded but some words stand out: surprisingly, security folk haven't washed out what seems to be either a query or accusation, directed at a former 'Hon'ble' governor of Manipur, Ved Prakash Marwah. 'Rs 38 crore … 5 year scheme … one crore con'—the word is incomplete, and I possibly cannot hazard a guess as to whether it spells out as contract or confusion or simply a 'con' on the people—'special security…'

'Honourable graffiti,' I point out to the young couple.

The Assam Rifles guard nearest to us turns to check, frowning, what the laughter is all about. We aren't concerned. We're happy to disturb the peace, such as it is.

24

In praise of Vision 2020: 'I sing softly-softly, nah, brother?'

'O! Beautiful Moreh
O! Beautiful Moreh
For the generation's Best
We would work with Zest.'

The giddily worded banner sponsored by the 31st battalion of Assam Rifles greets us as we walk towards the border with Myanmar at Gate Number 2, after taking the left-hand fork at Moreh police station. The first two lines of this message are at present an outright lie, but following through with the remainder could help redeem it.

Moreh, the last point on Highway 39—or the first, depending on whether you count Numaligarh as the beginning or the end—is a decrepit jumble of houses and shops of junked roofing sheets, clapboard and slap-up concrete that wouldn't look out of place as a truck stop or market zone amidst the decrepitude and filth of any number of Indian towns.

This is winter though already it is warm enough at noon for me to walk about in this market town in a T-shirt and light cotton travelling pants; my travel-worn Made in Myanmar canvas floppy hat, bought in Imphal nearly two years earlier for the modest sum of Rs 60, is a blessing in the sharp sunlight. In summer months, this lowland valley town turns into a dusty, steaming sweat bowl alive only for the prospect of trade.

The narrow street is choked with Suzuki minivans, clunky Tata Sumo variants. Further back from the lane are small trucks and rattletrap buses. In a few short hours these will in turn be choked with goods bought in the markets across the border, and carry back to all parts of Manipur—for further transport to Nagaland and Assam—the ubiquitous blankets; gaudy cushions; mattresses; cheap electronic goods; LED lamps; denim jeans and export reject clothing; shoes; cigarettes; combat clothing, low-tech combat boots included, in enough variety to outfit an entry-level rebel group or re-stock an existing one; sometimes, narcotics en route from the Golden Triangle region farther east where Myanmar, Thailand and Laos come together; and, I am reliably told by security experts and locals, occasional shipments of arms and ammunition, grenades and other explosives.

Kuki and Naga armed groups 'have frequently clashed in the past for control of the lucrative heroin trade route through Moreh, an Indian outpost close to the Burmese border', I read in a document put out by United Nations High Commission for Refugees as far back as 1999, capping the decade of major clashes between Kuki groups and NSCN-IM—which has for long accused these groups of collaborating with Indian authorities. 'Both groups have a powerful vested interest in prolonging communal conflicts in order to divert attention from their profitable smuggling of timber, gold, and heroin. Both the Kukis and the Nagas see this trade (especially heroin), as the best way to finance their guerrilla wars against the Indian government.'

The trade in Moreh is the reason why everyone wants to control it, I hear from security observers. All the Kuki groups want it. The Meitei rebels want it. Naga rebels want it but can't conclusively have it. The Indian and Myanmarese security establishments keep a watchful eye over it; and their crooked make a killing from it. Moreh is a pie for all seasons, and reasons. Everyone wants a share.

This place isn't about the beautiful. It's about the brash.

Three of us are travelling together. Basanta Wareppa, the researcher with Human Rights Alert with whom I had gone to visit Vidyarani, needs to track down two youngsters suspected of being roughed up by Assam Rifles. And Oinam Doren, a happy-go-lucky film-maker and photographer from Imphal, who is among other things engaged in shooting a documentary about my musician friend Rewben Mashangvah. Neither has earlier been to Moreh. When they heard I wanted to travel there they decided to come along.

I had no reason to complain. There is safety in numbers in a place like this. Besides, Basanta and Doren are Meitei. There isn't any problem with their presence in Moreh. Going with Kuki travel companions would be all right too, this being in the Kuki territories within Chandel district. Few Nagas would be willing to make the journey unless expressly taken by Kuki friends, and such relationships aren't yet the norm.

I remember well Rewben telling me a couple of years previously of an experience in Moreh. He went in with the protection of some Kuki friends; and Kuki community leaders were told of Rewben being in Moreh. They didn't mind: Rewben is all Tangkhul Naga, but he is also all gypsy soul; a lover of music, people and drink. And so it is in these parts: those of music can sometimes travel to places others cannot.

Rewben was warned not to speak a word in any Naga dialect, and be discreet after dark. He kept to speaking in Meeteilon—spoken widely by Nagas in Manipur—and English. He sang his songs, in Tangkhul, to a couple of friends behind the firmly closed door of his small hotel room.

'I sing softly-softly, nah, brother?' he told me. 'You understand, nah?'

Other than Naga dialects, all languages appear to be welcome. On the two-hundred-metre walk to the border along the crushed lane I hear along with Meeteilon, Tamil, Punjabi, Nepali and Hindi. There was even some Bhojpuri—Rabindra Thakur, the gaunt gentleman from Siwan in Bihar who earlier in the morning gave me a quick shave at his five-feet-by-three tin shed barbershop spoke it to his colleague. Thakur said he has lived in Moreh these past fifteen years. In the greater scheme of things in this town, Thakur would be newly arrived.

Nepalis have lived here ever since World War II, remnants and descendants of soldiers of the Gorkha battalions who ultimately fought the Imperial Japanese army to standstill. The Tamilians and Sikhs came across as part of the exodus when people of Indian origin were made unwelcome in Burma.

The middle-aged Sikh gentleman who runs the Indo-Myanmar Friendship Store, selling a range of knives, lighters and hip flasks commonly found in the tourist traps of Thailand and Cambodia, says they were given a choice around 1965 by the emergent military regime: stay and assimilate without question, or leave. 'Seventy per cent of us chose to stay back,' he tells me in Hindi, nursing a broken foot encased in plaster. 'Many of us who came over here have stayed on nearby. We still have family in Burma.'

We hear conversation in Burmese: bazaar talk between Myanmarese shoppers of Indian brass and stainless steel goods and utensils, woodwork—beds, chairs, shelves—household plastics, all manner of medicines, biscuits, juices, aerated drinks, chocolate, toiletries, towels, and so much more that shops along this sort-of-golden-mile stock to the rafters.

We aren't permitted to carry mobile phones or cameras into Myanmar. There's a small grocery store a few metres from the border run by a Nepali family that keeps these for us at ten rupees per phone, and twenty rupees for a camera; small, signed and numbered chits of paper the only indication of this trust. It seems safer than leaving the gadgets behind at our poky hotel, De Khunai Resort, although, as Basanta says, it is owned by a policeman. The dingy, filthy room for two hundred and fifty rupees a night has a broken window.

The last structure on the Indian side is a heavily barricaded Assam Rifles post, with troopers peering from a lookout. A Gypsy-load of troopers is parked outside the gate, facing Moreh; a trooper points a roof-mounted machinegun in the same direction. From what I can see through some trees, fencing and the wood customs and immigration checkpoint straight ahead, there is no such fuss on the Myanmarese side.

The cracking blacktop gives way to a short stretch of packed earth. Indian policemen and officials sit about on plastic chairs under the shade of a tree, by the sight of India's flag that flies robustly across from the Myanmarese one. They cursorily check those coming into India; one official takes cash from a returning Indian weighed down with a sack of what the government and polite economists call goods of 'informal trade'.

Myanmarese officials are polite enough. Basanta deposits his election identity card, and that acts as enough surety for Doren and me as well. We are a 'party', a smiling official explains in English. He patiently writes down our names and that of our fathers neatly in English in a register, makes us sign, and writes our names again at the back of the visa receipt—it costs ten rupees per person. It's getting to noon. We need to be back by 4 p.m. Myanmarese time, an hour earlier by Indian clocks, to return the receipt for Basanta to reclaim his ID.

There will be no proof of our visit to Myanmar except anything we buy, any Myanmarese currency we choose to retain, and our memories.

The regime that Nobel Peace Prize winner Aung San Suu Kyi has chosen to battle prefers it that way.

~

We step into the large bustling market village of Nan Phar Lon. It stocks everything Indian travellers and traders carry back with them; it stocks, for example, what the aptly named Burma Bazar in Imphal does, but at rates 50 per cent and more expensive than here.

The place has a festive atmosphere that such places, living on hard commerce, often have. Modest restaurants are doing good business. At one, the crowds, with either glasses of tea or beer in front of them, are taking in a DVD of wrestler-turned-actor Dwayne Johnson, who goes by the colourful moniker of The Rock, beating the daylights out of black gangsters to the rhythm of frenetic rap. An old man claps his hands and cackles as each bad guy dramatically collapses.

Tamils in full-sleeve cotton shirts and longyi—the lungi this side of the border—offer to exchange currency: the ratio of one rupee to twenty kyat is attractive but pointless for us small-timers. All establishments in the radius of several kilometres accept Indian rupees. If we are given some kyat as change, I know I will keep a few as souvenirs for my daughter.

We ignore the bustle of the market. Basanta is clamouring for local food. I can't wait either. Whatever I have eaten of several kinds of regional Myanmarese cuisine—at the hands of citizens who have escaped imprisonment or worse at home—are outstanding. Besides, this is for me a get-a-feel-of-the-place jaunt: might as well enjoy it.

We clamber onto a shared taxi cab built around an old Chinese motorcycle for the fifteen-minute ride to Tamu, the nearest town across the border. The road is under repair. We rattle across crushed stone and dirt and across a bridge. Villagers bathe and wash clothes in the inviting blue-green waters of the Mahuyah rivulet. Children collect pebbles. There isn't a sound except of a few vehicles like ours, and mopeds and motorcycles going to the border or away from it. It isn't exactly busy at this time of the day. The crush of traffic will likely begin nearer the time of closing of the border gates.

For a short distance the Indian border runs parallel to the road here, across a stretch of field. Basanta explains after a quick chat with a fellow Manipuri on his way to market in Tamu to buy gold jewellery that there's a checkpoint near here too, just before the bridge, for those who choose to use Gate Number 1. It is possible to then walk across to the road we are on now, and wave down a tong mai, the local taxi, for a ride.

After five minutes we come to a tri-junction to join the Indo-Myanmar Friendship Road, the planned first step in an ambitious blueprint to turn this area of Myanmar into a thriving communication and trade hub with Manipur; but the blueprint is dislocated by conflict, continuing apathy, and pressures of geopolitics. This road would be a bridge, as it were, between Northeast India and Southeast Asia through Myanmar. India's Border Roads Organisation constructed this road in 2001, linking Tamu with Kaleymo, a railhead to the commercial city of Mandalay in central Myanmar, and Kaleywa.

BRO continues to maintain the road: I see a BRO truck pass us on its way from Moreh. There is a proposal to build another road from Moreh all the way east to the Thai border town of Mae Sot—one of my favourite regions of Thailand—through the town of Bagan in Myanmar. This will be quite an undertaking: 1,360 kilometres along and through jungles and hill ranges. Were the BRO to attempt it, there is no doubt it would get done; the outfit that comes under the direction of India's Ministry of Defence routinely redefines the word 'possible' along India's western borders with Pakistan, northern and eastern borders along the lower and higher Himalaya, and parts of India's large inverted-U border with Bangladesh. They have even built roads in parts of Chhattisgarh where no civilian contractor is willing to work citing threats from Maoist rebels—but that is another story in another dimension.

The little I see of the 160-km blacktop on the ten-km ride to Tamu is a work of art compared to the nightmare stretch from

Imphal to Moreh during which Highway 39 is transformed into a deeply existentialist phenomenon, all the more puzzling for the scant stretches of whole, smooth tarmac that occasionally appear. I wonder what India's foreign minister at the time, Jaswant Singh, must have thought of the two differing experiences as he arrived to officially 'hand over' the road in February 2001 as part of India's ongoing but patchy make-nice gambit to draw Myanmar's junta a little away from China's increasingly tighter embrace.

On his brief journey the minister would have noticed, as I do now, how clean the place is. That small-town Tamu has a civic heart bigger than Imphal—indeed, bigger than most cities and towns of India.

We turn left and enter Bo Gyoke Road, Tamu's main street and market area.

There is a fire station with what to me seems like 1950s- or '60s-vintage fire tenders, and further on, rows of shops to our right. A large gold-painted Buddha is seated to our left. Basanta has eyes, however, only for an eatery.

'There!' He points excitedly to a place further along the same side of the road as the Buddha statue. 'We eat first!'

Doren, still rattled from our early-morning departure from Imphal and then, Highway 39, grins.

We eat first.

It's a little feast in the no-name restaurant, identified only by the billboard above the shop for Myanmar Premium Quality Lager Beer. There are several competing billboards nearby—grocers, chemists, and gift shops—advertising Red Ruby Cigarettes, Fresh Lipo Energy Drink, E-zee F-1 detergent, Brand Royal Whiskey, and Owl Brand Tea.

The food is easy to figure out: in the manner of small eateries in Southeast Asia, cooked dishes are neatly laid out in stainless steel containers, fronted by a cover of transparent plastic. We merely have to point at what we want and the smiling lady and her young son—with sandalwood paste on their cheeks, a common practice among women and youngsters—nod to record the order.

Seated around a plastic table on plastic stools, we get a large bowl of soup with mustard leaf and a kind of spinach, small bowls of stir-fried morning glory, stewed and curried pork, some hot kidney beans with squash, a dish of pumpkin, and cucumber to cool things down. And, of course, steamed local rice. After several repeat orders, our bellies pleasantly full, we pay the equivalent of Rs 280 using Indian money.

'Tomorrow,' Basanta implores Doren and me with his trademark grin, fondly looking at the empty bowls and plates on the table, 'we come back to eat before we leave for Imphal, okay?'

Doren and I happily agree.

Tamu doesn't try to be what it's not. It's an easygoing market town. I've also been told Tamu is what it is not supposed to be: a convenient transit point close enough to the border for several rebel groups from Manipur to maintain a discreet presence in this town, with an understanding with authorities here of absolutely no fuss, or else…

There are UNLF camps in these parts, security briefs advise me. They are believed to even help out with local security. In 2009, when Myanmarese top brass visited, cadres had 'undertaken security for the outer cordon and even general sanitizing', I heard a buzz among intelligence types. Some ULNF brass even maintain apartments and houses here, but I haven't the wherewithal in Tamu to be taken on a guided tour, on the lines of what an acquaintance from India's military intelligence had done for me in Dhaka some years earlier. As he drove us around in his car with diplomatic number plates, he gleefully pointed out the apartments of several ULFA leaders in up-market Dhaka localities, even an apartment of a mistress of one of the leaders, casually explaining away a car that followed us all the way back to his residence as his 'tail'—watchers from Bangladesh's Directorate General of Forces Intelligence.

Basanta needs to return to Moreh to record interviews for his organization, so we keep the tour of Tamu for the following day, restricting ourselves to taking a short stroll around the market. As much as the market at the border that caters to visitors who cross over from Moreh, Tamu is also evidently a major market town for locals for a handsome radius. Except for the absence of filth around the market, the pavement stalls of vegetables, fruit, fish, fresh spice, groceries, household goods, longyi and clothing wouldn't be out of place at Imphal's Ima Keithel.

They are similar in another respect as well. Several stores are full of all manner of Indian packaged products from toiletries and medicine to food and junk food. Even a quick glance over shelves can't miss some household names in urban India: Parle-G and Krackjack biscuits, Cadbury's chocolates, Coke, Fanta and Sprite in plastic bottles—I ask for one and see a factory address label in Meghalaya—Maaza mango drinks, Appy apple drinks, Real brand fruit juices, Pepsodent and Colgate toothpastes, vast ranges of soaps and shampoos from Unilever, Colgate-Palmolive, and the Himalaya company.

It could be a store in India.

The chemists', likewise, could be in India. Entirely.

Along with Luojia mopeds from China, the preferred modes of personal transport appear to be Honda and Hero-Honda motorcycles from India, along with a few from Bajaj Auto.

There is a comment about trade in the *Vision 2020* document prepared for the Ministry of Development of North Eastern Region, Government of India, and North Eastern Council. 'Despite improvements in infrastructure linkages at points like Moreh, very little trade benefits seem to accrue to the NER [North East Region] states,' the document mentions at one place. 'This is probably due to the fact that existing trade agreements [like the one with Myanmar] are restrictive towards trade in agricultural products.'

This may be true. But the trade in other types of products seems to offer great potential if only indicated by the sheer variety of Indian products in this one small town. There is also the point about improved 'infrastructure linkages' in the same section of the document. So far, infrastructure constitutes the existence of a 'Land Customs Checkpoint' at Moreh, like Sutarkandi at the border of Assam and Bangladesh, Dawki in Meghalaya for trade with Bangladesh, and Zokhawthar in Mizoram—another legal point of entry into Myanmar several hundred kilometres to the south of where we are now. And, of course, there is the beacon of the BRO road from Tamu that travels deeper into Myanmar.

If together these constitute improvement, the well-meaning planners must be content with little. There is no indication of any improvement in 'infrastructure linkages' on the Indian side along the entire 110 kilometres from Moreh to Imphal. And why stop there?

The point, as always, seems to be the gap between suggestion and implementation, fantasy and reality: imagine how much more trade there could be, if attitudes were to be fixed along with the roads, conflict abated, repressive measures lifted by government, corruption lessened...

'In fact,' the generally upbeat *Vision 2020* document concedes with a tone of despair and understatement, 'troubled relations in Manipur have made even the relatively more developed Moreh trading post relatively redundant, to the extent that informal trade will need greater incentives to convert to legal trade and formal trade is unlikely to divert via Manipur in the place of West Bengal.'

But it's good to dream.

25

Walkabout in Moreh: the Wild East, and other stories

'AR picked me up when I was playing football,' Ingo Singh tells Basanta in Meeteilon. 'They asked me to say I was UG.'

'Please ask him which UG,' I request Basanta.

'UNLF,' Ingo says. 'They told me, "If you say no, we will shoot you." I told them I am a student. Even if you kill me I won't say I am UG.'

It's a good thing Assam Rifles didn't take the boy at his bravado. He'd be dead. It wouldn't be the first time for AR.

We are seated outside a tiny mud hut in a back lane of Moreh. It's on the way to the town's hospital a few minutes' walk behind our hotel. A chained mongrel which appears to have a splash of German shepherd genes settles down near us. A pup dodges between the legs of a lady in tattered clothes carrying a snot-nosed infant.

Ingo's father Ibungo lives in Thoubal with his wife, Chamurai. Three of Ingo's brothers share the tiny compound of two huts. The eldest is a carpenter, the second a tailor, the third a daily wage labourer. At seventeen, Ingo is the youngest. Ingo wears distressed jeans, held up by a belt which spells Versace at the buckle and has its counterfeit logo, and a torn T-shirt.

He was arrested in November 2009, between 2.30 and 3.00 p.m., he tells us, while he was playing a football match at the grounds near his school. The arresting team from 31 Assam Rifles stationed in Moreh was led by a captain. They took him to the local camp near the fire station. Ingo says he told them if he were to be taken home he would show them his student ID. They kicked him instead, he says.

'They told me, "You are UG, nobody will come forward to help you." I told them they should go to my school and my neighbourhood. People from there will help me.'

He found out later that the headmaster of his school and the president of Moreh's Meitei Council had visited the Assam Rifles camp to plead on his behalf and have him released.

Ingo says he was blindfolded and, except for a few hits on his back with rifle butts, left alone for a couple of hours. They interrogated him again after a break, Ingo continues, his head lowered, fists clenched as he squats on the packed-mud floor outside the hut, a thatch roof sheltering us. He was asked, he says, to spill the names of 'Underground' folk in the area.

'I said if you know of them you should arrest them. They hit me.'

Then they asked him to run away from the camp, Ingo tells us. Wise to the ploy of fake encounters, he said: 'If you want to release me, release me at the football ground.'

It was past 9 p.m. when they offered him some food. The president of the Meitei Council and his family and neighbours had by then gathered outside the camp. Later that night Ingo was marched to the police station and handed over to the police.

'I am afraid I will be arrested again,' he tells us. 'They finally agreed I was a student, but I feel scared seeing Assam Rifles. I still don't know why I was arrested.'

Two of his friends were also arrested, he says. He offers to take us to the house of one, Thangjam Sunil, eighteen.

The house in Ward No.7 is as decrepit as the one we have just left. Sunil has come back from work early today, so we are able to meet the gaunt, wiry youngster. He works as a manual labourer. When he can, he also loves to play football.

The day the Assam Rifles patrol came to arrest Ingo, and asked about for his friends Sunil and Thangjam Robert, they ran scared. Some AR troopers chased them down. They caught up with Sunil and Robert near Moreh police station.

They were made to sit in front of Moreh police station as angry AR troopers kicked them and beat them with rifle butts. As his mother watches teary eyed, Sunil tells us that he was beaten some more after being taken to the camp separately from his friend. There he was blindfolded and his hands tied. His sins: friendship with Ingo, and running away.

Doren keeps four children busy with images in his digital camera as we talk. It helps to distract the family who are clearly nervous with our note-taking. Basanta's repeated assurances that he works with 'human rights' help a little. These are wary people—dirt poor, messed with.

'Then I was taken in a Gypsy and moved to another camp,' Sunil whispers.

Fortunately for him, members of the Meitei Council and the local Meira Paibi—the fearless group of women that seems to knit Meitei society—had showed up, and helped to negotiate his release. Sunil is grateful for the support. He doesn't have the benefit of a student ID and a headmaster vouching for him. It was his word against Assam Rifles'.

'I hide now when I see them,' he tells us, looking away.

His mother cleans rice.

Thangjam Robert, the last of the friends, is seventeen. He drives an autorickshaw. He is not home at the dark walk-up room the family calls home in Ward No. 6 on the Moreh Tali Road.

A young girl, Robert's sister, is studying math under the light of the one lamp at a small table squashed into the clutter of the soot-streaked room that is bedroom, kitchen, and family area as well.

Robert's mother Renu runs a small grocery. She has only just returned after shutting shop. It's seven in the evening—eight, just a few hundred metres east in Myanmar. Renu is willing to talk. Her story is fuller than what the two boys have thus far managed to recall.

There was only five minutes or so remaining for the match to end, she says, as we sit cross-legged on a threadbare carpet by a large bed. 'I saw the entire incident.'

When the Assam Rifles patrol showed up at the ground, women spectators tried to prevent them from taking anyone.

'Women threw stones at Assam Rifles. There were some gunshots. I took shelter. Later someone told me my son was in the middle of the crowd. I saw his slippers on the road.'

After running from Assam Rifles, the boys had tried to enter the compound of Moreh police station. But the police had closed the gates, she says. Angry, the boys saw a signboard that displayed numbers for an Assam Rifles helpline. They picked up stones and hit the signboard. That's when the chasing patrol caught up with them.

'Since you arrested my friend, we hit your signboard,' that's what Renu says Robert told them. Her son narrated to her later that he was blindfolded in the camp. They beat the soles of his feet with a stick.

Around seven in the evening, Renu, a group of Meira Paibi and representatives of the Meitei Council had reached the Assam Rifles camp. Robert was released after some discussions, but not before he was 'made to sign a piece of paper with another piece of paper covering most of that paper'.

'I saw bruise marks on my son's back,' Renu says. 'All over his back. We mocked them,' she adds. '"You have to change your signboard." They said UG was behind it all.' She shakes her head.

'Are you afraid of Assam Rifles?' I ask her.

'Yes, I am. If they pass by us, I feel scared.' She wipes a tear, and then notices that Robert, in a woollen cap, T-shirt and Bermudas, has quietly come in and sat by her. She strokes his hair, his back.

'He is my child,' she whispers. 'My son.'

~

Basanta, Doren and I go for a walk. It will be full moon the next day, and the border-market will be shut in keeping with the Buddhist practice of marking a holy day on such occasions. Gate Number 2 will also be shut; we shall have to find an alternate route to Tamu.

We walk the main street of Moreh in the bright light of the moon, heading west towards the Khujairok River that marks the beginning of town. The decrepitude of the day takes on a surreal cast at night. A lady sits forlorn at Lily PCO. Children play football on the patch of tarmac near the small, half-empty Cynite Computers, which offers 'Basic Computer Course @ Reasonable Price'. The shabby dark cavern of the closed Great Eastern Hotel—there's a dream in a name—passes to show the aptly named and crowded Border Tailer, its intent not at all dampened by spelling.

A Tata Spacio, a sort of downmarket cousin of the clunky Sumo, is stacked at least fifteen feet high from the ground with blankets, pillows, chairs, cushions, folded clothes racks, bundles of sarong and longyi. The rear seats have been removed to make space for goods. The seats are strung with nylon rope along the rear windows.

It's too late to travel back to Imphal. The highway is shut down by police and Assam Rifles before sunset. 'Troubled' area tactic.

There will be a frenzy of traffic moving either way the next morning. Shoppers and others will leave Moreh as early as possible. They will drive up the steep slope into the hills and stop for a minute at the temple of Ima Kondong Lairembi Khubham, goddess of the forest, to offer prayers and thank her for bringing them this far—and now, could you please ensure we reach home safely?

They will need such divine intervention. At Khudengthabi, about ten kilometres up Highway 39 from Moreh, they will encounter a 31 Assam Rifles checkpoint. It will be manned by its 'A' Company, which will greet them with a dramatic message on a billboard: 'National Integration Through Cultural Interaction.'

Then the troopers, under standard operating orders, will strip search the vehicles though not always the passengers they carry, poke through gunny sacks of clothes and blankets and pillows with long iron spikes, looking for signs of narcotics or explosives, listening for the 'thunk' of something harder—weapons, or perhaps an innocent metal rack. Or, they will use long knives, more machete than bayonet, to hack through what they wish. If the taxi and bus drivers and their helpers, and the passengers are slow to move, they will be heckled with shouts of 'behnchod' and 'madarchod'—sisterfucker and motherfucker—to speed things up; a sort of cultural interaction with the local population using India's national language to its greatest emotive extent.

After several minutes—or hours, depending on the severity of checking, which in turn will depend on both the mood of the commanding officer at the post and a fragment of intelligence as to the possibility of a drug or arms run—the vehicles will be let off. If any goods are damaged: tough. This is not a time or place for recompense. Some goods or money could remain at the post as a placatory offering for being so thoroughly checked. Besides, as most of the trade at Moreh is thus far either black or grey, it will merely be a further black, or grey, skim of the total value of the trade.

The travellers will then strive, after passing the Chothe village of Chongkhang, to reach the highest point of the 110-km route at Tengnoupal, where a large camp of 29 Assam Rifles will greet them with a sign proclaiming the force as a 'Friend of the Hill People'; but the word 'hill' will be painted over with a neat rectangle of white. Possibly this will have been done by a local commandant realizing that Assam Rifles should be a friend of 'all' people, not just people of the hills, but as he lacks the power to change the motto birthed by Verrier Elwin, he would adopt his own clever process of public relations-oriented editing.

Travellers will usually be spared a check at this place.

From Tengnoupal they will descend to the lower hills and to Bongyang, where vehicles will be checked, this time by a company of 20 Assam Rifles. Then they will quickly descend to the plains, and the filthy town of Pallel, which acts as a traffic control point for Moreh.

From here it will be more or less a straight run to Imphal, past Khongjom, the site of a major Anglo-Manipuri war; Wangjing; chief minister Ibobi Singh's home constituency of Thoubal, a decrepit town beyond which Highway 39 revives into relatively decent tarmac; and then Lilong. Imphal will be within easy reach, depending on the time of day and traffic. Should any of the travellers have read the *Vision 2020* document, they might smile indulgently at the description in one of the sections: 'Some important tourist circuits in North East India: Imphal-Thoubal-Chandel-Tengnoupal-Moreh-Imphal.'

The travellers will arrive exhausted. It will have been quite an expedition to the Gateway to South East Asia and back.

The Khujairok River smells of garbage and faeces. We turn back.

We find momentary solace at a roadside stall run by a Meitei lady. She is nearly done with her stock of tasty boiled gram, but we manage to get three servings. Here, sitting on a bench made from the wood of packing cases, sipping sweet black tea, listening to a recording of sonorous Bible worship at the Kuki Baptist church just off the road, we are for a while cocooned in our own thoughts.

I'm restless, I finally tell Basanta and Doren. I don't know about you lot, but I feel like a drink. They accompany me in my search. We haven't far to travel: there are several options openly available in Moreh at every other grocery or eatery. It's a town that works by its own rules. There's Skol beer from Dagon Breweries, Myanmar

Premium Lager 'Proudly bottled and brewed by Myanmar Brewery Limited', strong Dali-brand Chinese beer, and two of my favourite beers from Thailand, Singha and Chang, in cans.

There's Old Most Rum and Goldpiper Whiskey as well, thinly camouflaged rip-offs of Old Monk rum and Bagpiper whiskey, among India's best-known brands of alcohol.

In deference to border trade and the pleasant side-trip to Tamu, I purchase several bottles of Myanmar Premium at Rs 80 a bottle. Basanta buys leaf-wrapped smoked fish from a street-side vendor, and Doren some wafers and bottled water. This will be dinner.

We march back to our hotel, glad for the end of the long day's travel to this town—a place of trade in both real and counterfeit goods, and again, an outpost of a state where democracy is made counterfeit.

There's a banner from 31 Assam Rifles, clearly an outfit that habitually breeds peerless irony, to show us the way:

'I am the Moreh

You are the Moreh

The Moreh is Dying

Only You and I can make it Alive.'

26

'National integration through cultural interaction'

We take a slightly roundabout route to Gate Number 1, past the Shree Angala Parameshwari Muneeshwar Temple, bedecked in figurines and rainbow colours. The lane leading to it is redolent of fresh idli and pungent sambhar, but I can't get Basanta and Doren interested in some Tamil-style breakfast. I'm also a little disappointed to be just a few days late for the fire-walking festival at the temple. Anyway, it's something to return to, catch up with some mysteries of Moreh.

The lone, armed Assam Rifles trooper at the barrier before Gate Number 1 doesn't mess with us as we walk up to him, except asking, in Hindi, 'Where have you come from?' and 'Why do you want to cross the border?'—perfectly legitimate queries. After all, there isn't any other Indian official present here today to do the asking; and, as the main market is closed, there's no rush.

My smiling reply of 'Bas, thora ghumney, aur kya?'—just a little sightseeing, what else?—is enough to mollify him. Basanta and Doren are described as friends from Imphal, which is true enough. The trooper is helpful: he points to an autorickshaw some distance ahead, and says we must cut a left from where it is parked and walk a little to reach the Myanmarese immigration checkpoint for our visa 'ticket'. We realize that only a little further on we shall meet the road we took the previous day, and be able to wave down a ride to Tamu.

Basanta and Doren look surprised. It isn't the sort of interaction they are used to with Assam Rifles—most locals prefer to remain quiet out of both fear and anger. Maybe it's our chit-chat in Hindi that does it, and the fact that I do not look like an ethnic Manipuri. It suddenly strikes me that for the past two days I've fronted all exchanges we have had with security personnel, using my non-Manipuri features, Hindi and ID to smoothen the way.

Basanta is excited to meet a couple of middle-aged ladies from Imphal on the aged pickup truck-taxi into Tamu. They explain that the previous day they paid seven thousand rupees to harvest an entire tree of giant green beans near Tamu; and they are going to collect.

Even after paying off border officials, police and Assam Rifles sponges, and transportation from Imphal to Tamu and back, they will make quite a killing with these delicacies. Four of the foot-long beans cost a hundred rupees in the markets of Imphal. With a laden tree, they will still clear several thousand rupees for two days' work.

'I love these giant beans,' Basanta says longingly.

'You're in the wrong line of work, my young friend,' I joke with him. 'You should do what these ladies are doing. In this human rights business you'll likely end up in jail.'

Basanta doesn't take to the joke. I don't blame him. Being threatened, arrested or jailed isn't an unknown phenomenon among activists in Manipur.

Kapia—that's what his name sounds like, and there's no way I can get him to spell it for me—takes us for a ride around Tamu on his 'Dagon Jeep', an old tong mai.

Basanta can make himself understood by speaking Meeteilon; our driver can understand many of the words and a lot of the meaning that resembles his dialect of Tiddim Chin, so it's not too much of a problem. We settle for him to take us around Tamu for a few hours for Rs 450 and then deposit us back at the market for lunch. Kapia first offers to show us a place that Basanta translates as 'we go to a place with many fish'.

We drive through to the end of Bo Gyoke Road, past single and two-storey buildings of homes and an office of Myanmar Economic Bank. As soon as we take a turn to the south, concrete gives way to clusters of wood and bamboo houses and hovels, some on stilts. The walls are of woven bamboo or rough wooden slats, the roofs tin. Tarmac gives way to earthen track; town to village.

We come to one of Tamu's smaller, lesser known, quite neglected temple enclaves. It's a curious mix. On a hillock a small stupa of brick and mortar displays five seated figures of the Buddha all around, all quite worn. Figures of a tiger, elephant, fish, cow and mouse are in a recess below each likeness of the Buddha. I don't get to look any further as our guide calls out to us, pointing to a square tank, evidently The Place with Many Fish. That's what he has brought us to see. He seems a bit put off that I've gone nosing around someplace else.

Another, and more elaborate and well-kept Buddha, head a little tilted to the right, is seated facing east in the middle of the tank, which we reach by a walkway of planking and bamboo. The walkway has remnants of fish food—grain husk—that earlier visitors have let be. We pick up handfuls to throw into the pond, and hundreds of red carp-like fish, quite cleverly reposing under the shade of the walkway, dash out to feed. Our guide smiles.

He has no explanation though for the curious temple that we saw on the way up to the small stupa. It has a larger-than-life likeness of a huge moustachioed man holding a sword in his right hand. A white elephant stands by his side. To the man's left stands a statue of a lady, also holding a sword, by her side a white horse. Remnants of incense and spilled oil from long-ago worship stain the dusty floor of the temple. We can't make out what deities the temple is for; and our guide demurs. The forms, though, wouldn't look out of place in a temple complex in Tamil Nadu.

Kapia saves the pièce de résistance of Tamu for the last, for which we travel ten minutes south on the Indo-Myanmar Friendship Road, and then turn right onto the Golf Club Road. About six or so people are in the sun-shade placed by the nearest green—well, brown, scorched by the dry-season sun. The parking area of the small clubhouse has a sprinkling of scooters, motorbikes and cycles and one large SUV.

The large Aw Nam Mae temple complex emerges at the end of the road. A tall cement statue of the Buddha, plastered in white, greets us at the entrance. To its right is a giant spiralling snake with a dragon head.

The place is packed with devotees and monks and nuns to celebrate the full moon, and a festival of piety. Children run about under multicoloured strings of prayer flags. Some hold balloons on strings. Some are absorbed with orange ice lollies. Others queue to climb up a tower. Several dozen Buddhist monks and nuns walk slowly in line on a circular pathway that rings the sanctum holding a golden Buddha, as numerous devotees, mostly women, stand with bags of rice. As each bhikku passes, a devotee tips a token spoonful of rice into a wooden bowl, and finishes with a tiny bow.

The talk of elders and the shriek of children are drowned out by the sonorous chanting of prayer greatly amplified and shared through loudspeakers. These are placed around the compound that looks to be several acres in area.

In this country there is no public exchange of views without fear of censure. There is, therefore, no freedom of speech in the manner that several hundred million urban Indians increasingly take for granted. There is no news available besides what the state puts out; in Tamu, news meant the *Crime News Journal, Internet Journal*—which seemed to be for the elite, with advertisements for laptop computers and PlayStation games denominated in US dollars—and *Football Kicker Sports Journal*, with a cover photograph of Manchester United star Wayne Rooney, and the 4-0 defeat by that club of Hull, another club in the English Premier League. I couldn't figure out the content beyond photographs and advertisements as it was all in Burmese.

A pastor we met a day earlier had bemoaned the tightly controlled access to the internet ('No, government very strict'), satellite TV ('Very restricted') and education ('Government very strict, state school only'). Indeed, the tightly controlled access to anything. But the pastor, who admitted to visiting Imphal once 'in the black way'—crossing the river, not the checkpoint—was glad for some leeway the military regime permitted in the practise of religion, he said, and showed us a Lai Siangtho, the Holy Bible in romanized Tiddim Chin, printed at Swapna Printing Works in Calcutta and distributed by the Bible Society of Myanmar. But he had to be discreet, the pastor told us; he couldn't really go to town on behalf of Christ.

But here today at Aw Nam Mae, it is as if the mandated quiet of Myanmar has been given the day off.

We climb to the top of the tower negotiating the crowd of mostly children that descend the steep, corkscrew steps. Eighty steps, my aching bones tell my brain. After acknowledging the seated Buddha which has grains of rice in the slightly cupped palm of the left hand, two young girls praying at his feet, and records of visitors on scarred whitewash—'I love you Myat Thi'; 'Thank you Lord'; 'Yumnam Shanta with his family from Imphal Date 12-01-07'—we take in the view of Tamu.

It is a lovely 360-degree view of a sea of evergreens and palms, low hills to the east, west and north. Only a few roofs, some flat concrete, some peaked aluminium, show through the green. There's a haze of heat in this vast valley, the sun harsh in its brightness.

It is difficult to imagine part of the proposed Trans-Asian

Highway system snaking through this sleepy place run, as the country is, by the whim of generals. The point is not so much the generals, who seem happy enough to take any roads, railways or ports that come their way through the competing funds of China or India, both countries eager to extend and maintain hold on dirt-poor, resource-rich, strategically located Myanmar.

For this trade and strategic highway to make sense from the Indian point of view—as the Trans-Asian Highway would traverse India—conflict needs to completely die down in all parts of northeastern India. For the proposed highway going east from 'Mainland' India, all Assam needs to be at peace, and prosperous. All Meghalaya. All Nagaland. All Manipur.

The other great Asian Highway network plan calls for a link to snake eastward from Kolkata, cut across restive Bangladesh with its on-again-off-again relationship with India, arrive in the restive Indian state of Tripura, head northeast to the railhead of Silchar in lower Assam, turn east to Jiribam, and Imphal—where the railway could one day extend to. And then, merge with the last stretch of Highway 39 to Moreh and the border with Myanmar.

India's Ministry of Road Transport and Highways has recently been talking about renaming stretches of Highway 39 and other highways in the northeastern region to make them part of a more systematic national highway grid—and, of course, part of the multi-nation Asian Highway One and Two. The renaming will be the beginning of a dream. But whatever the name—basically, maps being worked over and distance markers being painted over—the state of the road and the state of conflict will for several years ensure that for all practical purposes it remains Highway 39.

'Shall we have lunch?' Basanta asks.

~

I lose my temper at Khudengthabi.

Maybe 'Ted' had something to do with it, young Ted from Imphal escorting young Anna and Janice. Ted in full rapper chic, in Moreh for a Bible fellowship programme, and then to visit one of his fellow student 'friends from Bee-lore' in Tamu. Bee-lore: once-Bangalore, now Bengaluru.

We met them, youngsters of the Kom tribe of the Kuki, on the way back from Tamu. They were at the Myanmarese immigration kiosk where we had stopped by to reclaim Basanta's ID. Hulking Ted had been lit up like a beacon in a fluorescent yellow T-shirt and baggy shorts of the Orlando Magic basketball team, yellow Nike sneakers, a flashy New York Yankees baseball cap rakishly back to front on his head, large white-framed shades and a kilo or two of white metal bling around his neck, wrists and fingers. More bling: a huge crucifix on a necklace outshone all other shine. The two pretty girls, thus spotlighted, were content in simple T-shirts and denim jeans.

We wanted to walk back into Moreh the same way we had arrived, but Ted suggested to Basanta and Doren that we ride their taxi further up, directly into the border-market village and then simply hop across the compound of a house into Moreh. I was outvoted.

The taxi deposited us and pushed off into the bowels of the now-empty market town. Ted led us all, came by a locked gate, then took us into a cul-de-sac with fencing as high as two medium-sized people, and declared he was lost. I think I muttered something like 'Why trust a guy dressed like that?' to Basanta and Doren before giving in to half an hour of walking around in the maze of the village.

Ted took to first requesting, then shouting at householders to let us into their homes so we could jump the fence into no-man's land and walk across to India. Nobody obliged. The one compound we found open had a fence far too high for us to cross. When Ted asked for a ladder, we heard someone laugh.

In the end, feeling like strangling Ted, I suggested to the hot and freely perspiring party that we retrace our steps east to find the road to Tamu, find our way back to somewhere near the immigration checkpoint near Gate Number 1, then head west and cross over.

'How do you know east or west?' Ted asked.

Silently, I pointed to the angle of the blazing sun, and went off, not caring to look if anyone was following me. A few turns later, I realized they were.

About halfway back to the immigration kiosk, we noticed a string of locals across a parched field heading west—our intended direction. We followed them and, in an anticlimactic and welcome ending, crossed two narrow lanes, a small field, a no-man's-land stretch filled with plastic trash—and onto a lane by the large Tamil temple we had seen earlier that day on our way to Tamu.

Shining Ted and the two pretty girls left us. I caught Doren looking wistfully at them.

They are stopping every vehicle at Sibong checkpoint. We get out of the tiny Suzuki van and walk towards the barrier with three of our co-passengers. Our small backpacks and their shopping—dozens of cushions and blankets, dozens of cartons of cigarettes—are piled into the surprisingly spacious luggage area and on the carrier, giving the van the look of a squashed white bug. That it can negotiate these roads with such a load is a certificate to the van's durability.

Then I hear the familiar tones and language of 'National Integration Through Cultural Interaction'.

Sisterfucker. Motherfucker. Gandu—ass fucker. And other such, all addressed by two troopers to the driver and passengers of an overloaded Tata Spacio a little ahead of us.

'Samaan neechey la, behnchod.' Bring down all the stuff, sisterfucker.

I move too quickly for Basanta and Doren to stop me. Before I realize it, I'm standing in front of one of the troopers, a large person who looks to be from somewhere close to India's western border with Nepal.

'Please stop it,' I tell him in formal Hindi. 'Speak to them properly.'

He asks me: who do I think I am, sisterfucker? He points a large iron spike at my stomach. He then tells me to go away. His companion, with features from India's Hindi-speaking 'heartland', smirks.

'Put that down,' I snarl at the first trooper, pointing to the spike. 'Stop cursing me. And stop cursing these people. Speak to them properly.'

'Udhar ja,' he tells me, the spike still pointed at me, indicating the barrier with his head; there's a sandbagged guard post there. He's now really angry with me. But I couldn't care less, with my own anger boiling over.

'Kiska order hai?' I ask him.

'Officer ka.'

Then call the bloody officer, I shout, lapsing into English.

The trooper disgustedly throws the spike on the road and stalks off to talk to a superior standing by the guard post. He looks at us—I notice Basanta and Doren have stuck by me all along. The trooper yells at me to come to the guard post. I refuse, and again ask for the officer.

Meanwhile, I notice that a couple of troopers have started to strip-search the van we are travelling in. Our bags and all the goods are on the road. Floor mats are removed, the engine cover raised. They look into every space. I don't bother. It's what Assam Rifles does at this checkpoint anyway. Everybody is guilty of being a rebel, insurgent, and carrier of drugs or weapons, unless proven innocent. It's the abiding rule of this zone.

After a minute or two a trooper with chevrons on his uniform shows up, and tries to mollify me.

'Who are you?' he politely asks.

'I'm an Indian,' I fume at him. 'If this is India, if these people are Indian, we can come and go with some respect.'

They've been on duty since 5.30 a.m., he ignores my temper to politely explain. 'We must have checked 250 vehicles by now, all coming from Moreh.'

He tells me of how they wear fourteen kilos of bullet-proof plating—this I know, convex plates weighing seven kilos in front of the chest and seven kilos to protect the back. We get tired, he says.

'We are far away from home for many months. There is tension for us, tension for our families. You know there are hathiyar'—weapons—'carried on this road.'

I nod. It's true enough. But more are moved along trails that have meandered for hundreds of years through these rolling hills.

'UG log ley jaatein hain.' The Underground moves weapons.

'Bhai-saab, it hurt me when you said you're an Indian,' he complains to me. 'Am I not an Indian too?'

Don't you see? I beseech him. That's the whole point. Why do you have to treat people badly to begin with? You may hate them because you are posted here, but don't you understand that what you do makes them hate you? Hate India? Why doesn't your officer give an order to first catch a culprit and then do whatever it is you want—you people will do that anyway, won't you, with the Armed Forces Act?

He stands mute. There's nothing more to say.

We shake hands and part. Our van has been checked, and rolls up to where I'm standing. Everyone inside looks a little stunned.

The trooper knows it and I know it—I tell myself as we drive off: nothing we say will matter until political royalty in Imphal and Delhi get it right, and the czars of the economy of conflict permit a righting.

'National Integration Through Cultural Interaction' will simply have to fend for itself.

27

Imphal-Delhi-Imphal: tea with a bureaucrat

I have a meeting at noon with D.S. Poonia, chief secretary of Manipur, but he has asked me to check with Gopendro, his assistant, from time to time as to when he can actually meet me. It's Martyr's Day—30 January, the anniversary of the assassination of Mohandas Gandhi—and there is a slew of official engagements for the top bureaucrat of the state. Secure in the knowledge of delay, I decide to go walkabout, my favourite pastime in Imphal.

I had planned to again visit Kangla Fort, to see how this former redoubt of Assam Rifles was doing since the ejection of the troopers by the government's palliative decree, its sop after the mess created by the Manorama incident in 2004. I also wanted to see how the two giant statues of the mythical beast, Kangla-sha, were coming along. When I earlier visited the fort in 2007, they had been little more than intentions in straw packed onto a frame, the beginnings of a move to symbolically reclaim Meitei heritage after long occupation by both British and Indian forces. But Kangla, a fascinating repository of Meitei history, is closed to visitors for the day, I discover as I arrive at the gates after completing a long circuit of central Imphal.

I go elsewhere, look for other commemoratives. The towering Shaheed Minar near the western wall of Kangla seems like an appropriate pit-stop on this day. As ever, this martyr's memorial is touched by the sickening irony that is everywhere present. The memorial is dedicated to Tikendrajit Singh and Thangal General, who, after the defeat of Manipur by the British in 1891, were hanged at this spot.

The commemorative plaque could have been a mirror of sentiment and events of the twentieth century and these early years of the twenty-first. They were hanged, as I read, 'in front of eight thousand white-clothed women in order to subjugate Manipuri defiance and pride. The attempted humiliation failed when Thangal General laughed aloud before being hanged in a gesture of radiant defiance against oppression. The Government of Manipur has dedicated this Shaheed Minar to the memory of the martyrs who have exhibited sterling qualities of courage and sacrificed themselves for the dignity and independence of Manipur.'

That was in 1980. I wonder if some day in future there will be a memorial similarly worded, replacing the word 'British' with 'Indian'; 1891 with 1949—the year Manipur signed the pact of accession to India; and the names of Bir Tikendrajit and the General with the names of those murdered in Malom, and of the dead such as Manorama, Sanjit and Rabina. It will come some day: a day of reckoning if not a day of reconciliation—an apology by default wrenched from India as an apology has never been voluntarily offered for anything.

The second occasion of irony occurs as I cross the road back to the western gate of Kangla, in the process breaking through a cordon sanitaire of regular police and police commandos using my ID. The elegant structure near the crossing I have just left behind, a mix of Manipuri and British colonial styles, is the Gandhi Memorial Hall, which fronts the road along which the Republic Day parade passed a few days earlier. Both carriageways are closed to traffic and pedestrians. Several police Gypsies are parked near the Hall, and several dozen more arrive, plump with commandos tasked to protect Manipur's VIPs—all from the government—who arrive in their white cars with flashing red lights. They are joined by numerous army and Assam Rifles vehicles and personnel in combat gear, tasked to guard local armed forces heavyweights. The compound of Gandhi Memorial Hall is bristling with police commandos and soldiers. The governor arrives last in a motorcade of outriders, guards and staff.

A siren sounds off at 11 a.m. Then another, two minutes later. It marks the death of the Father of the Nation.

Inside, they begin to sing *'Raghupati Raghav Raja Ram'*, a bhajan beloved of Gandhi that invokes peace, wisdom and the benevolence of the gods. The commandos and soldiers keep away citizens; now the singing that plays over loudspeakers scares some crows into startled flight. There is some chatter in Meeteilon—I can recognize the words 'Mahatma Gandhi' spoken several times. There are then some short speeches in English with the same key words. The rulers of Manipur invoke a man of peace in a place made a fortress with all the automatic weapons and automatic attitudes at their command.

In minutes, the clot of security around Gandhi Memorial Hall, in kaleidoscopic olive-tan-black, begins to disperse in a roar of engines and the swish-swish of fast-paced cars that, led by the governor whose official residence is just few hundred metres away, disappear to the south. Others, many of them of the army, blitz to the north.

Traffic, gridlocked all this while along the city's major roads that lead into the Kangla area, is released in a snarl of engines and honking of horns—the weapons of impatience and irritation.

The ritual of peace is over for another year. It is as if Gandhi had never been.

~

My entry into the Old Secretariat is discreet. As is sometimes the norm for visits beyond official 'visiting hours', no entry is made in a register, no pass issued. Surprisingly, there isn't even a security check, as Gopendro efficiently whisks me away from the cramped reception area to the chief secretary's suite of offices almost immediately to the left. I'm called in after a short wait in a small anteroom. There's loud, tympanic noise of carpentry. It's 12:20 p.m.

Poonia, the trim, sharp-faced top bureaucrat of Manipur, holds court in a sprawling room. He is seated in front of a regulation photograph of Mohandas Gandhi. To Gandhi's right is a regulation photograph of Pratibha Patil, India's president; the other flank is taken up by Manmohan Singh, the regulation prime minister. In front of the wide desk are black office chairs in several rows—I'm seated in the front row directly across Poonia. His chair is clearly designed to dominate the room, the visitors. To my right is a wall-to-wall painting of a Meitei dancer.

Poonia looks smooth and suave; not a hair out of place. A navy-blue tie with a white strip sits on a plain shirt. His fingers are steepled. A pen stand and pencil holder are nearby. Files are neatly stacked to his right. As we speak, a clerk arrives to thump a new stack of files, neatly, to his left. Impressed, I neatly line up my phone, tape recorder and notebook on the desk, and lean forward to explain what I'd like to ask him:

It's a no-brainer that Manipur is a state in conflict, but I need to go beyond that—and Poonia smoothly interrupts.

'Why the conflict?'

'Why the conflict,' I agree. He presses a concealed buzzer and an attendant arrives. Poonia orders tea for both of us.

'The 1949 merger with India—some sections of the people were angry with that. But even then for several years it didn't have any effect. The first group that came up—was it UNLF or was it PLA?—one of them...' He trails off. '"You are weak, we will help you..."' Poonia resumes in his staccato manner, articulating the standard-operating-procedure cant of rebels and revolutionaries to both potential recruits and the general public.

'And pick up weapons to fight the state,' I add my two-bit.

'There were more and more groups getting into that.' Poonia's fingers move hypnotically. 'Groups splitting into factions.'

Is it just the economics of insurgency? I attempt to draw him elsewhere, to see if he will spout state theory, or something else.

Poonia ignores me. '[The] leadership lives mostly abroad, in fact, entirely abroad. Public statements are distributed locally.'

He then launches into a rambling, nearly incoherent speech on the tribal culture and customs in the Northeast, saying how people 'miss out on a lot of progressive situations ... but there is a progression', and 'social pressures'. I try to jolt him out of it, moving to a query about human rights issues. It works.

'Let's come back to what we were saying,' Poonia resumes. *'Why this social discontent?'*

The root is, of course, ethnic to some extent, he explains. 'Ethnically they are different so they never felt one with what is called Mainland India. If you recall, Mizoram's chief minister Lalthanhawla went to Singapore to attend some conference. There he said, "I feel more at home here than in India." That does convey a lot. In the Northeast there is an affinity to Southeast Asia: the food, the people—most importantly the features.

'Then there is the annexation part.

'Thirdly, in the initial years of our planned development, the investment till the Sixth Plan'—the Planning Commission of India's sixth Five Year Plan period that ran between 1980-85—'was very low in the Northeast. India wasn't putting enough money for development.'

People in this region were literate earlier, they are more literate now. They are conscious, Poonia continues. 'They read, they have access to information, their aspirations are higher, hmmm?' The explosion of television and information technology has brought exposure to events as well as lifestyles, he says. 'They want that, but quite often it does not come easy; that disconnect remains. For them it's still by and large grants and aid. The economies don't generate their own sustenance for individuals, society or the government.'

Poonia steeples his fingers, and lowers his sight from a point above my head to bore into my eyes. 'And what happens in practical terms—when the flow of funds from the Centre to the state happens, in each state certain people would have access to those resources. Quite often it is skewed: somewhere more and somewhere less. And when it is skewed, the people who get left out, or don't have access to those resources, they want their share.' He smiles, and brings militancy into the loop along with what I take by implication to be a reference to political masters. 'This extortion is one of [the ways] to get access to [resources]. And the gun also helps get access.'

The gun is a powerful instrument, I agree, for both the state and rebels.

'And then there are the larger governance issues. How good…?' He steps back from the snare I've been attempting to set up for a while, and then walks right in. 'By and large, not so much Central government, but the state government. Democracy has positives but it also…'

To my irritation, Gopendro arrives to show in a man carrying some files, and airline tickets, and ruins the moment. Poonia signs a receipt. The interruption continues for several minutes with a flurry of files being signed. He looks at the screen of a laptop by his side, a Sony Vaio with a crocodile-hide pattern in dark brown, taps the cursor pad a few times.

I look around the room, sipping tea that has meanwhile arrived, served in a transparent glass set. Behind me is a map of Manipur in such wonderful detail that I immediately hanker after it. I launch into a telling of my experience from some months ago when I went to the tourism department and surprised them—they weren't really expecting anyone to ask for maps...

'Why?' Poonia is not amused. 'They have maps.'

'They do, but those are maps with little detail, of little use.' Even India's map companies don't bother with smaller states of northeastern India. Manipur, Nagaland, Mizoram, Tripura and Meghalaya are all clubbed into an overall 'Northeast Map' along with Assam, unlike any other part of India. Anyway, I say, we got sidetracked with the interruption of paperwork. We were talking about issues of governance in the context of the present day.

'Ya,' Poonia resumes. 'It's all about how the Central grants get used, and who has access to this assistance. Where roads are to be made; how well or how badly it is done—people are affected.' He switches track yet again, inadvertently using failures of the state to finally introduce a reference to anti-establishment emotion. 'Your ladies'—Meira Paibi, I imagine—'are not protesting lack of water or lack of power supply...'

'I too find that surprising.' The hum in Imphal is from generators that power some shops, a few hotels; electricity in Manipur is mostly three or so hours of power every twenty-four hours. Municipal water supply is usually a trickle or nothing.

'That's the surprising part,' Poonia dismisses my implied sarcasm. 'Tolerance levels are very high in certain matters and then tolerance levels can really break'—he waves his hand—'heh, heh.'

'It's interesting that you say it.' I smile to cover a sense of disquiet. I'm not sure if I should bring up the fact that people take unkindly to being raped or killed by representatives of what is seen as an oppressive, callous power; it can't quite be equated with stunning lack of infrastructure—disruptive though it is. So I try another tack. Even if we assume what you say about the insurgency or the Underground is true—I tell Poonia—as in, they live for the economics of it through extortion or otherwise, but how would you then tackle the non-insurgency issues, as it were, the emotional ones, which you touched upon right now. There seems to be these peaks the administration has to face every now and then, when there is a physical excess by agencies of state, followed by great public reaction, and then things get dislocated for weeks and months. There is bad press. The whole atmosphere is muddied. It takes forever to extricate from it…'

'But it doesn't happen so very often,' Poonia interrupts me.

'But when it does happen, it seems to go at a high pitch.'

'I get the impression,' he says softly, '[that] they almost revel in that.'

'Really? Why would you say that?'

'You create situations and then the government will sort it out.'

Before I can break in to clarify this vague assertion, Poonia has moved on in a rush, in his manner of making disjointed points to both admit establishment errors and at the same time, blame it all on insurgents and protesters. 'It's purely fire-fighting—it's an almost 24/7 activity. You're not doing very systematic governance … the state government does do development work, [but] I put it down to lack of systematic governance. You are not even-handed in dealing with all sections. There are so many ethnicities, so much diversity. To balance all that a politician really has to be shrewd. The Planning Commission told our chief minister: "You are dealing with a very difficult situation. I wouldn't want to be there." There are skewed benefits…' Poonia pauses into his explanation. 'Those who don't get it—every time they raise a voice, they get something. Interest develops in doing that. As I said earlier, various militant groups will start splitting into factions. Just as the nexus between politicians and…'

He briefly pauses, then plunges back in. 'No politician or MLA gets elected without the support of some group or the other—more than one or two, maybe, different shades of it. Most of that is bought. Where does the money come from?'

I don't offer comment to this rhetoric.

'Once that is there,' he says, 'the allegiance—would he not then have to perforce subvert executive authority? Here again,' Poonia explains, 'in the city, there are lots of hospitals coming up, buildings—hotels coming up. Where is this money coming from?'

'You tell me.'

Poonia chortles. 'I was asking a rhetorical question.'

'But I would say it to you anyway.'

'My presumption is that it's the same funds that get extorted or siphoned out of the system which comes back in the form of investments. The institutions which flourish increasingly are those which probably have [this] money, either individually or as a group. In the long-term it's a positive thing, because it's getting into the system. Once you're in a system you want to protect that. The hotel or hospital runs if you're in a peaceful environment…'

'That's a contradictory loop,' I offer.

'…The resistance to the system would then wear away.' Ergo: stolen, extorted or 'bad' money, when pumped back into the system becomes 'good'; and this will finally being peace.

But ultimately something has to give, I insist, unwilling to accept this cynical argument. It can't go on in this vicious loop. Why steal in the first place? There is no need for a warped route to peace when the simple step of governance would do.

'The pressure from society is increasing,' Poonia acknowledges. 'Governance has to improve. The accountability of public representatives has to improve. Accountability of the bureaucracy…' He stops cold.

How do you break the chain of perception that exists about Manipur? I ask to cushion the awkward moment. How do you turn the perception game—perception inside Manipur as much as the perception of Manipur outside? When I talk to people here, it's nearly all despondent—'we don't see any light at the end of the tunnel, the politicians must reform themselves, they must repeal AFSPA.'

Poonia ignores the hook. 'Manipur doesn't have several advantages, such as minerals. It doesn't have a market that can sustain a lot of economic activity. There has to be interdependence. There is no use looking at only the Valley trying to live by itself or trying to make a dent in the Indian economy. The Finance Commission talks about sharing Central revenue between the Centre and the states. The share of Manipur in that is 0.34 per cent.' He laughs. 'So ... but that's non-Plan. Plan money is much better.'

'It comes back to this emotional pitch,' I try again. 'If you repeal AFSPA will the problems vanish overnight? What is your view?'

'Because of those provisions they [the Underground] feel the heat,' he says, 'the pressure from security forces. They use NGOs and human rights groups to highlight what happens once in a while because of the militancy situation. Security forces may overreact or may abuse their authority. That gets magnified.' Poonia next cants the official line. 'The objective is only to build them in the bad light so you can have it withdrawn. Even this film they talk about nowadays, this *AFSPA 1958.*'

It won the National Film Award for Best Non-feature Film for 2009 only a short while ago, I remind Poonia. The awards are given by India's Directorate of Film Festivals, which operates under the Ministry of Information and Broadcasting.

'Award toh unhiko milta hain, na?' he snaps in Hindi.

NGOs and human rights groups didn't get the award, I point out. A film did.

'Awards are given for offbeat things.' Poonia smiles and points to a stack of files. 'What is the award for clearing these files? You can get an award for writing a book that is different or controversial, but you will never get an award for writing about government schemes. That's the reality.'

'Tell me...' I begin, only to be interrupted.

'I have always wondered, as a person, the people who sing songs and play musical instruments get awards at the national level, are given awards by the president. They have distinctive personalities, they get noticed. We are part of a cog—a cog in the wheel.'

For a reserved, intensely controlled person like Poonia, this is akin to an outburst. I seem to have touched upon a nerve—the AFSPA nerve, the most delicate in Manipur.

I tell Poonia that I saw *AFSPA 1958* the previous evening, right here in Imphal, at the Imphal Press Club.

Two senior media persons, B.G. Verghese and Sumit Chakravarty—Verghese for long also involved in policymaking—have been in town these past three days for a recce on media freedom in Manipur on behalf of the Editors Guild of India. Arun, the editor of *Ireibak*, had phoned while I was on my way back from Moreh, reminding me of a function at the club that would use the presence of these two gentlemen to felicitate the crew of the film. There would also be a screening. *AFSPA 1958* had been doing the rounds of several film festivals in India and overseas. I was determined to catch up with the film which had created for itself a buzz for its gutsy portrayal of the events surrounding the death of Manorama in 2004.

It is one of the most wrenching, disturbing documentaries I have seen. The work of several camerapersons and skilful editing, event merges into event with minute breaks provided by scrolling information. The angry naked mothers of Meira Paibi in front of Kangla Fort, demanding the Indian Army rape them as the army stood accused of raping and killing Manorama ... nonsensical clarifications by the state ... the anger of the crowd that spread from the epicentre of Imphal across the Valley ... young boys raising slogans and throwing stones at police, paramilitary and Assam Rifles ... public hatred and scorn against Indian symbols ... forces battering the public with kicks, batons and rifle butts ... screams and cries and tears everywhere ... the sound of automatic weapons firing ... a policeman firing a machinegun at the feet of approaching, unarmed protesters, men, women and youngsters—unarmed, always unarmed, even though government authorities describe all this as being driven by the Underground ... a ricocheting government bullet hammers into an unarmed boy, he silently becomes a U-shape and collapses ... chased by paramilitary, an old lady hides in a gutter...

The censored version of the documentary approved for public viewing runs to seventy-one minutes. Mainly a gathering of journalists and writers, we saw the uncensored version that had ten more minutes of anguish, anger, confusion and conflict in one hellish reality that refuses to go away, refuses to be put down by platitudes of the masters. After the movie ended, as I began again to be aware of my breathing, I recalled something Ramananda told me. Each time something like this happens the state learns a lesson, said this man who speaks of heartbreak in the softest of tones. It learns to kill less brazenly, Ramananda said, and so the numbers of the dead gradually become less.

It's a cynical, numbing equation driven by the blinding ego of the government and the counter-balancing emotion of citizens. The man now in front of me is part of both the 'X' and the 'why' of that equation.

I can't help thinking of the senior Imphal-based journalist who broke down the previous evening in front of Verghese and Chakravarty, the point-persons sent by the Editors Guild. *'Tell* us,' he requested of these men. *'When* will all this stop?'

The answer, expectedly, was silence.

'You've been to Moreh?' Poonia asks. 'A Kuki boy disappeared.'

I nod. 'I was there yesterday. There was a flap.'

'The papers talk about fire-fighting. They don't talk about the explosive situation [over the disappearance],' Poonia speaks in a burst. 'People there know who took the boy away, but the media will moderate it, won't take names, or it will become a communal issue. The boy has been taken away by non-state actors; the state doesn't have much leverage to do something. An emissary has gone. It shows the state cares. The people feel happy someone has come to listen to their grievances. And it settles after a while.'

Apunba Lup took much longer—he speaks of the agitation that began in July 2009 and ended in the second week of 2010. But it was just the same in the end, he says.

'The day they decided to come forward and withdraw the agitations ... Why did they withdraw?' Poonia fans his fingers in a query to me, but I realize it as his habit of rhetoric. 'They were so worked up: "nothing doing, we want the head of the chief minister, we want this, we want that"—ten demands. Then they said okay, let Ibobi continue as chief minister, but we want the DGP to change, the SP to be thrown out of the state, the police commandos who were suspended should be put behind bars; we want a three-member judicial commission.'

He leans forward. 'So I asked them about all these demands, consistently denying dialogue—at CM level it was almost through once, but it went back because of MHA's [Ministry of Home Affairs] public statements. Once, there was public information that the chief minister has been summoned to Delhi. [Protesters] get emboldened—"he has been summoned and now they are going to throw him out". Media people told me that he would be removed, but sitting in government I knew that nothing like that would happen. But [as] the perception was different, it set the clock back a good one month more.

'What happened finally?' Poonia again asks rhetorically. 'None of those demands were insisted upon. The only significant thing was that the high court would direct the Central Bureau of Investigation to take up investigation [of Sanjit and Rabina's death]. On a Friday they came in and they just said we will suspend our agitation and schools will reopen from Monday'—11 January. 'It was like a magic wand.'

Poonia stops to catch his breath.

'I thought the state government deliberately stretched out the agitation by playing hardball,' I say, 'holding back on demands to dissipate the agitation.'

I continue: It would be enormously difficult for a disparate group of protesters with key leaders jailed or being continuously hounded—and these are everyday citizens, not trained guerrillas—by the combined might of police, paramilitary and army, and yet display perennial staying power. The fact that they held out for several months is a major display of public anger; the theory of support from Underground groups can only take the explanation part of the way. Either way, the truth of disaffection cannot be denied. (Besides, while I am not really surprised, it is still unsettling to hear the blame being poured only one way without acknowledging the bizarre, brutal killing of Sanjit and Rabina by the police.)

'The explanation is all there in the media.' Poonia shrugs off my intervention. 'Their own analysis said that it was led by militant groups. Or, after a certain point in time, because schools and colleges were closed on account of the boycott there was pressure from senior citizens and parents on these groups to withdraw. But for a long time the militant groups didn't allow them to withdraw. They would have discussions. It's not a secret. The state government knows. They [militant groups] also know that we know ... intelligence agencies...' He checks himself again on the verge of giving away too much. 'This is reflective of what happens all the time.'

He takes out printouts of tickets from an envelope.

Where are you off to? I ask.

'Delhi.' Poonia smiles. 'Where else?'

28

Interlude: walkabout with Meitei soul

It is morning, the sun is out, and the pair of Kangla-sha dazzling white. I can see the representation of this mythical creature a couple of hundred metres away along a narrow tree-lined road, foreshortened through the arch of the western gate of Kangla Fort, and serenaded by two rows of lush trees. I'll get to them. There is no rush. It's a pleasure to be out in the open after a night spent without electricity, in the company of persistent mosquitoes, the smell of sewage, and then be jolted from nightmare slumber with the chanting of 'Hare-Krishna' at 4.30 in the morning. A voice had soon overlaid that, a soundtrack presumably run by a combative teenager from the next-door jumble of houses, joining the battle of loudspeaker faith—'I'll consume the living and the dead. I'll see to it'—like some bizarre heavy metal retake of Ishtar's threat from the *Epic of Gilgamesh*.

Remnants of Kangla in its many avatars are everywhere.

The skirting of shishu, rubber and kadam trees cannot hide the barracks and stores to the left, painted brick-red, topped with greying asbestos and aluminium. A marble plaque by Llewelyn & Co. of Calcutta commemorates the 'proud memory' of all ranks of 4th Assam Rifles 'who lost their lives in the Great War 1914-19'. Nearby is another memorial to the officers and men of the 4th who died during World War II. In the profusion of Nepali names—Thapa, Gurung, Limbu, Chhetri, Rai—is a sprinkling of 'Tangkhul', 'Kuki' and 'Paite' and 'Haukip', but no Meitei forms: perhaps it was too soon after the Anglo-Manipuri wars to die in the name of the conqueror's queen and later, king. Anyway, the memorials mark soldiers from a time before Assam Rifles came to be accepted in these parts as much an enemy of the public as protector.

To my right is an immense parade ground, now marked with rusted viewing stands and a shed marked 'V.I.P TOILET'. Such accoutrements of modern-day privilege overshadowed other, older markers, such as the 'Nunggoibi' that lies along my route. It is a spot where the heads of slain enemies were buried after rites performed by the Maibi, priests. In 1891, a marker informs me, 'five British officers including Mr Quinton, the Chief Commissioner of Assam were beheaded and their heads buried at Nunggoibi'.

It was, of course, a short-lived commemoration for the kings of Manipur. They soon lost the war, Kangla—and with it, all Manipur.

History and heritage join me at every turn. A curve to the right at the Kangla-sha brings me to the brick ruins of the old Citadel, Kangla's innermost defences around a complex of palaces, built by King Chandrakirti in 1873. A little to the right, a bungalow I had seen even in 2007 lies demolished, officers quarters for someone from Assam Rifles, now just hedgerows and driveway shattered by weed. I arrive next at the temple to Shri Govindajee, or Krishna, and the stately beithab, a monument dedicated to the deity. Renovation is in progress. The pillars and structures of the curiously Romanesque beithab are scrubbed, patched and painted pale ochre. The nineteenth-century temple, now bereft of cocooning plaster, is being readied for a makeover. Rafters are being replaced, treated and painted by workers from 'Mainland India'.

This area is important for tourist brochures and practitioners of Vaishnavism, but there are sites that lie farther to the north of this more than two-hundred-acre symbol of Meitei heart and soul—

consecrated here, legend says, from the time of King Pakhangba in the first-century AD. The seven ancient Meitei clans which lore describes as having settled the Valley have their separate enclosures here. This is the place of the Manglen, where Manipur's kings were interred or cremated; Bodhachandra, who died in 1954, five years after Manipur formally came into India's possession, has his decorative Manglen here.

I stroll past the ghosts of history, from a time charged with empire, its dissolution, and deal-making for a new one. Alongside residences of British officers in still-neat compounds, is also the low, sprawling one which was the sometime home of William Joseph Slim, later Field Marshal and the first Viscount Slim, the hero of the war against the Japanese in the Burma and Manipur theatres.

The forgotten tomb of Sir Mohammed Saleh Akbar Hydari, the architect of an early peace deal between India and the Nagas—the doomed Hydari Plan tripped up and ignored by India—lies amidst a patch of mango and banana trees. The governor of Assam at the time, Hydari died at Waikhong while on a visit to Manipur in December 1948.

I look around. The sun is sharp. Light reflects off the several holy ponds, or pukhri, mostly to the northwest. Visitors stroll in a small rose garden with the nearby eastern hills crowning, and crowding, the Valley. The noise of Imphal is banished by breeze and birdsong. The mostly ugly buildings around Kangla are nearly obscured by the line of trees—what they cannot keep away, distance blurs.

The trees too hide from this spot the memorials to the thirteen dead by police firing one day in June 2001, when tens of thousands of Meiteis in Imphal protested the implication of India's ceasefire with NSCN-IM. An announcement after a round of peace talks suggested the ceasefire extended to all Naga areas, including those in Manipur, and was taken to be an indication that large swathes of

Naga-majority territory in Manipur would be included into the Greater Nagaland demand of NSCN-IM. The Government of India rapidly backtracked, but by then Meitei society had more martyrs. They lie at the northeastern fringe of Kangla.

At one of the small temples shrouded by a banyan, a family is at prayer. Short prayer flags striped red, yellow, black, white, purple and green flutter on bamboo poles as a Maibi leads a chant. Everybody bows low to touch foreheads to the packed-earth floor. It is a private moment, and I feel I am intruding. I move away, and stroll back to the Kangla-sha.

The huge creatures tower over me, from toe to staghorn tip nearly three compact storeys tall; they would dwarf an elephant. Seemingly part dragon, part lion, part deer, the original statues that fronted the Uttra, a structure in which Manipur's kings were crowned, were destroyed twice over: during the Anglo-Manipuri wars and later, at the time of Japan's push through the Valley. Few except Meiteis recognized and respected it as the destruction of Manipur's state emblem.

There is now a sign of rebirth. A sign of belated admission proclaims it at the entrance to Kangla Fort. 'Respecting the cultural, religious and political aspirations of the people of Manipur, Kangla was handed over by Assam Rifles to Government of Manipur on 20 November 2004.' But it includes an obstinate proviso of a defensive state. The message speaks of Kangla being 'occupied' by the British; but of various complements of Assam Rifles—the 4th, the 17th, the 30th, the headquarters of the inspector general of Assam Rifles, North and South—over several decades merely 'staying' here.

Uttra, I see, already has a new concrete shell; maybe it will be painted and filled by the time I revisit. Standing in the protective shadow of the Kangla-sha, it is easy to imagine how the entire southern portion could one day become beautiful parkland and manicured garden with gazebos, ponds and promenade, as a luridly colourful schematic of a fantasy Kangla Garden is shown on a signboard at the edge of the parade ground.

It used to be a place of power, war and hatred. It now seems to me to be a place of peace, of longing. For the first time in several weeks of travel, I feel completely calm.

29

'General weakness. Pain in private part after electric shock'

Ramananda has asked me over home for lunch. Nandini is cooking—a happy thought. They live in Chingmeirong, just down the road from the mammoth new Assembly complex under construction. After greeting his parents at the porch of the modest house and quizzing Nandini about the menu, I follow Ramananda to a patch of garden around a small rectangular pond. There's a rough-hewn picnic table and bench, surrounded by runners of herbs, and a wall of woven bamboo on one side. We bask in the welcome sun and sip tea from Tamenglong—always a pleasure. It's the place he does his thinking in, Ramananda tells me.

There's a fair amount to think through, from what I hear. Ramananda says there is a move by several activists to find a place in Kolkata and—or—Delhi for people from Manipur who have suffered aggressive incarceration and torture. There's a person, whom Ramananda describes only as Bikram, who can't sleep well; and when he does, he wakes screaming from nightmares. He says Bikram was given electric shocks eight times. He now suffers from physical handicap. Another person the associates are thinking of helping has a major drinking problem—but drink cannot help him forget his time in jail. Just two among so many who Ramananda says have lost their zest for life.

I ask after Yumnam Jiten Singh, whose situation I inadvertently came into contact with in September 2009, after police and paramilitary plucked him from Tulihal airport. Jiten had been on his way to Kolkata, and then to Bangkok to attend a conference on the United Nations Framework Convention on Climate Change, not an unusual activity for this activist. A copy of the arrest memo signed by the district magistrate of Imphal West and several other documents had reached me within days of his arrest, thanks to friends in the region. Next to 'Reason of Arrest' it was written in jumbled cases: 'being an Active member of P.L.A.'

The documents present a fascinating account of how the state does business with those it decides to go after. In this case, it turned out to be a ploy to break the agitation by Apunba Lup. It would have seemed different were it not for the fact that eight people—all men—were arrested the same day, including Jiten. He is an office bearer of Citizens' Concern on Dam and Development, an organization that has given grief to the Manipur government over the mammoth Tipaimukh hydroelectric project, located in southwestern Manipur bordering Mizoram. He is also a founding member of a Philippines-based NGO, Asia Pacific Indigenous Youth Network. Whatever the sins of Jiten, and the seven—members of All Manipur United Clubs Organisation—the primary one appears to be their association with Apunba Lup and the agitation after Sanjit and Rabina's killings in July 2009.

Those were charged times. Shaken by public protests, the administration had on 4 August imposed Section 144 of the Code of Criminal Procedure, and barred gatherings of citizens based, ironically, on the 'likelihood of causing serious breach of the peace, disturbance to the public tranquillity and grave danger to the human lives and properties in the areas'—including the Municipality area and Greater Imphal—'because of the unlawful activities of some antisocial elements for furtherance of their evil designs'.

This allowed police to wade into the protesting crowds. But how do they grab perceived instigators of protest to break the back of the movement? A barrage of law.

They were hit with Sections 121 and 121A of the Indian Penal Code, with the key phrases 'attempting to wage war' and 'conspiring to commit offences against the state'. Then came Section 16/18/39 of the Unlawful Activities (Prevention) Act, which deal with 'unlawful acts of supporting or motivating' insurgents; and Section O of the Official Secrets Act, for 'leaking information to others', whatever that signified. By the time the district magistrate got around to issuing orders for detention, several more names had been added to the laundry list of the arrested—and a section of the National Security Act, 1980, had also been applied against Jiten and some of the company.

Based on a confession from Jiten obtained by the arresting police officer—neither Jiten's handwriting nor signature form any part of the confession—the district magistrate of Imphal West spun an official web of partial truth and conjecture that trapped Jiten and several associates; and also extended the official lies and obfuscation related to the deaths of Sanjit and Rabina.

The district magistrate in his order first established, truly enough, that Jiten joined an NGO called Committee on Human Rights in 2007 and that, subsequently, he participated in numerous rallies and protests including those asking for the repeal of AFSPA. It then stated, again correctly, that COHR was part of Apunba Lup, described as a conglomerate of thirty-two organizations; and identified the organization's office bearers. The order then went into statement mode.

'That, on 23-7-2009 at 10.30 hrs Chungkham Sanjit ... a bailed out PLA and a pregnant woman namely, Rabina Devi, were killed in a shootout between the State security forces and armed militants at Khwairamband Bazar. In the shootout another 5 persons sustained bullet injuries.' It switched to truth. 'Consequent upon the incident, a Joint Action Committee (JAC) against the killing ... were formed at their respective residences. The JACs were fully supported by the COHR, AMUCO and Apunba Lup. They claimed the killing was a cold blooded murder and demanded to take stern action against the Police Commandos who were involved in the killing...'

After briefly describing plans of agitation, the document went into a stream of consciousness mode without offering any basis whatsoever. 'That, the agitation launched by the so-called Apunba Lup, including COHR, were financially supported and back [sic] by the banned organization namely, People's Liberation Army (PLA in short), United National Liberation Front (UNLF in short), and Peoples Revolutionary Party of Kangleipak (PREPAK in short). The agitation are [sic] headed by the COHR, AMUCO, Apunba Lup and the meira paibis of various locals.' It speaks of protesters deflating tyres of vehicles, pelting police with stones and pebbles flung from catapults, and taking out torchlight processions during hours of curfew. PLA is blamed for nearly everything. And Jiten is blamed for his involvement in protests that involved the PLA and other underground parties.

I received another document along with all these. It was of Jiten's record of medical examination on 18 September 2009 at J.N. Hospital in Porompat, Imphal. 'General weakness,' the prognosis went. 'Pain in private part after electric shock.'

'Jiten looks okay,' Ramananda tells me casually. 'He's just a little highly strung.'

I can't help wondering at his calm; I know Ramananda escaped Imphal around the time of Jiten's arrest fearing for his own arrest. Babloo Loitongbam, who heads Human Rights Alert, was away on work; I know he delayed his arrival to Imphal as well. Babloo is related to Y. Joykumar Singh, the current director general of police of Manipur, but by his own admission the relationship is a little sour these days. The police chief hasn't forgiven him for his part in the damning report on Manipur published in 2008 by the international agency Human Rights Watch.

Nandini calls out to say lunch is ready. Ramananda's parents have already eaten. The meal is compact, superb. Sticky rice, a soup of vegetables from the garden, pork stir fried with ginger leaf, some salad.

Sated, we head out to Ramananda's office in Paona Bazar. He is meeting Jiten and Babloo there. They plan to discuss ways of publicizing cases of torture and to rehabilitate the victims. There is no question of discussing this on the telephone. They believe their phones to be tapped.

~

Jiten is gaunt. His sunken cheeks highlight darting eyes behind thick steel-framed glasses. A turtleneck sweater hangs on a reed-thin body. Simple trousers and worn shoes complete the ensemble. We talk indoors as Babloo and Ramananda move out to a balcony to catch the sun, work a plan.

Jiten speaks in quick bursts, his cup of Tamenglong tea mostly forgotten.

The thirty-three-year-old tells me in an absolutely flat tone: 'They would blindfold us before interrogation and torture.'

Manipur Police commandos picked him up at the airport and took him to commando barracks for the initial interrogation and 'softening up'. He was thrice given electric shocks and beaten once. They pressed him to confess links with the Underground, which Jiten denied. They took him to Imphal West police headquarters where he was again interrogated. Meanwhile, he complained of uneasiness and was sent for medical check-up. He contrived to have his medical report smuggled out—a copy of which I received.

'I was in for four months. It is good other people were with me so we could talk, discuss things. Otherwise a person could go insane.' They were twenty to a cell at Imphal's Central Jail.

The preferred methods of torture are electric shocks, Jiten tells me, and beatings—with truncheons and sticks on the back and front of the torso and soles of feet. Sometimes, they put a cloth over the face and then pour water over the nose—the technique that acquired global infamy as 'waterboarding' after American gaolers practised it on Iraqi prisoners and Al Qaeda suspects during and after the second Gulf War. Sometimes they use pliers to squeeze a body part, Jiten says; maybe yank out nails—but the yanking out part is generally discouraged as it leaves telltales. 'The focus is on inflicting maximum pain and psychological pressure and intimidation without leaving obvious, visible marks.'

All this brings it up to Stage Two of interrogation. Stage Three 'is with joint forces in a hideaway in Kangla, which ordinary Manipuris still largely shy away from'.

Bikram had it worse than him, I hear. The interrogators played back recordings of his phone conversations, showed him intercepted e-mails. He was given electric shocks eight times besides being thrashed. Once, Manipur Police commandos took him to the statue of the elephant near Khwairamband Market, kicked him out of the vehicle, kicked him back in, kicked him out, placed him against the pedestal and beat him again. I'm told Bikram still cannot pass the place without going to pieces. 'I wonder what he feels,' Jiten says softly.

Bikram arrives then. A compact fellow, he offers me a firm handshake. But his eyes are everywhere and nowhere. He goes to a corner of the room and sits quietly on a chair, and looks away from us.

Once a young man, now an island.

30

What Uncle Muivah thinks, Uncle Muivah does

After several months of trying I finally hear at the end of April 2010 that my meeting with Thuingaleng Muivah, the general secretary of NSCN-IM—the 'M' in the 'IM'—has come through. A Naga friend in Delhi, where I am to meet Muivah, sends me a text message: 'Good news! The meeting with Uncle Muivah is on!'

The message arrives as I'm on my way back to Bhawanipatna in Kalahandi district of Orissa after visiting the zone of a controversial alumina refinery project by metal and mining giant Vedanta Resources Plc. There at Lanjigarh, across a slim stream, lies the imposing skyline of the Niyamgiri Hills, sacred to the Dongria Kondh tribe. They believe Niyamraja, their god, lives there. About two hundred hamlets of the tribe are embedded in the range.

The state government of Orissa awarded the hill to a subsidiary of Vedanta to mine bauxite to feed Vedanta's proposed alumina plant at the base of the hill, without asking what the Dongria Kondh thought of it. As I visit, the Dongria Kondh swear they will fight Vedanta and the government as long as they live. For Vedanta executives, the gods of ore are in Bhubaneshwar, Orissa's capital, and in New Delhi. These gods, and their corporate supplicant, plan to wear down a people, and then a mountain. The approach has, thus far, been the norm in India. And it's why I have been visiting:

to record for my column 'Root Cause'—on conflict and the convergence of business and human rights—for the New Delhi-based business paper *Mint*.

It feels strange to be in the middle of among the most dispossessed and poverty-stricken areas in India and instantly receive communication on account of India's booming telecommunications networks. Then, travel for several hours over wretched roads and, while doing so, conduct a seamless transaction over the phone with an Internet-based travel agency to book a ticket from the nearest airport—Raipur, the capital of the Maoist rebellion-riven state of Chhattisgarh—to Delhi. And, more so, make the appointment well in time to meet a rebel leader who for decades emphatically went to war against India. He is at present resident in New Delhi courtesy of the Government of India as talks during the thirteenth year of ceasefire drag on, seemingly without end.

As it happens, I have to wait. My appointment is for 3 p.m. on 29 April, but Ashang, Muivah's assistant, sends a text message to say something has come up. The meeting is then fixed for 5 p.m. After a few minutes, I'm told it's to be 7 p.m.—'Really sorry, but Mr Muivah has to visit the doctor, so sorry.' But do come, Ashang assures me; he'll leave word at the gate of 61 Lodi Estate.

The place is a standard-issue Delhi official bungalow—gate, guard house, driveway, low main building with an outhouse—but in a state of relative disrepair. There is no nameplate at the gate. The white exterior is faded, the lawns untended. Quite unusual in an area that typically proclaims a resident, usually a senior or influential MP, or senior armed forces officer, in shiny, large brass letters.

The bungalow crawls with police in uniform and plainclothes armed with pistols and automatic rifles, and folks in safari suits who, a friendly policeman tells me, are 'IB'. The Intelligence Bureau. For India, Muivah is a 'spook' operation most of the way, handled directly by the Ministry of Home Affairs, the parent ministry of all spooks except the bizarrely worded Research & Analysis Wing of the Cabinet Secretariat, or R&AW, in recent years a bit of a toy of the National Security Advisor or the Prime Minister's Office, depending on which ego-centre chooses to wield the reins.

One 'IB', a Sikh gentleman, takes my business card, asks my business, and looks surprised when I politely tell him that I have an appointment with Muivah. Another tells me Muivah isn't in. I ask him to check again, and that it would help to give the card to Muivah's assistant. He can either do that, I tell him, or I will phone Ashang and ask him to have me fetched.

To be fair, I'm being a little uncharitable. Guarding Muivah is a tricky business. If anything were to happen to him under India's watch, Naga regions in Nagaland, Manipur, Arunachal and elsewhere would explode. But I'm tired with the games that even junior IB folk indulge in by dint of habit, escalating the simple matter of an appointment into a few minutes of power-play.

The IB person returns with my card and Ashang. All is well.

The drawing room in the IB safe house that is now Muivah's Delhi camp is sparse. A large flag of Nagalim on a wall to the left, crossed spears, and an arrangement of sofas and a table provide décor. I don't have to wait long before Ashang ushers Muivah in.

His eyes look tired behind the steel-rimmed glasses. His left cheek has a patch of surgical gauze held in place by transparent surgical tape, from a minor operation earlier in the day. The trim, compact man is the very essence of the cliché of a rebel leader with a formidable reputation usually turning out to be smaller in stature than one expects. He looks his years: seventy-six. He smiles warmly and shakes my hand. The grip is firm.

As I wait for Muivah to compose himself for our interview, I recall the comments of an editor-in-chief of a middling, New Delhi-based English-language newspaper chain at a major investment conference hosted by Deutsche Bank in Mumbai two months earlier. We had shared the dais to discuss matters related to internal security. Unlike me, this gentleman loudly proclaimed to an audience of bankers and investors from Asia, Europe and North America as to how India is perfectly safe from jihadis; that the Maoist rebellion and the gargantuan ills of India they ride upon are illusory; rebel groups everywhere in Northeast India were and continue to be no more than a bunch of cheap thugs, and the people of that region fonder of Indian dole than Indian democracy.

'We pay for them,' he had sneered, to some laughter. 'Right now one so-called leader is in Delhi, staying in a government house. His bills are being paid for by India. His security is provided by India. *These* are your rebels. They live on government money.' He opted for grandstanding a parrot-patriotism and leveraging partial truth into the whole truth instead of addressing issues that had burnt large tracts of India for decades before this conference, and would continue to simmer for years after it. 'If India wanted,' he offered as overstatement, 'we could have finished all these fellows in two days.'

A few minutes after our session ended some key bankers and investors from Southeast Asia, a few of Indian origin, had queried me as to whether the particular editor-in-chief was close to government, or had some personal stake for his near-propaganda in telling the world that absolutely everything was well with India. Because their data and reality showed—despite undeniable growth and progress—a vastly poor as well as disenchanted side to the country; and people from these sections who have since Independence repeatedly raised their heads to hit back at Indian notions of governance and development.

Instead of feeling vindicated by my own presentation and interaction, it brought home to me yet again a sense of how easily Indian power-players ride waves of delusion, use the mantra of well-being as a bulldozing, talk-is-cheap gimmick, and treat those away from India's good news party as mere irritants instead of acknowledging what it is that makes such folks irritated in the first place. This time-honoured tradition of misgovernance has taken tens of thousands of lives, Indian as well as rebel-Indian.

The editor's position also highlighted the absence of queries to the timeworn cliché of 'If India wanted…'

India, through its politicians and security paraphernalia, has tried its best—or worst, if genocide counts as worst.

The simple point is: putting down is not always the same as keeping down. This ageing man in front of me—the resolute leader of a rebel entity—is living proof of it.

~

How do you see the future of your people, I ask him. The future of your movement. The future of what has brought you to New Delhi—these talks that are now in their thirteenth year as you and I speak. And, the reconciliation process among Naga factions that we have been seeing for the past two years?

Muivah speaks in a rasp, in obvious pain after the surgery to a growth on his cheek.

'We have our own history; we go by that. Our political philosophy is that we Nagas will have to decide our own fate.'

Then he perks up with a little India-bashing. 'You see, before, of course, the reality is that there were lots of problems, many people died. But today it is really a problem with a big nation like India. They feel it is below their dignity to respect our rights. In the name of the largest democracy they like to dismiss the rights of the Nagas. And naturally, there will be no end, you know. Nehru was in his prime, and strong enough to talk as he wished.' He grips the armrests of the sofa. 'Our leaders talked with India and explained the history of the Nagas. But unfortunately he was never prepared to respect the truth of the Nagas, the realities. That became the issue. We were told that when…' Muivah pauses, recollecting the time of the early Naga wars with India... 'they sent in their forces and the whole [area] went to pieces, the Nagas were living from hand to mouth, eating rats ... and [Nehru] slapped on the table, saying that it would be a matter of a few days for the Indian armed forces to crush the Nagas.

'Nehru sent more than 200,000 troops to occupy the land,' he tells me. 'Killing was on a daily basis. Tch!' He clicks his tongue. '*So* much. The Nagas resisted; it's more than sixty years now. There's a big difference between high claims and reality. So ...' Muivah self-explanatorily spreads his hands. 'The Nagas *did* survive.'

He shakes his head. 'If that is the attitude of the leaders of India, there can be no solution. There can be no understanding between the two because the gap is too wide.'

Preliminaries over, Muivah moves to the meat.

'It was 1995, I think, the government intention was to talk. It publicly announced that military solution was no longer possible. They wanted to go for political resolution. They admitted that fighting was of no use. From that time onwards up to this day is the first stage of talking and it has been going on for more than twelve years. We could propose—and in some ways Indian leadership admitted—the invincibility of the Nagas.'

India's leadership has never said that aloud, but talks to reach out for a ceasefire with NSCN-IM did begin around that time, during the Congress-led government of which Narasimha Rao was prime minister for a five-year period until 1996. During the following two years, the Congress government gave way to a chaotic coalition of what was until recently the Opposition. A few months before the ceasefire deal was announced in August 1997 I had, as an editor with *India Today* magazine, and as a part of a media team, accompanied Prime Minister H.D. Deve Gowda to the annual meeting of the World Economic Forum at Davos. It was in late January of that year.

On our way back, we were made to wait at a hotel in the outskirts of Zurich for a couple of hours before leaving for the airport to embark the flight designated Air India 001. The prime minister needed rest, we were told. Only, there were far too many delegation officials, known Indian spooks, and faces that looked to be from either Indian's Far East, or Southeast Asia, around Deve Gowda's suite of rooms. It was too busy for a premier who had the unfortunate and embarrassing habit—for other Indians, at any rate—of frequently napping at meetings, public functions, even in Parliament.

Gentle quizzing of friendly officials from the Prime Minister's Office and friendly spooks let slip the fact that the NSCN-IM leadership were visiting. Querying the reason led to the answer that something big was in the offing. We knew it had to either be a peace deal, or outright surrender—though unlikely, as there was then no pressure as in 1971, when some Naga Army leaders were arrested after they lost sanctuary in East Pakistan after the 'Bangladesh war'. At the very least, many media persons were certain, there would be a ceasefire. That ceasefire agreement came into effect from August 1997.

When I mention my being around in Zurich to Muivah, he laughs delightedly. 'Is it so?'

And immediately launches into easy rhetoric, looking somewhat less troubled by the surgery. 'Now, in this political stage, after six years of talking they admitted the history of Nagas is unique. The situation is also unique: so—officially signed, admitted.' He skims one palm against the other to make a small slapping sound, a trademark gesture to mark the climb down of the Indian position after several decades of war and aggressive manoeuvring.

'So, on that basis we have been talking.' Muivah fixes me with a professorial stare. 'But you know: they want to do things for their interest, at their convenience, hmm?'

The way India has played it all these years since 1997 has been straightforward—from the Indian establishment's point of view.

Basically, the approach has been: give up all ideas of Nagalim or Greater Nagaland; accept the suzerainty of the Indian Constitution; and, to show you we care, we are willing to amend the Constitution to accord Nagaland special status beyond the status it already enjoys, for instance, as a state that pays no government tax.

Every year when it came around to the time of extending the ceasefire for another year, there would be stepping up of rhetoric from both sides. The same approach would be followed before a round of peace talks between representatives of the government and Naga rebel leadership. Indian negotiators would stick to their guns. NSCN-IM's leadership would suggest the whole exercise as pointless, and threaten to break off ceasefire. It took on a more urgent tone from 2001, when NSCN-K separately signed a ceasefire agreement with the Government of India. S.S. Khaplang's faction now provided India added leverage to try and keep NSCN-IM at bay.

Indian and NSCN-IM negotiators would skitter around points like which side was breaking rules of ceasefire. Both have, quite freely, from Indian troops arresting IM cadres and impounding weapons, to IM operating openly in areas of Assam, Manipur and Arunachal Pradesh where the ceasefire is technically not in force. IM has never shied away from the reality that it imposes what amounts to a parallel administration; certainly in Nagaland, and also in Naga-dominated areas in the three adjacent states.

Each side would probe and needle the other, come to the brink of a break, and then pull back. The implicit threat of the resumption of conflict has liberally been used as a bargaining ploy by both sides.

By 2005, things had changed remarkably, going by the record of this conflict. In a BBC interview with veteran journalist Subir Bhaumik late that year, Muivah was candid about twice revising NSCN-IM's proposals and to have 'come down from our original position'. Among others things, that involved passing up the initial cast-in-stone demand of absolute sovereignty; agreeing to the joint defence of Nagaland, which includes a Naga force for internal security; leaving foreign affairs issues to India unless they were of direct interest to the Nagas, in which case the Naga leadership would be consulted, and, to accept Indian currency.

There is little in this that India's political and security establishment would find objectionable or, at any rate, something they couldn't over time whittle down further. The sticky point continued to be the merger of all Naga territories into one. As India cannot pressure Myanmar into ceding its Naga territories to this enterprise, it would mean pulling together the contiguous Naga-inhabited territories in Manipur, Arunachal Pradesh and Assam into a Greater Nagaland. The last time someone tested the waters on that issue, Prime Minister Atal Bihari Vajpayee during the National Democratic Alliance government in 2001, the valley areas of Manipur erupted in protest and several dozen died in the consequent rioting, and firing by police.

In spite of this bottleneck, in July 2007, peace talks between India and NSCN-IM were actually held for the first time on Naga soil, in Dimapur, instead of the usual neutral locations like Bangkok, Amsterdam or Zurich. The Dimapur meeting was a 'big deal' by any yardstick of conflict resolution. Muivah, who stayed at his group's Hebron Camp, led a twenty-two-member delegation for the talks held at Dimapur's Circuit House. Besides the government's official interlocutor at the time, K. Padmnabhaiah, the Indian delegation included Union minister Oscar Fernandes, a veteran of such discussions outside India—sometimes following up hard talk with a meal along with their spouses, even singing a hymn or two to the great delight of the solidly Baptist NSCN-IM. A Northeast in-charge from the home ministry made up the third member of the Indian delegation for the meeting at Dimapur. And, unsurprisingly, a representative of the Intelligence Bureau rounded off the Indian team.

That year, they decided to indefinitely extend the ceasefire, provided everything remained ceasefire-worthy on the ground.

So far, so good. But the absence of war is mostly a tense, tricky peace.

~

'In terms of making concessions or amendments in the Indian Constitution…' Muivah slowly stirs his cup of tea. 'We don't accept that. The issue is between two separate entities. And so, it cannot be looked at from the perspective of the Indian Constitution.'

He leans forward to rest the cup on the table, and I do the same. 'We can talk, understand each other, recognize the position of each other. Take steps to come closer to each other. That should be the way. But if you start talking in terms of Indian institutions, or in terms of amendments to the Indian Constitution that will not be acceptable to us.' He waves aside the Indian approach: 'Up to this stage that is the way.'

I begin to understand the position this rebel leader and his organization is in: he cannot be seen to give in; and, at the same time, he must deflect flanking manoeuvres that India and other Naga factions bring to bear. (It would pretty much be the same position for his former colleagues in the other NSCN faction, led by S.S. Khaplang. Rebellion chess.)

'Nagaland was never a part of India as far as we are concerned. We know the relationship, the nature of the relationship in terms of the agreement we have. That is the only way. Otherwise…' He shrugs. 'They [Indian negotiators] say, "Some new ways must be explored." "Yes," we say, "we'll cooperate with you. But so long as you say you will not talk about sovereignty, or independence or self-expression…"'

Before I can intervene to remind him that his organization has climbed down from the point of total sovereignty, he carries on: 'Of course they say that Nagas must accept the Indian Constitution, become part of the Indian union. But on this basic point we do not think there will be any permanent solution to the issue.

'Two months back we came from Europe and had talks with the prime minister [Manmohan Singh]. He said there must be a solution and that solution must be honourable, and acceptable to both, and it must be through negotiation.

'Yes, Mr Prime Minister, that has been your commitment—well and good,' Muivah recalls a message conveyed away from the standard 'photo-op' of gifting Prime Minister Singh a Naga shawl and a set of spears in a gesture of studied courtesy, 'but your people who come and talk to us across the table don't talk along those lines. They start explaining Indian institutions and the Indian Constitution. And your home minister [P. Chidambaram] openly stated that the Indian Constitution must be accepted if there is to be any solution.'

Muivah seems to be working up to anger, and continues the telling in a playback mode. 'But the talk is without any precondition. How is it that your officials are imposing the Indian Constitution on us? That is a contradiction. With all respect to your commitment, this is the reality. When they don't respect your own commitment, I don't think it's proper.

'So,' Muivah tells me as he told the prime minister. 'The problem is from your side; it's not from our side.'

'No, whatever may be is in the past,' Muivah speaks colloquially on behalf of the prime minister.

'Okay, past may be past,' Muivah is back speaking his reply. 'Let us look at the future. There must be a solution in the shortest possible time, and it must be acceptable to us. It must be honourable.'

That's what he also said publicly at Hebron Camp in March 2010, just a few weeks after arriving in India for talks, and a month before our meeting in New Delhi. The day was 21 March, celebrated as the thirtieth Republic Day for NSCN-IM as taken from 1980, the year the undivided NSCN was formed.

After hoisting the organization's flag—accompanied by a display of explosion-expertise by the group's demolition squad—Muivah announced to the gathering of his cadres, officials and several civilians from the area, that the prime minister had said 'the past is past', and that 'a solution would be honourable and acceptable to both sides'.

Dressed in a dapper grey suit, waving an emphatic forefinger, Muivah had reserved special opprobrium for Chidambaram. 'Mr Chidambaram,' he had thundered, 'the Nagas will *not* accept imposition of the Indian Constitution. We will *not* accept any imposition. The Nagas will only accept an honourable settlement.'

I had been in Dimapur then, trying to keep up with Muivah's itinerary, to understand what was going on, to try and meet him. He's too busy, I was told, and doesn't at this time want to meet anyone from media, or 'writers of books'. There were too many meetings both planned and sudden, too much to be done for peace talks, for the Naga reconciliation process currently under way. I received similar feedback from his adversaries in the Unification camp—as the Khaplang grouping was officially identified at the time—to my request to meet Muivah's counterpart, N. Kitovi Zhimomi, who was coincidentally in the area. His faction had their own Republic Day to celebrate as well. General Secretary Kitovi too had a packed calendar of meetings—on account of the reconciliation process—with similar groups as met Muivah.

There had been a flurry of activity for Muivah. First, he enforced religious fasting for all his kilonser, or ministers, and senior staff who were called to Hebron. Nobody would mess with Muivah when he suggested fasting was good for the health. Wags had gone to town, insisting it was Muivah's message to the kilonser and NSCN-IM fat cats to 'shape up'.

Alongside, he received a host of visitors, from several Naga tribes, members of the Forum for Naga Reconciliation, a visiting team of Quakers—along with Baptists, long-time Christian evangelists-turned-interventionists for Nagas. Muivah had even met the apex Kuki Tribal Union, a sign of how far things had come since the Kuki-Naga bloodletting of the 1990s. NSCN-IM had put out a note of Muivah's assurance to the group, that 'Nagas and Kukis were living together and will live together as our fathers had worked in NNC time', implying that the wedge had since been imposed between the two communities—neighbours in the hills of Manipur—by vested interests. Late on 25 March 2010, Kitovi and Muivah met for a low-key tête-à-tête. Things unimaginable even two years earlier were happening.

But there was a fair amount of buzz too—not all of it pleasant in the charged atmosphere of bonhomie and to some extent, media-hyped hope—that filtered back to me through sources and friends.

Mobilization has started, Naga friends told me, confirming some strong reports from New Delhi from some friends in India's intelligence apparatus that NSCN-IM had begun a robust recruitment drive in all Naga areas, especially in Ukhrul district of Manipur and the southern Tirap and Changlang districts of Arunachal Pradesh. And that 'Mt Gilead', the group's main training ground in Indian territories, was as active as ever. The reason for it was not so much to prepare a bulwark against Indian forces—although that was never a distant intention—but more to recoup losses on account of defections, and to guard against any current and future grouping against what is today known as NSCN-IM.

In late 2009, some senior functionaries of NSCN-U, specifically from the faction that had violently broken away from IM to ally with Khaplang—the core group that in private has spoken of the political aspect of Naga reconciliation being a case of 'winner takes all'—established contact with officials at the Ministry of Home Affairs. The ministry reciprocated. The implication from the government perspective is easy enough to understand: try and minimize the reality, even with declaration of indefinite ceasefire and ongoing talks of groups reconciling, that NSCN-IM is still overwhelmingly the largest group in play; and, continue to initiate flanking manoeuvres to outwit it and weaken it. Besides this aiding the Indian position, for NSCN-IM's opponents within the Naga armed movement any weakening of this more powerful group would be of great use in any future negotiation, and jockeying for positions in a scenario of reconciliation.

As a corollary, there was already talk about the theoretical coming together of the two main NSCN factions, and future leadership, after the time of Isak Swu and Thuingaleng Muivah on the one hand, and S.S. Khaplang on the other. Alongside jockeying for positions with or against India, there was concurrent jockeying for position first within each faction, and then the theoretical future of a merged Naga armed group.

Moreover, even if there were to be no outright conflict, either among the factions or with India, perceptions of strength and weakness would prove crucial in determining positions of power and influence in the overarching, as yet theoretical, entity of a united 'Nagalim', one in which fragmented territories and people come together. And, failing that, determining positions of power in the present-day territory of Nagaland, in which former rebels would, theoretically, join the political and administrative mainstream.

But it is no secret that unity among Nagas without Indian influence isn't something Indian mandarins are overjoyed about in the first place.

Wheels within wheels.

'Bhangilay bhangibo,' Muivah had said during an earlier visit to Hebron in 2007, using a phrase in Nagamese to suggest that if talks with India break down, there is nothing to be done about it. It's a sentiment as easily applied to talks among Naga armed groups.

If Nagas want peace, there will be peace, Muivah is said to have spoken in closed-door meetings during his visit to Hebron in March 2010.

And if Nagas want war, he declared, we will have war.

~

I ask Muivah about a leap of faith, and if such a thing is possible both among Naga factions as well as with his group's discussions and negotiations with India.

'Between Mr Nehru's time and now,' I also ask, 'do you feel that besides the cessation of hostilities, there has been a greater level of understanding from the Indian side—the leadership as well as those who negotiate with your organization? Or is it a similar attitude put in different words, with a little more civility?'

'They admitted the fact that military solution is not possible,' Muivah again says, underscoring the huge change from India's stand in the belligerent decades right after independence. 'A political solution must be negotiated and acceptable to both.' He shakes his head a little, hitches up the minimally rolled shirtsleeves a little. 'We should say that changes are there, but until the final solution can be worked out, nothing can be settled.'

To me it seems there are still too many contradictions to be ironed out before settlement can be arrived at—I query Muivah—the issue of Greater Nagaland being one. For instance, on the one hand, you talk about Nagas deciding their own fate. On the other, the Indian side—politicians, bureaucrats, R&AW, IB—seems determined to prevent an approach that meaningfully reaches out to that future, as for them a future must be within an Indian construct. 'And, what about the future of the Naga people in general, especially keeping in mind the reconciliation talks that have been going on for the past year and more, including,' I try levity to negate perceived slight, 'all those football matches in Chiang Mai?'

Muivah laughs out loud, and then stops short as he realizes there's a surgical patch on his face.

'Among the Nagas ourselves, there are differences,' he says soberly. 'But the differences are not beyond solution. There are some problems over which we cannot yet arrive at a solution. But if people in any camp, or if there are some those who doubt the process, say we cannot accept the recipe of the international observers, it can be solved among the Nagas themselves. Immediately after the Shillong Accord, Mr L.P. Singh and Mr B.K. Nehru when they were interviewed said, "The longest insurgency in Southeast Asia is solved once and for all."' Muivah laughs again, this time in derision. 'But after nearly twenty-five years after the Shillong Accord, they realized...' He leans forward. 'The fact is that the Naga issue cannot be dismissed ... I think that will be an illusion.'

When Nagas were earlier fighting 'mighty India', he says, 'some external friends approached us...' He lets that hang for a few moments for the implication to sink in before adding: 'Nagas can still be a force.'

I nod in understanding. China, as much a spiritual destination for Muivah as Christ, provided rebels of the Naga National Council with training and arms. When Muivah broke with that organization after the Shillong Accord to co-found NSCN in 1980, the contact remained, though diminished compared to the 1960s and 1970s.

Pakistan's long-time role in providing sanctuary to rebels in former East Pakistan was revived in the 1980s with the arrival in Bangladesh of a series of hard-line governments with an increasingly open anti-India stance, a posture further intensified in the early 1990s during the tenure of the Bangladesh Nationalist party-led government of Khaleda Zia. According to Indian intelligence sources, both military and non-military, Pakistan's Inter-Services Intelligence (ISI) coordinated with their counterparts in Bangladesh, the Directorate General of Forces Intelligence, to support several underground groups from eastern India, including, of course,

NSCN-IM, People's Liberation Army from Manipur, United Liberation Front of Asom and the Bodo Security Force.

Two NSCN-IM battalions of its Alee, or overseas, command, are still located in Bangladesh, according to Indian intelligence sources. This is in spite of the recent thaw in Indo-Bangladesh relations. This relative cosying up between the Government of India and the Sheikh Hasina-led Awami League government has since 2009 led to the arrest and handing over of several top ULFA leaders, for instance, from former sanctuaries in Dhaka and elsewhere in Bangladesh. But NSCN-IM endures.

Closer home, NSCN-IM has maintained ties with the Communist Party of India (Maoist), a carryover from the days before 2004 when the Maoist conglomerate was formed by the merger of the two largest extreme leftwing factions, the Communist Party of India (Marxist-Leninist) People's War, and Maoist Communist Centre.

Muivah may be weakened by time and defections, but he knows his positions of strength are still ample for the competition, India in general and other Naga rebel groups and political entities in particular, to conclusively work against him.

I press him on a couple of points, aware that I might be pushing too close to the bone. 'To me the Indian government seems to just want to wait things out, play a waiting game.'

'Yes!' Muivah immediately sits straighter, and I plunge on, realizing I've touched a nerve.

That's usually how the government plays it, I say, and we see it being played a lot. The other thing is: I see and sense so much energy among Naga people. It's now the second, third, fourth generation since this movement began, since the wars began. So many changes have taken place among the Naga people. I see so much hope and aspiration among Naga youth—so much positive energy to want to move ahead. And—leave India aside for the moment—all this talk of reconciliation among the Nagas is so hopeful. Hope that there may finally be an end to conflict, a time for Nagas to take charge of their aspirations that must lie beyond conflict.

'Wouldn't it be incumbent,' I plead, 'wouldn't it be right, after so much sacrifice and torment all around, to offer your people a greater root to that hope?' For me to say it any plainer in front of Muivah—for heaven's sake, stop fighting and start living—would be impolite. 'In your presence,' I add, gently alluding to his mortality, and the transparently shrewd Indian ploy of waiting for the present aged leadership of all Naga rebel factions to pass on.

I appear to have upset Muivah.

'We never think that Indians would do the best for us,' he enunciates slowly, a flush creeping into his face, 'that they would have the greatest love for us. We don't think that. They want to wear us out, for days, for years.' Muivah's face darkens in anger. 'They do not learn from the bitterness of their failure, the failures from which they suffered. They are going to repeat the same mistake. Do you think the movement will end with Mr Muivah? Who am I?' He raises his voice. '*Who am I?*

'No,' he rasps. 'That is a serious mistake. You may not like to hear it, but this is a fact: more than a thousand people will come and do much better than what we have done. We have that kind of belief, faith; that Nagas will become stronger all the time. Let us see how strong the Indians will be.

'Do you know, Mr Padmanabhaiah,' Muivah segues into his habit of making a point by recalling conversations during various meetings and negotiations, this time with India's interlocutor for peace talks. 'Mr Nehru claimed big, *big* things. He went to the extent of saying, "No, the Chinese will be *thrown out* of Indian soil, in 1962." In two weeks' time Chinese forces reached up to the banks of the Brahmaputra. Do you want to repeat the mistake of Mr Nehru today also? Do you think China has become weaker and you have become stronger?'

I sit absolutely still.

'Nations rise,' Muivah points to what he implies as India's arrogance. 'Nations fall. This time also if they cannot take positive steps forward soon, Nagas will take steps.' He slap-slides his palms again with a loud smack. 'Yes, yes...' He smiles grimly. 'We know the techniques. We have tried it before. They won't be able to wear us out.'

With a laugh Muivah declines my request for a photograph, even one with the good side of his face turned in profile.

'Next time,' he promises, as he gifts me a sleeveless Tangkhul jacket that Ashang, his assistant, has brought from another room. I try it on: it's a perfect fit.

As we say our farewells, Muivah and I talk about his home in Ukhrul district of Manipur, in the Tangkhul Naga village of Somdal. I tell him that I've been unable to make it to Somdal, but have seen it across the valley from Ngainga village, which I had visited to pursue the story of the Luingamla kashan.

'Is it so?' He smiles broadly.

It would be interesting were he to visit Somdal, I tell him as we shake hands. If he ever did, I would like to be there.

He nods in a noncommittal manner. 'I haven't been to my village for forty-seven years,' he says softly. 'I'm thinking to go there.'

31

Mr Muivah's difficult homecoming, and other ongoing stories

Within days of our meeting, Muivah travels to Dimapur and on to Kohima. His team sets itself up at the village of Visvema close to Nagaland's border with Manipur. The date for his visit to the Naga areas of Manipur is fixed for 3-10 May 2010. The plan calls for him to cross over into Manipur at Mao Gate, into the largely Naga-inhabited territory of the state's Senapati district, make his way to Imphal, and then to the districts of Tamenglong, Chandel and Ukhrul. He would weave in a visit to Somdal on 8 May.

Villagers put up a banner at the entrance to Somdal. 'Welcome home Avakharar,' it proclaims, in anticipation of the visit of Elder Father. Muivah's family home in Somdal now belongs to his elder brother Shangreihan; but that is a matter of detail: all Somdal is home. Plans call for Muivah to stay a while, visit the graves of his parents, attend prayer meetings, and mark a vastly sentimental—and vastly political—homecoming.

All hell breaks loose before that.

At a mid-afternoon meeting on 30 April, the Manipur Cabinet votes to prevent Muivah's entry into the state. Not long after I receive a text message from a contact in Kohima: 'Manipur cabinet decds to bar Muivah fm entrng state!'

'Oops,' I text in reply, 'but xpctd.'

'ya lets c what happns!'

We get talking a few minutes after this exchange of text messages, and this person reminds me of a senior NSCN-IM official losing his cool at a meeting at Hebron to discuss the extent of Naga territory. He claims this took place during Muivah's visit to Hebron Camp in March 2010. 'If this time the Manipuris—the Meiteis—create roadblocks we will just invade Imphal Valley. What can they do? Nothing.' The official was calmed down by his colleagues, my friend says, but after the decision of the Manipur Cabinet to bar Muivah and his party, patience has, in any case, frayed dangerously thin.

Later on 30 April, Manipur state minister and spokesperson of the Congress-led Secular Progressive Front government tells media that the decision was taken to limit 'possibilities of disturbances threatening peaceful coexistence of the communities if the NSCN-IM leader comes to Manipur'. Besides, he adds, the ceasefire between NSCN-IM and the Government of India doesn't extend beyond the geographical boundary of Nagaland state. In Manipur, Muivah is technically still a hostile, his organization technically still at war. The minister said his government's decision had been faxed to India's Home Minister P. Chidambaram.

It comes as little surprise that the Manipur government would override the Ministry of Home Affairs' request to Manipur's Director General of Police Y. Joykumar Singh to provide Muivah security during his travels in the state. NSCN-IM had formally sent the request on to the ministry through India's newly appointed interlocutor for peace talks, R.S. Pandey. According to the Indian Constitution, a state has the call on law and order unless it is seen as having irrevocably failed to uphold it; and the Manipur administration decided to invoke its right. Beyond this technicality, however, the memories of 2001 are still fresh in Manipur.

On 14 June that year, at the conclusion of talks between NSCN-

IM leadership and the Indian side in Bangkok, India's interlocutor at the time, K. Padmanabhaiah, announced that the extension of ceasefire for another year would be 'without territorial limits'. It made impeccable sense in the realm of logic—among other things, it would alleviate the imbecility of the ceasefire as it exists, in Nagaland but not elsewhere in Naga-inhabited areas—but the realm of politics in this region possesses its own impeccable credentials when it comes to logic. For the non-Naga people of Manipur such as the majority Meiteis and those of Kuki-Chin tribes, by implication such an announcement amounted to virtually ceding the Naga regions of the state—in the hilly districts of Senapati, Ukhrul, Tamenglong, Chandel and some parts of Churachandpur district inhabited by the Zeliangrong Nagas. The eventual Constitutional paperwork for it would be a fait accompli.

Imphal Valley erupted, all the more remarkable as the state was at the time under President's Rule—basically, New Delhi and its military, paramilitary, police and intelligence community cohorts could do pretty much as they pleased without a care about local sensibilities. Several tens of thousands of mostly Meiteis took to the streets of Imphal and other large towns of the Valley on 18 June 2001. In Imphal mobs stormed the State Legislature and set fire to it. Government vehicles and buildings became a target. Eighteen people died in retaliatory firing by security forces. Local media slammed the Central government. Local youngsters, heads tonsured in sympathy for those who had died in the firing, swore to die to save the territorial integrity of present-day Manipur. On 24 June, the prime minister at the time, Atal Bihari Vajpayee retracted the Bangkok announcement, in effect limiting the ceasefire with NSCN-IM to the state of Nagaland.

It had been touch and go. As Guwahati-based mediaperson Wasbir Hussain wrote in *newspapertoday.com*, an online paper I edited at the time for India Today Group, V.S. Atem, the former commander of NSCN-IM's army, threatened to go back underground and resume war if the ceasefire was not extended across all Naga-inhabited areas.

Similar trouble has now returned nine years later, but this time, Naga organizations, both in Manipur and Nagaland, decide to stick it to Manipur, further polarizing an already deeply polarized situation.

The influential ANSAM, or All Naga Students' Association, Manipur, had already sparked economic blockade to protest the Manipur (Hill Areas) District Council Act, 1971 (3rd Amendment, 2008), which has been used to propose long-delayed elections to autonomous district councils in the hills. This was seen by Naga organizations as elections to force the state's agenda using puppet candidates, reduce the power of village councils, and a setback to Naga aspirations; as it could also lead to the bifurcation of Senapati district into Naga majority and non-Naga majority areas. This blockade effectively reduced transport of goods along Highway 39, and Highway 150—the one that snakes northeast from Imphal to reach, by way of Ukhrul, the borders of Nagaland.

By 5 May 2010, several trucks headed to Imphal on Highway 39 are torched by Naga activists—Manipur media shouts that it is at the instigation of NSCN-IM and sharply criticizes Home Minister Chidambaram for precipitating the crisis in the first place. In turn, Muivah criticizes the Government of India and the Government of Manipur.

On 6 May, when Naga organizations from Nagaland, among these the United Naga Council, Naga Students' Federation and several women's organization show up at Mao Gate to protest Manipur's bar on Muivah, and try to walk through massed Manipur Police commandos and regular police, emotions are at fever pitch. The protesters are charged and fired upon. Three die and close to a hundred are injured even as Manipur's chief minister rushes to Delhi for meetings with Chidambaram, Congress heavyweight and Finance Minister Pranab Mukherjee and Defence Minister A.K. Antony.

Naga organizations in Nagaland and the hill districts of Manipur totally shut down the two highways in protest. Within days, Imphal Valley, the redoubt of Meitei life and opinion, is squeezed for lack of essential supplies. The only other way into the Valley, the node of three main highways criss-crossing Manipur, is through Highway 53, from Silchar and Jiribam to the west; but that is, typically, barely navigable in the monsoons that have now arrived.

Meanwhile, by early June, Muivah moves from Viswema east to Pfütsero in the region of Chakesang tribes, ostensibly to try and reach Ukhrul using NH 150. His team calls the move a 'peace mission', but by now it is clear to everyone what it is: a political play to reinforce the idea of Greater Nagalim and NSCN-IM's stake in that stand. The Manipur government attempts to pre-empt that by rushing several hundred police to the villages of Liyai Khumour and Jessami near the state lines; the Border Security Force too deploys personnel, driven by a now exasperated home ministry that instructs forces to prevent Muivah from entering Manipur. As New Delhi contemplates the airlifting of essential supplies, including medicine, into Imphal, Bharatiya Janata Party officials visit Chidambaram to insist that the territorial integrity of Manipur be protected—adding to the already volatile circus of opinion and emotion.

Another crucial byplay takes shape along the sidelines of Muivah's will-he-won't-he visit to Manipur, besides several Kuki organizations expectedly panning Muivah's moves. Angami Zapu Phizo's daughter Adinno, the leader of a faction of Naga National Council and the so-called Federal Government of Nagaland, in an email interview to Manipur's Hueiyen News Service lashes out at Muivah and NSCN-IM. Among several insults, she contemptuously terms Muivah a 'nonentity' in Nagaland affairs, and claims that 'as the keeper of the soul of Naga nation, NNC has the final say on war and peace'.

Kughalu Mulatonu, the senior functionary of NSCN-Unification whom I met several months earlier at the group's Kehoi Camp near Dimapur, announces in an interview with the India Abroad News Service agency: 'Muivah is a terrorist and his terror designs were reflected when he used hundreds of innocent Naga civilians as a human shield to try to enter Manipur and visit his birthplace.' Muivah has 'no business to curb the human rights of the people of Manipur,' Mulatonu adds, a position that goes against NSCN-IM's stand, and appears to play into India's hand at the same time. 'We warn Naga civil society groups not to hold Manipur to ransom by blocking trucks from entering Manipur via Nagaland … you cannot do that as it violates all basic norms of human rights … We want that the Meiteis of Manipur and the Nagas cohabit without any animosity.'

More bitter words are exchanged. The Forum for Naga Reconciliation's attempts for peace among the factions lie, for this time, in tatters.

By the time ANSAM lifts the blockade on 18 June 2010—the first of several such 'lifts' and re-impositions over the following two months—the plains areas of Manipur are mired in panic and despair wrought by scarcity and hyper inflation and, with the anger that must follow, seemingly ready for retaliation. A headline in Imphal reads: 'Torture of 2.5 million Manipuris by ANSAM.'

The mood affects even the tiny universe of this book, the reason I have come into contact with several layers of people among Nagas and Meiteis. My Naga friends who live in Imphal call to tell me they are heading into the hills—Naga strongholds in the Manipur hill districts—for safety. I receive outraged emails from Meitei human rights activists who speak of the Nagas' need to secede being at the root of all ills. Some acquaintances and friends, Naga and Meitei, who routinely and together take on the governments of Nagaland, Manipur and India on issues related to human rights, and displacement of project-affected people now turn on each other; issues of identity rather than change and reconciliation are brought to the fore.

The decision to lift the blockade comes after a meeting attended by representatives of Naga Students Federation, the apex Naga Hoho, United Naga Council of Manipur, and Naga People's Movement for Human Rights. The presence of these organizations takes the issue far beyond the scope of a students' organization protesting a set of elections. A soberly written article in *The Telegraph* of Kolkata from the following day sums it up:

> In a joint statement, the Naga organisations said they took the decision to 'temporarily suspend' the blockade in deference to the request of Prime Minister Manmohan Singh, Home Minister P. Chidambaram and leader of Opposition Sushma Swaraj.
>
> However, the meeting endorsed the United Naga Council's decision to declare the ADC polls in the Naga areas of Manipur as 'null and void' and sever all ties with the state government. It demanded that the Centre make alternative arrangements for the Nagas in Manipur. It also urged the Centre to remove Section 144 CrPC and withdraw state forces from the Naga areas. Condemning the declaration of UNC and ANSAM leaders as offenders, they decided that the agitation would continue till the aspirations of the Naga people were fulfilled.

Muivah leaves for Delhi on 15 July, with significant public loss of face, but with NSCN-IM's agenda intact. And the Meitei-Naga divide is reinforced in Manipur, perhaps irrevocably.

But there's something for Muivah and his colleagues to chew on, perhaps something they expected—indeed, expected as inevitable in spite of the various interventions for reconciliation.

On 7 August 2010, Muivah's and NSCN-IM's rivals come closer. That day, the united Khaplang-Unification faction of NSCN declares a merger with Adinno Phizo-led NNC/FGN. The attempts at encircling the NSCN-IM by relatively less powerful rivals and the squeezing of its will are on. The Government of India, a willing inheritor of the British policy of divide and rule, watches, and waits.

And the blockades, they thrive.

Postscript

Stories are ongoing. But a book has to end somewhere. So it is with *Highway 39*.

The telling in this book ends in mid-2010. While some situations remain static, others have moved on, in the dynamic nature of things.

Highway 39 is today renumbered in several ways in accordance with a new system of designating highways in India. But the distance and direction from Numaligarh to Moreh remains the same—and so does the fractured landscape of conflict and conflict resolution in Nagaland and Manipur this route traverses. Contentious state borders still exist, as do security checkpoints, harassment by state agencies, ethnic insults, blockades, and a share of the spoils that government rogues and rebels—both ideologically driven and rogue—alike skim off citizens, businesses and budgets. Politics and attitudes aren't as easily painted over as distance markers to record a new highway.

To a few changes. For example, a police officer mentioned as being in Senapati is posted to Imphal as I write this; and could be posted elsewhere as you read this. The director general of police of Manipur, Joykumar Singh, has been removed from his post. Brigadier Anil Chauhan of 59 Mountain Brigade, whom I met in Senapati, has shipped out. Others have taken their place, and they continue to play out the script in an ongoing reality play that can only be changed for the better with definitive, and positive, intervention of those who rule India. The same applies to some officials I met in Nagaland. Quite simply: jobs change, especially jobs in government.

And, even, in rebel groups. Maj. Gen. Phungthing of NSCN-IM is now chief of its army. He is now 'General' Phungthing.

More Kuki groups have been brought under wing of SoO—or suspension of operations—which basically means the state (army, paramilitary, police) won't go after them, pending talks of ceasefire and surrender. The United National Liberation Front exists, but is greatly challenged with its iconic leader, Rajkumar Meghen, perhaps better known by his nom de guerre, Sanayama, in India's custody and in an Indian jail; he was arrested in end-2010. But rebellion against the state continues. And justice is still not delivered for the Malom 10, Manorama, Rabina and Sanjit—or young, traumatized Vidyarani. AFSPA continues to bind Manipur; the establishment will hear nothing of removing it.

Meanwhile, some interesting things have taken place in the Naga construct. Even as I was travelling for *Highway 39*, I was struck by the unanimous resolution adopted by the Nagaland Assembly in November 2009. Urged by Chief Minister Neiphiu Rio the 60-member Assembly, including Opposition Congress MLAs, acknowledged that the underground had 'selflessly worked, fought and sacrificed for the aspirations and the rights of the Nagas', and doffed the hat to those who 'continue to follow the tradition of selfless sacrifices for the common cause of the Nagas'. Rio added: 'It is the desire of the Nagas to live together as one family.'

As I wrote in an essay in *OPEN* magazine in late-2010, '...besides reaching out to various rebel factions, it seemed like preliminary groundwork for future power sharing within the Naga construct—should unity among factions come about; and later, ceasefire turns to peace. The message also implicitly reached out to Nagas in Manipur and Arunachal Pradesh. I've even heard of unofficial moves to press for autonomy in the Naga-inhabited areas in these parts. Theoretically, the merging afterward of Naga territories even within the ambit of the Indian Constitution wouldn't be far-fetched. All of this is yet to be, but the point is: the Naga people are deciding their future. India will need to keep its establishment egos away, and work to keep the Nagas as friends. It could have happened in 1947.'

I believe this last implicitly, but my belief and realpolitik are two different things. Reconciliation talks among rebel groups floundered, and the ceasefire drags on without conclusion in sight. Meanwhile, the wheels churn. The Unification group of NSCN, formed after a breakaway from NSCN-IM was compelled to join the rival Khaplang group of NSCN, has broken. Mulatonu, the rebel leader I met in Kehoi, has, after a split in the Unification group, signed up with the Myanmar-based Khaplang. More will change. More will remain the same.

As for Thuingaleng Muivah's quest: he is yet to visit his home in Somdal. It is quite possible I shall visit it sooner than he.

References

GENERAL (BOOKS, JOURNALS, DOCUMENTS)

'Army in Nagaland', *Economic and Political Weekly*, 24-31 August 1996

Alemchiba, M., *A Brief Historical Account of Nagaland*, Kohima: Naga Institute of Culture, 1970

Allen, B.C., *Gazetteer of Naga Hills and Manipur*, New Delhi: Mittal Publications, (Reproduced) 2009

Angami, Z., *Rules for the Administration of Justice and Police in Nagaland*, Kohima: Novelty Printing Press, 2008

Ao, Temsula, *These Hills Called Home: Stories from a War Zone*, New Delhi: Zubaan/ Penguin, 2006

Arambam, Sophia, translation of Arambam Somorendro's poem at *thangta.com*, 2000

Bajpai, Kanti, 'Diversity, Democracy and Devolution in India', in Michael E Brow and Sumit Ganguly, eds, *Government Policies and Ethnic Relations in Asia and the Pacific*, Cambridge: MIT Press, 1997

Barpujari, H.K., *The American Missionaries and North-east India (1836-1900 A.D.): A Documentary Study*, Guwahati/ New Delhi: Spectrum Publications, 1986

Baruah, Sanjib, *Durable Disorder: Understanding the Politics of Northeast India*, New Delhi: Oxford University Press, 2005

Baruah, Sanjib, ed., *Beyond Counter-insurgency: Breaking the Impasse in Northeast India*, New Delhi: Oxford University Press, 2009

Comptroller and Auditor General of India, *Civil Report, Nagaland, 2007-08; Manipur, 2007-08*

Dhar, Maloy Krishna, *Open Secrets: India's Intelligence Unveiled*, Delhi: Manas Publications, Third Impression, 2008

Fernandes, Walter and Barbora, Sanjay, eds, *Land, People and Politics: Contest over Tribal Land in Northeast India*, Guwahati: North Eastern Social Research Centre, Copenhagen: International Workgroup for Indigenous Affairs, 2008

Fernandes, Walter, ed., *Search for Peace with Justice: Issues Around Conflicts in Northeast India*, Guwahati: North Eastern Social Research Centre, 2008

Ganguly, Rajat, 'Democracy and Ethnic Conflict', in Sumit Ganguly, Larry Diamond, Marc F. Plattner, eds, *The State of India's Democracy*, Baltimore: The Johns Hopkins University Press, 2007, and the National Endowment for Democracy

Gill, Preeti, ed., *The Peripheral Centre: Voices from India's Northeast*, New Delhi: Zubaan, 2010

Government of India, Ministry of Home Affairs, *Report of the Committee to Review the Armed Forces (Special Powers) Act, 1958*, 2005

Government of India, Second Administrative Reforms Commission, *Fifth Report, Second Administrative Reforms Commission: Public Order (Justice for each...Peace for all)*, June 2007

Government of India and North Eastern Council, Ministry of Development of North Eastern Region, *North Eastern Region: Vision 2020*, 2008

Government of India (coordinated by the Indian Council of Social Science Research, New Delhi), study commissioned by Ministry of Minority Affairs, *Baseline Survey of Minority Concentrated Districts: District Report, Ukhrul*, Guwahati: Omeo Kumar Das Institute of Social Change and Development

Government of Nagaland, Department of Parliamentary Affairs, *Naga Referencer: Orientation Programme for Legislators of Nagaland*, Kohima, 2006

Gundevia, Y.D., *War and Peace in Nagaland*, Dehradun, New Delhi: Palit & Palit Publishers, 1975

Haksar, Nandita, *Rogue Agent: How India's Military Intelligence Betrayed the Burmese Resistance*, New Delhi: Penguin Books India, 2009

Hazarika, Sanjoy, *Strangers of the Mist: Tales of War & Peace from India's Northeast*, New Delhi: Viking, Penguin Books India, 1994, 1995

Hazarika, Sanjoy, 'Banner of Revolt', *India Today Millennium Series: 100 People Who Shaped India*, Sudeep Chakravarti, ed., 2000

Iralu, Kaka D., *Nagaland and India: The Blood and the Tears*, Kohima: Privately Published, 2003, second edition

Jeyaseelan, Lazar, ed., *Conflict Mapping and Peace Processes in Northeast India*, Guwahati: North Eastern Social Research Centre, 2008

Keyho, Biseto Medom, *My Journey in the Nagaland Freedom Movement*, Kohima: Privately Published, 2008 (banned by Naga rebel groups)

Konthoujam, Indrakumar, *Alternative Perspectives: Economy, Polity, History & Culture, (Vol. III Issue IV), Colonialism and Resistance: Framework, Administration and Democratic Movements*, Manipur: Centre for Alternative Discourse, 2008

Majumdar, Nivedita, ed., *The Other Side of Terror: An Anthology of Writings on Terrorism in South Asia*, New Delhi: Oxford University Press, 2009

Mehrotra, Deepti Priya, *Burning Bright: Irom Sharmila and the Struggle for Peace in Manipur*, New Delhi: Penguin Books India, 2009

Naga Peoples Movement for Human Rights, *People and Guns: Naga People's Struggle for Peace*; 2009, DVD: 90 minutes

Ngangom, Robin S., *The Desire of Roots*, Cuttack: Chandrabhâgâ, 2006

Rammohan E.N., *Insurgent Frontiers: Essays from the Troubled Northeast*, New Delhi: India Research Press, 2005

Saikia, Jaideep, *Terror Sans Frontiers: Islamist Militancy in Northeast India*, New Delhi: Vision Books, 2008 (revised edition)

Sengupta, Dipankar and Singh, Sudhir Kumar, eds, *Insurgency in North-East India: The Role of Bangladesh*, New Delhi: Authorspress, in association with Spandan, 2004

Shimray, Atai A.S., *Let Freedom Ring: Story of Naga Nationalism*, New Delhi: Promilla & Co., Publishers, in association with Bibliophile South Asia, 2005

Singh, Karam Manimohan, *Nupi Lan [Women's War of Manipur]*, Imphal: K. Premlata Devi, 2000

THINK-TANKS, RESEARCH ORGANIZATIONS, NGOS, POLITICAL AND ARMED GROUPS

Central Institute of Indian Languages; *ciil.org*
Centre for Development and Peace Studies; *cdpsindia.org*
Institute of Defence Studies and Analyses; *idsa.in*

Ministry of Home Affairs, Government of India; *mha.nic.in*
Naga Peoples Movement for Human Rights; *npmhr.org*
South Asia Terrorism Portal; *satp.org*
United Nations High Commission for Refugees; *unhcr.org*

MEDIA

bbc.co.uk
CNN-IBN; *ibnlive.com*
DY 365
Eastern Mirror; Sunday Mirror
Economic and Political Weekly; *epw.in*
Hindustan Times; *hindustantimes.com*
Hueiyen Lanpao; *e-pao.net*
Imphal Free Press
jstor.org
mainstreamweekly.net
Meghalaya Times
New Delhi Television; *ndtv.com*
NETV News
Nagaland Post; *nagalandpost.com*
siroy.com
thang-ta.com
The Assam Tribune
The Morung Express; *morungexpress.com*
The Hindu; *hinduonline.net*
thesangaiexpress.com
The Sentinel
The Shillong Times; *theshillongtimes.com*
The Statesman; *thestatesman.net*
The Telegraph; *telegraphindia.com*
The Times of India; *timesofindia.indiatimes.com*

Author's note: Media references have been provided here in grateful acknowledgement but without specifically naming articles, as these have mostly been used for corroboration of events, dates and background. Articles (and TV programmes) are specifically acknowledged where they appear in the narrative.

Index

Adinno, 24, 365, 367
Aier, Reverend Wati, 51
Akhan, Captain, 41, 44–47
Anglo-Manipur War, 1891, 134, 305, 318
Anita Devi, Thongatabam, 152–53
Ankang, Stephen, 112
Ao, Temsula, 4–6
Apunba Lup, 140, 155, 216, 218, 225–27, 231, 251, 329, 337–39
Armed Forces (Assam and Manipur) Special Powers Act, 1958. *See* Armed Forces (Special Powers) Act (AFSPA) 1958
Armed Forces (Special Powers) Act (AFSPA) 1958, 115, 133, 210, 212, 223, 228, 230, 232, 234–36, 248, 251, 252–63, 282, 316, 325–27, 338, 370
Arthashastra, 101
Arun, Irengbam, 144, 146–49, 327
Arunachal Pradesh, 46, 56, 58, 59, 63, 108, 204–05, 252, 256, 267, 344, 349, 350, 354, 370
application of Armed Forces (Special Powers) Act, 256

Assam, 265, 298, 349
application of Armed Forces (Special Powers) Act, 256
Assam Rifles (AR), 13, 59, 63, 66, 78, 80–81, 86, 91, 97–98, 100–03, 106, 111–15, 120, 124, 128, 132–33, 151, 169, 173–74, 187, 191, 231–32, 236, 247, 256, 266, 277, 280, 282–83, 287–88, 290, 292, 299–306, 307–08, 315, 317, 319, 327, 331–32, 334
Atem, V.S., 45
atrocities (rapes and abductions) by armed forces and police, 29–30, 57, 63, 72–78, 120, 136–43, 154–55, 174, 184, 228, 247, 262, 314–15, 327–28. *See also* Armed Forces (Special Powers) Act (AFSPA)
Aung San, General, 54

Bangladesh, 59, 241, 269, 294, 297–98, 312
war, 348
Banian Repertory Company, 144
Barooah, Rajib, 159–64, 167
Baruah, Sanjib, 229
Basanta. *See* Wareppa, Basanta

Bengal Eastern Frontier
   Regulation 1873, 12
Bhagat, H.K.L., 95
Bharatiya Janata Party (BJP), 164, 231, 365
Bhaskar, D. Vizai, 144
Bhaumik, Subir, 349
Bhogal, S.S., 116
Bhutan, 207, 267
Bishnupur, 121, 133
Bodo groups, 110, 267
Border Roads Organisation (BRO), 294, 296
Border Security Force (BSF), 124, 161, 256, 259, 273
Bose, Subhash Chandra, 54, 132, 187
Boyd, Deirdre, 162–64
Brahma Raatha, 144
Brahmaputra, 265, 269
Braja, 215–16, 217
Brajabasi, Paona, 118
bureaucracy, 14, 17, 35–36, 47, 62, 70, 76, 84, 91, 147–48, 153, 162–64, 181–82, 185–86, 192–93, 217, 219–20, 224, 251–52, 254, 256, 271, 325
Burma National Army, 54
Burma. *See* Myanmar

Cambodia, 291
   war, 52
Camp Hebron, 10, 40, 41, 46, 196
ceasefire, 2, 43, 44, 53, 58–59, 61, 63, 102–04, 107–09, 110, 112, 113–14, 117, 168, 184, 203, 333, 343, 347–50, 354, 362–64, 370–71

Central Bureau of Investigation (CBI), 156
Central Industrial Security Force (CISF), 149
Central Reserve Police Force (CRPF), 59, 78, 120, 124, 222, 256, 273–74, 277
Centre for Youth and Social Action, 188
Chakesang Naga, 26
Chaman Lal, 172
Chandramani, S., 133
Changlang, Arunachal Pradesh, 58, 256, 354
Chanu, Vidyarani, 121–30, 131, 152, 290
Chauhan, Anil Brigadier, 92–93, 100–01, 103, 105, 117–19, 369
Chhattisgarh, 95, 231, 262–63, 294, 343
Chidambaram, P., 60, 112, 259, 352–53, 364–65, 367
China, 54, 63, 267, 295
Chinglensana, Thockchom, 139, 141–42
Chophy, Azheto, 10
Cinema Paradiso, Imphal, Manipur, 270, 272
Colah, Zasha, 72–74, 76
communal conflicts, 289
Communist Party of India (Maoist), 61
Communist Party of India (Marxist-Leninist), 61
Constitution of India, 20, 71, 181, 255, 257–58, 349, 351, 353
corruption, 84, 163, 178–80, 229, 231, 274, 281–82

Council of Nagaland Baptist Churches, 16
counterinsurgency operations (CI), 73, 101, 103
Criminal Procedure Code (CrPC), 258, 261

Damu, Thockchom, 139–42
Dantewada, 231
Deboo, Astad, 150–51, 157–58
Desai, Morarji, 20–24
Deve Gowda, H.D., 347–48
development funds, misappropriation, 84
Dhansiri river, 6, 10, 40
Dima Halam Daoga (J), 107
Dima Halam Daogah, 107
Dimapur, 2, 3, 7, 10–11, 14, 32–33, 37, 40–41, 46, 50, 63, 66, 68–69, 79, 83, 108, 159–67, 173, 350
Diphupar Gate, 8, 40, 196
Directorate General of Military Intelligence, 109
divide-and-rule policy of British, 55, 281, 368
divide-to-rule approach for conflict resolution, 205
Doren, Oinam, 290, 292, 295–96, 301, 303, 305–08, 313–15
Dorendrajit, 238–39
Doulo, Neichute, 26, 27–39
Dubey, Second Lt. Sanjeev, 76–77

Elwin, Verrier, 111, 305
Entrepreneurs Associates, 27, 33
extortionists, 118

Federal Government of Nagaland, 16, 50, 170, 365
financial inefficiency, impropriety and fraud, 36–37. *See also* corruption
Foreign Contribution Regulation Act (FCRA), 34
Forum for Naga Reconciliation (FNR), 50–51, 191, 200–01, 353

Gandhi, Indira, 20, 95, 132, 138, 157, 221–22, 242
Gandhi, M.K., 21, 134, 138, 157, 273, 279, 317
Gandhi, Rahul, 279
Gandhi, Rajiv, 138, 157
Gandhi, Sonia, 148, 157, 236, 279
Gopendro, 317, 320
Gorkha Janamukti Morcha, 61
Gorkhas, 102, 118
governance, government forces, 108, 324–25
  Indian notions of governance and development, 345–46
Government of India and Nagaland
  Angami Zapu Phizo and, 17, 22
  conflicts sponsored by, 12
  divide-and-rule approach for conflict resolution, 205
  grants-in-aid to, 35–36
  handling of Naga issue, 60, 65, 71, 86, 178, 180, 182–83, 185–86, 201–07
  human rights violation, 182
  and NSCN-IM, ceasefire agreement, 44, 59, 61, 112, 117, 362
  reconciliation process, 52–53

Government of India and Manipur, 221–24, 236, 241, 364
Government of the People's Republic of Nagalim (GPRN)/NSCN, 42, 50–51, 59, 106–09
guerrilla operations, 57

Haralu, Tsibu, 69–70
Hasina Wajed, Sheikh, 160, 358
Hazarika, Mrinal, 267
Hazarika, Sanjoy, 253, 263
heroin trade control, Kukis nagas clash over, 289
Hmar People's Convention (Democratic), 106–07
Hmars, 226, 278
Ho Chi Minh, 146, 148
Human Rights Alert, Imphal, 120–21, 213, 290
human rights violations, 112, 115, 124, 182, 247, 256, 308, 343
Hungyo, Sgt Major Salmon, 111
Hydari, Mohammed Saleh Akbar, 333

Ima Keithel—The Market of Mothers, 98, 134–35, 209
Ima Kondong Lairembi Khubham, 303
Immanuel Grace Academy, 122–23, 128, 130
Indian Army, 42, 63, 90, 114, 165, 171, 327
Indian National Army (INA), 132
Indian Oil Refinery, Numaligarh, 14
Indian Peace Keeping Force (IPKF), 64, 207
Indian Penal Code, 212, 261
Indian Reserve Battalion (IRB), 66
Indo-Myanmar Friendship Road, 294, 310
infrastructure, lack of, 37, 297–98, 323
Inner Line Permit (ILP), 11
insurgency and terrorism, 229, 260, 271
Irabot, Hijam, 136, 223, 239, 242
Iralu, Kaka D., *Nagaland and India: The Blood and the Tears*, 29
Ireibak, 144–45, 327
Islamic National Front, 107

Jain, Akash and Khushboo, 280–86
Jamir, Alemtemshi, 162–66
Jamir, S.C., 172, 268
Japfü peak, 15, 31
Jeevan Reddy Commission, 236, 252–57, 259, 262
Jeevan Reddy, Justice B.P., 236, 248, 252, 259, 263
Jinnah, Muhammad Ali, 200
Jonghan (Khaplang), 50
Joseph, Josy, 247, 250
Just Peace Foundation, 210

Kangla Fort, 134, 137, 209, 218, 236, 247, 273, 276, 278, 317, 327, 331, 334
Kanglei Yawol Kanna Lup (KYKL), 106, 226, 231
Kangleipak Communist Party-MC cadres (KCP-MC), 108
Kangpokpi (KPI), 98–99, 105–06
Kanhailal, Heisnam, 209, 240, 243
Karbi Anglong, 41, 161, 267, 269
Kargil, 63

Kaupru, 106
Kautilya, 101, 235
Keishing, Rishang, 232
Keyho, Biseto Medom, 20, 24
Khaplang faction. *See* National Socialist Council of Nagalim–Khaplang (NSCN–K)
Khaplang, S.S., 50, 60, 62, 166, 355
Khasis, 62
Khatkhatti, 162
Khongjom War Memorial Society, 278
Khonoma, 16
Khordak Ichin, 121
Khujairok River, 303, 305
Khwairamband Bazar, 221, 246, 338, 341
Kikon, Mmhonlümo, 67–70, 177, 187–93
Kithan, Mhathung, 180–86, 192–93
Kom tribe of the Kuki, 313
Koupham Valley, 106
KREDDHA (International Peace Council for States, Peoples and Minorities), 44
Kuki and Naga armed groups, clashes, 93–94, 289–90, 354
Kuki Baptist Church, 93
Kuki National Front (P), 106
Kuki Revolutionary Army, 106
Kuki(s), 14, 84, 92, 97, 106–07, 109, 226, 278, 289, 354

Lalhouba Amagee Mama, 214, 250
lalup system, 246
Lee Myung-bak, 276
Leibakki Wa, 144

Liberation Tigers of Tamil Ealam (LTTE), 60, 64, 206
Loitongbam, Babloo, 339–40, 387–88
Lokendro, Arambam, 209–14, 221–22, 224, 234–35, 238–43, 245, 249, 259, 261
Loktak lake, 94, 121, 131, 146, 148, 269, 277, 282–86
Longkumer, Chubatola, 187
'Look East Policy', 55
Lotha Nagas, 68, 176, 177, 187, 191
Lotha Women's Hoho, 190
Lotha, Major S.Y., 178–79
Lotha, Y. Vandanshan, 168–75
Lotha, Yambamo, 169–71
Luingamla, 72–78, 83, 87–91, 360
Lungshimla, 75
Lyngdoh, Robert 'Bob', 164

Mahabharata, 236, 238
Mahasweta Devi, 209, 211, 213, 245, 247–50
Majaw, Lou, 271–72
Malamnganba, 130
Malom massacre, 227, 318
Mangol Devi, Yumnam (Ima Mangol), 211, 245–47, 249–50
Manipur, 14, 56, 58, 63, 72, 75, 79–80, 217, 325, 349
  All Naga Students' Association (ANSAM), 364, 366–67
  Armed Forces (Special Powers) Act (AFSPA), 223, 234–36, 251, 259, 260
  Centre relations, 326
  conflict and violence, 237
  history, 237–38

integration into Indian union, 239, 318, 320
movement for statehood, 221–24
Nagas, 14–15, 46, 58, 79, 205, 226–27, 290
Poumai Nagas, 223
underground revolutionary movements, 222–44
war against Burmese, 242;
women's movements, 245–51
Manipur Police, 128, 133, 136–37, 140–41, 151, 153, 272, 277, 280, 286, 340–41, 364
Manipur Rifles, 78
Manipuri theatre, 209
Manorama Devi, Thangjam, 132, 227, 228, 234, 247, 252, 317, 318, 327, 370
Maoism, 68, 150, 231, 281
Mary Kom, M.C., 135
Mashangvah, Rewben, 75, 77, 78, 82, 98, 290
Maxwell, Lt. Col. H. St. P., 246
Meeteilon, 80, 125, 127, 144, 150, 152, 153, 218, 222, 235, 248, 290, 291, 299, 308, 319
Meghalaya, 259, 267, 269, 298
application of Armed Forces (Special Powers) Act, 256
Mehrotra, Deepti Priya, 211, 248, 249, 260
Meira Paibi, 210, 219, 230, 235, 246–48, 301–02, 323, 327
Meiteis, 14, 75, 80, 92, 94, 97, 105, 106, 119, 125, 239, 317
Meitei Pangal, 94, 102, 121, 134
Memcha, Ningthoujam Ongbi, 123, 125–29

Memchoubi, 242
Metha, K., 187–88
Mizo National Front (MNF), 241
Mizoram
application of Armed Forces (Special Powers) Act, 253, 256
movement for statehood, 241–42
Mokokchung, 174, 187
Mooshahary, Ranjit Shekhar, 259–60
Moreh, 79, 159, 233, 276, 278, 280, 288–92, 294–95, 297–98, 299–306, 307, 312, 313, 316, 327, 328, 369
Meitei Council, 300, 301, 302
Mount Tiyi College, 179, 187–88
Muivah, Thuingaleng, 62, 86, 166, 203, 342–67
Mulatonu, Kughalu, 195, 198–207, 366, 371
Muslim migrants from Bangladesh, 196
Myanmar, 54, 59, 288–89, 292–93, 298, 312
and Manipur, similarities/relations, 296–98

Naga(s), 2, 11, 14, 16, 18–23, 26–32, 35–38, 46–47, 106, 108, 111, 165
administrative division, 55
Army, 42–48, 57–59, 63–64, 85, 89, 113, 170, 174, 197, 268, 348
(in) Arunachal Pradesh, 46, 204–05
autonomy, 52
civil society, 223

cultural festival, 162
divided aspirations, 199–200, 357
economy, 32–33
factions and India, 62, 65, 69–71, 202, 205–07, 253, 333, 346–60
food, 47
guerrillas, 63
(in) Manipur, 14–15, 46, 58, 79, 205, 226–27, 290
and Meiteis, divide, 227
(in) Myanmar, 50, 54
national movement, 5, 24, 56–62, 181–86
reconciliation process, 52–53, 60, 62, 106, 191, 200, 204, 208, 346, 353–55
unity, 53, 71
wars with India, 15–16, 28, 52, 194, 347
Naga Common Platform, 200–01
Naga Hills, 1, 4, 6, 11, 100, 193, 241, 268
Naga Mothers' Hoho, 8
Naga National Council (NNC), 17, 24, 107, 133, 202, 354, 357, 365–66, 368
Naga Peoples Movement for Human Rights (NPMHR), 111, 114
Naga Yuya, 50
Naga Student Federation, 2, 364, 367
Nagaland
application of Armed Forces (Special Powers) Act, 253, 257
statehood (1963), 17, 21, 41, 60, 184, 241

Nagaland Aids Control Society, 188
Nagamese (language), 8–9, 46, 181, 191, 355
Nakade, S.B., 252
Nandini, Thockchom, 209, 215–20, 245, 336, 340
Naorem Ganga Tombi, 248
Narayanan, M.K., 235
National Cadet Corps (NCC), 278; Air Wing, 30
National Democratic Alliance (NDA), 350
National Rural Employment Guarantee Scheme (NREGS), 121, 178
National Security Act (NSA), 155, 228, 261, 338
National Security Guards (NSG), 259
National Socialist Council of Nagalim (NSCN), 17, 111
National Socialist Council of Nagalim (Isak-Muivah) (NSCN-IM), 2, 10, 24, 40–42, 44–46, 50–51, 58–59, 61–63, 85, 87, 92, 102, 103–04, 106–09, 111–14, 133, 160, 166, 168, 170, 190–92, 195, 203, 232–33, 268, 289, 333–34, 342, 349–55, 358, 362–65, 367–68
Alee Command, 59
parallel administration, 177–80, 182
Town Command, 178–79, 188, 191, 192
Valley-based insurgent groups (VBIG), relationship, 92, 106–10

Index

National Socialist Council of Nagalim-Khaplang (NSCN-K), 10–11, 24, 42, 61, 103, 106, 195–96, 349, 351, 353
National Socialist Council of Nagalim (NSCN) (Unification), 11, 42, 195–97, 353
Naxalite movement, 61, 66, 213
Nehru, Jawaharlal, 20, 26, 30, 60, 138, 157, 253, 278, 347
Nepal, 97, 207
Ngaimu, 72, 76
Ngainga Baptist Church, 88
Ngainga, 72, 82–85, 87–88, 91, 360
Ngangom, Robin S., 157–58, 188
Ngully, Nyambemo, 191
Nibedon, Nirmal, *Nagaland: The Night of the Guerrillas*, 28
Nikhil Hindu Manipuri Mahasabha, 238
Nongmaikhong Mayai Leikai, 121
non-government organizations and human rights groups in Nagaland, 33, 326
North Cachar area of Assam, 107
North Eastern Council, 223, 297
North Eastern Hill University, 4, 157
North-East Region Commonwealth Parliamentary Association, 260
Nuh, V.K., 16
Numaligarh, 14, 159–62, 190, 288, 369
nupi lan—women's war, First, 246; Second, 246–47

Official Secrets Act, 261
Operation Durga, 102
Operation Ijai, 101
Operation Red Poppy, 102
Orchid Textile Centre, 123

Padmanabhaiah, K., 359, 363
Pakistan, 294
  geopolitical manipulation, 91
Panglong Agreement, Burma (1947), 54
Pan-Manipuri Youth League, 241
Paona Bazar, 134, 209, 259, 340
Patel, Sardar Vallabhbhai, 54, 138
Patil, Shivraj, 259
Patkai Christian College, 10
'Peace Camps', 43
People's Liberation Army (PLA), 106, 127, 137, 231, 241, 337
People's United Liberation Front (PULF), 102
People's War Group (PWG), 61
Phanitphang, Sgt A.S., 111
Phanjoubam, Pradip, 225–33
Phizo, Angami Zapu, 16–25, 71, 170, 223
  and Morarji Desai in conversation, 20–24
Pillai, G.K., 65, 112, 181, 199
Planning Commission, 286, 321, 324
Poonia, D.S., 317, 320, 323–27
Purul community power project, 102

Rabina Devi, 134, 136–43, 152, 154, 156, 157, 227, 230, 259, 318
Ramananda, 216, 245, 248, 250, 328, 336–37, 339–40

Ranjeeta, 120–30, 131
Rao, Gen. K.V. Krishna, 232
Rao, P.V. Narasimha, 55, 169, 347
Rashtriya Rifles, 172–73
Ravi, P.N., 259–60
rebel groups, 105–09, 345
  Bodos, 267
  Kukis, 109
  from Manipur in Myanmar, 296
  Maoists, 34, 43, 52, 231, 294, 345
  Naga factions, 8, 55, 57, 60, 101, 111, 180–83, 253
Regional Institute of Medical Sciences (RIMS), 116, 129
religion, 237–38. *See also* Sanamahi
Republic day celebration in Manipur, 274–77
rice export issue (Second Nupi Lan), 246
Right to Information (RTI) Act, 178
Rio, Neiphiu, 14, 180, 192, 201, 370
Robert, Thangjam, 301–03
Ropianga, C., 256
Ruivah, Zamthingla, 73–78

Sak-Khangkhidaraba Lanmee, 242
Salwa Judum, 262
Sana Devi, L., 133
Sanamahi religion, 144, 213, 237–238, 250
Sanamatum, 129–30
Sangma, Agatha, 260
sanitation, lack of, 69, 135–36, 270, 273, 279, 305
Sanjit, Chungkham, 137–38, 152–57, 219, 227–30, 318

Sanjit Joint Action Committee, 152–54, 156
Saramati Hotel, 51
Sayeed, Mufti Mohammed, 95
self-determination, 55
Sema groups, 60
Sema, Hokishe, 60
Sen, Justice D.M., 172–74
Senapati, 28, 92–94, 100, 105–08, 117–18, 120, 232, 361, 363–64, 369
Senpilo, Rebecca, 174
Seyietsu, Khrisanisa, 16, 29
Shaheed Minar, 317–18
Shangam, Maj. R.S., 86
Sharma, Smriti, 189
Sharmila, Irom, 133, 135, 210–13, 221–22, 245–46, 248–51, 260
Shastri, Lal Bahadur, 138, 187
Shatsang, Seth, 82–91
Shebna, Lt M., 86
Shillong Accord (1975), 60
Shimrang, Phungthing, 49–66, 200
Shree Angala Parameshwari Muneeshwar Temple, 307
Shrivastav, P., 252
Shullai, Sam, 164
Singh, Ingo, 299–301
Singh, Jaswant, 295
Singh, Karam Manimohan, 246
Singh, L. Achaw, 253
Singh, Lt. Gen (Retd.) Mandhata, 58, 168
Singh, Mandhir, 72–73, 76–77
Singh, Manmohan, 112, 150, 169, 234, 248, 259, 260, 279, 320, 352, 367
Singh, Meino, 238–39
Singh, Okram Ibobi, 14, 38, 138,

140, 147–48, 155, 218–19, 225, 227, 230–32, 284, 305, 329
Singh, Raman, 231
Singh, Salam Ningthemba, 122, 126–29
Singh, T. Mangibabu, 284
Singhajit, Irom, 211–13, 215, 246–47
Sircar, Badal, 240
sociopolitical organizations of the Tangkhul tribe, 112
Somorendro, 210, 233, 237, 239, 241–43
South Asia Forum for Human Rights, 123–24
sovereignty, Nagas' fight for, 11, 166, 170, 181, 184–86, 199, 201–04, 206–07, 349, 351
Soyingbeni, 168, 172, 175
Special Operations Group (SOG), 124
Springdale School, 188–90
Sri Lanka, 60, 64, 206
State Intelligence Bureau (SIB), 35
Suilei, 75–76
Sümi tribe, Nagaland, 60, 75, 174, 196–97
Sunil, Thangjam, 300–01
Surchandra, prince of Manipur, 238
Susieyana, 168–69, 171
Suu Kyi, Aung San, 54, 292
Swu, Isak Chishi, 62, 166, 355

Tamenglong, 92–93, 106–07, 336, 340, 361, 363
Tamu, 295–98, 303, 306, 308–11, 313–14

Tangkhul Baptist Church, 93
Tangkhul Nagas, 72, 82, 232, 249, 290, 360
Tangkhul Naga Long, 112, 117
Tangkhul Shanao Long, 77
Tangkhul Women Society, 74
taxation in Nagaland, 10, 38
Technology Mission for Integrated Development of Horticulture in North Eastern States, 37
telecommunications network, 38, 343
Ten Innocents Memorial Park, 133
Tengnoupal, 304–05
terrorism, 258. *See also* insurgency
Thailand, 289, 291
Thangal Bazar, 135–36, 250, 270, 272, 273
thang-ta, 150–51, 278
Thimayya, Gen. K.S., 101
Thiyam, Rattan, 209, 243
Thoiba, M.C., 144
Thungbeni, 190, 194
Tiddim Chin, 309, 311
Tikendrajit, Bir, 134, 136, 139, 318
Tirap, Arunachal Pradesh, 58, 354
Tonsija Devi, Irom, 215
'track-two' initiative, 50
Trans-Asian Highway system, 312
Tripura, 189, 257, 312

Ujjwal, Nishit, 118
Ukhrul, Manipur, 28, 59, 72, 76, 78–79, 81–83, 85, 89, 110–13, 115, 117, 129, 354, 360, 361, 363–65
Underground (UG), 79, 80, 84, 118, 132, 133, 181, 184, 186,

225, 231, 242, 270, 273, 275, 282, 299–300, 302, 316, 323, 326
unemployment, 71, 207
Ungbi Memi, Thockchom, 139
UNICEF, 34
United Liberation Front of Asom (ULFA), 110, 160, 265, 267–68, 296, 358
United National Liberation Front (UNLF), 106, 110, 121, 210, 226, 242, 296, 299, 320, 339, 370
United Nations, 29, 202
  Development Programme (UNDP), 162
  High Commission for Refugees (UNHCR), 289
  Mission in Nepal, 43
Universal Declaration of Human Rights, 45
United Progressive Alliance (UPA), 235–36, 260
United Socialist Revolutionary Army, 106
Unlawful Activities (Prevention) Act, 1967, 257, 261
  Amendment 2004, 257–58

Vajpayee, Atal Bihari, 350, 363
Verghese, B.G., 327
Vidura Jang Bahadur, 98
Vietnam war, 52
Village Development Board, Nagaland, 179–80
Vyasan R., 191

Wanghying (Khaplang), 50
Wareppa, Basanta, 120–30, 131, 290, 291–97, 299, 301, 303, 305–06, 307–09, 312–15
Wokha, Nagaland, 68, 70, 123, 176, 176–79, 187, 189, 190–92, 193
Wonchibeni, 171
World War, Second, 54, 97, 291
Wungnaoshang, 89–90

Yambamo Lotha Brigade, 170
Yanger, Sentila T., 74
Yanthan, Khodao, 23
Yepthomi, Ato, 164-65
Yikhum, Wokha, Nagaland, 177, 179
Yumnam, Jiten, 216–17, 337–41

Zeliangrong Students Union, 71
Zeliangrong(s), 41, 69, 250, 363
Zhimomi, Kitovi, 166, 196, 353–54
Zomi Defence Volunteers, 106
Zomi Revolutionary Army, 106

Acknowledgements

This begins with my publisher, HarperCollins India, and its editor in chief, Karthika, V.K., who believed in the need for such stories to be told—and enabled me to tell this story.

To my Naga 'younger brother'—you know who you are—for opening doors and minds in Nagaland, Manipur and Delhi; and the hours explaining history, politics and society.

Ningreichon Tungshang, who opened doors in Ukhrul and Imphal, and without whose intervention this book would not have been complete. Seth Shatsang, who ensured that these doors stayed open. Rewben Mashangvah, for his friendship, his searching music, and his patience in explaining nuances of history and folklore.

Keith Wallang and Anungla Longkumer, for friendship, food, and helping me to understand so many facets of the 'Northeast'. And, ensuring I would be welcome in many places and by many key people.

Thockchom Nandini and Ramananda Wangkheirakpam: their love for Manipur paved the way for my understanding of it. And how can I forget endless cups of Tamenglong tea at Jupiter Yambem Centre?

Babloo Loitongbam at Human Rights Alert, Imphal—and his colleagues, the indefatigable Basanta Wareppa and Ranjeeta Sadokpam, my companions on some travels, and for their help and patience.

Temsula Ao and Robin S. Ngangom, who took time in rain-swept Shillong to share their anguish and their hopes for their people. And for their work, which enriches mine.

Sravan Marur, officer and gentleman, for pointing me in the right direction on *Highway 39*.

Sanjoy Hazarika, senior colleague and friend, who made the way easier for many of us by writing books on the gas leak in Bhopal and the 'Northeast', which showed years before long-form journalism became fashionable in India, that it is also necessary.

Some people who appear in this book as single alphabets in capital letters (revealing their identities any more may jeopardize their positions and, in some cases, their lives).

Samrat Choudhury and Venita Coelho for their sensitive reading of the manuscript.

Shantanu Ray Chaudhuri, my editor at HarperCollins India, for his sensitive handling of the manuscript, and for numerous helpful suggestions.

And, finally, to all who shared stories this book lacks the privilege of including. Hopefully, I shall soon have more opportunities to share these—through future books and essays, in media, at every possible forum. In any case, I hope I have been able to absorb your thoughts in this work.